ON THE ROAD WITH MIKE DREW

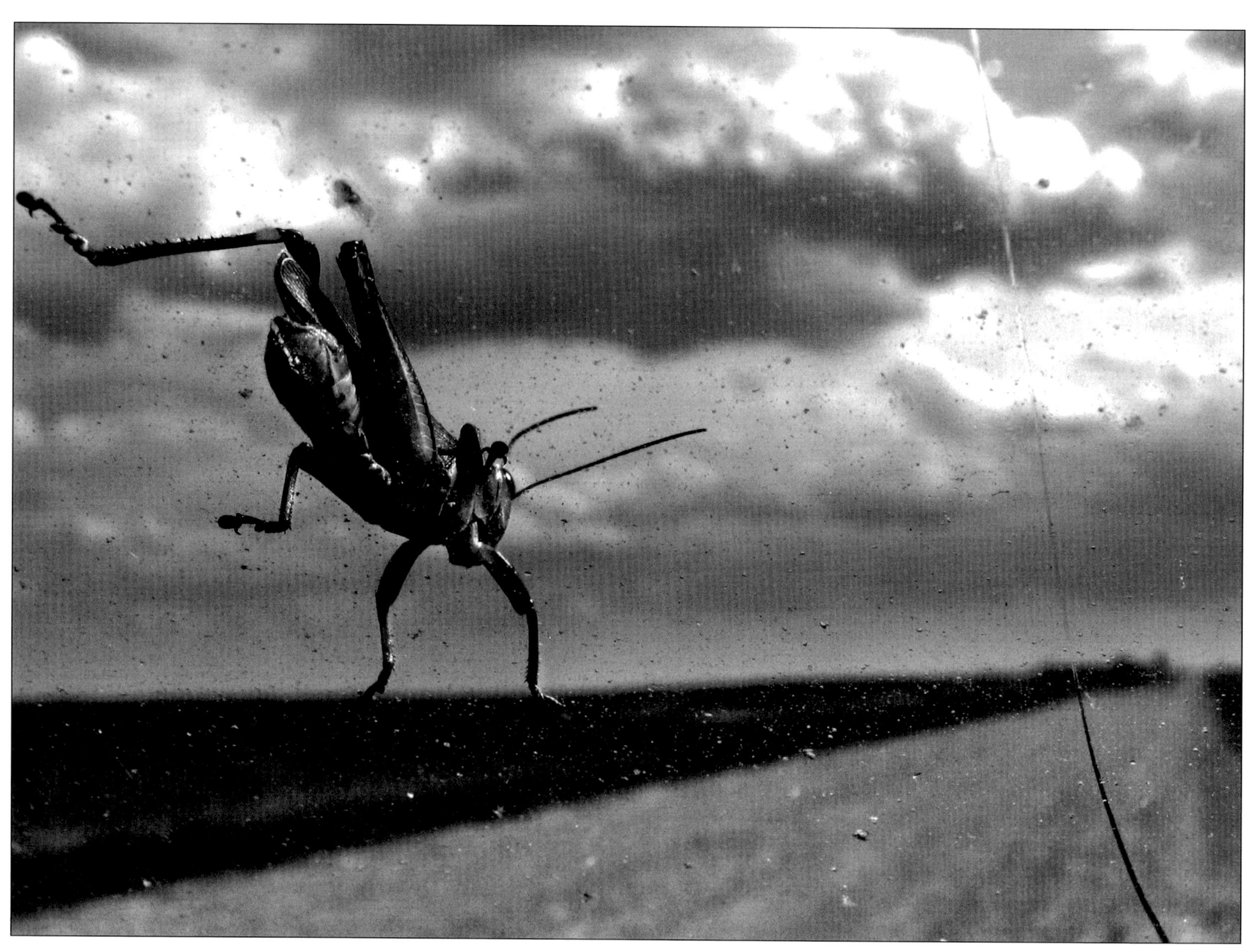

On the Road with Mike Drew

Collected Photographs and Stories from Central and Southern Alberta

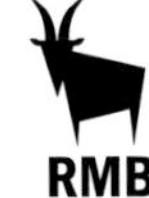

RMB

First Edition

RMB | Rocky Mountain Books Ltd.
rmbooks.com
@rmbooks
facebook.com/rmbooks

Cataloguing data available from Library and Archives Canada
ISBN 9781771602044 (hardcover)

Printed and bound in Canada by Friesens

Distributed in Canada by Heritage Group Distribution and in the U.S. by Publishers Group West

For information on purchasing bulk quantities of this book, or to obtain media excerpts or invite the author to speak at an event, please visit rmbooks.com and select the "Contact Us" tab.

RMB | Rocky Mountain Books is dedicated to the environment and committed to reducing the destruction of old-growth forests. Our books are produced with respect for the future and consideration for the past.

We acknowledge the financial support of the Government of Canada through the Canada Book Fund and the Canada Council for the Arts, and of the province of British Columbia through the British Columbia Arts Council and the Book Publishing Tax Credit.

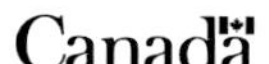

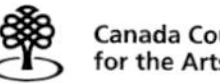

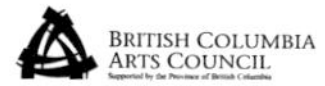

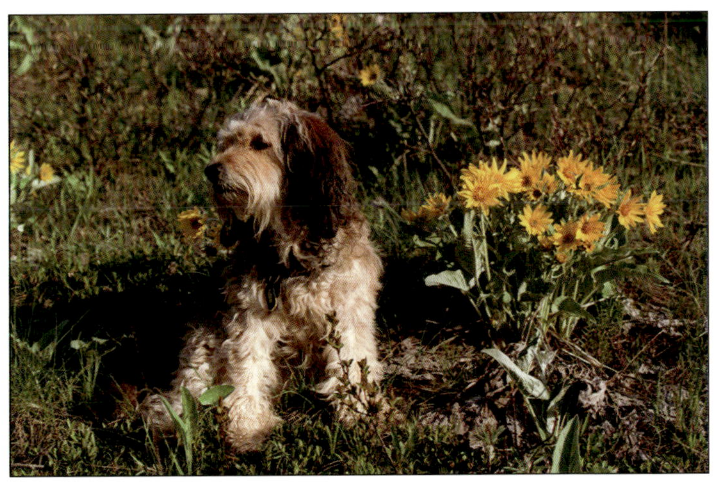

For Ansey, 1980 to 1996, the best friend a boy could ever have.

CONTENTS

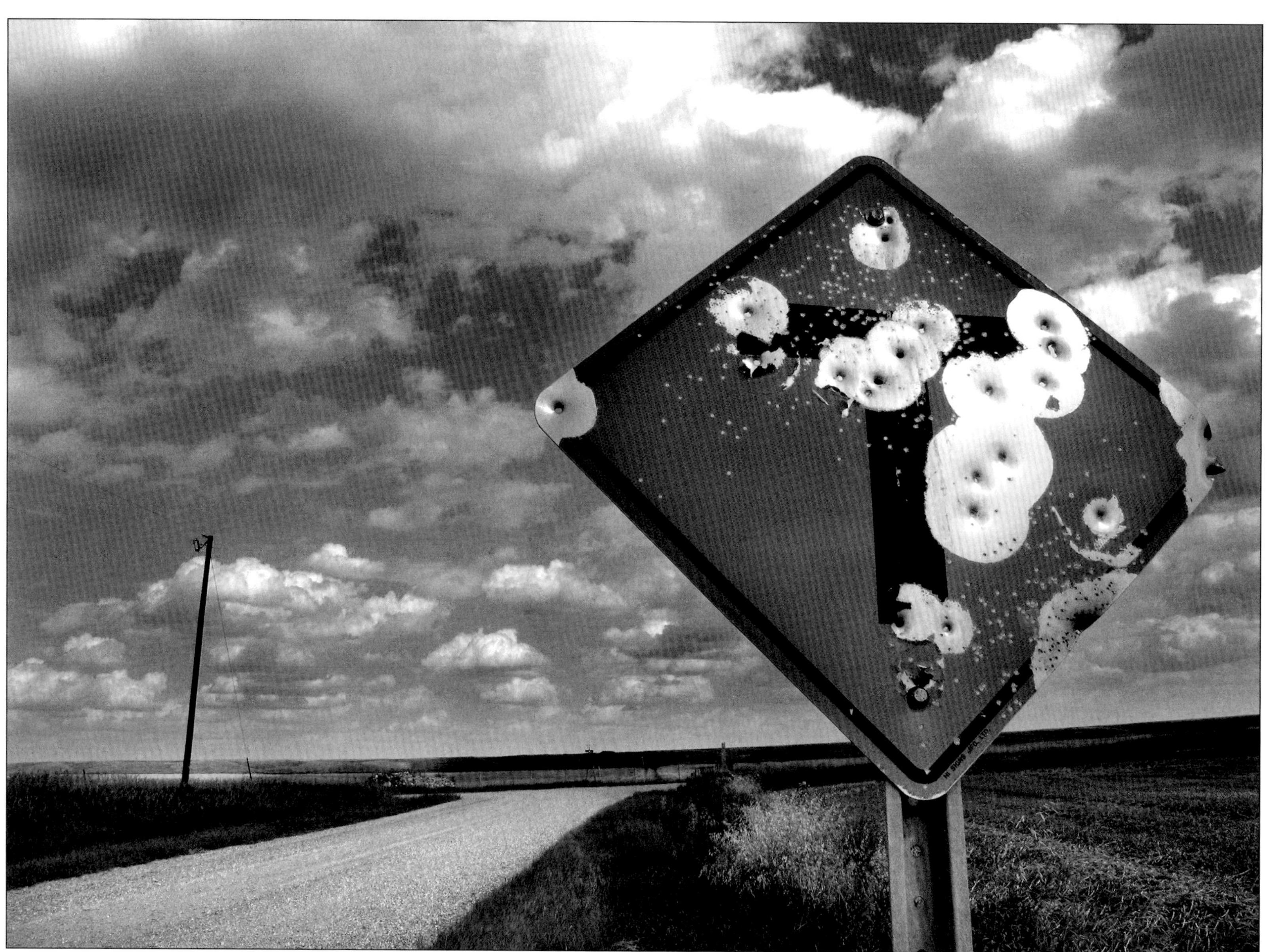

INTRODUCTION

ABOUT GETTING LOST

I DON'T REALLY GET LOST. True, sometimes I don't know exactly where I am, but I'd rather call it exploring than lost.

So let's just say I was exploring when I topped the mountain ridge between Pierce and Headquarters, Idaho.

I'd left Calgary the previous morning, determined to go fishing somewhere, and ended up crossing most of western Montana and sliding into central Idaho over Lolo Pass and down the Lochsa River. Darkness found me near Orofino, a small town in the gold-rush area of Idaho, and I pulled over, crawled into the back of the truck and went to sleep.

Next morning I pulled out just before dawn and headed into the mountains. I knew where I wanted to end up – Kelly Creek – but the last time I was here, maybe a decade ago, I came in from the other side. But I knew it was only a mountain range or two away so I headed up the widest gravel road I could find.

It got narrow pretty quickly and then dropped down to just a couple of ruts with grass growing up in the middle.

But it was going in the right direction so I stuck with it. The morning light lit the dew that glistened on roadside ferns and dripped from cedar boughs, and at the top of the trail it cast reflections in ponds and brightened meadows filled with late-summer flowers.

The road was skinnying up pretty good, but after only about half a mile I came to an intersection and turned onto a road that led back down the other side of the mountain. It widened as quickly as the first road narrowed, and 20 minutes later I came out on a lovely jade-green river.

I headed upstream. I could see trout dimpling the long, flat runs and splashes of red from spawning kokanee salmon flashed from the shallower eddies behind boulders. I still wasn't sure which river this was – one of the forks of the Clearwater was my best guess – but it didn't really matter. There were trout to be caught.

Why drive the 800 km to Idaho to catch the same fish I could catch here? I don't have a good explanation for that. The fishing is no better there than here, and gas prices are only marginally cheaper. It's beautiful there but not any more so than our neck of the woods. Cheaper fishing licences than BC, though.

No, the best reason I can think of for heading to Idaho is that I just felt like turning right at Missoula, Montana, and this is where I ended up.

Turned out this was the North Fork of the Clearwater River and at the head of the long valley was Kelly Creek, one of the best cut-throat trout streams in Idaho. I drove slowly along, knowing now that I was on the right track, and took in the scenery.

The valley was narrow and the river strewn with boulders. Deep runs held the promise of fish, and when I stopped by a meadow to make a few casts I caught a fat cutthroat right away. At the next run I tried I caught a couple more. Just what I'd hoped for.

I watched a mother elk and her calf ford the river a bit farther upstream and found a whitetail doe staring at me from the trees. Snowshoe hares bounced along the road and one paused long enough for a picture. The whole place reminded me of the Elk River valley near Fernie. But with cheaper fishing licences.

I fished my way up to Kelly Creek, which turned out to be less than stellar fishing. I blame it on the sudden change in the weather. That rain that blasted Calgary on Monday started over near Idaho.

But I had a fine day on the Clearwater until then, and I went to sleep with Idaho sky full of clouds and awoke to a lovely misty morning.

I rolled on back through Wallace and on to Coeur d'Alene – with a side trip through another mountain range on muddy roads – and then back into Montana as the sun broke through clouds and lit up the Cabinet Mountains with peach-coloured light.

By the time I got back to the house I'd travelled just under 2500 km. You may feel free to wonder why I would drive that far in three days just to catch a couple of fish – that I put back in the stream anyway.

Well, I just like getting lost, I guess.

No, better make that "exploring."

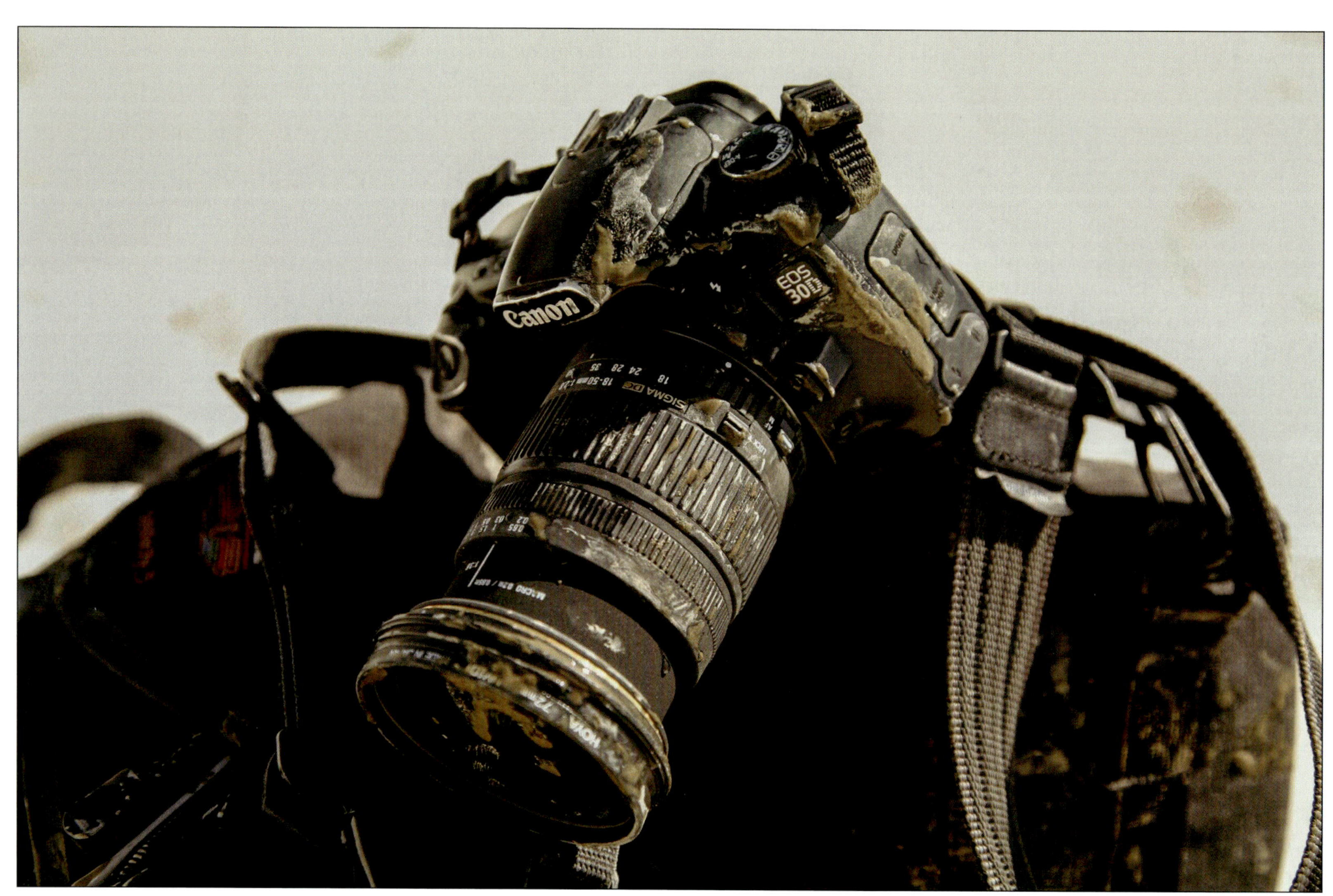

Always make sure your gear is in tip-top shape!

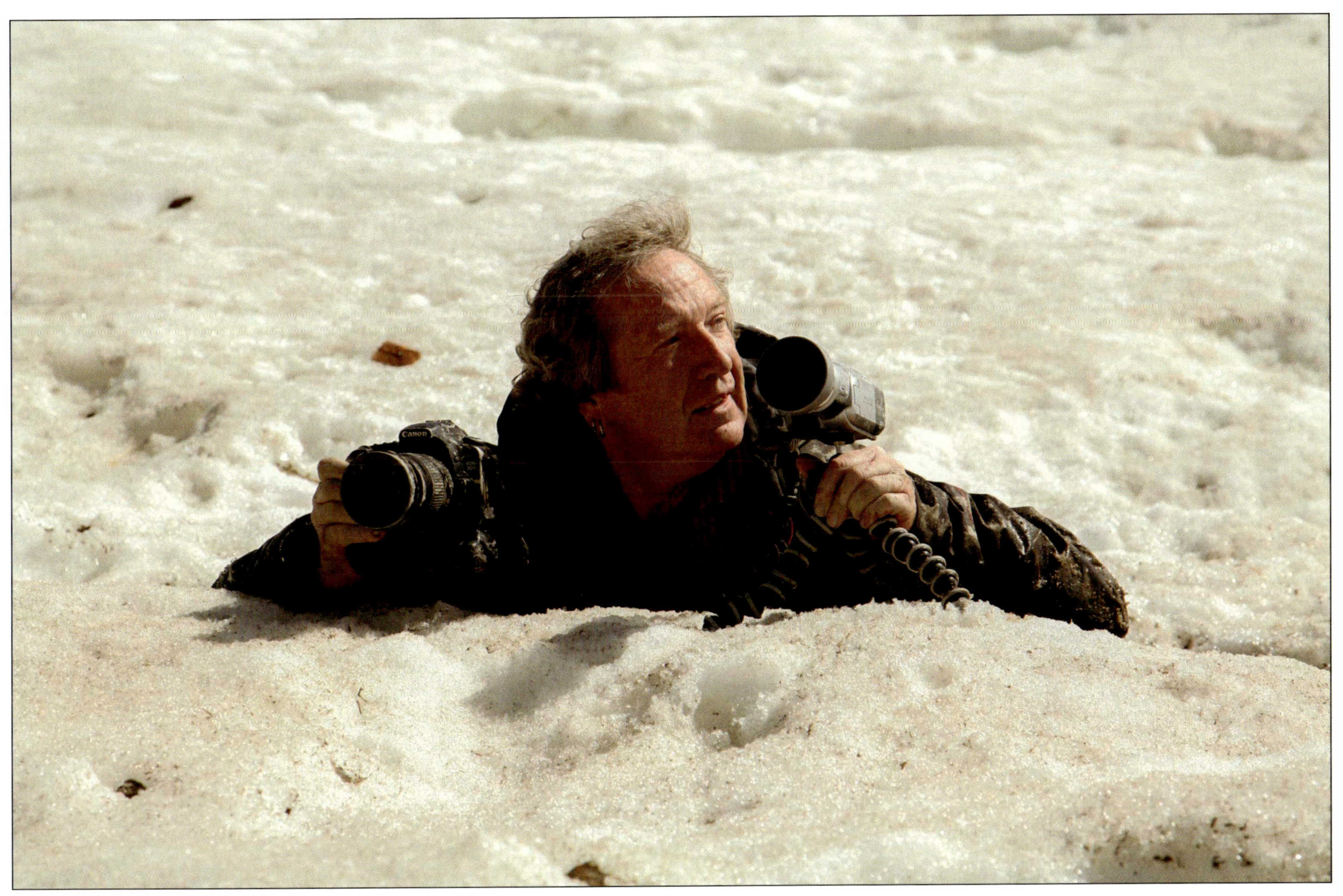

Crawling out of a crack in the melting ice along the Bow River.

ABOUT PHOTOGRAPHY

I WAS LYING ON MY BACK, slathered in mud with ice water dripping in my face when I suddenly realized that I was staring straight up at three or four feet of unstable river ice.

I'd crawled into a melted-out space to shoot some photos and video of the nifty natural ice sculptures and the coloured light filtering through cracks in the huge slabs of ice still piled up on the banks of the Bow downstream from the city. The hollow was maybe 20 feet from front to back, about ten feet wide and varied in ceiling height from about three feet where my face was to just a few inches at the back of the hollow.

The floor was covered with river cobbles and slimy mud that smelled of a kind of fishy staleness, and icicles hung from the ceiling and dripped water constantly. Outside the temperature was pushing 20°C but in here I could see my breath.

The light that made it through the thick ice was soft and shadowless, and when I rolled over onto my back to take pictures of the detritus stuck in the ceiling I could see that the ice was yellow in some spots and blue in others, black and grey in a couple of places.

And it was when I was looking up that I suddenly realized how stupid it was to be here.

I was alone east of the city lying under a three-ton slab of unstable, rotting ice. No one knew where I was. There were rocks embedded in the ice big enough to crack my skull. I couldn't move quickly even if I had to because of the tight space and slipperiness of the rocks and mud.

I eased myself back out into the sunshine.

I looked around. There was a pair of pelicans flying by and a prairie falcon screeching directly overhead. Robins were on the ice picking off bugs. Ducks and geese both on the water and in the air. But no people.

Don't get me wrong. I like it that way. And yeah, I do dumb things all the time.

But as I was lying there in that ice cave I suddenly had the feeling that this was a stupid thing to do. I'm 56 years old. I should know better.

And I do. But this insatiable curiosity – and my boyhood obsession with getting as filthy as possible – keeps me doing things like crawling around under unstable ice.

And the ice looks so cool at this time of year. It builds up all winter, surface ice being pushed up by the current layer after layer along the river until cliffs of it ten feet high soar above the open water.

When it starts to melt it looks even more amazing.

Surface meltwater seeps into cracks and expands them until it reaches the rocky shoreline underneath, where it runs under the ice to the river. The water erodes away the undersides of the ice slabs like meltwater below a glacier, and soon tunnels and caves form.

On the top, leaves and other detritus that have blown onto or been frozen into the ice and then exposed by melting accelerate the melting process on the surface. Being darker than the surrounding ice, they absorb the sun's energy rather than reflecting it like the white ice. The ice directly beneath these objects melts away and soon the rocks, leaves, twigs, even feathers sink into the ice. The meltwater they create erodes the ice even more.

Air pockets left under the slabs of ice shoved around by the river gain heat from the scant sunlight seeping through, and as soon as the hole melts through, the ice erodes quickly as the warm air circulates.

All of this makes for pretty nifty pictures but it also makes the ice incredibly unstable. From the surface you can't tell where the ice is thin and you can fall through at any time.

The ice this time of year isn't above water – the river pushed it here and then went merrily on its way – but falling into a metre-deep hole and twisting a joint or breaking a bone isn't something you want to do. Be very careful walking on any ice this time of year.

And please, don't crawl underneath. Yeah, I like the pictures I took but really, they're just pictures. In the long run they don't matter at all.

Would I crawl back under the ice to shoot some more? Yeah, I would. But I'm just a big, dumb 56-year-old kid who loves to get dirty. I'll tell someone where I'm going and when I'm going to be back next time, though.

Please, do as I say, not as I do. The ice is nice but don't be dumb.

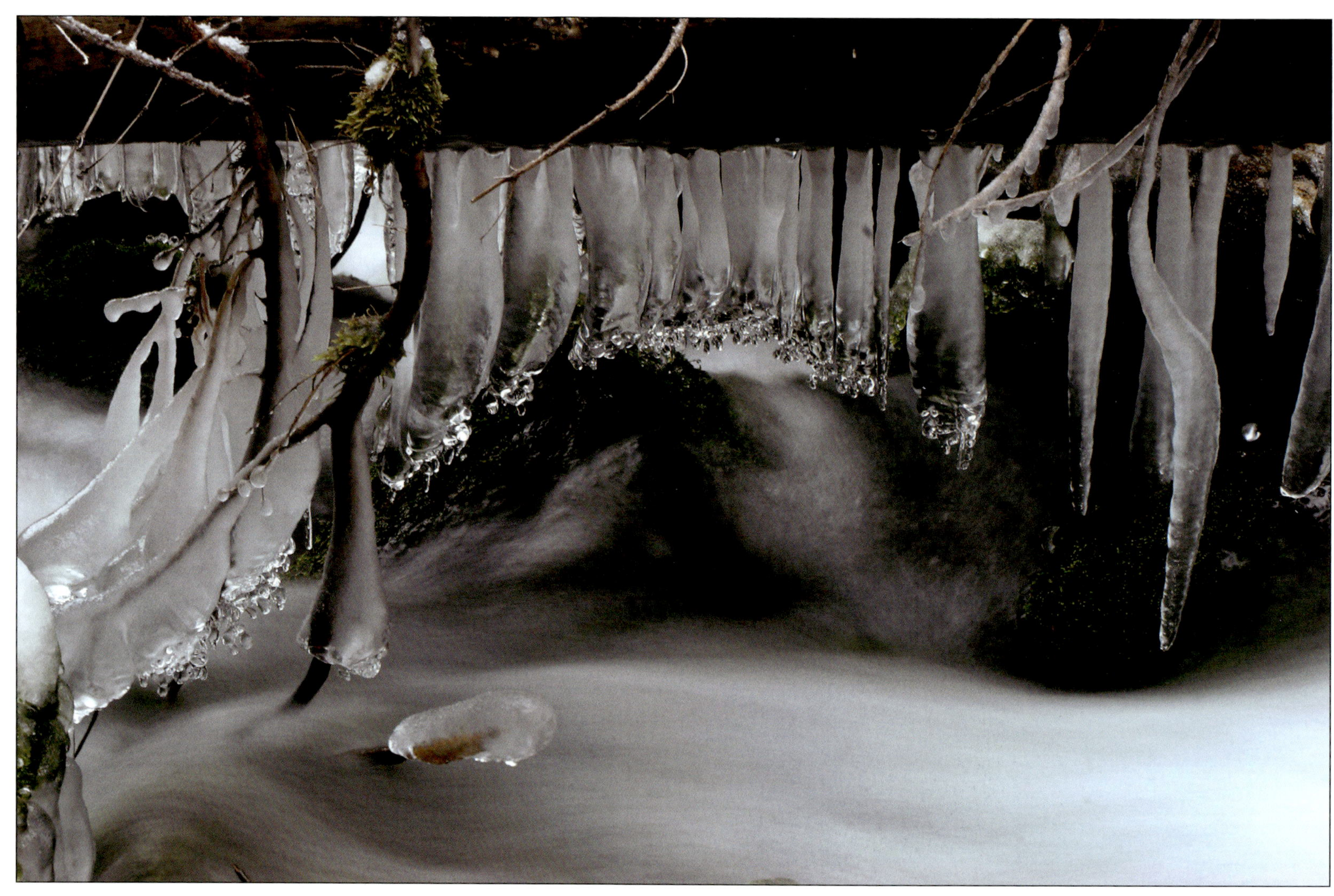

Ice bells on Spurling Creek.

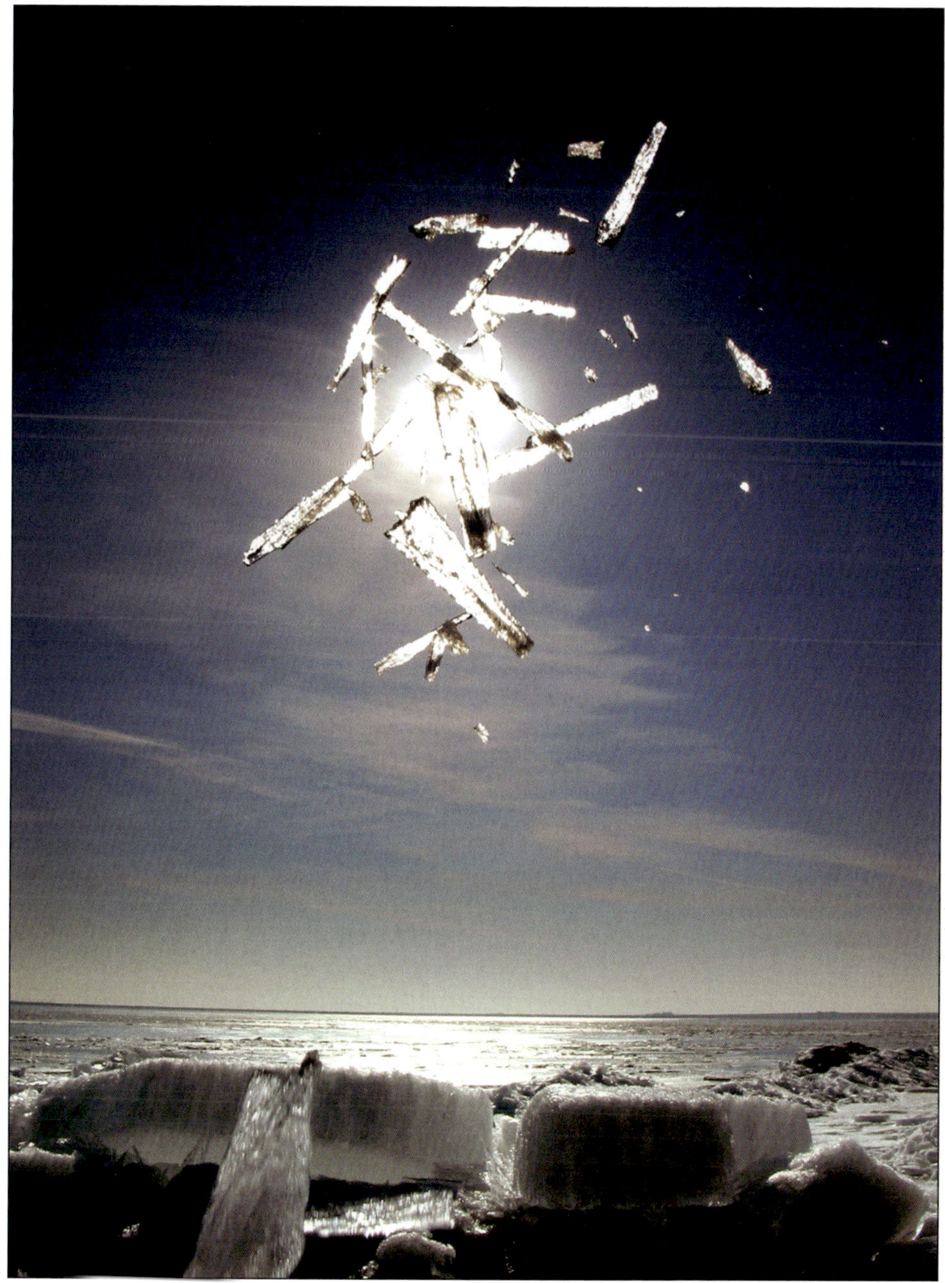

Tossed ice at Keho Lake.

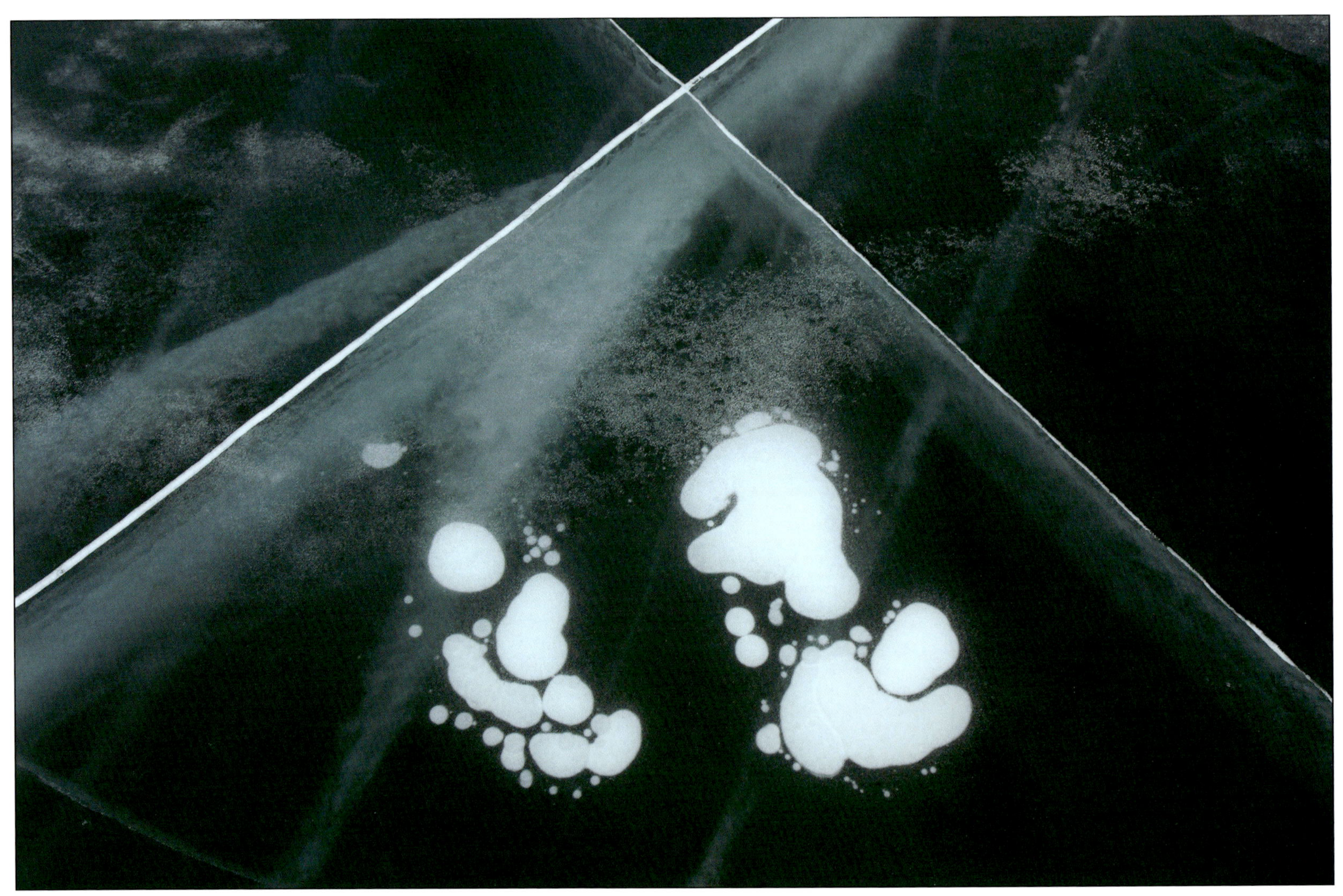

Bubbles and cracks in thick but clear ice on Gap Lake, about 90 km west of Calgary.

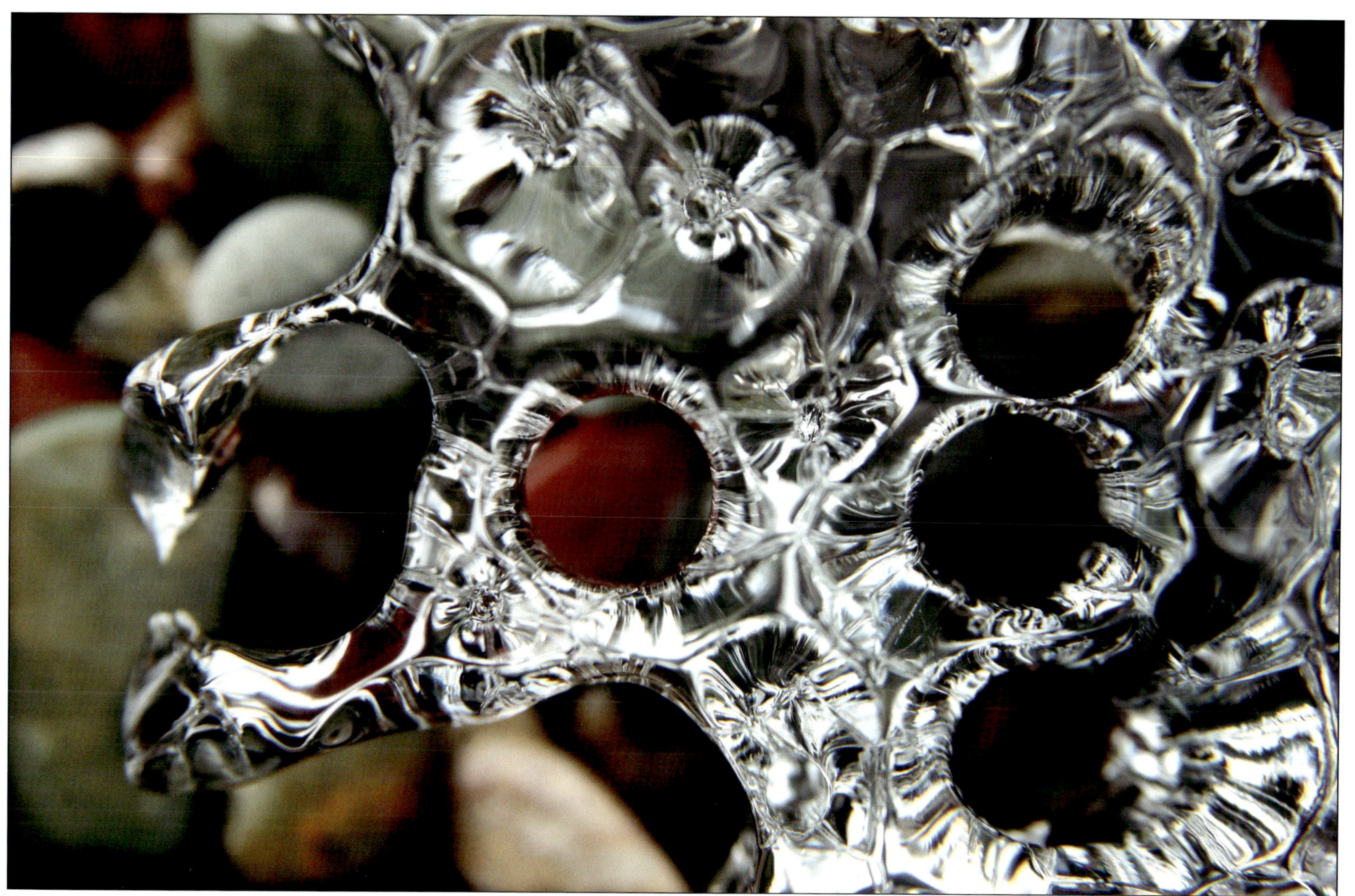

Melting ice and pebbles at Waterton.

ABOUT PHOTOGRAPHY—BLACK AND WHITE

I PREFER NOT TO THINK OF black and white photography as the antithesis of colour.

I look at it more as colour distilled to its elements.

The tones of a good black and white photo represent the subtleties of the colour scene it records and leave the viewers the option of filling those colours in for themselves. The shades of grey in a sky are actually blue, the darkness of grass is green.

Textures become simply textures. The bark of a tree, wrinkles on a face, the vastness of a forested hillside, the clouds in the sky.

Without the cues that colour brings, textures and shapes are allowed to evoke their own emotions. Landscapes especially benefit from this approach but it's effective with people, too. It's hard to imagine Ansel Adams in colour even though he dabbled in it. Same with Karsh or Herb Ritts.

But more than anything, black and white just looks cool.

Out here in the west, with the big bold landscapes we have, it looks especially good. The soft curves of the badlands, the sawtooth edge of the mountains, thunderstorms – oh my, but I love thunderstorms – billowing up over the prairies, the gnarled bark of cottonwood trees along a winding river valley, it all looks so stunning in black and white.

And with all the digital options we have just a loop and a click away we have the luxury of shooting in colour and then converting to black and white just to see what it looks like.

Sometimes of an evening I'll flop on the couch with the laptop open and pick stuff from my archive just to see how it would look with the colour taken away. I don't do anything elaborate, none of that lab colour, grab-a-channel Photoshop stuff, I just desaturate and play from there. I never convert to greyscale, though. Too much information hits the trash that way.

Then I work the levels, brighten and darken here and there – the usual darkroom-ish stuff – and then add a bit of warm tone just because I like how it looks on the screen. If you're making digital prints you can control that better through ink selection anyway, so the warm tone is just cosmetic.

It's fun to do simply as an exercise, and sometimes you come up with some interesting results. I tried it with a picture I took of a girl named Carol Melting Tallow at a powwow a few years back, and I'd be hard pressed to choose which version I like best, the colour or the black and white.

But generally when I feel like shooting black and white I just set my cameras up to record that way.

I don't belong to the Cult of Raw – yes, I've heard the arguments, but I'm not convinced the differences are visible as long as your exposures are right – so when I shoot black and white that's the way it records. Works for me but everyone has their own preferences.

There's no second guessing that way. You look at the tones and shapes and textures as you shoot and make your decisions based on those criteria. The green of a cottonwood leaf is a different tone from the green of sagebrush. The green of a prickly pear cactus pad is different from the green of grama grass. Granite is different from limestone, sand is different from sandstone, river water is different from lake water. And skies change all day long.

There is an infinity of shades in black and white, but in colour we tend to key on the major tones – blue, red and green and the brighter combinations of those three. They are all beautiful, and I can't imagine a sunrise or sunset or a parrot's plumage or a powwow dancer's costume without them. We see in colour and judge our world through its many variations.

But there are times when black and white is just plain better.

I'm looking at one right now as I peck out these words.

I'm in deep southwestern Alberta near the town of Cardston, and off to the southwest the great square massif of Chief Mountain rises out of the snow-dappled hills behind a foreground of wind-powered generators. It's near five in the afternoon and the light is an even hazy blue. Chinook-blown cloud rolls close over the mountain and lenticular clouds form higher up where the winds are even more fierce.

In colour, it's a somber scene. In nice, warm-toned black and white, it looks soft and quiet. To me, anyway.

In the dim and unenlightened past Paul Simon sang about Kodachrome giving such nice bright colours. Can't argue with that. But he also sang that everything looks worse in black and white.

The boy needs to take another look.

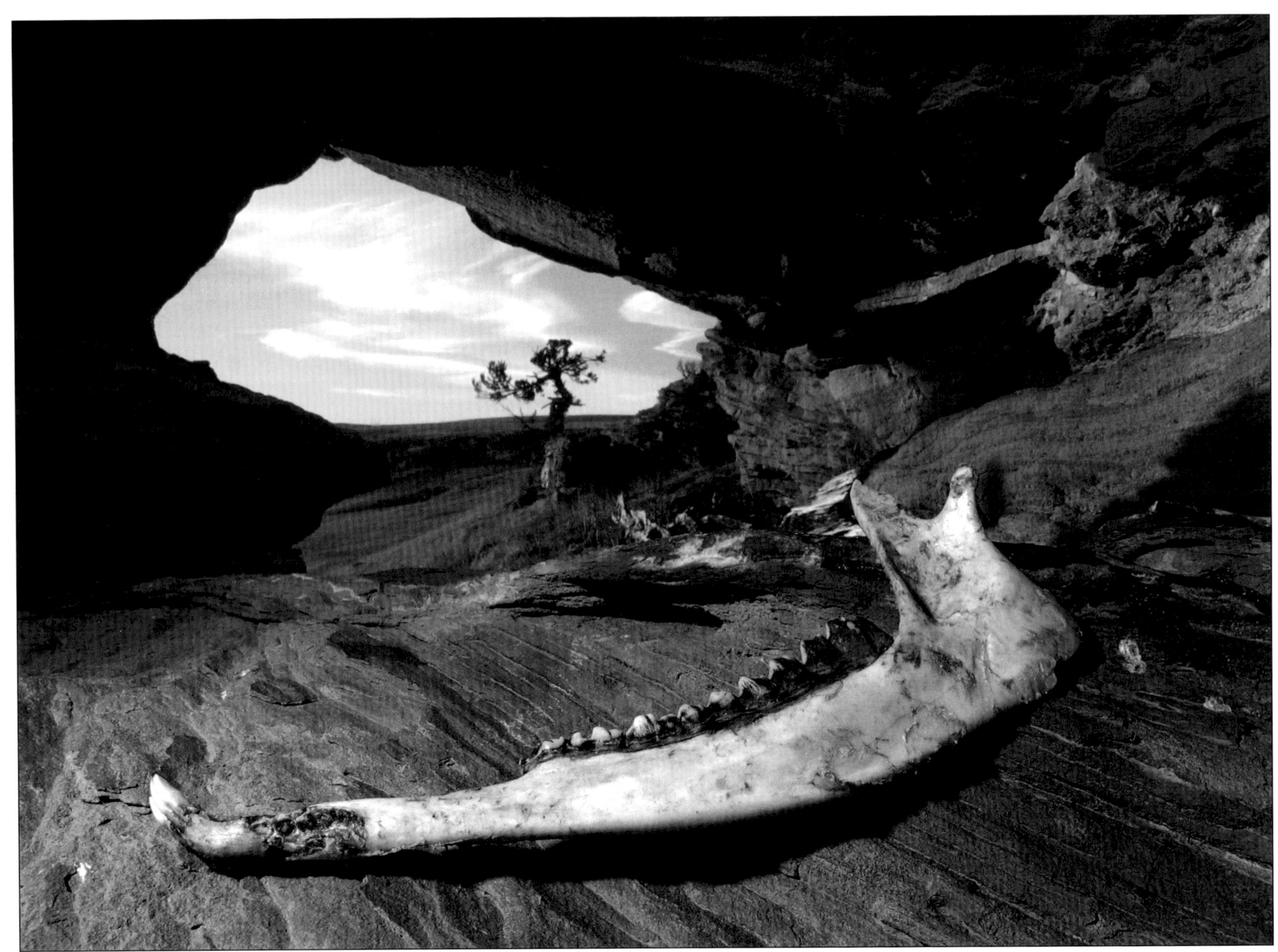

Deer jaw and my favourite limber pine in the Porcupine Hills.

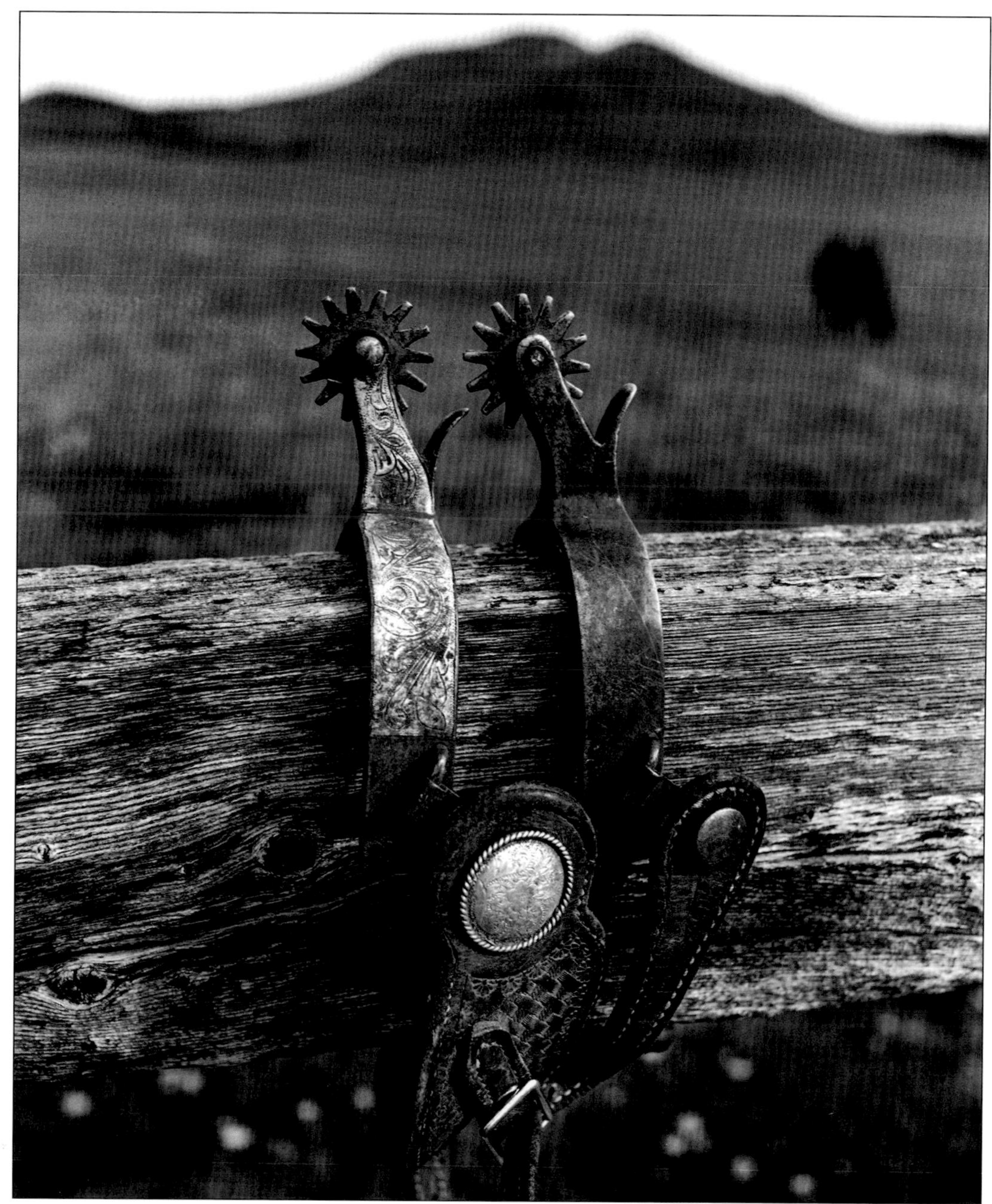

Spurs at the OH Ranch west of Longview.

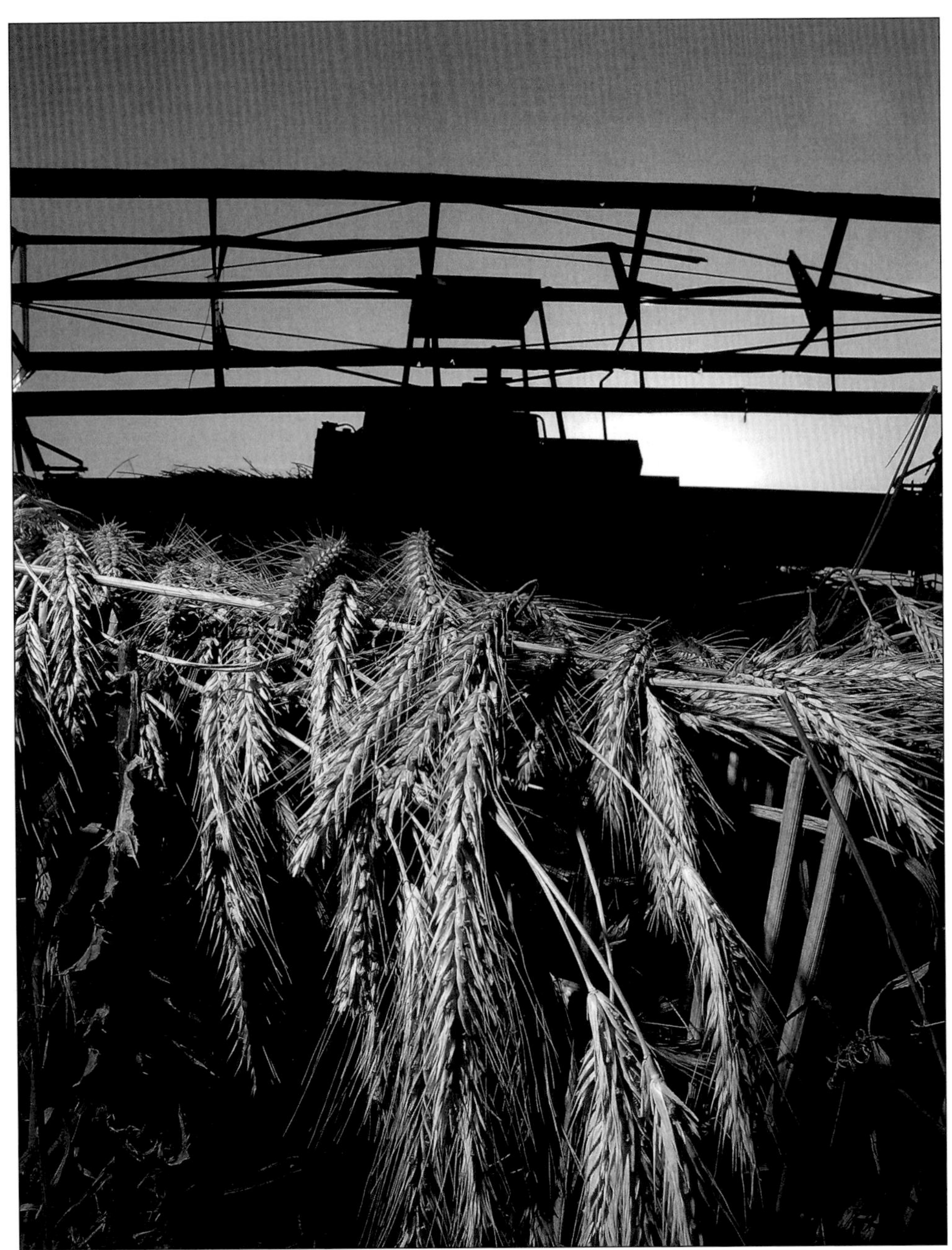

Barley hangs on the cutting bar of a swather east of Parkland.

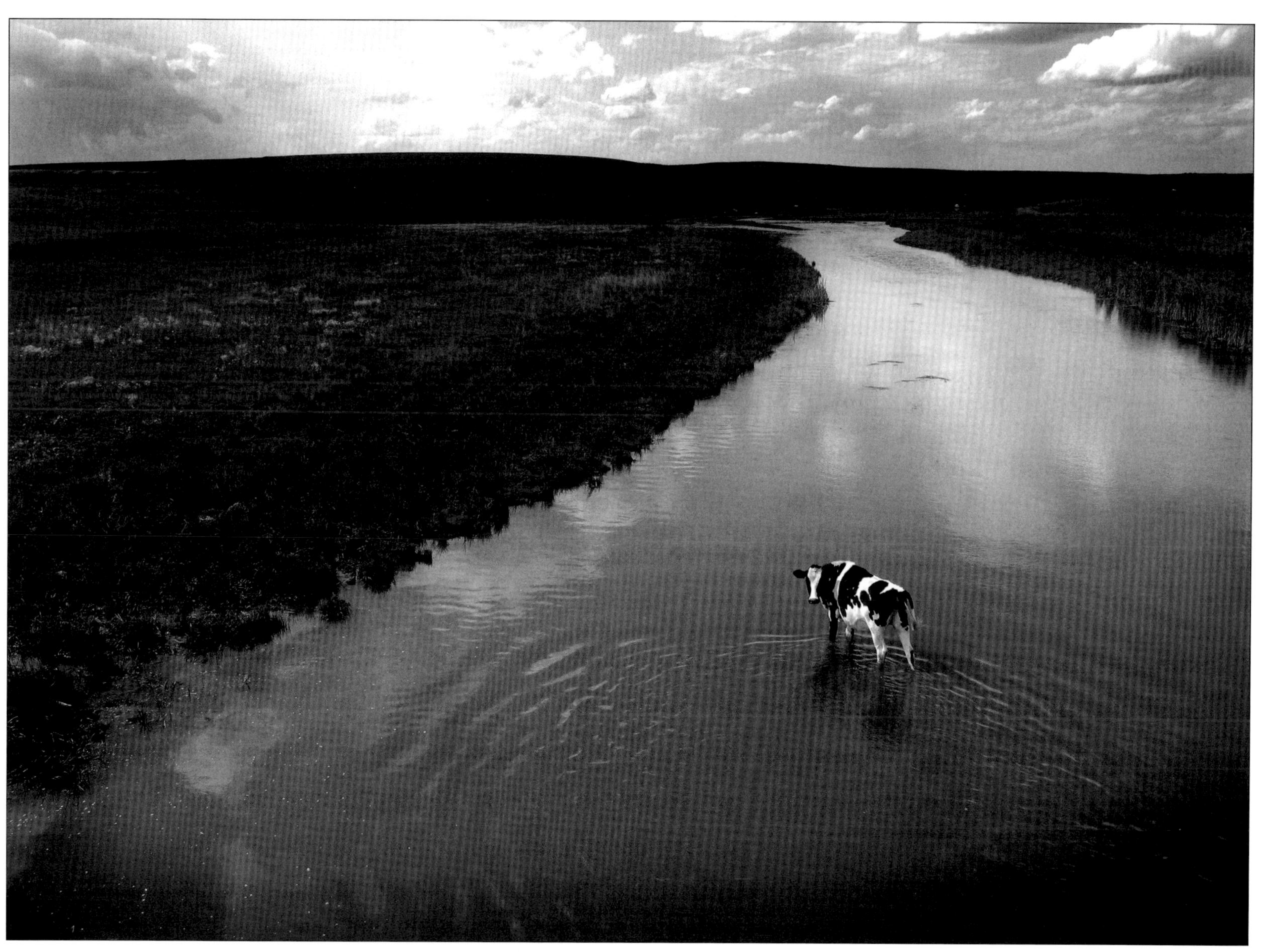

A cow stands in the low summer flow of the Little Bow River east of Nanton.

S P R

I N G

BLUEBIRDS

It's nice to have the sun come up early enough so I can get out of town ahead of the morning traffic.

Even if I'm just barely getting out of town.

I've been on holidays for the last couple of weeks, but because I'm going on a big trip in June I decided to stay close to home this time. To me, close to home means limiting myself to as far as I can drive during daylight hours. That translates to about a 900 km round trip on most days.

So this past week as I drove along the traffic jam-free streets of the city, I decided to check out a spot maybe not a 900 km drive away. I headed just a dribble past the city limits.

As I've said many times before, we're mighty darn lucky to live where we are. Even though the city is spreading like a stain in every direction, once you get yourself to the edge, you're home free. The satellite communities are still far enough away to leave some open space – let's keep it that way, okay? – and instead of heavy industry we have farmland. Pretty sweet.

So I breezed through town and headed southwest to the edge of the Ann and Sandy Cross Conservation Area.

The wind hadn't yet come up as I drove along the eastern boundary, and the sounds of morning filled the air. I could hear robins and other birds singing as I rolled down the window to shoot a few pictures of a group of bull elk grazing on a hillside. The drone of traffic and planes flying overhead filtered through but it was still heavenly.

Chinook clouds were building in, but once the rising sun cleared the lower layers, soft sunlight filtered through the trees. Aspen catkins caught the light with their silvery fur, and willows shone bright white as if they had their own power source.

Poplars are still a bit behind as far as flowers go, but the resin on the buds is beginning to swell. One of my favorite scents is the smell of balsam poplars, so I stepped out of the truck and pinched a bud and gave it a sniff. Wonderful. A week or two of warm weather and we'll have leaves starting to show. The forest will be perfumed by their scent.

I rolled up out of the valley onto the hay fields along the ridge. There was still a lot of snow up there from the storm earlier in the week and it gave the hills a wintery look.

But it didn't feel wintery. True, it was cold and there was frost on the ground and a crust of ice on the puddles. But the soft light changed the character enough that it felt more like spring. An Alberta spring, to be sure, but spring.

There was a bit of a breeze starting to come up now that I was out in the open, but a breeze was all it was. I could still hear chickadees in the shrubbery and geese flying overhead. A flock of starlings came chattering by.

There seemed to be a hawk – redtails, mostly – in every tree and I even saw a pair perched by an old nest. Kestrels and merlins were hunting the treelines while harriers patrolled the pastures. I have yet to get a good picture of one of those guys.

I cruised up by the Leighton Centre and photographed wisps of spider web sparkling prismatically between the trees. Lots of spiders on the move. And the willows up there are a mosaic of white catkins and red stems.

And there were bluebirds, lots of bluebirds.

They were pretty cautious, and for half an hour I tried to photograph them, but every time I moved they flew off, the females the pale blue and grey of the sky to the east and the males like the bright blue sky overhead.

But finally I found a pair that would tolerate me, and as I shot I could hear that lovely tinkling call they have as they discussed, I don't know, household matters, maybe?

By now the wind was starting to gust and the soft morning sunlight slipped back into the thickening clouds. And the traffic was getting thick as well. I bet I saw a vehicle every 15 minutes. Time to head back to town.

It was a short drive back. And yet while I was up in those hills it felt like I was a world away. Elk, bluebirds, ducks, geese, springtime wafting through the foothills.

And all so close to town.

I'll never stop my wandering, exploring far-flung places, driving five hours to photograph a flower.

But sometimes it's good to stay close to home.

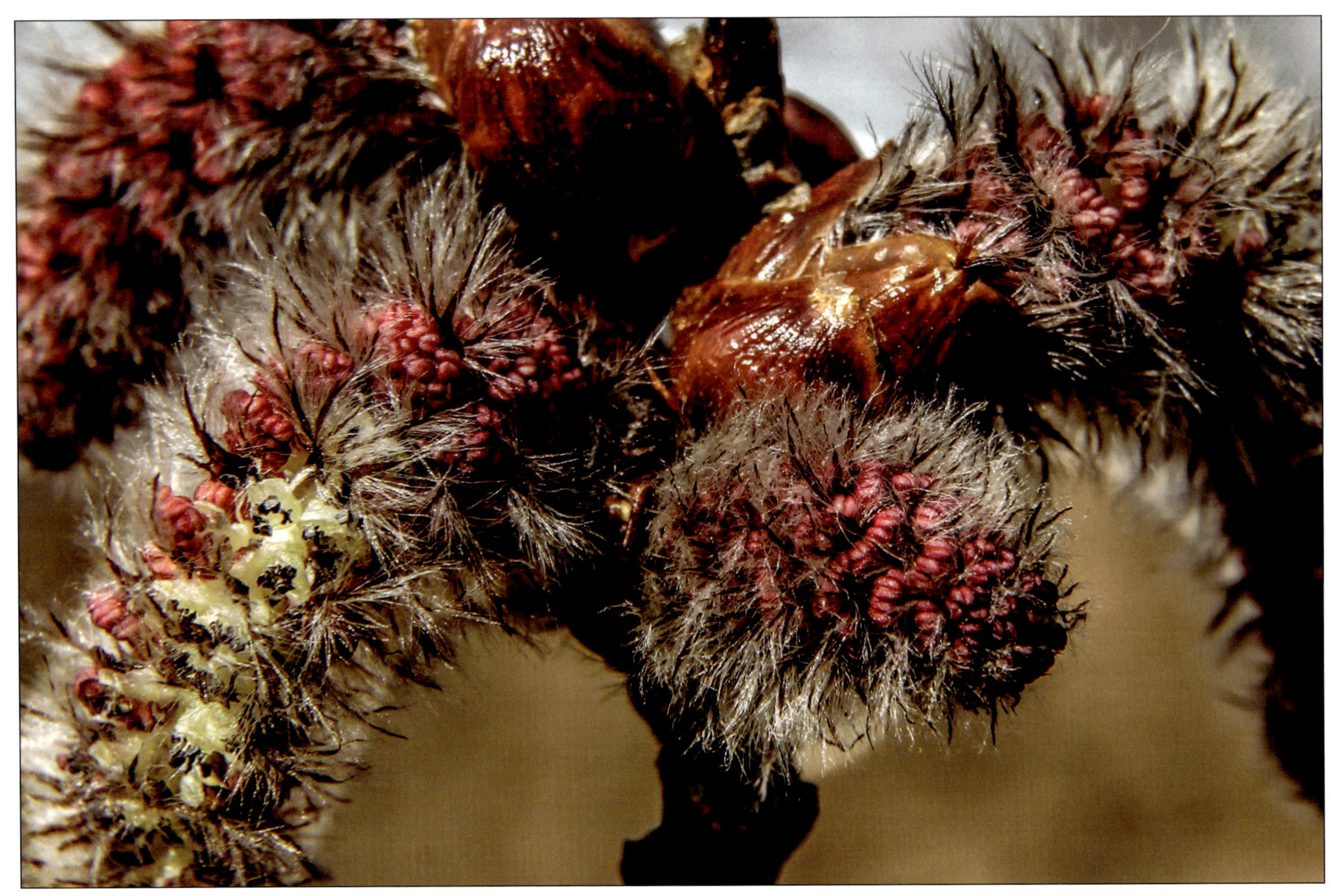

Close-up of male aspen catkins in full bloom in the foothills west of Calgary. Unlike many tree species, aspens come in separate male and female varieties.

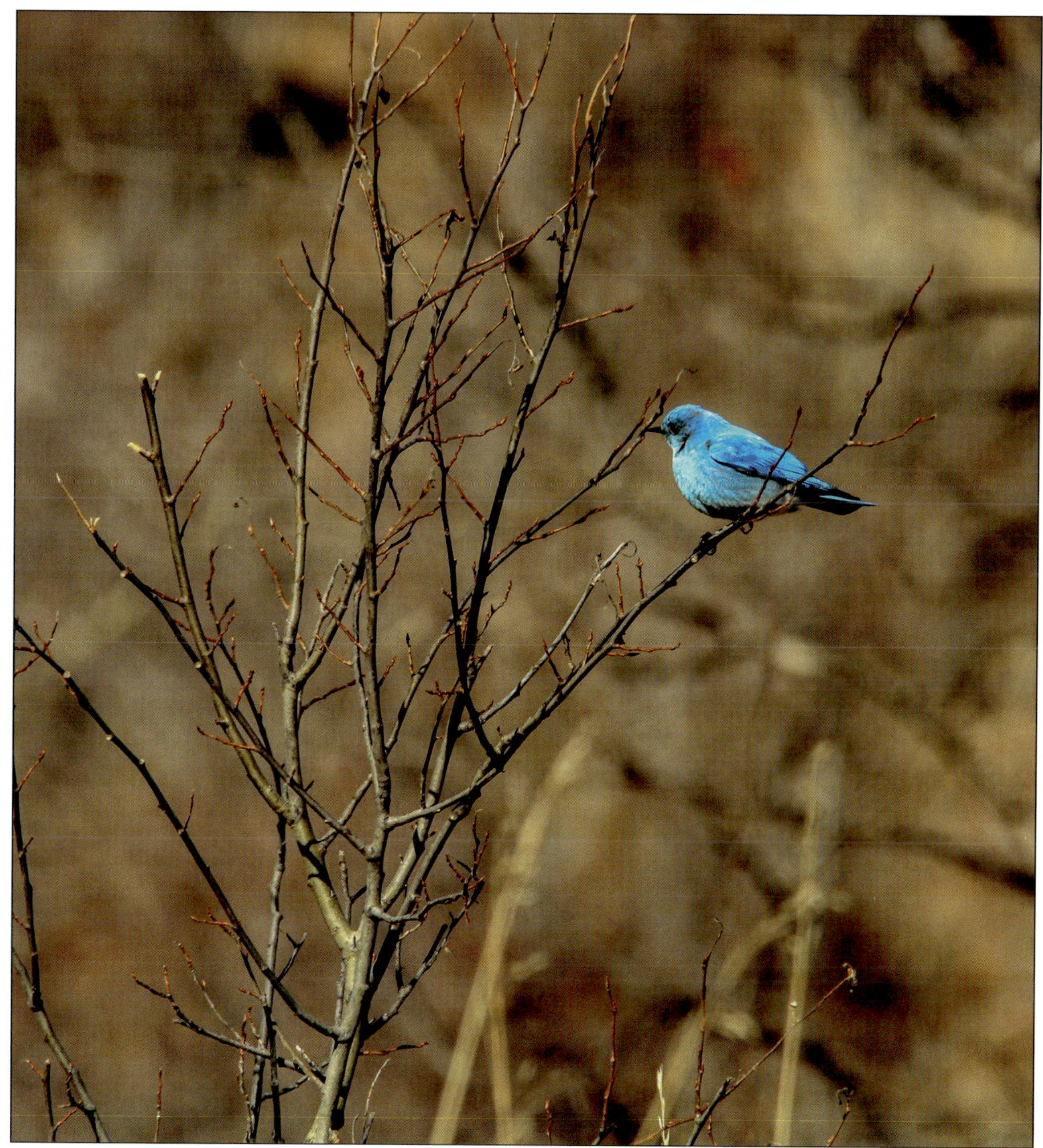

A male mountain bluebird hangs out by a nesting box in the foothills just west of Calgary.

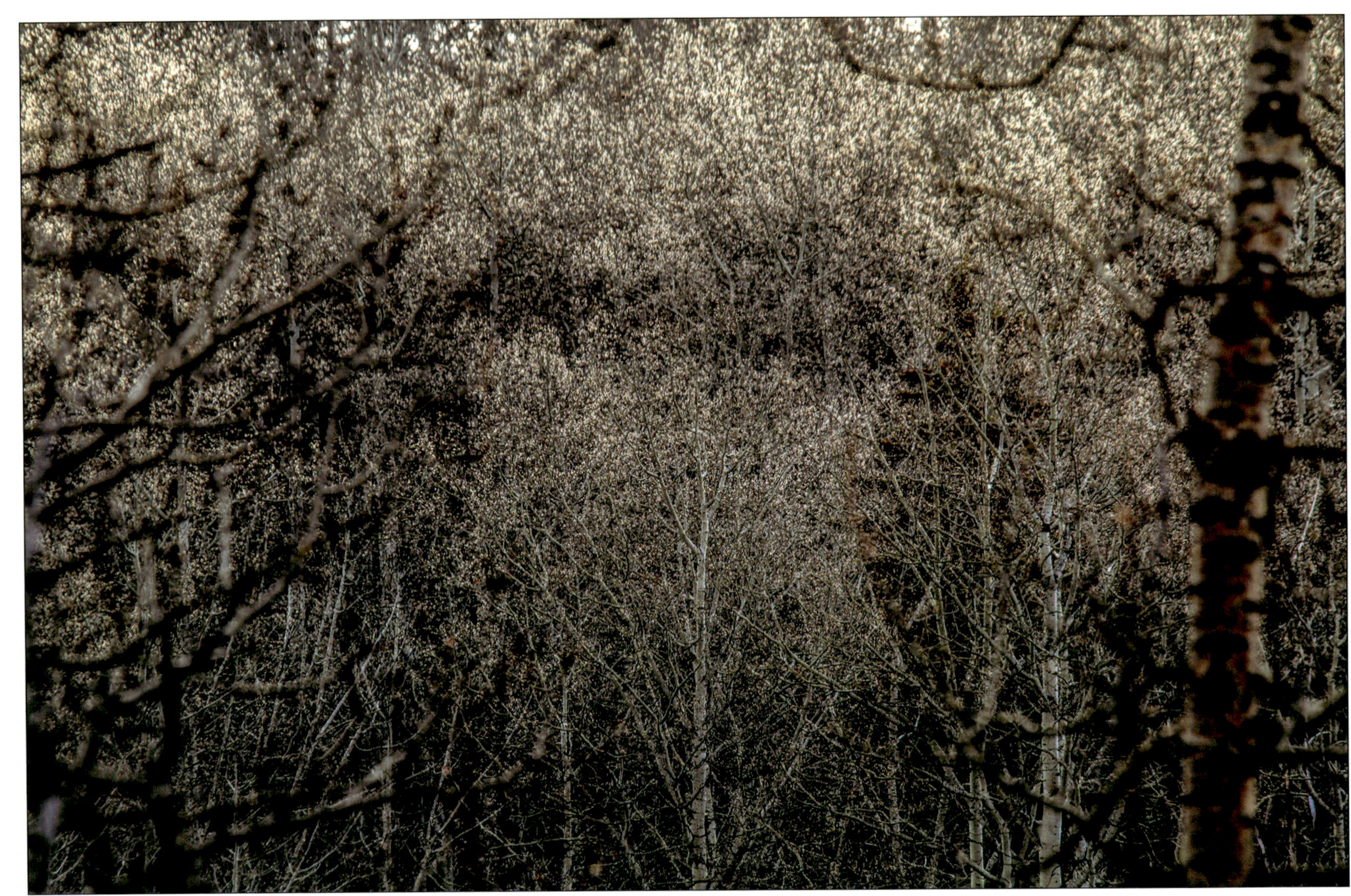

Aspen catkins in full bloom in the foothills west of Calgary.

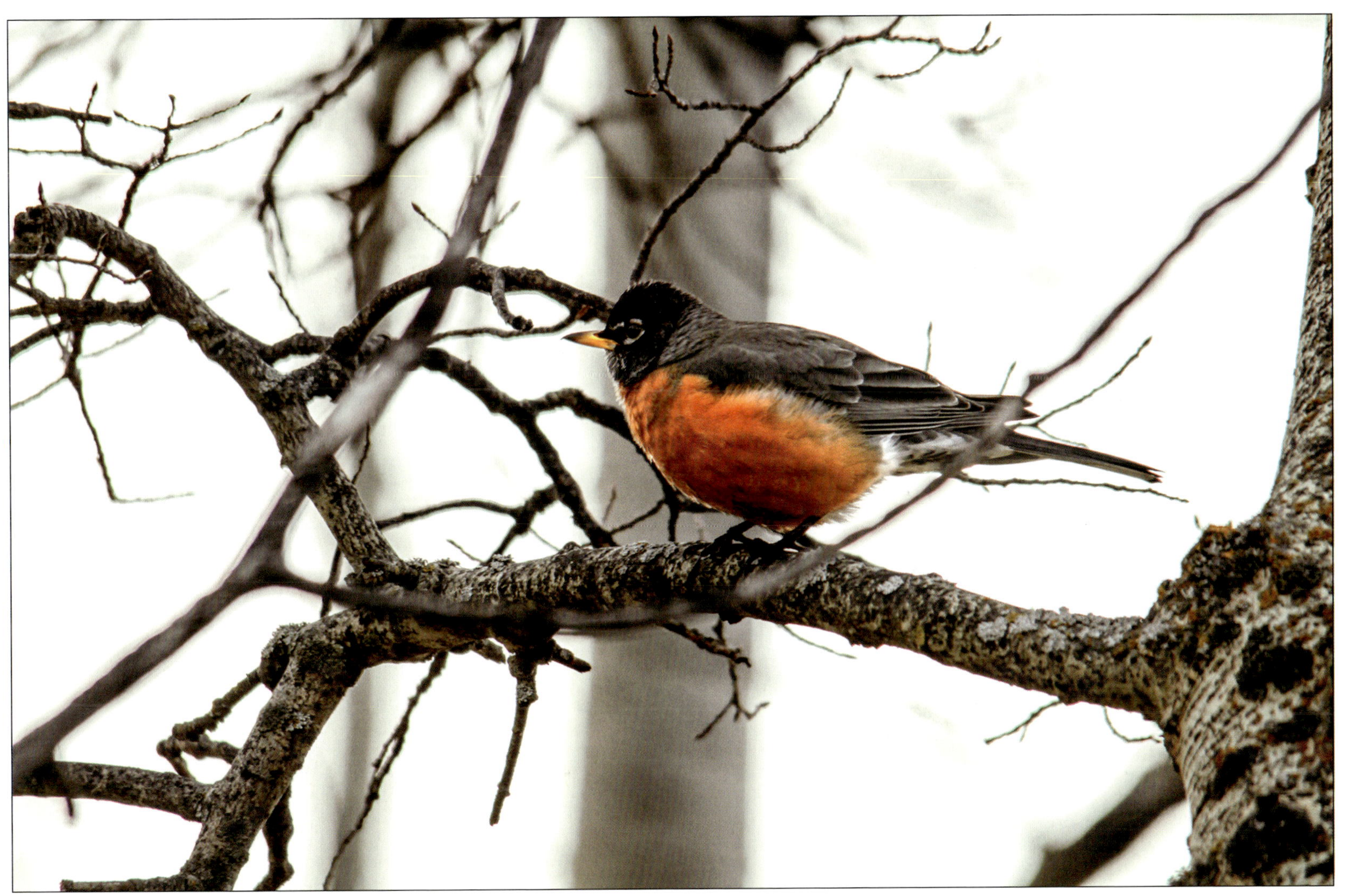

A robin perches on an old aspen tree just west of Calgary.

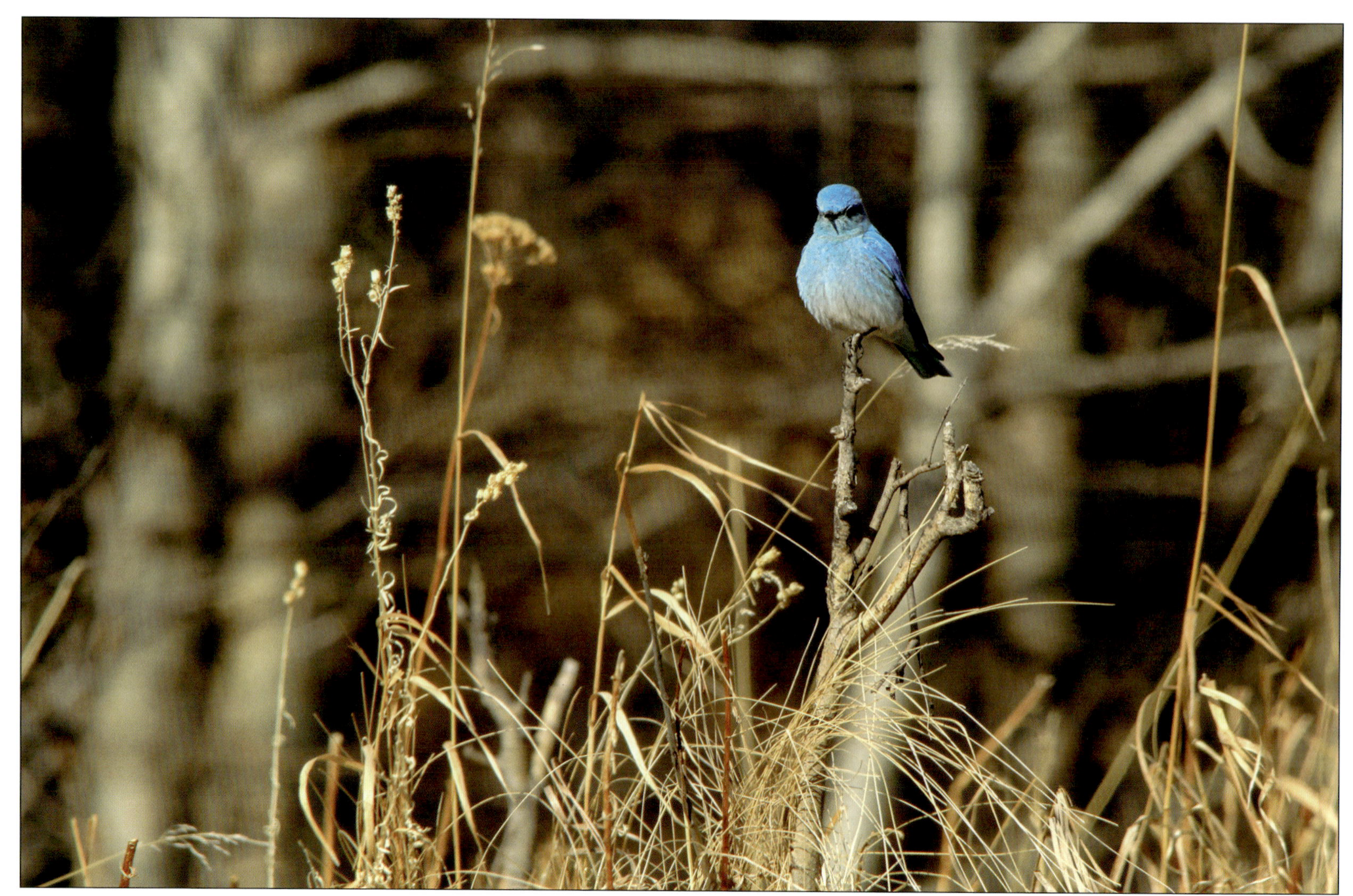

A bit of sky broke loose and perched on a twig southwest of Calgary.

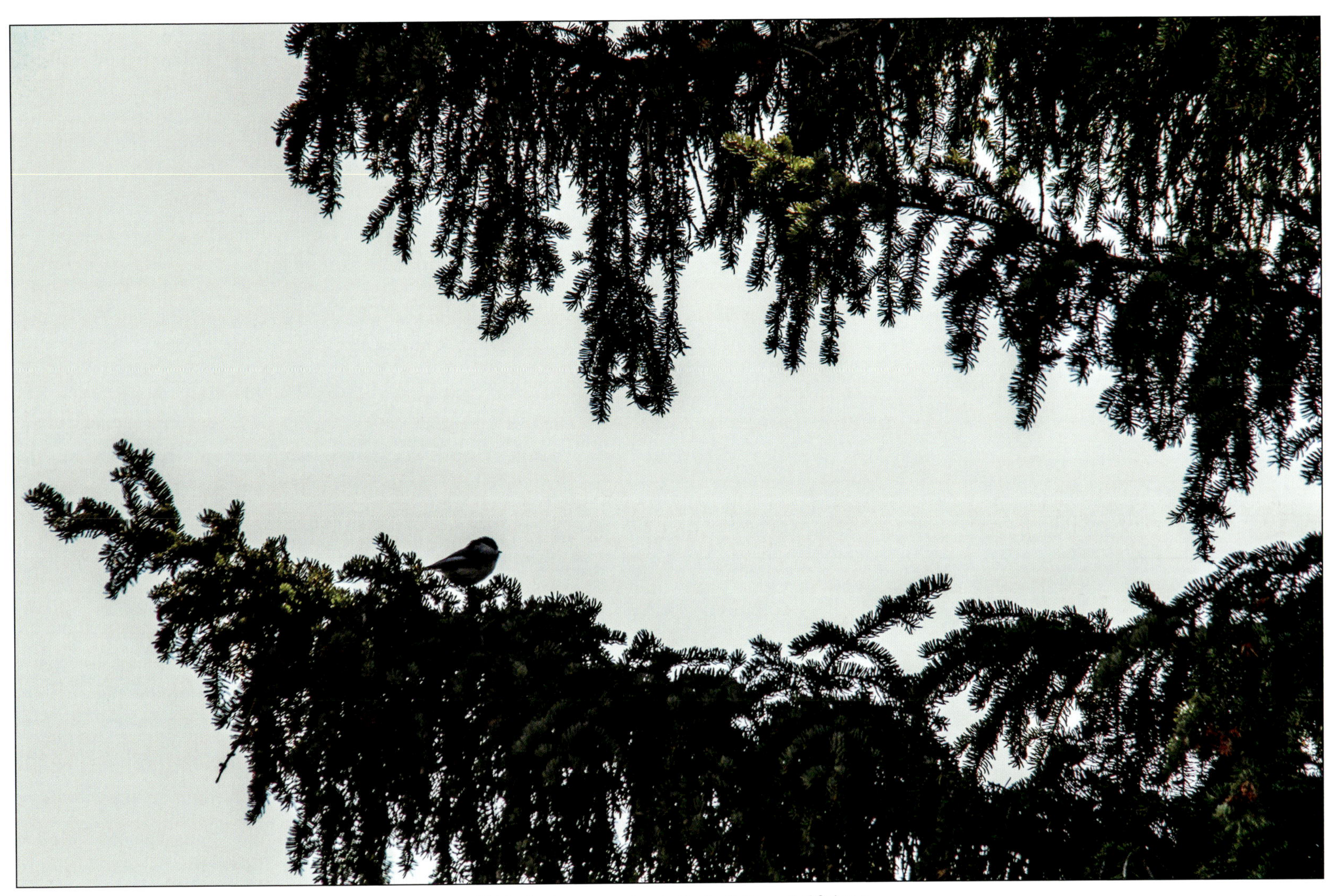

Chickadee in a spruce tree in the foothills west of Calgary.

CROCUS

I CAN NEVER DECIDE IF THESE guys are purple, mauve or magenta.

But whatever colour they are it's sure nice to see their little faces poking up through the winter-flattened grass.

I found these crocuses out on the prairie north of Cluny along Crowfoot Creek but they're showing up everywhere these days in spite of the not very springlike weather. The sun has been strong enough to thaw the ground, and as soon as they can, crocuses open their petals to the sky.

It was cool and rainy – with bits of snow pellets coming down, too – as I headed east on Tuesday. The sky was spectacular, jammed with every shade of cloud from snow white to nearly black, and I passed through rain showers and back into bright sunshine as I drove along.

The meadowlarks are back, too, and I saw several perched on fenceposts and declaring their territorial claims in song. Nearly every copse of trees had a pair of redtail or Swainson's hawks and every pond with even a splash of water was covered with pintail and shoveller ducks.

Tundra swans floated like icebergs on the bigger bodies of water, most of which were still mostly ice-covered. Geese grazed in stubble fields gorging on green grain and grass shoots. Flocks of ducks, crows and blackbirds wheeled through the stormy skies. Bees streamed out of their boxes near alfalfa fields and crawled on the plastic coverings that kept winter cold at bay, soaking up the solar heat.

But it was crocuses I was looking for. And I found them pretty easily.

In truth I didn't have to drive 120 km east of the city to look for them. They're blooming right here in town on Nose Hill and Tom Campbell's Hill in Bridgeland. They're just as pretty there as they are along Crowfoot Creek, but honestly, I'd rather poke around Crowfoot Creek.

I found the first batch on top of a windblown hill beside a gas site access road. They were barely out of the ground but the blossoms were wide open, the sunny yellow centres pointed toward the sky. There was nothing else green around them except for a couple of fresh shoots of rough fescue grass and some low pasture sage, but the silvery brown of the old grass made a happy contrast to the colour of the blossoms.

Time to belly crawl.

I removed all the junk from my jacket pockets, slapped a macro lens on the video camera and an extension tube on the still camera and flopped on the dry grass. Three sneezes later – dust, spores and dry grass tickle my sinuses – I started exploring the flowers.

The first thing you notice when you get close to crocuses is how furry they are. And they're furry for the same reason animals are – to keep in the heat. During the day the sun heats the ground and everything close to it. That's one of the reasons that crocuses bloom when the stems are so short.

As long as the sun is shining everything is relatively warm. But when it goes down and all that daytime heat gets sucked back up into the prairie sky it can get pretty chilly. Crocuses know this and when the blossoms close at the end of the day their fur coat keeps them warm enough to face the cold of dawn.

Up close the colour of the blossoms is intense, not only the purple – mauve, magenta – of the petals but also the bright yellow of the pistil and stamens inside the flower.

In fact, it's these colours along with the general shape and early blooming that led to these flowers being called crocuses. They look similar to European crocuses – the source of the spice saffron – but they're actually members of the anemone family, not true crocuses at all. In the states they're called pasque flowers because they bloom around Easter time.

Anyway, the colour is brilliant up close, especially with sunlight streaming through the petals and illuminating the bright yellow of the flower's interior. Add a scatter of bright, sunshiny pollen and it's just breathtaking.

Insects like it too. I watched one bug climb around the petals for a bit. Looked like a hunter but I'm a bit behind on my entomology. Couldn't tell you what that bee-like insect rolling around in the pollen was either but they both sure seemed to like hanging out among the flowers. The ladybug nearby was easy to identify, though. And I know it was on the hunt.

I rolled around on the grass for a bit and then ventured farther east. The storm I'd photographed from a hilltop near Blackie seemed to have siblings blooming up all over the place, and I drove through rain and snow showers past Makepeace and on east from Hussar before heading back west again through the high country north of Standard.

Deer were moving out of the coulees up onto the flats for their evening meal when I stopped by a south-facing hillside covered with crocuses. They were just closing up for the day, wrapping their fur coats around their shoulders and going to sleep. I took a couple of pictures and headed home to do the same thing.

Purple, mauve, magenta – the name of the colour doesn't matter. The crocuses are blooming. Springtime is here.

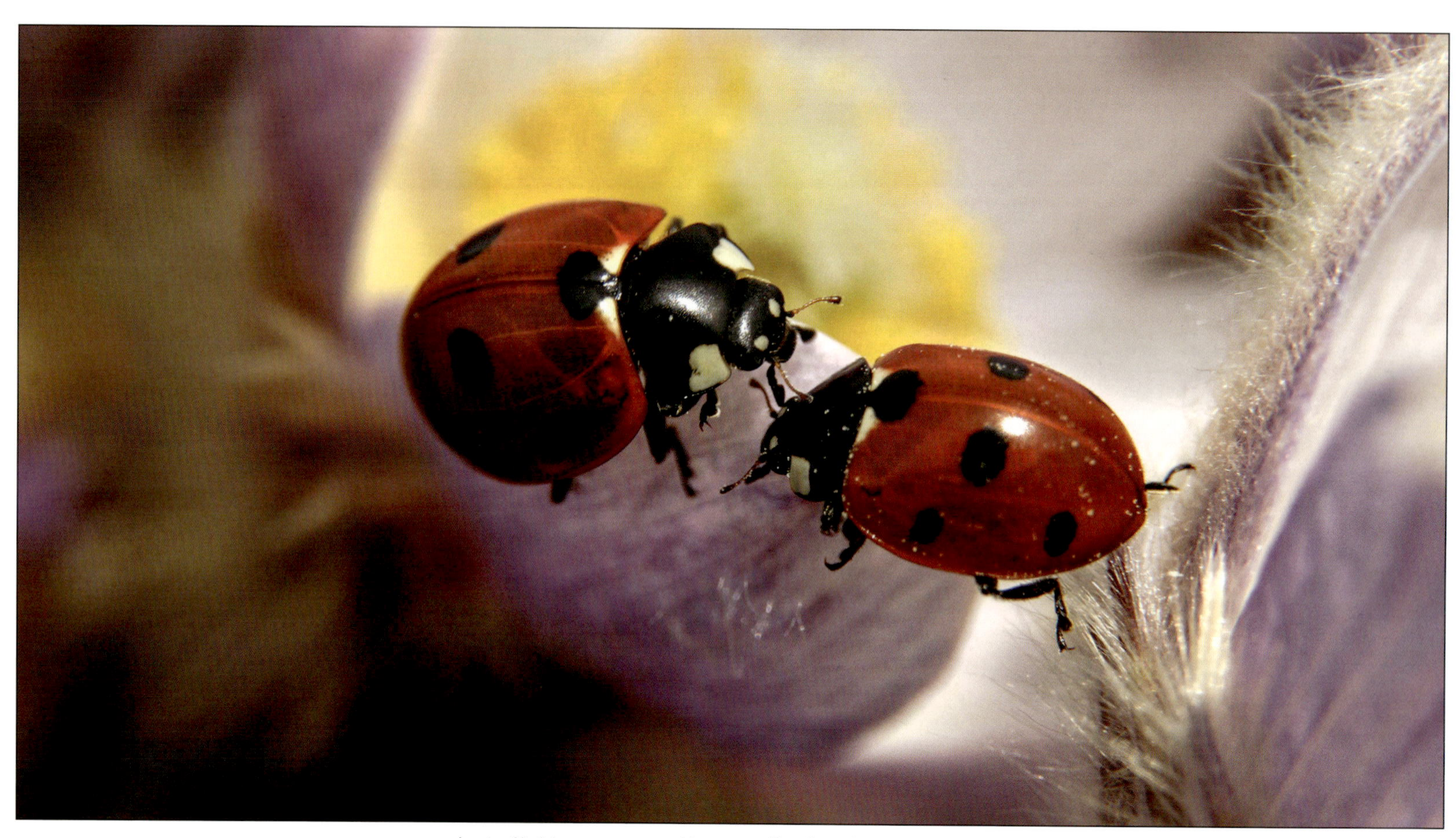

A pair of ladybugs on a crocus blossom on Tom Campbell's Hill in Calgary.

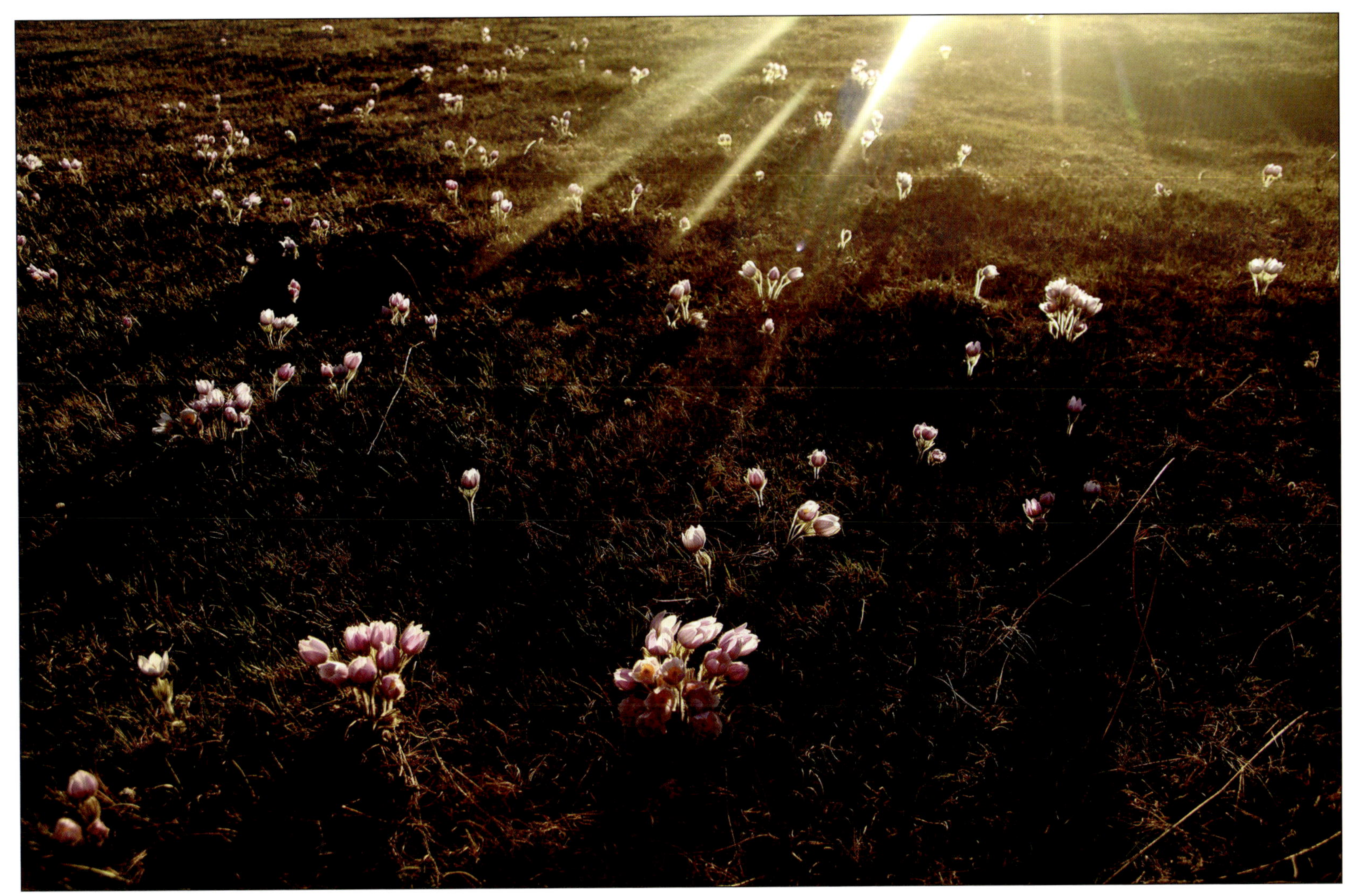

Crocuses photographed with a dirty lens near Carseland.

FOXES

I really thought the baby foxes would get up with the sun.

I figured they'd be out bouncing around as the amber light swept across the plains and kissed the summit of the Porcupine Hills. I was sure they'd be yipping and wrestling and biting each other's tails as the robins and meadowlarks sang their morning songs.

I was absolutely certain that I would pull up and they would stare at me, curious but unafraid, as I peered back at them through the lens on my camera, a happy smile crinkling and deepening the wrinkles on my face.

Well, at least the morning sun laid a smooch on the Porcupine Hills. Beyond that, all I saw was an empty pasture.

I've known about the generations of foxes that have denned here near Nanton for several years now, but I have never been able to catch them. My timing was always off – like this morning – or I didn't make it out that way before the family had dispersed.

But a friend had sent me an email a couple of days before letting me know the babies were up and about – thanks, Andrea! – so I set the alarm for 4:30 AM to make sure I was there for first light.

Now I will never complain about driving in the country as the day begins. No matter what time of year, dawn is always special. The way the light moves and colours change, the way sound travels, the way cool air settles in the valleys and hides in the shadows as the day warms up. I love it.

And I almost always have it to myself.

So as I drove south with Venus hanging bright in the bluing sky and the salmon tint of dawn brightening the eastern horizon, I knew it was going to be a wonderful day. And it's a good thing that I was feeling that way. An hour and half later, the Porcupines kissed and the sky gone from pink to blue, I kept on driving.

Foxless.

It was still just before 7:30 AM and the day was lovely and warm so I kept on going west and south.

Deer were everywhere. Whitetails and mulies thronged the pastures nibbling on new green grass, with a few of them taking advantage of the buds on the willows just starting to open.

Hawks patrolled the skies, Swainson's mostly out that way but I saw a few ferruginous hawks as well. Far off over a slough I saw a young bald eagle flying low with a contrail of ravens in pursuit. Why get your own breakfast when you can steal it?

Though the sun was warm there was frost in the shadows, and on the ponds out in the hills there was ice. I stopped to shoot some of the crystalline patterns illuminated by the low-angled sun, and as I stepped from the truck I was greeted by a wall of frog song. These guys really take spring seriously!

Aspen catkins caught the morning light as well, looking like frost on the branches. Won't be long before the fluff starts to fly. Up on the higher elevations there was still a lot of fresh snow from a couple of days before but it was melting rapidly as the day warmed. Bearberries left over from last year shone through while out in the more open areas great swaths of crocuses purpled the hillsides.

I saw my first Columbian ground squirrels of the year up the East Sharples Creek valley – talk about late sleepers – and a moose blasted across the road in a pretty obvious hurry.

Bluebirds were everywhere.

The males, all blue and looking so bright in their breeding plumage, stood guard against the incursions of tree swallows while their more drab mates gathered nesting material. They have the softest songs of any small bird, a kind of faint tinkling.

Their neighbours – and arch rivals – the tree swallows were roaring like a freight train in comparison. Not only were they fighting with the bluebirds for nesting boxes, they were fighting with other tree swallows. And whenever things calmed down, they fought with each other.

By now I'd made a circle and was heading back toward Nanton, rolling north again along the east side of the Porcupine Hills. The sun was high now and the day had warmed a lot. Heat waves danced off the road in front of me. I had a window cracked to keep cool as I drove.

And I was hungry. I'd been up for eight hours already and skipped breakfast so I was thinking about grabbing a bite in town. But first, a swing past the fox den.

And there they were, six little foxes not much bigger than kittens doing everything I had envisioned them doing. At 1:30 in the afternoon.

In the worst light of the day.

Heat waves made focusing a nightmare, shadows were harsh and unforgiving. And for video, the sound was horrendous with vehicles and wind making a constant roar. Forget about the amber light of dawn and the morning serenades of meadowlarks and robins.

But as I looked at them through my long lens the babies suddenly stopped and looked back at me. All at once the harsh light and cacophonous sound disappeared. My rumbling stomach didn't matter. The hours I'd been awake were of no importance at all.

And a happy smile deepened the wrinkles on my face.

The baby foxes had made my day.

But next time I go to visit them, I'm leaving at the crack of noon.

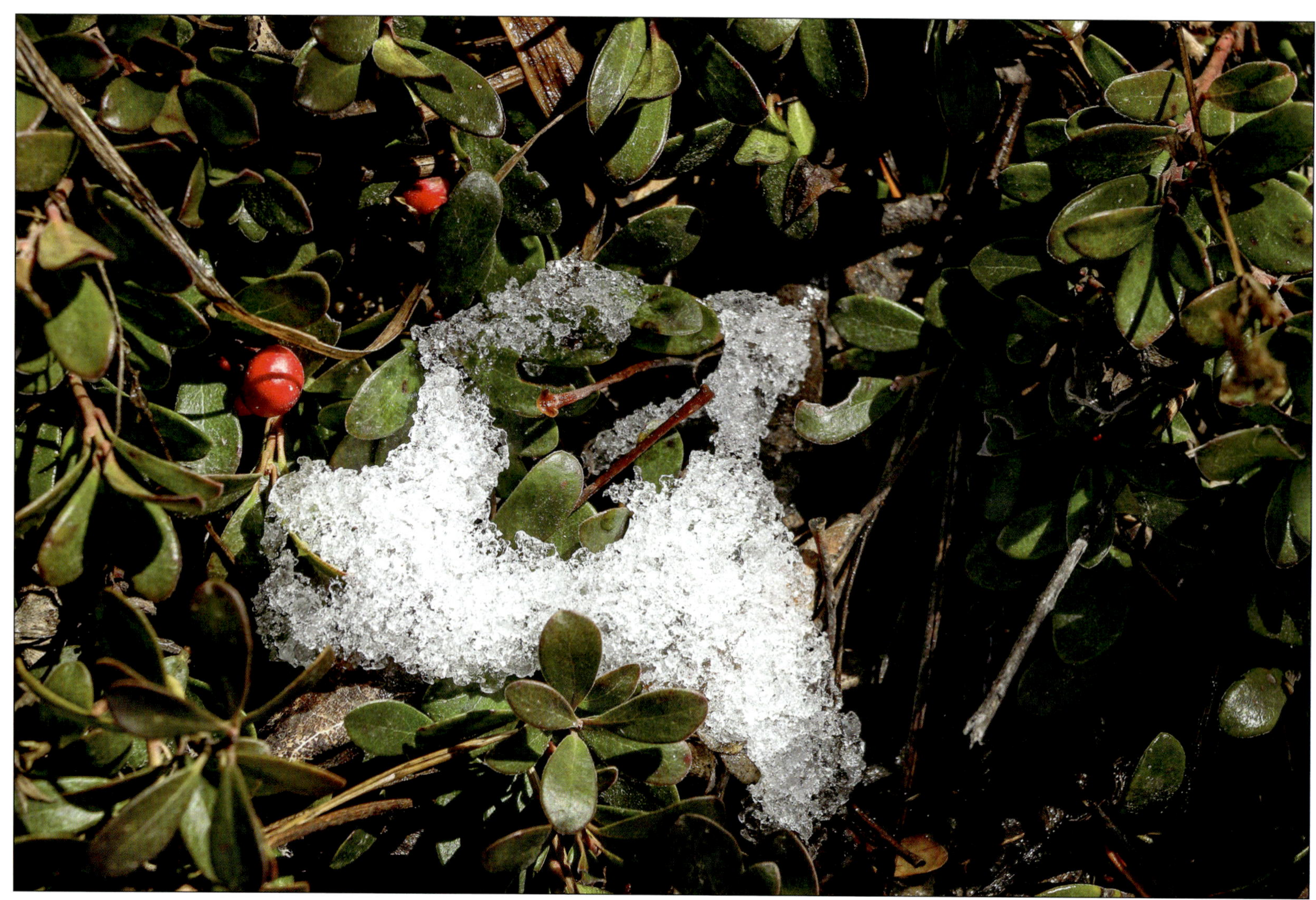

Fresh snow melts on bearberry in the Porcupine Hills near Nanton.

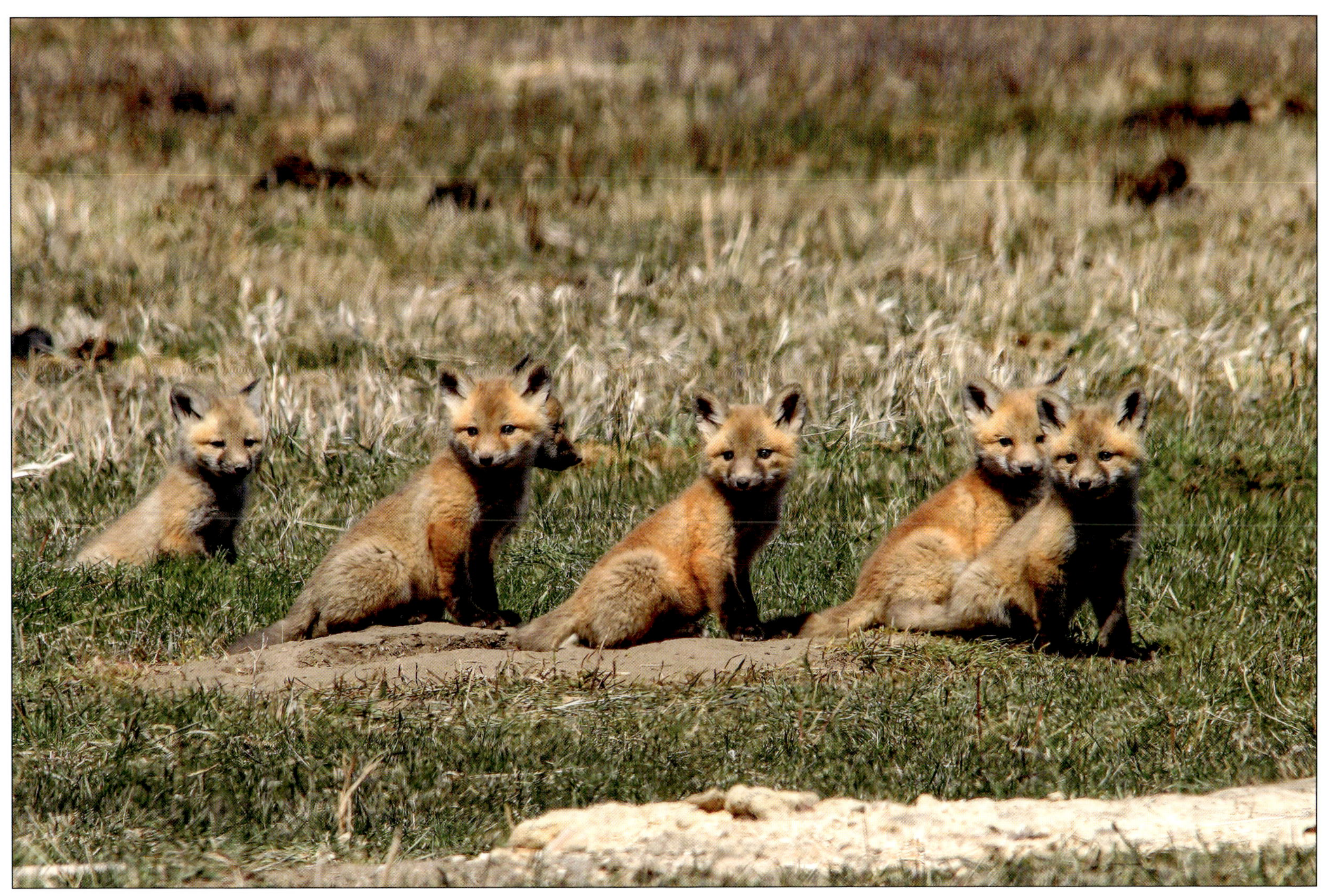

Baby foxes hanging out by their den near Nanton.

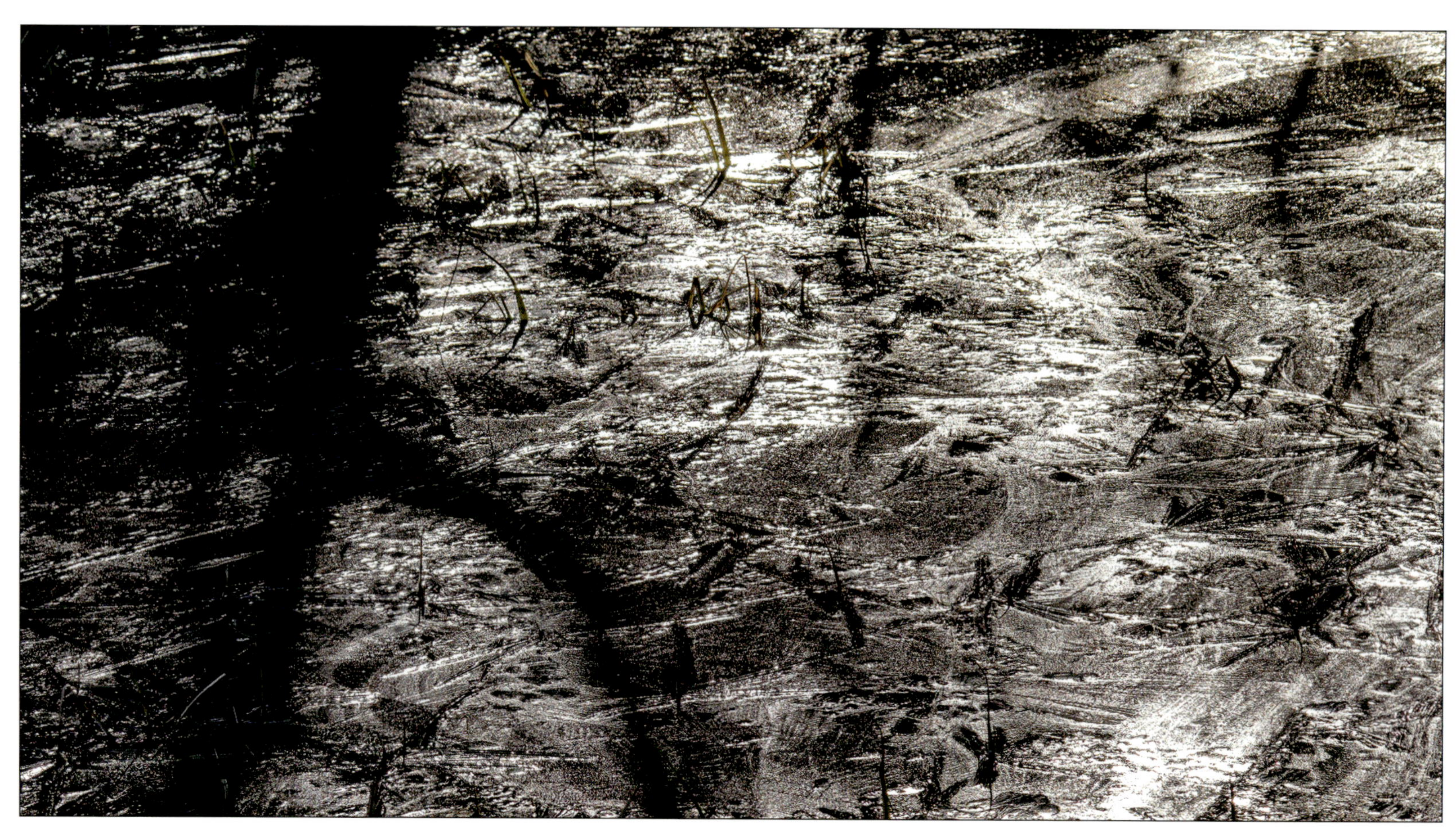

Cold spring mornings mean ice in the shadows in the Porcupine Hills near Nanton.

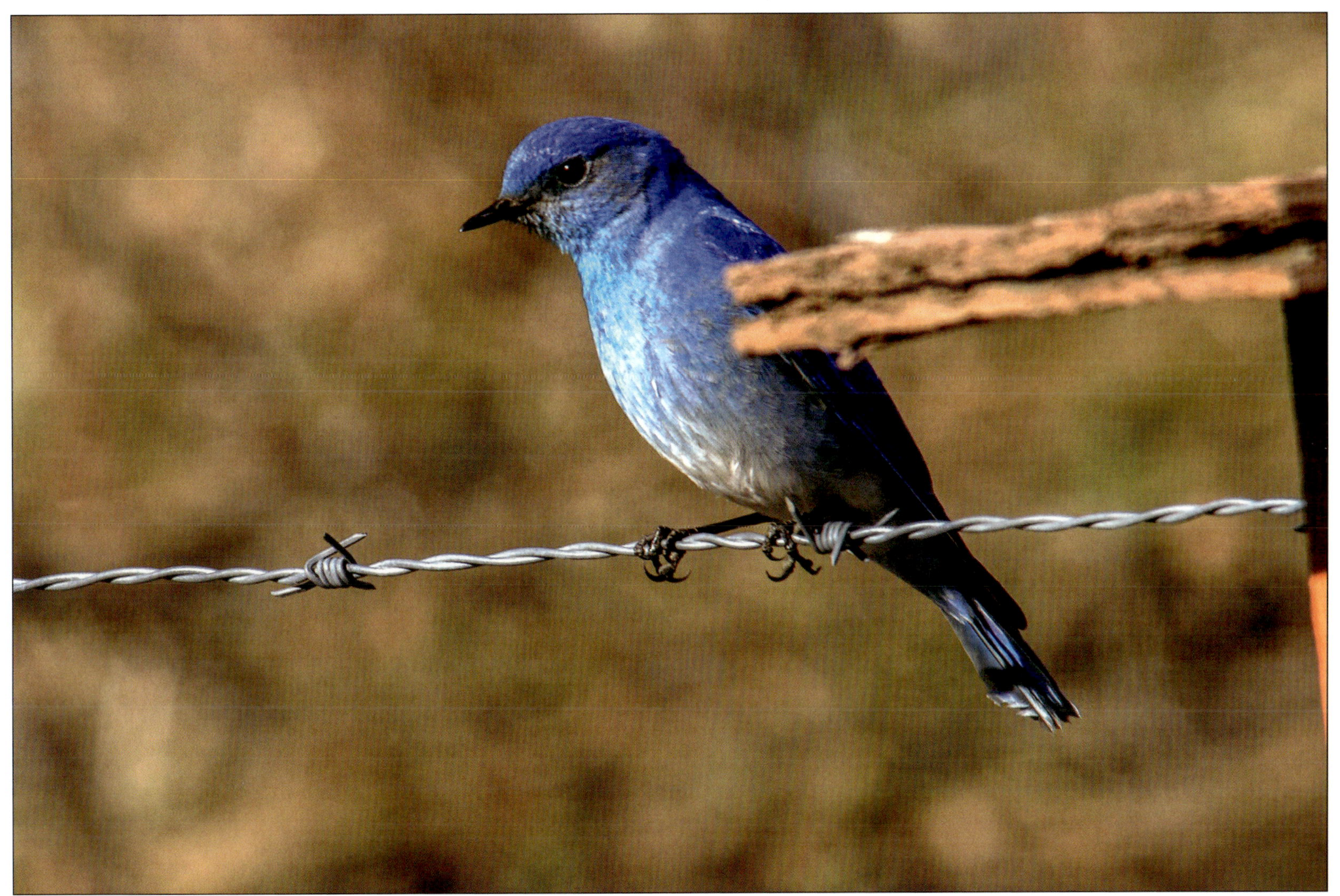

Male mountain bluebird keeps watch near a nesting box in the Porcupine Hills near Nanton.

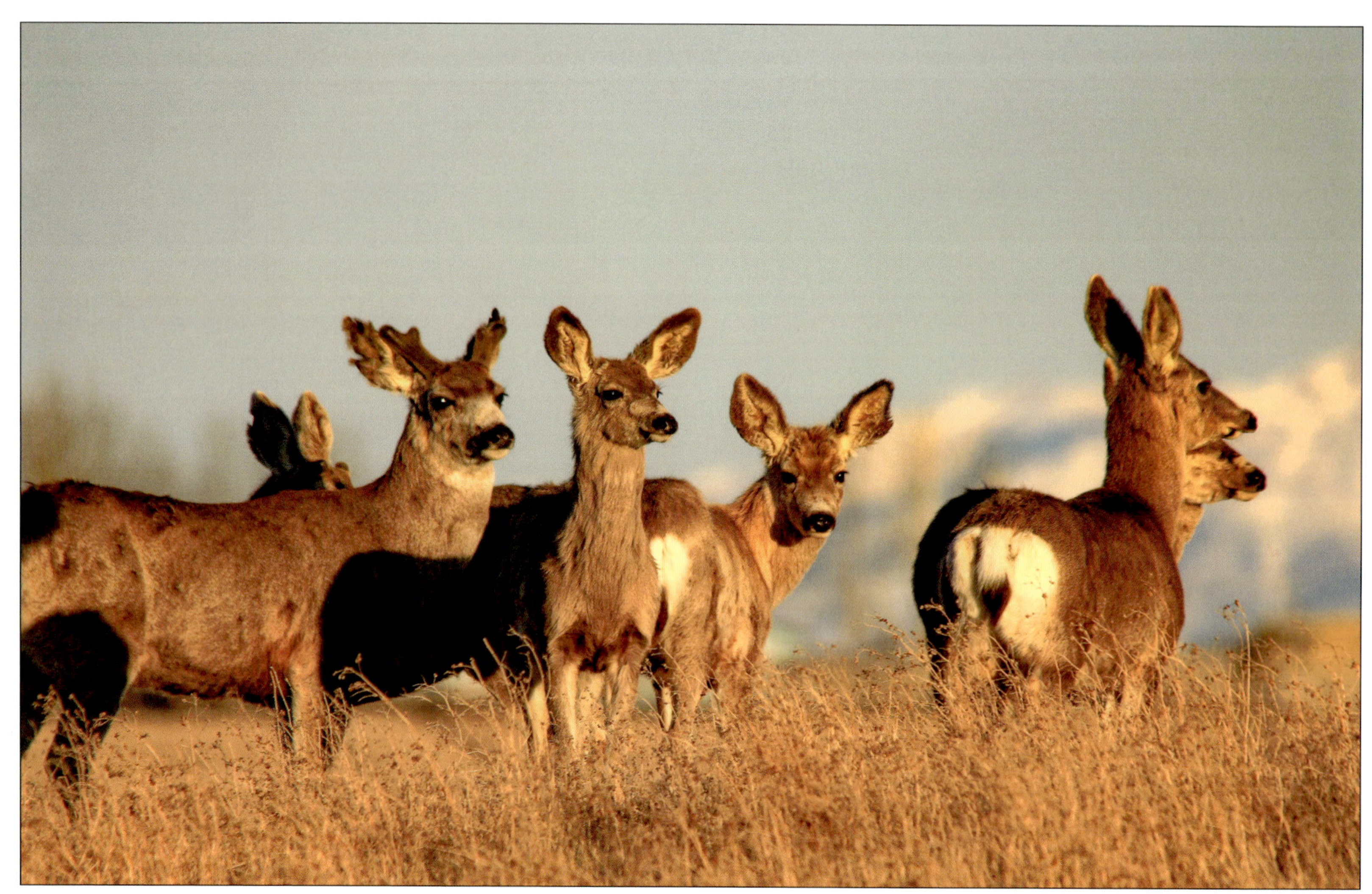

Mule deer in the morning light east of Nanton.

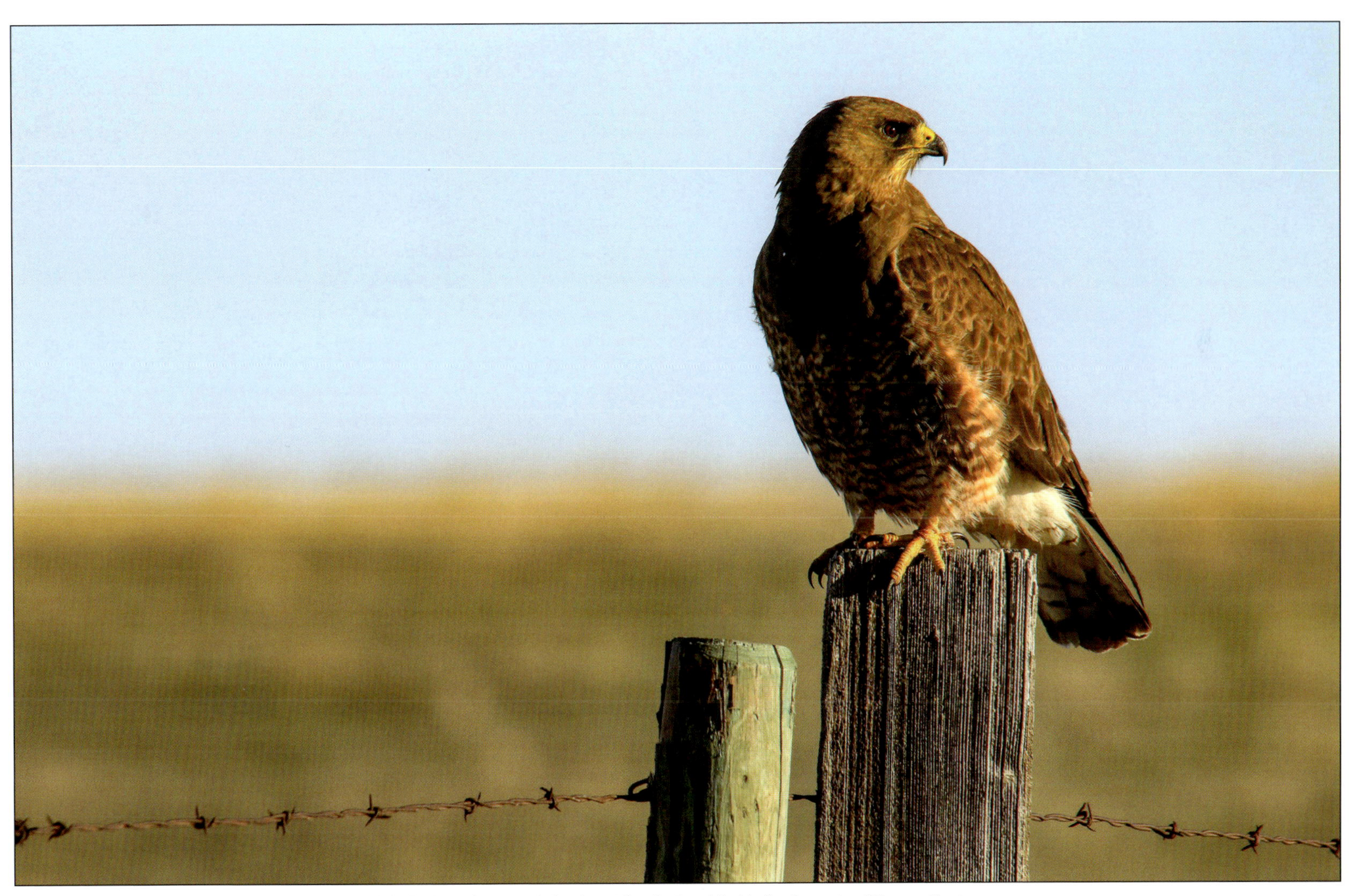

A dark-phase Swainson's hawk watches for breakfast in the Porcupine Hills near Nanton.

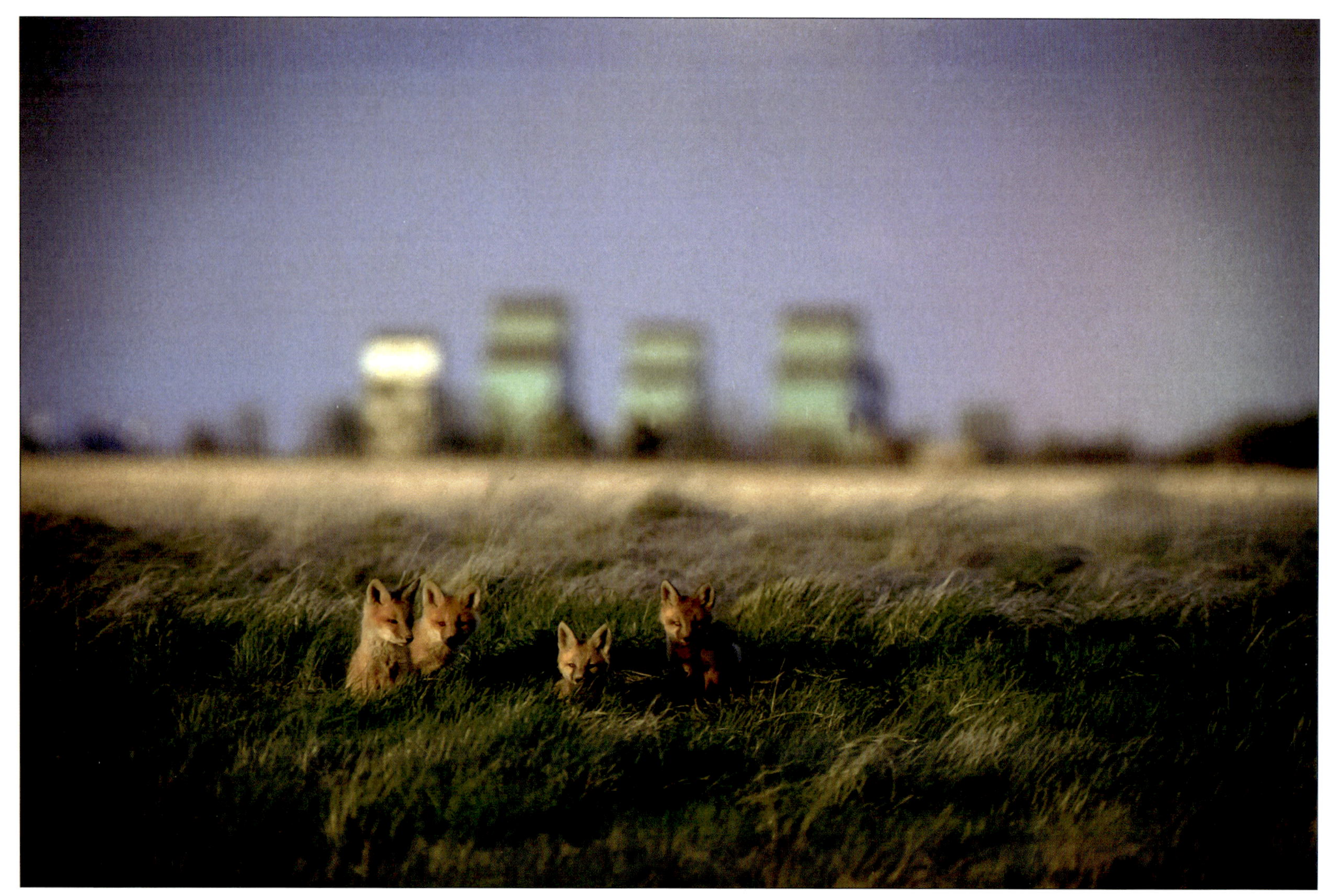

Foxes at Wrentham circa 1992.

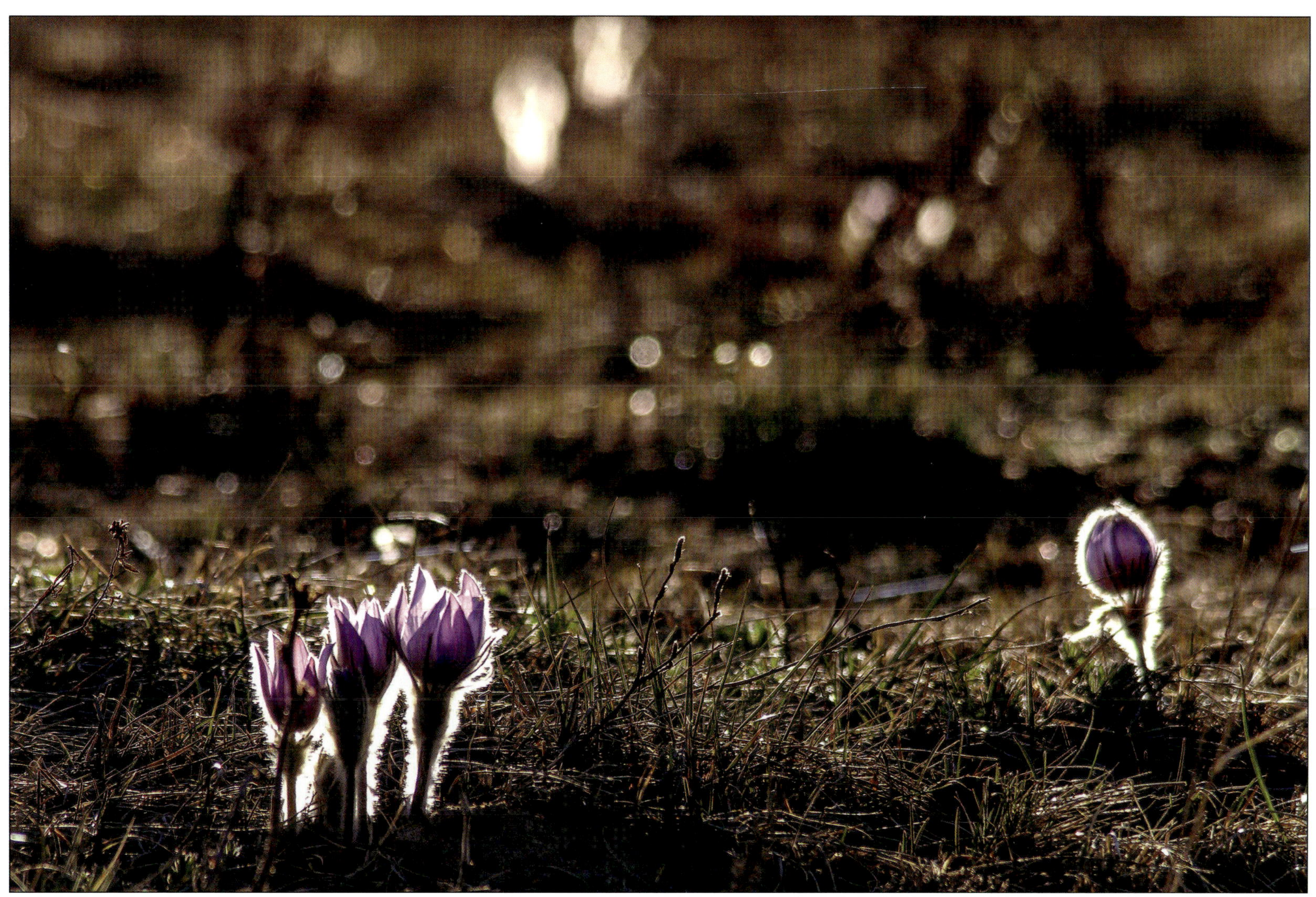
Crocuses bloom in profusion in the Porcupine Hills west of Nanton.

BEARS

I WAS UP IN THE HILLS between the Ghost River and the Bow to see what had happened to a dead deer.

I'd found it a little more than a week before, lying by the side of the road at the very summit of this plateau that divides the two watersheds. At first I drove right by it – you see a few winter-killed animals once the snow melts so it wasn't unusual – but I noticed something different about it so I stopped and walked back for a look.

I won't describe exactly what it looked like. Suffice to say that it hadn't been there long. There were cat tracks in the mud along the side of the road and the body was still warm.

I never saw what killed the deer – a cougar, I suspect – even though I waited down the road for three hours hoping it would come back. But a week later I was still curious about what had happened with the deer after I left so I went back for a look.

I headed out to catch the first light so it was barely 6 AM as I drove up the road to the height of the hills.

Mist hung in the valleys and frost on roadside grass glittered golden in the early light. The air was absolutely still.

There was no big rush to get back to where I saw the deer – whatever had happened to it was done now so another hour wouldn't make a difference – so I dawdled up and down the side roads.

The forest was full of bird song. I'm not great at identifying birds by their voices but I could definitely hear robins, red-winged blackbirds, song sparrows, flickers and the drumming of a ruffed grouse. I even heard the soft hooting of an owl.

Every little pond had ducks on it and geese grazed in the pastures among the horses. Whitetail deer stopped at the sight of my truck before bounding, tail flags held high, back into the trees. They're more easily spooked than their mule deer cousins but the dead deer I found was a mulie so maybe they're on to something.

I drove around the rolling hills and in and out of the trees for a while longer before finally heading up to where I'd last seen the deer. It was gone, of course. All that was left were a few patches of hair. I walked around to look for tracks and maybe some other signs of the hunter's identity but I found nothing. It was fascinating to see how the deer had been completely devoured, though.

I drove on down the road to have a look at the Ghost River valley. It was hazy and calm and scented with new leaves. There was ice on the ponds lying in the shadows. I stopped for a bit and then, dawdling, I headed back toward the summit.

I dawdled some more as I drove back toward the highway, stopping at a slough to listen to the birds and take a few pictures and then lingering to watch horses and magpies in a pasture.

And then as I drove by another road I saw something trot across it about a quarter mile away. I immediately thought about the deer killer, but no, I was sure that wasn't it. I'd only caught a glimpse but I was sure it wasn't a cougar. No tail.

I drove down to check it out anyway and as I crossed a little creek and glanced to my left I saw a pretty little cinnamon-phase black bear standing there with a mouthful of grass.

It looked at me for a few seconds and then looked around before dropping back on all fours. I expected it to take off running but instead it trotted over closer and stood on a fallen tree sniffing the air, still with a mouthful of grass, before heading into the trees. I followed in the truck for a minute but only caught one more glimpse.

I turned around and headed back to the main road, happy with the morning. It was not even 7 AM and I'd already shot a dozen pictures I liked.

So when I saw the weasel bouncing through the grass behind the squabbling tree swallows and bluebirds I was shooting near a nesting box on a fencepost, I was beginning to wonder if it might be a good day to buy a lottery ticket.

Truth is I see weasels with only slightly more frequency than I see bears. There's lots of them around but they're so furtive that you just don't see them. I just happened to stop in the right spot.

It seemed as curious of me as the cinnamon bear was, and I shot dozens of pictures as it stood up, ran a bit and dropped low in the grass before turning to look me in the lens again and again.

I walked back to the truck and stood listening for a minute before heading back down the main road. People were beginning to stir and in the still air I could hear their voices coming from acreages and ranches near by. I wondered if they knew what was going on in their neighbourhood, if they knew about the bear and the weasel and all the birds. I wondered if they knew about the dead deer and whatever killed it.

Yeah, I'm pretty sure they do. That's probably a good part of the reason why they live there.

I know that's why I go to visit. Especially early in the day. All this and I can still get back to town in time for breakfast.

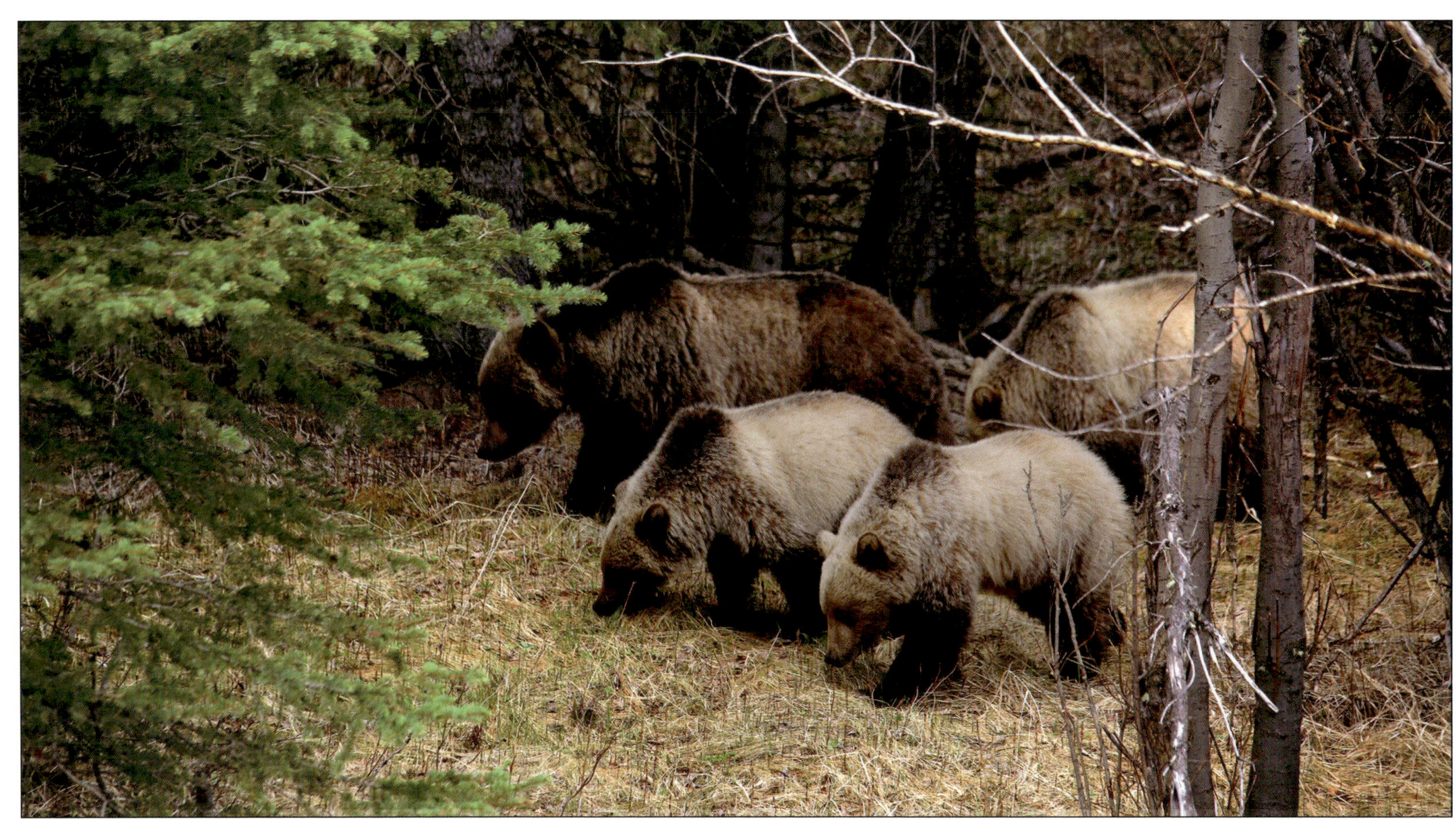

Mama grizzly and three cubs forage along the Kananaskis River west of Calgary.

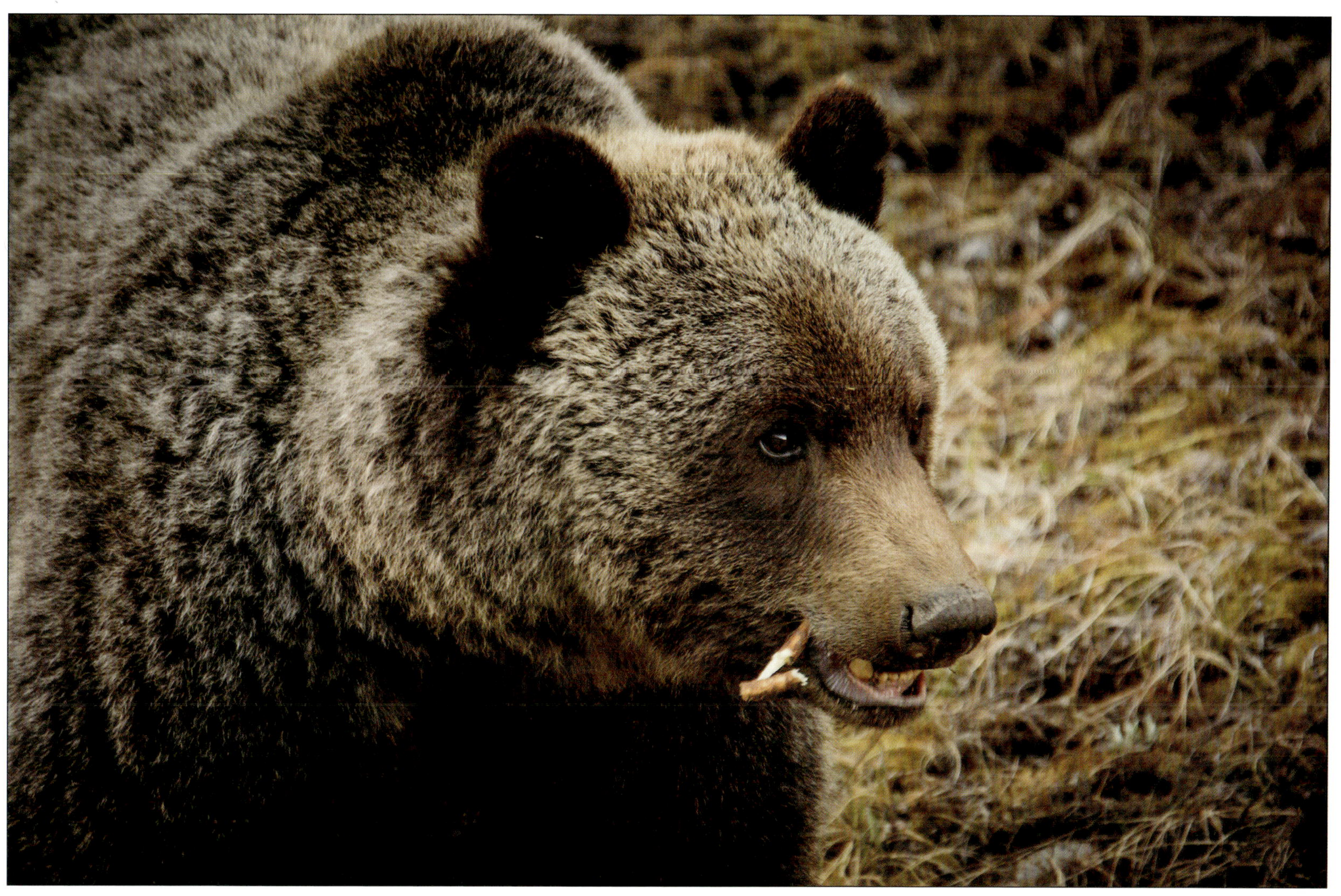

A grizzly bear snacks on spruce tree roots in Peter Lougheed Provincial Park.

CHEESY MOON

There was this big wheel of cheese hanging in the sky over the mountains. It was round and kind of mottled and glowed like a lamp with a too-small bulb.

I noticed it as I came over a rise above Jumpingpound Creek out west of Cochrane and I admit that it surprised me. I knew that a full moon was due any day and I was ready to look east to watch it rise just before sunset, but now, looking west just before 5 AM, I was startled a bit to see this big bright object in an otherwise dark western sky.

I'd hit the road around quarter past four in the morning because I couldn't sleep. Not for any particular reason. I just couldn't keep my eyes closed so I hopped into the truck and took off. Half an hour later and I was watching cheese float in the sky.

That in itself was pretty cool, but as I drove down a valley just a few kilometres down the road I found a family of trumpeter swans having a bit of breakfast. The sunrise sky gave off just enough light to brighten their huge white bodies, and the moon's reflection glistened off the dark water as they dipped their long necks looking for food.

Yeah, this was better than sleeping.

Nothing beats morning light; whether from the moon over the mountains or the first rays of the sun, it's the best. Especially on a morning like this.

It was cool, as most mornings are this time of year, and tendrils of mist rose into the air. Water lay flat and mirrored perfectly the surrounding countryside. By the time I got to Nakoda Lodge the sun had already brightened the mountains to the west and the shallow pond at the east end of Hector Lake kicked back an upside-down image of the shoreline.

Sprinklers along a street in Exshaw coated the lower limbs of trees with a layer of ice, and a robin took advantage of the wet ground beneath them to grab a beakfull of bugs for its babies. Just down the road an osprey brought a fish to its mate on a nest by the Bow River.

Bighorn sheep were just waking up on a hillside half in shade by Gap Lake, rams in one area and ewes in another. Magpies strode among them grabbing torpid insects stirred up by sheep's hooves. Mount Rundle rose into a tumble of cloud above Canmore but the Bow valley was bright, sunny and calm.

I stopped for a quick bite of breakfast and headed farther into the mountains as the sun rose higher in the sky. The moon had long since dropped behind the peaks and taken with it the morning glow, but the crisp shadows produced by sunshine slicing through cool, clear air were almost as nice.

I found a mule deer buck, its new antlers pushing up velvet-covered nubbins from above its eyes, nibbling on new buds on roadside shrubs and saw several elk high on a hillside doing the same thing. Past Lake Louise I found ducks squabbling on a pond and nearly got hit on the head by a yellow-rumped warbler chasing a mayfly as I stood in the shade of a spruce tree taking pictures. Guess it didn't see me.

A bit of haze had started to form in the Bow valley as I gained elevation, but it was still only just a little past 9 AM so the light stayed just fine. Ravens soared against the blue sky over Bow Lake and I had to shield my eyes from the glare coming off the still-frozen, snow-covered surface of the lake.

I stopped and looked round. The air was filled with bird song, as it had been all morning, with song sparrows trilling from tree tops, warblers and chickadees trilling in the brush and even ravens adding their coughs and cackles to the symphony. A chipmunk nibbled something in the shrubs just a few feet away.

The mountains glittered with snow and the sky, now turning milky as the mist rose in the warming air, started to fill with clouds easing in from the west. A feeder creek tinkled as it tumbled across a gravel fan before disappearing under the ice of the lake.

The moon that I'd seen kiss the mountains five hours before was now hanging like a cheese somewhere over the Pacific Ocean, on its way to becoming the full moon of the following day. By now, six days after I last saw it, the shadow of the earth has started to cross its trajectory, darkening it into its monthly eclipse before crossing off it again and letting its full glory shine.

A month from now there'll be another cheese hanging over the mountains, another nearly full moon racing the sunrise to the west. But it will be just a few days shy of summer by then, the swans will have moved on, the smaller birds will be on their nests and working hard to feed their babies, Bow Lake will be a glacial blue and the mountain snows will have melted back to higher elevations.

And I'll be here again. Because waking up at four in the morning because I can't sleep isn't a hardship this time of year, it's a blessing. I get to see the best part of the day.

Cheesy though that may sound.

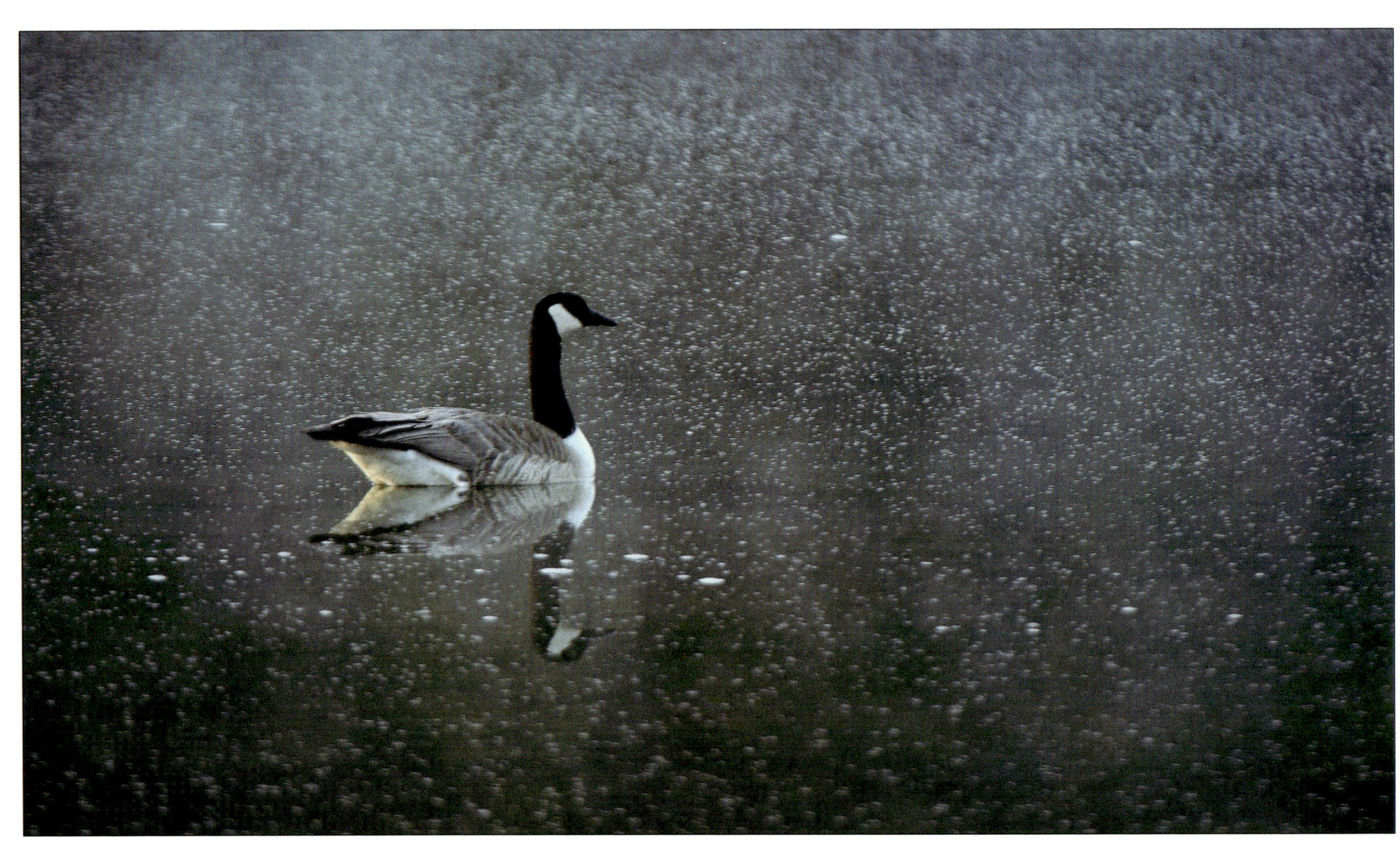

Goose in the mist at Hector Lake.

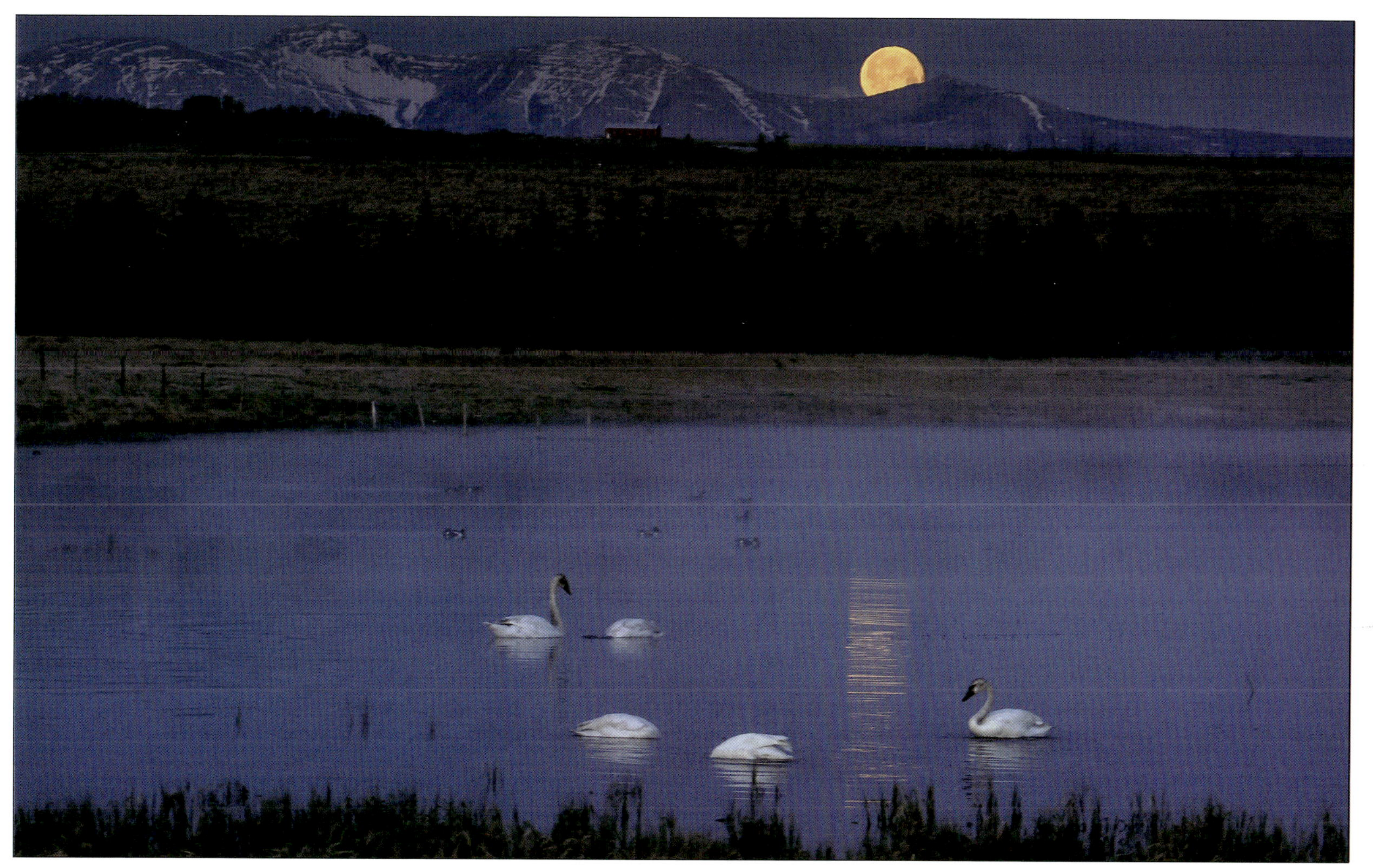

Trumpeter swans and the setting moon near Scott Lake Hill.

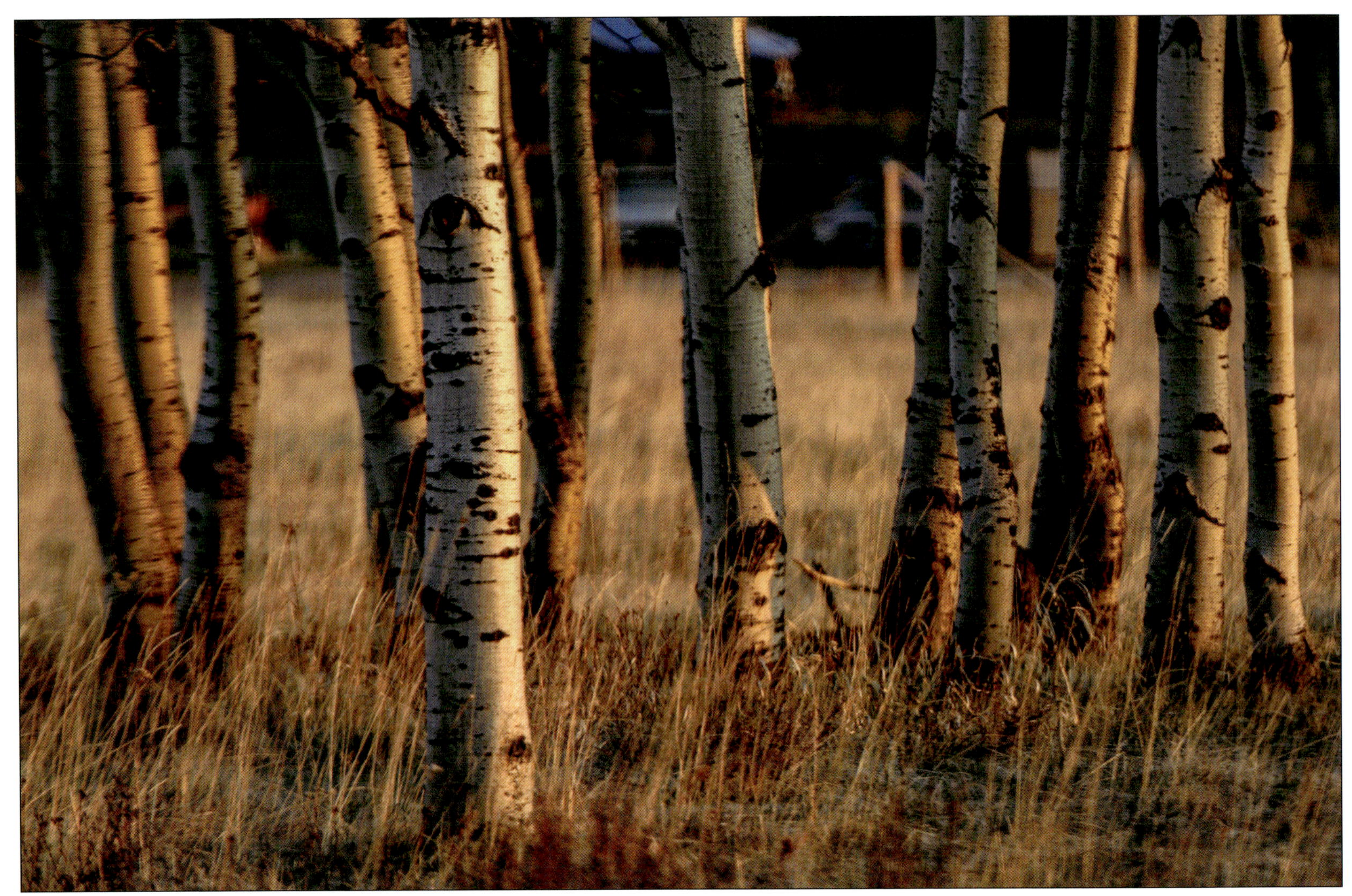

Aspens in the setting sun along Threepoint Creek near Millarville.

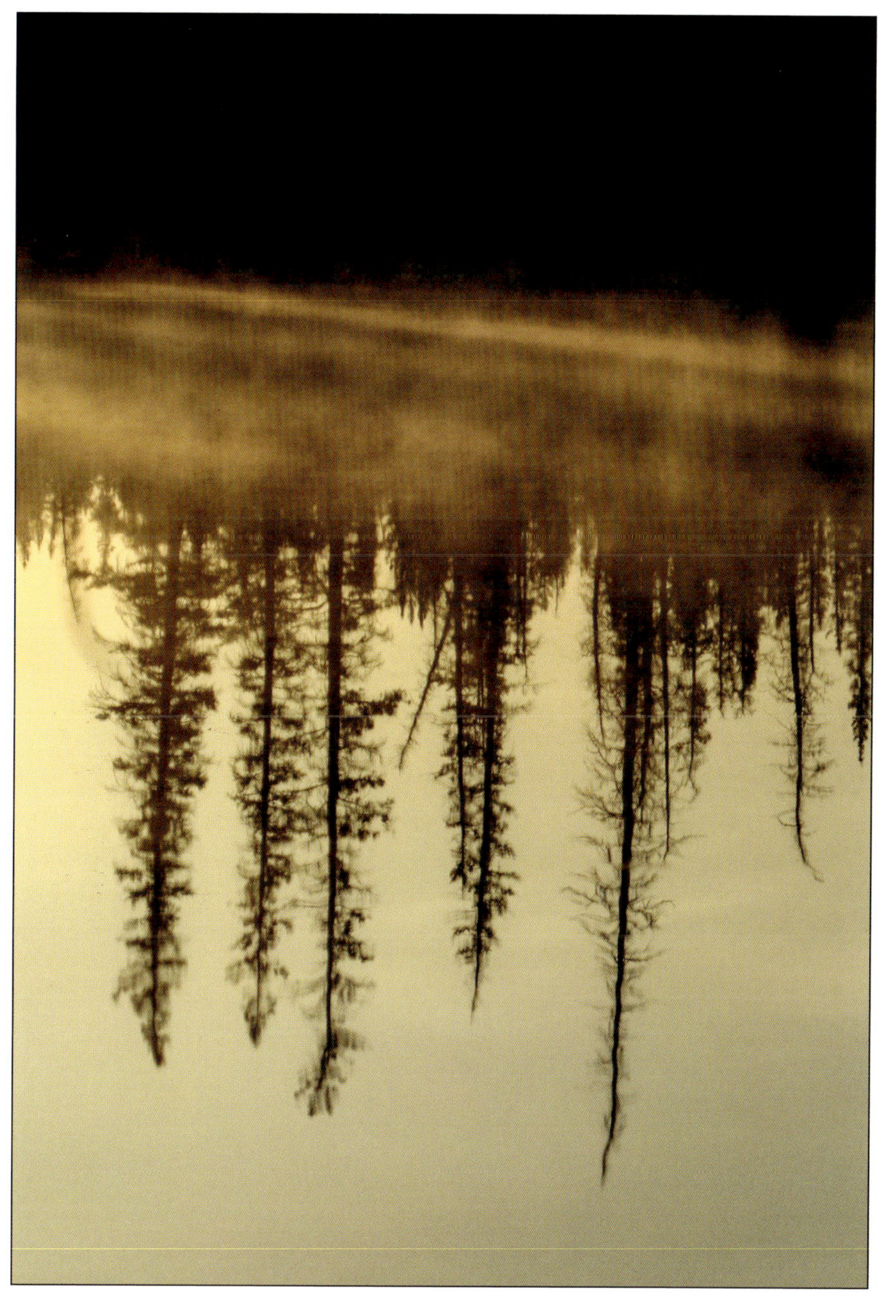

Mist on Hector Lake.

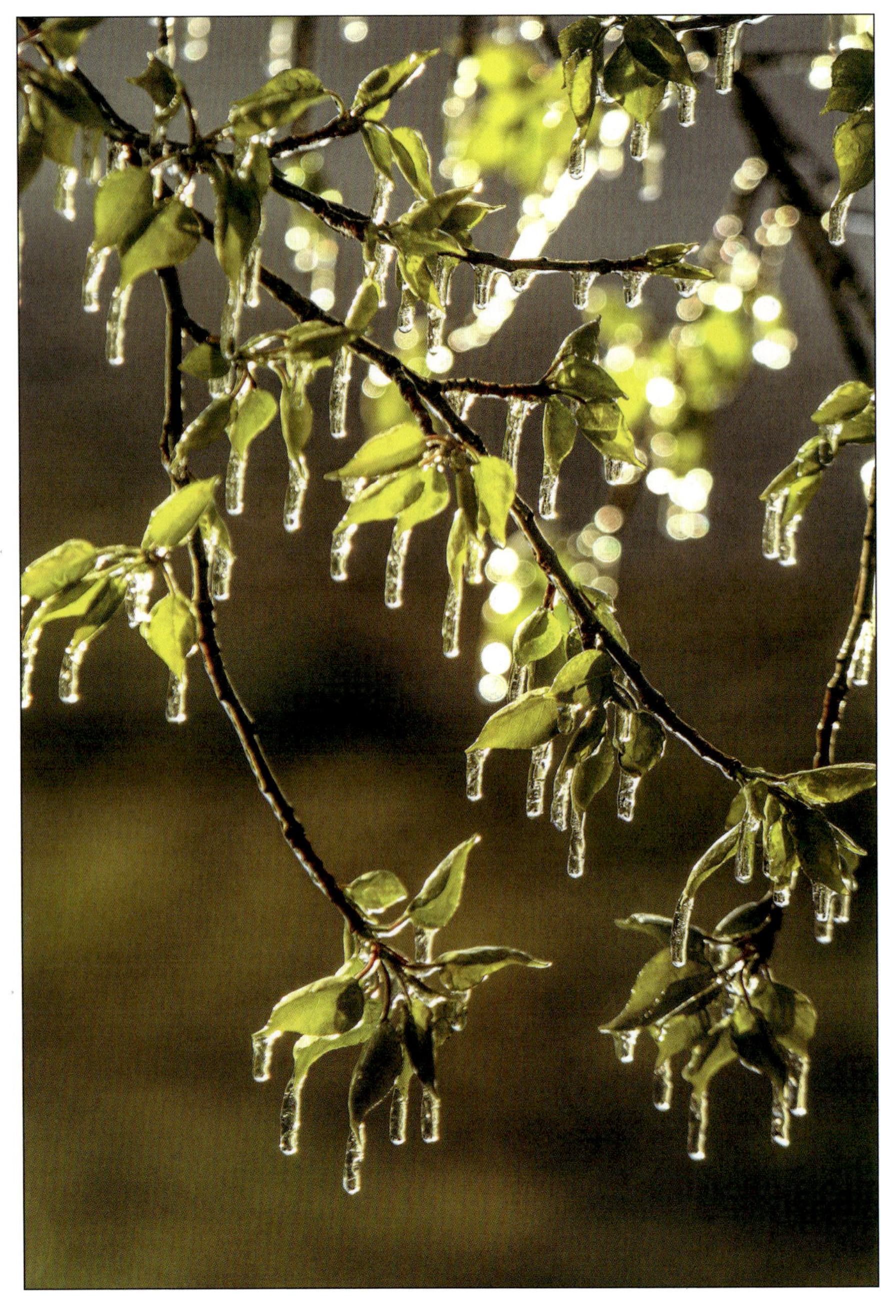

Early-morning sprinkler ice on poplar leaves at Exshaw.

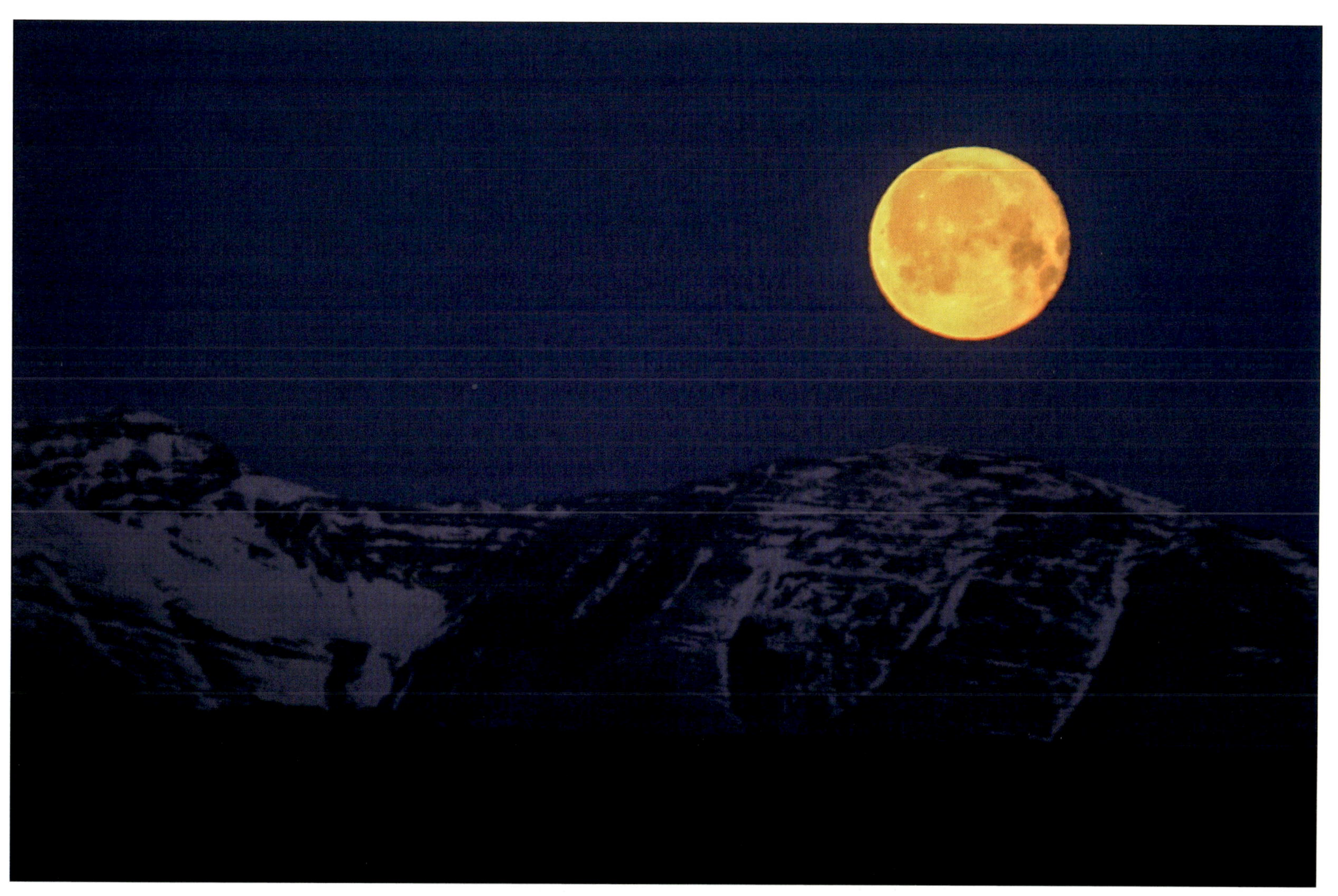

Moonset near Scott Lake Hill.

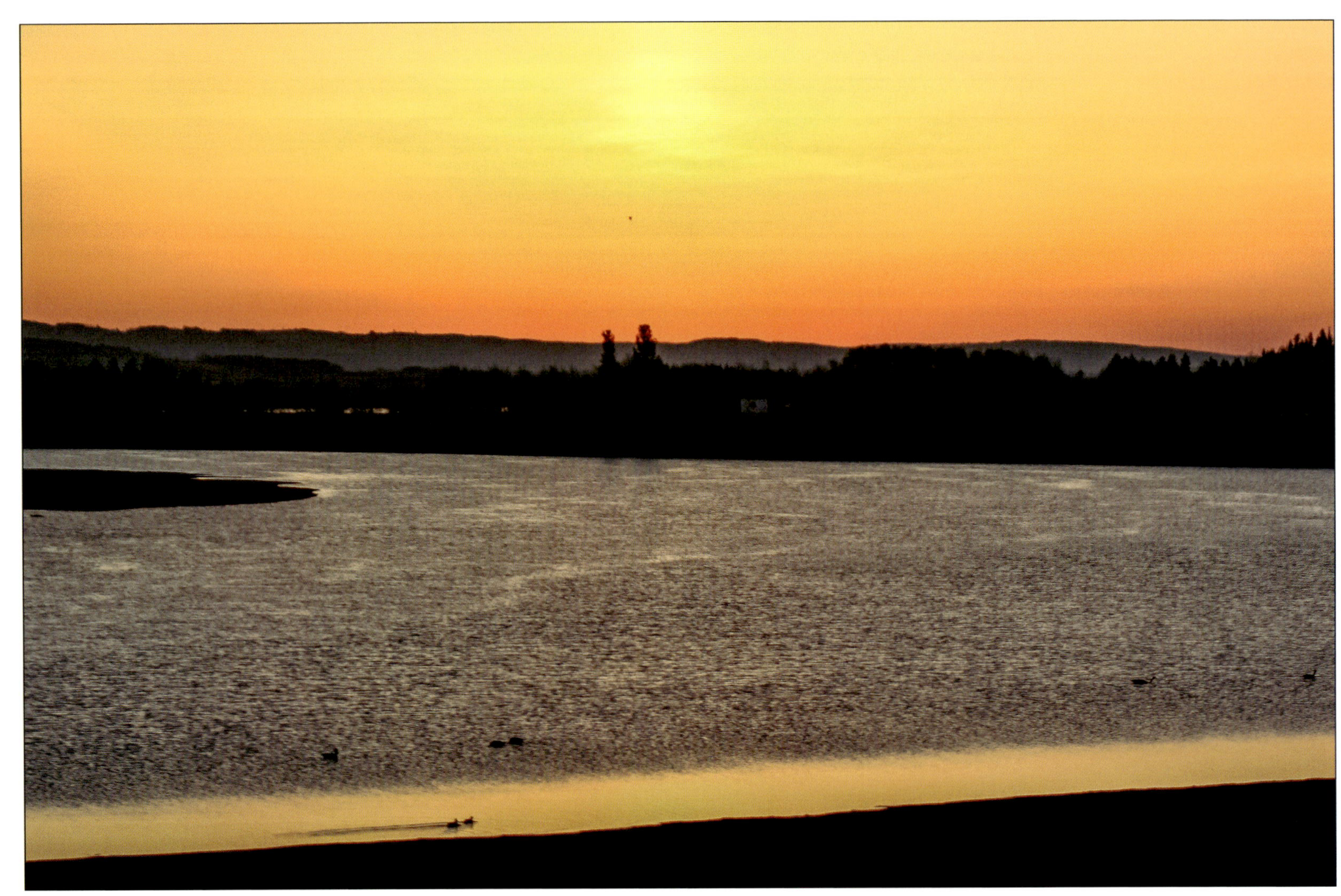

Sunrise on the Bow River at Morley.

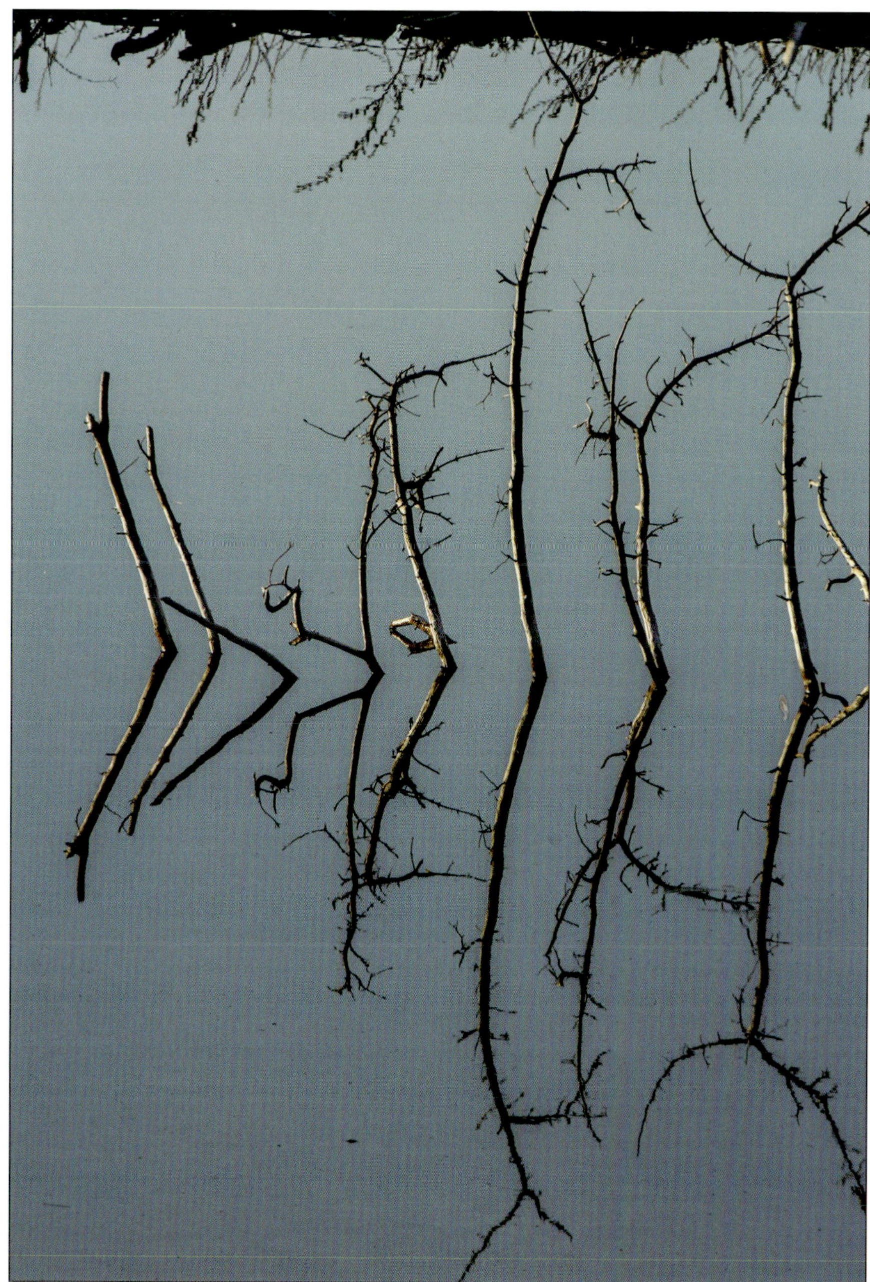

Sticks reflected in Hector Lake.

HIGH WATER

I LIKE MUD.

It's squishy and slippery and it makes a mess wherever it shows up. It covers things up and dries to a hard crust. It makes for tough driving and it sticks to everything.

But I like it.

For one thing, it's fun to play in. Who doesn't like to let that inner kid go and just head out stomping through the slop and getting as mucky as possible? Or go driving down a slimy road or through a big puddle – safely and with respect for other people and the land, of course – and making a big sloppy mess?

Okay, maybe I'm in the minority. I was definitely in the minority as I was kneeling in the slop along the Bow River at 7 AM on Tuesday morning.

But as I kneeled down and put my left hand into six inches of fresh river-deposited silt to brace myself while I shot a few pictures, I was happy as a pig in, well, mud.

The high water from last week's rains was subsiding as the level of the river slowly backed down toward normal, and as the water pulled back it left behind a nice fresh layer of silty muck.

People, we all-knowing beings who think our way is far better than nature's, generally hate this stuff. When the houses we build on floodplains that were dry at the time the home was built have their nicely manicured lawns covered with this stuff when the river inevitably bursts its banks, we complain to the heavens.

But rivers are living things and they set their own ever-fluctuating boundaries.

You can see those boundaries and their shifting nature when you look at the Bow River from the top of the valley east of the city.

Looking down at the brown river flowing below you can see where the water has run up into the grass and where old channels are flowing again. And you can see cottonwood trees.

Cottonwoods are the biggest trees on the prairie and they only grow along water courses. That's why you see them along irrigation canals as well as along river and creek valleys. They like to have wet feet.

And they need periodic floods to keep them thriving.

That muck along the river's shore? That's what cottonwoods need to help germinate their seeds. In fact, without occasional floods cottonwoods would cease to exist.

As trees go, they don't live very long, maybe 150 years. So those big trees you see all gnarled up along the Bow east of the city put their roots down sometime around the time the railroad made it to Calgary in the 1880s. Most of them are a lot younger. The ones in the city – in fact, most of the trees in the city – aren't much older than a lot of your grandparents.

So when you're standing on top of the river gorge out south of, say, Dalemead and you look down to the river, the cottonwood trees you see mark the lines of mud deposits from old floods. Where a stream has redistributed soil, cottonwoods grow.

Those riverine forests are full of life, especially at this time of year. Birds sing from every tree and the forest floor is covered with early spring flowers and perfumed by the scent of chokecherry and saskatoon blossoms. It's a beautiful place to be listening to the wind whisper in the new leaves with the high water of the river rushing by.

And there's all that life-giving silt sitting so sloppily along the riverbank. Robins and sandpipers poke in it for water-borne bugs and bits of food, worms crawl through leaving their trails. Kingbirds flit through the air after insects hatched from river-bottom nymphs whose life cycle coincides with the high water. Bits of shiny minerals carried here by water coming all the way from the mountains glitter along the shore.

And it feels good between the fingers, all silky and cold.

Floods and high water bring life. They may be inconvenient for us but they are part of the world around us. We too often forget that when it comes to a battle with nature, it's always nature – no matter how long it takes – that will win.

So if you're casting a covetous eye on a river-valley property shaded by cottonwoods chances are real good you're going to end up with silt on your lawn. You're not going to like constantly having wet feet.

But the cottonwoods will love it.

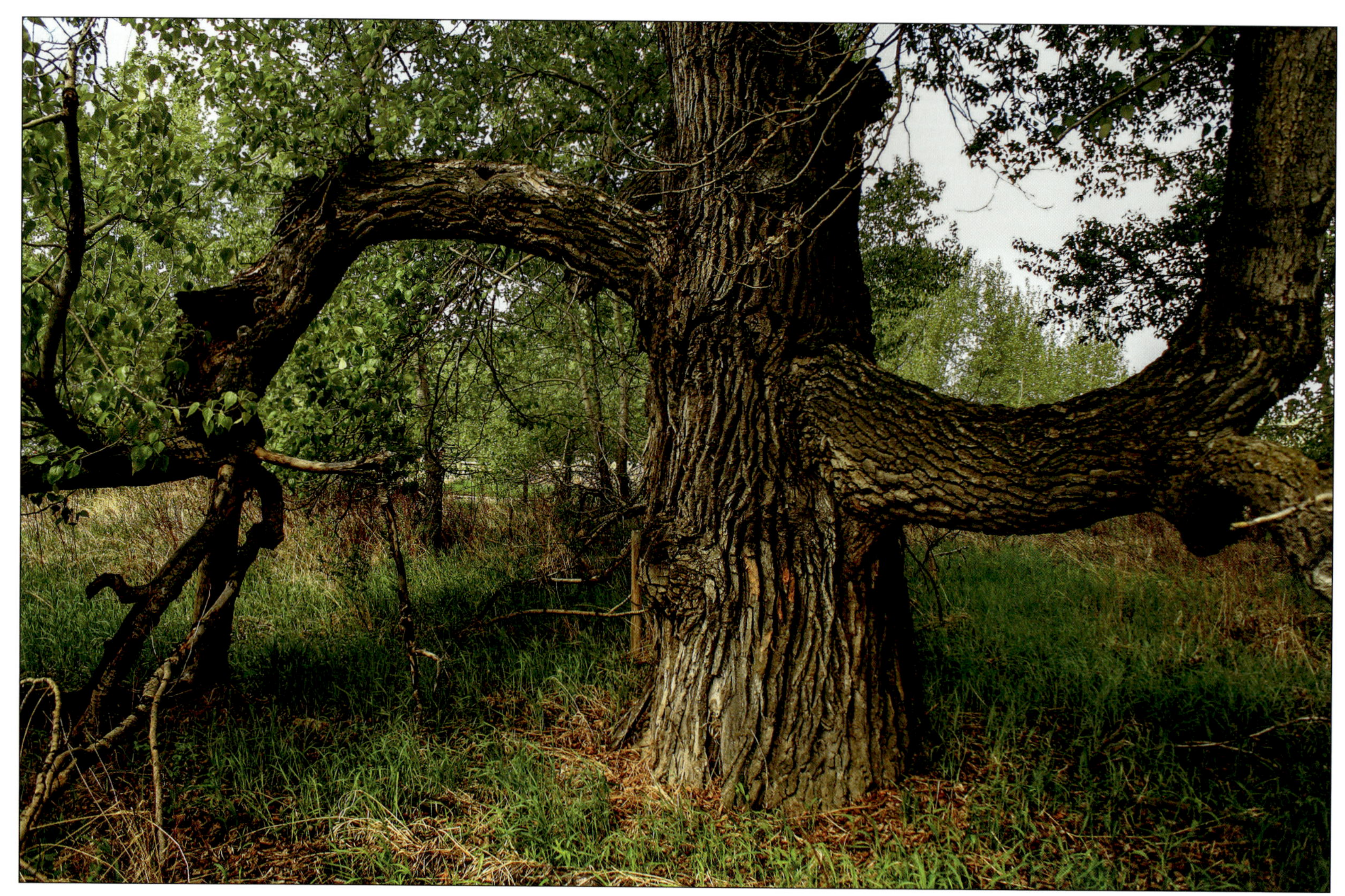

Cottonwood trees along the high and muddy Bow River.

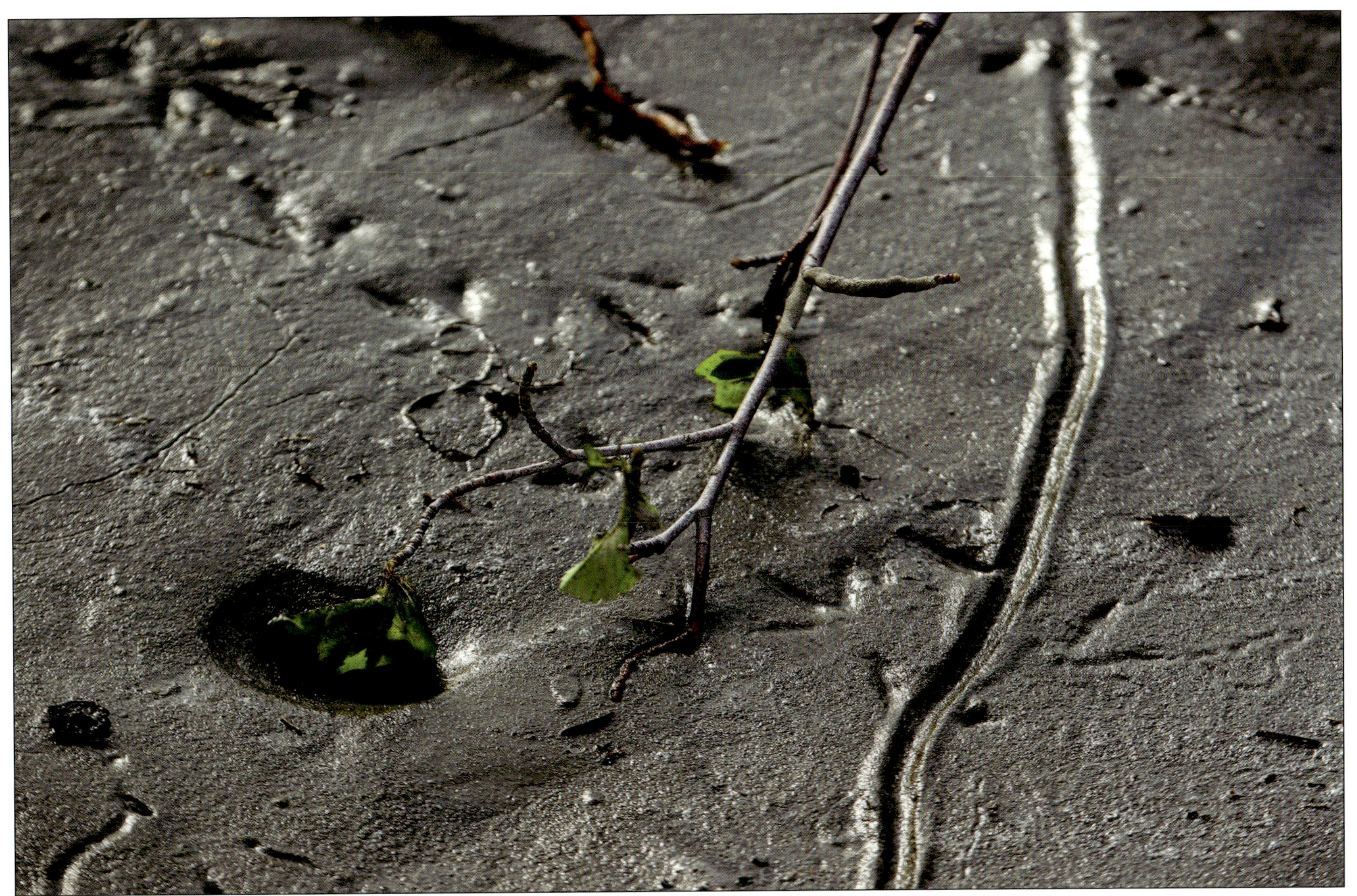

New spring leaves and worm tracks in the silty mud along the Bow.

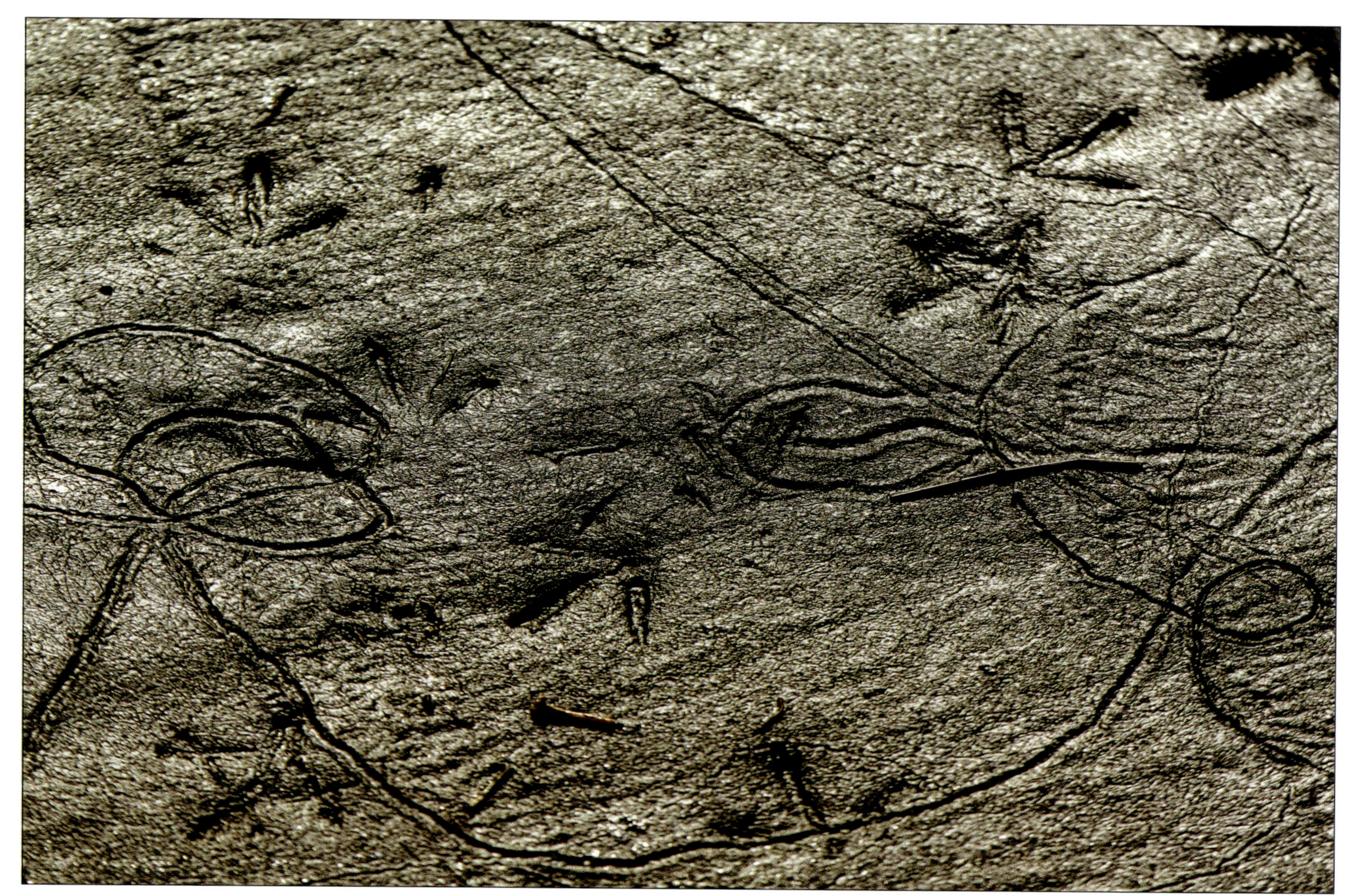

Worm and bird tracks in the newly deposited silt along the high and muddy Bow River.

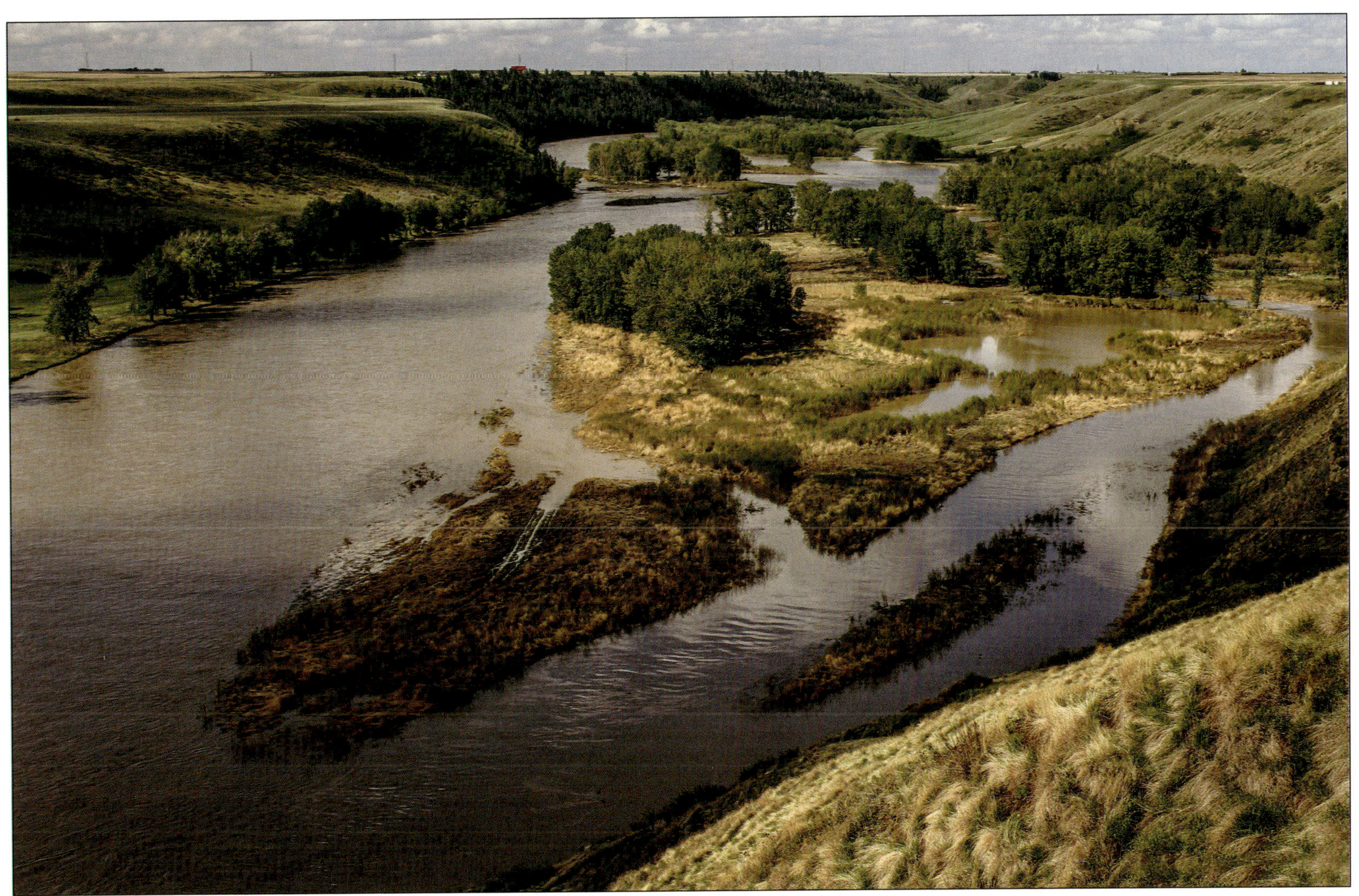

High water surrounds Legacy Island on the Bow River.

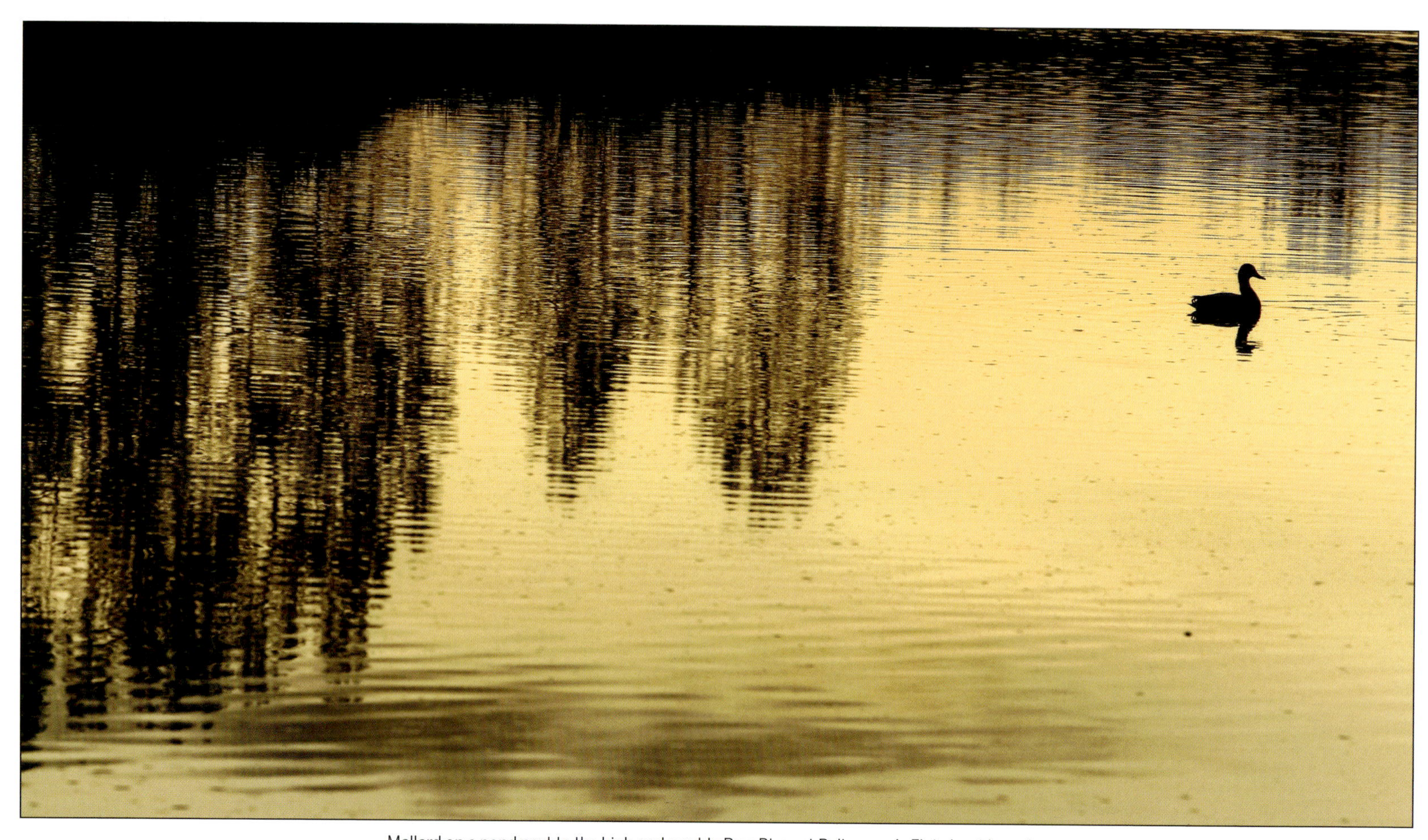

Mallard on a pond next to the high and muddy Bow River at Policeman's Flats boat launch.

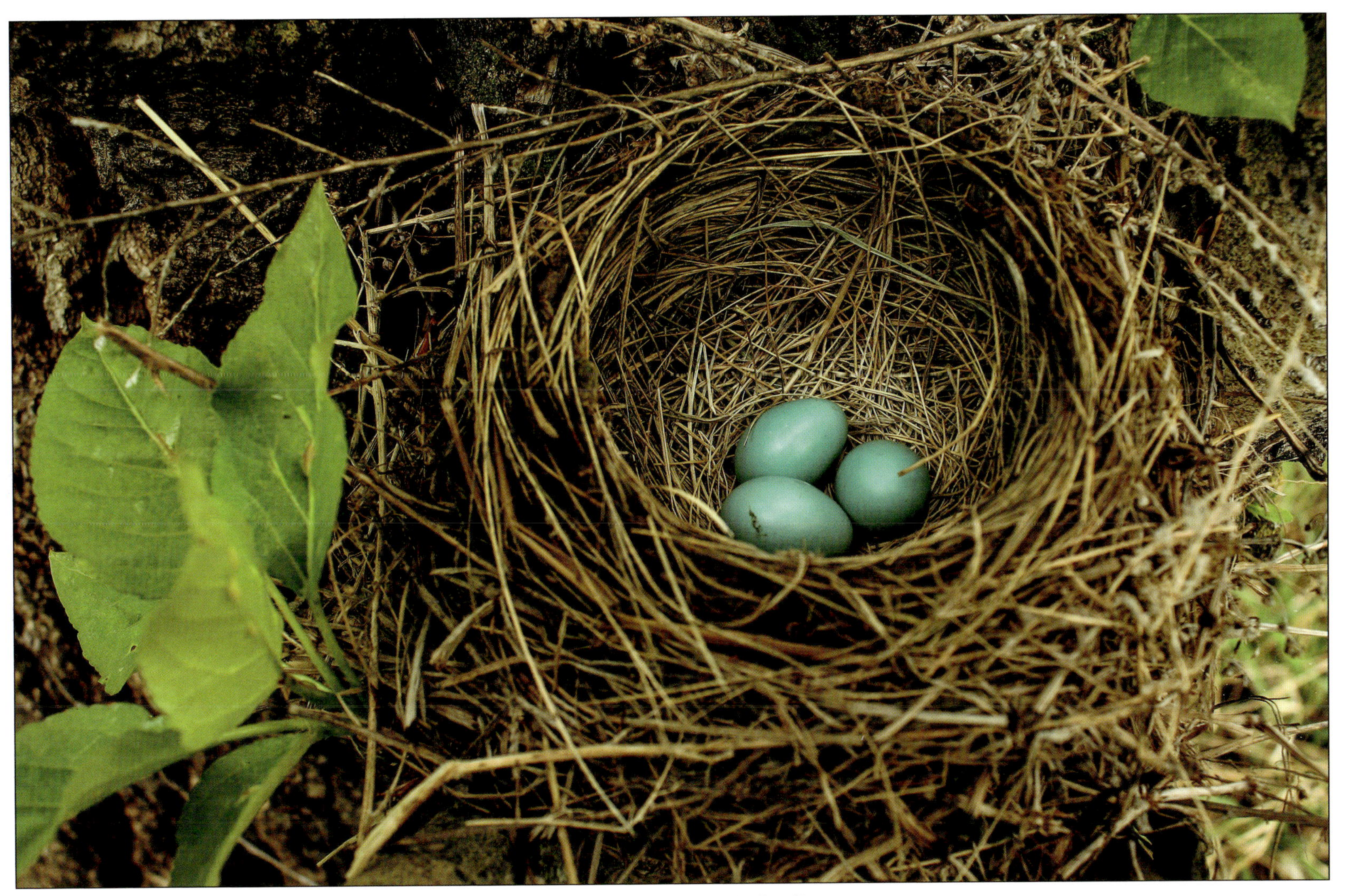

Robin eggs in a low nest along the Bow River.

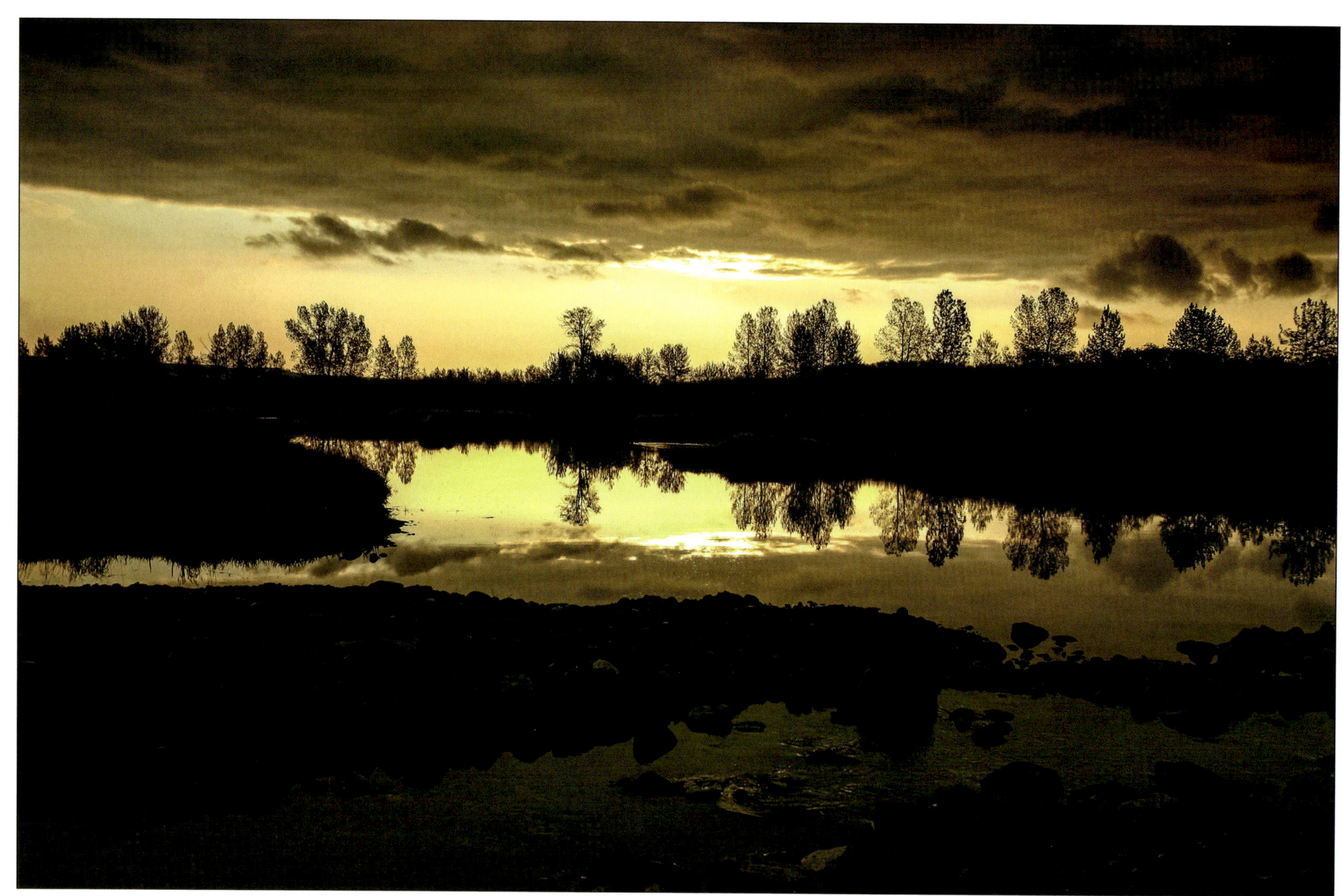

A pond next to the high and muddy Bow River at Policeman's Flats boat launch.

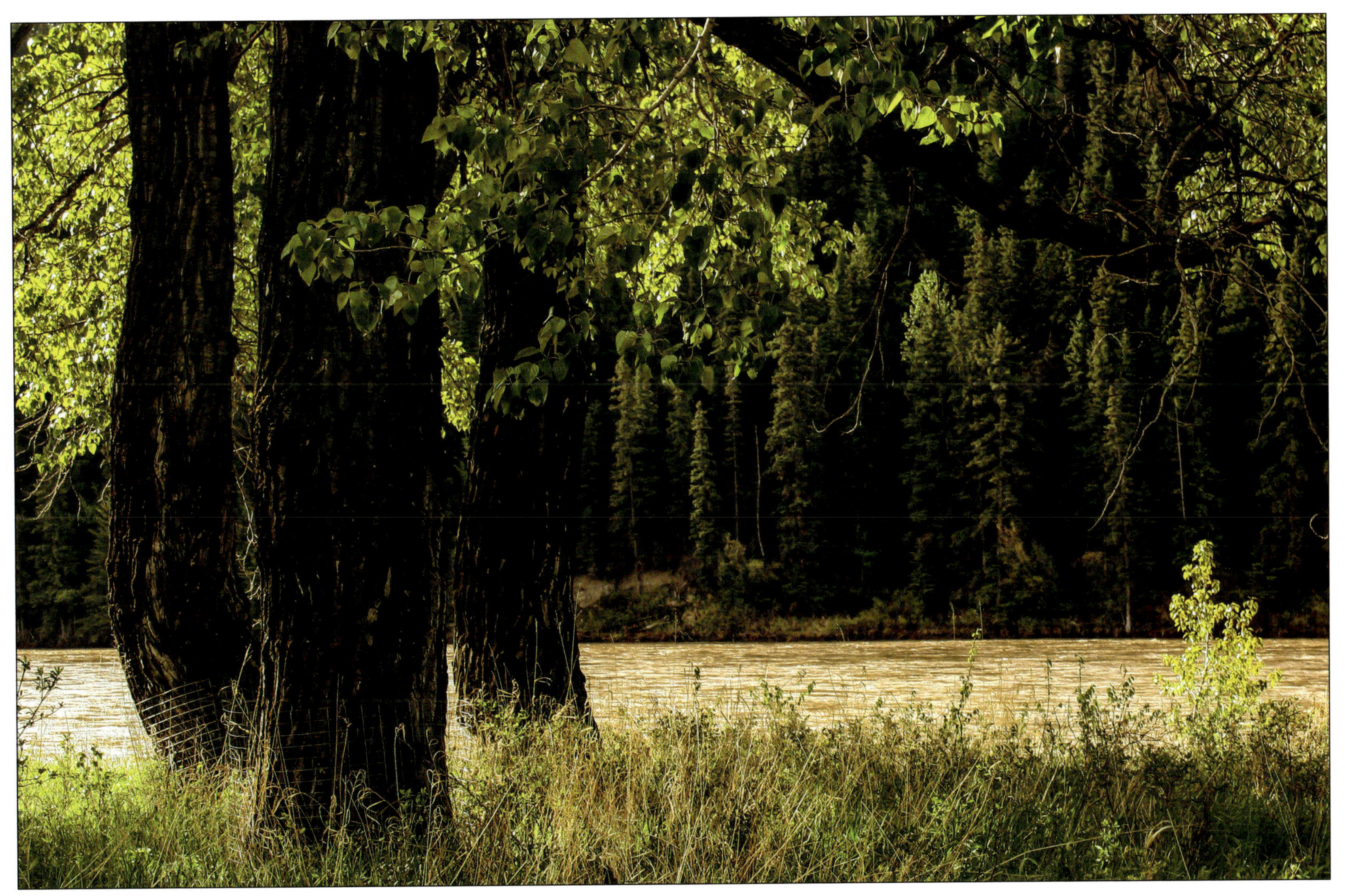

Cottonwood trees along the high and muddy Bow River.

PLAINS

THE PLAINS ARE MADE FOR Panavision. Or CinemaScope or Cinerama or any of the other super wide aspect ratios you see in movies like *Lawrence of Arabia* or *Bridge On The River Kwai* or *The Searchers*, where the horizon is as much a character as any of the actors.

Sometimes even more of a character. There's a scene in *Lawrence of Arabia* where Lawrence gallops his camel back to rescue a comrade. The scene starts with characters in the camp watching for him to return. Suddenly someone notices a speck on the horizon.

Instead of cutting to a tight shot, the director, David Lean, just lets the camera linger as the speck grows and grows on the ruler-straight horizon. It's a magnificent scene that uses the division between earth and sky to emphasize the insignificance of man in all this space and show the scope of Lawrence's accomplishment in finding his friend.

Yeah, the plains are made for the wide screen. At least that's the thought that popped into my head when I saw the antelope buck on the plains between Dorothy and Cessford. He was just standing there on a low hill looking around and there was nothing else but grass and sky.

He was just a speck on that vast horizon.

I'd gone out that way in hopes of seeing some burrowing owls. I'd spotted them out that way last year and I was hoping they might have returned to the same burrows. Needless to say I had no luck finding the little guys but that didn't really surprise me. They could have moved a hundred feet farther away and I'd have never seen them. They tend to blend in and it's generally just dumb luck that you see them.

But there's always plenty more to see out on the prairie, and I know the owls are out there somewhere. I'll find them next time. Maybe.

It wasn't a warm day but the bright sun heated up the ground anyway and shimmering heat waves softened the endless horizon. Cattle grazed on all the new green grass or congregated in fence corners where they ducked in between each other trying to get away from the clouds of mosquitoes.

It seemed as if every tree – all eight of them – or patch of buffaloberry hosted a Swainson's hawk nest. Baby Richardson's ground squirrels bounced around in the grass while their parents kept a lookout for hawks searching for a quick meal for their own babies.

There were mule deer about, and virtually every third fencepost featured a meadowlark belting out a tune. I watched curlews wandering in the grass probing for worms and bugs with their long bills, and every little pothole held teal, shovellers, mallards and pintails. Frogs sang for their mates.

I could see rain falling off to the north and east, long curtains of white hanging like sheets on a clothesline below dark-bottomed clouds, but where I was the sky was mostly blue with just a few puffy clouds. A light wind was blowing just hard enough to make it tough for thc mosquitoes to find me.

I drove out onto a community pasture and looked west to where the land sloped away to the Red Deer River. I could see nothing but a few cattle in all that velvety green edged with a line of cottonwoods along the river. Every bird was singing, from the insect rasp of clay-coloured sparrows to the falling skylark song of Sprague's pipits.

The evening light threw shadows into the coulees that set everything more than knee high into sharp relief. The heat waves that had shimmered at midday were gone as the land cooled down. I saw antelope here and there, mostly females about to give birth and looking for low spots to keep out of sight of coyotes.

The bucks were solitary, too, nibbling on grass as they wandered along. They have nothing to fear at this time of year and they were barely conscious of my presence.

So when I saw the buck on the low hill I had all the time in the world to compose my picture. And that's when I thought about *Lawrence of Arabia*.

The plains are all about sky and land, just like the Arabian desert. That they're covered with grass instead of sand makes little difference to the overall impression. And with that antelope buck posed there on the demarcation line that separates ground and cloud like Lawrence on his camel, well, I bet even David Lean would be impressed.

Lawrence of Cessford. In Panavision. I can see it all now.

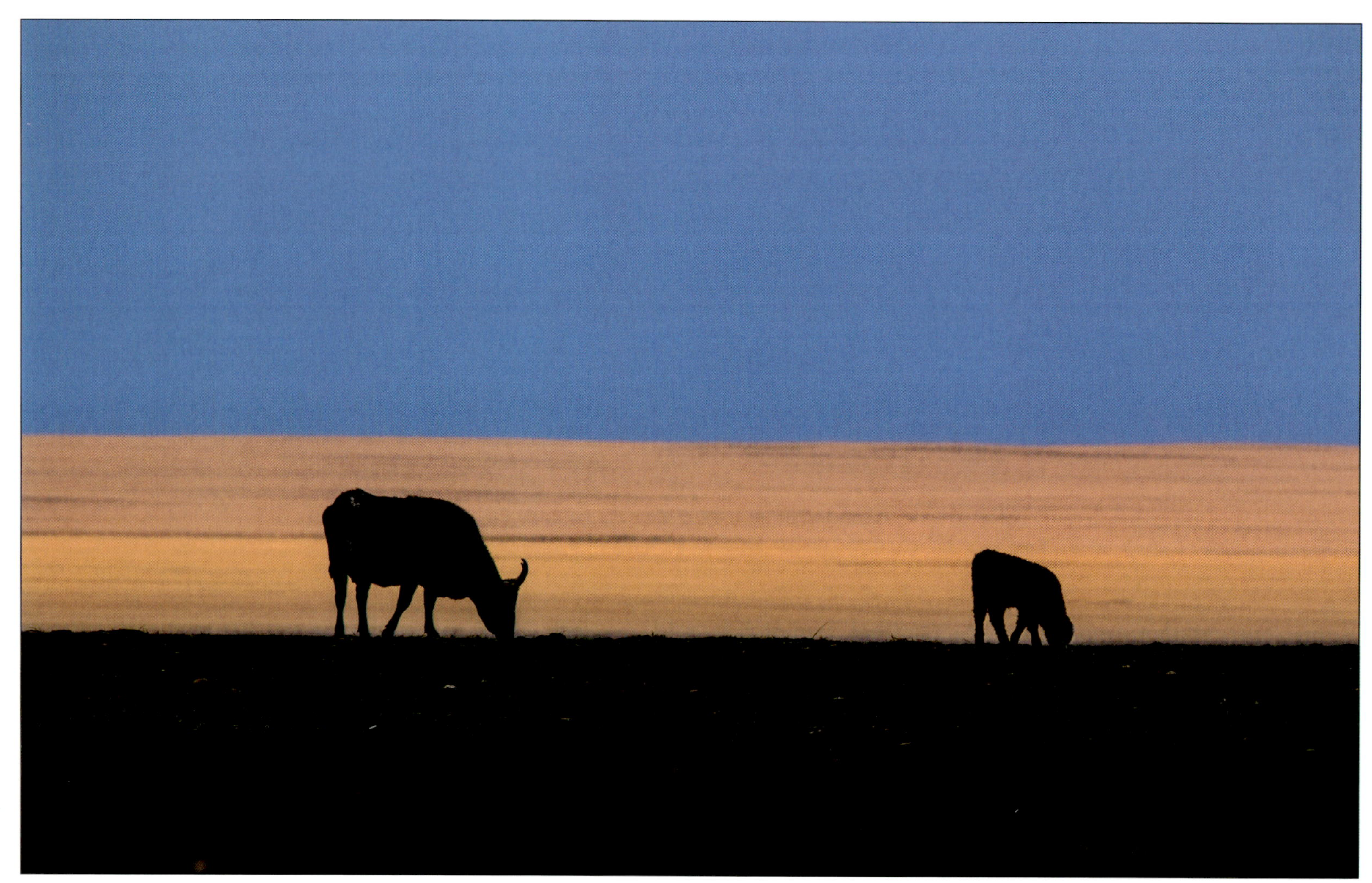

A patch of setting sun coming through the hazy clouds lights up a stubble field east of Granum.

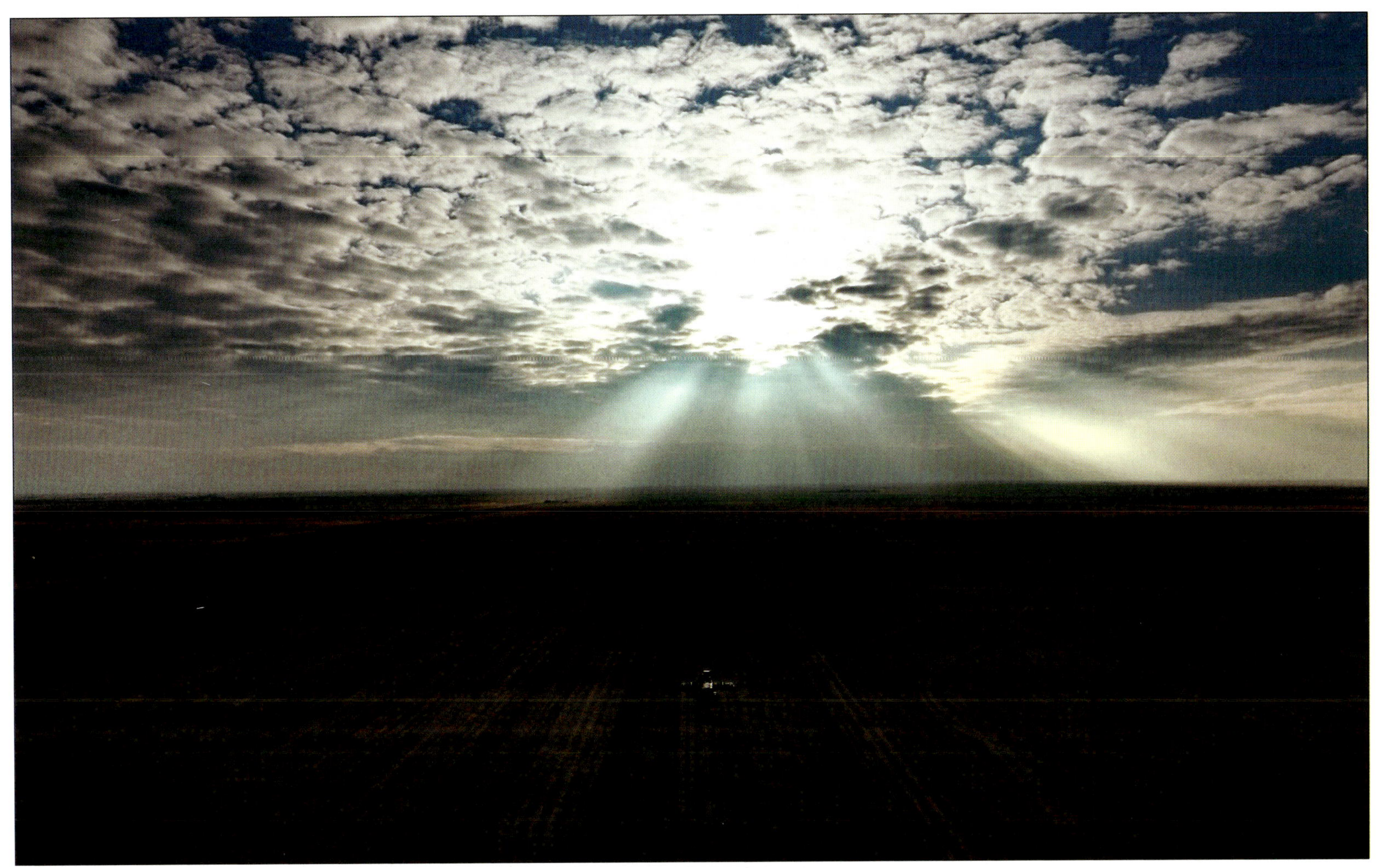

Seeding time east of Granum.

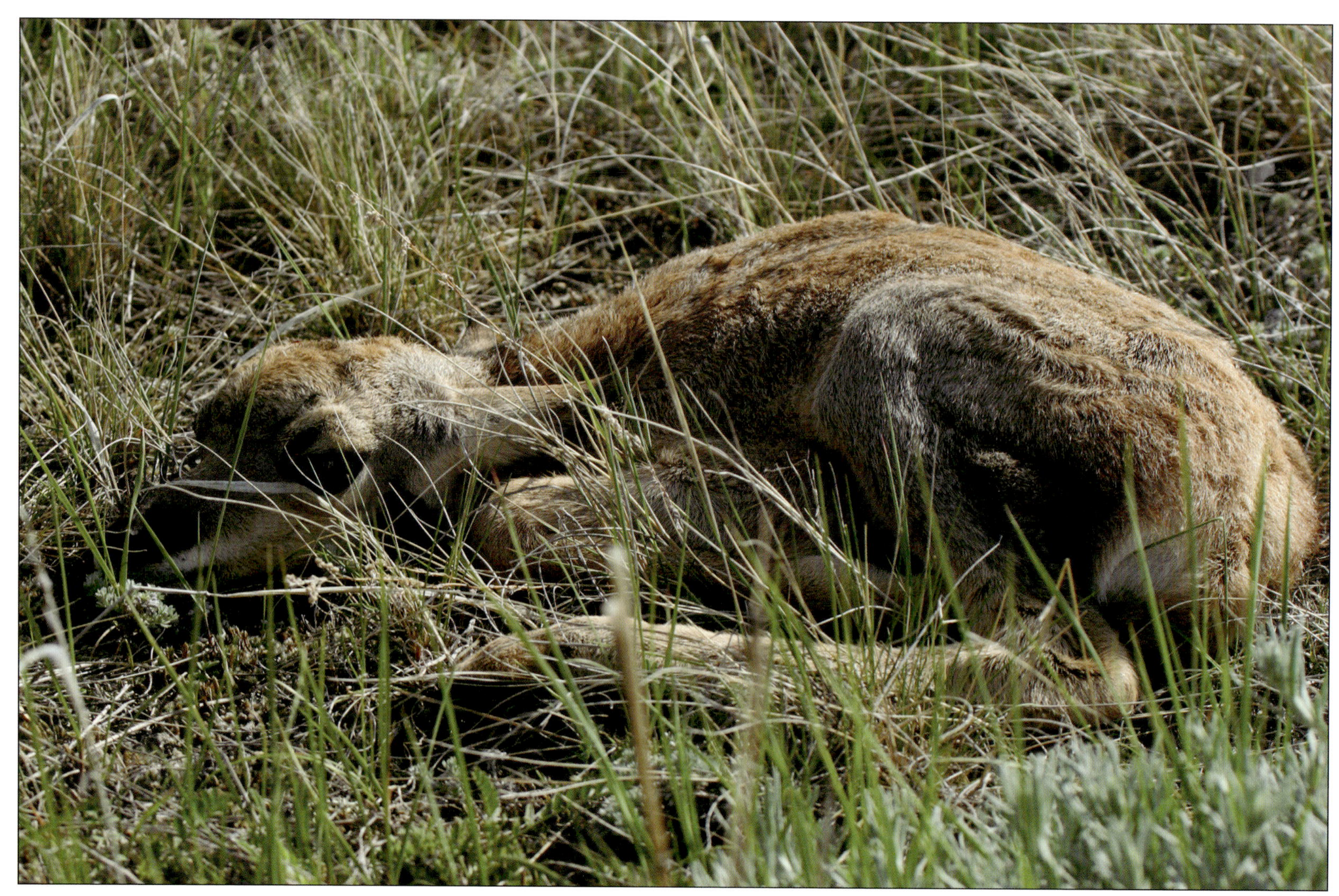

Newborn pronghorn on the prairie east of Tilley.

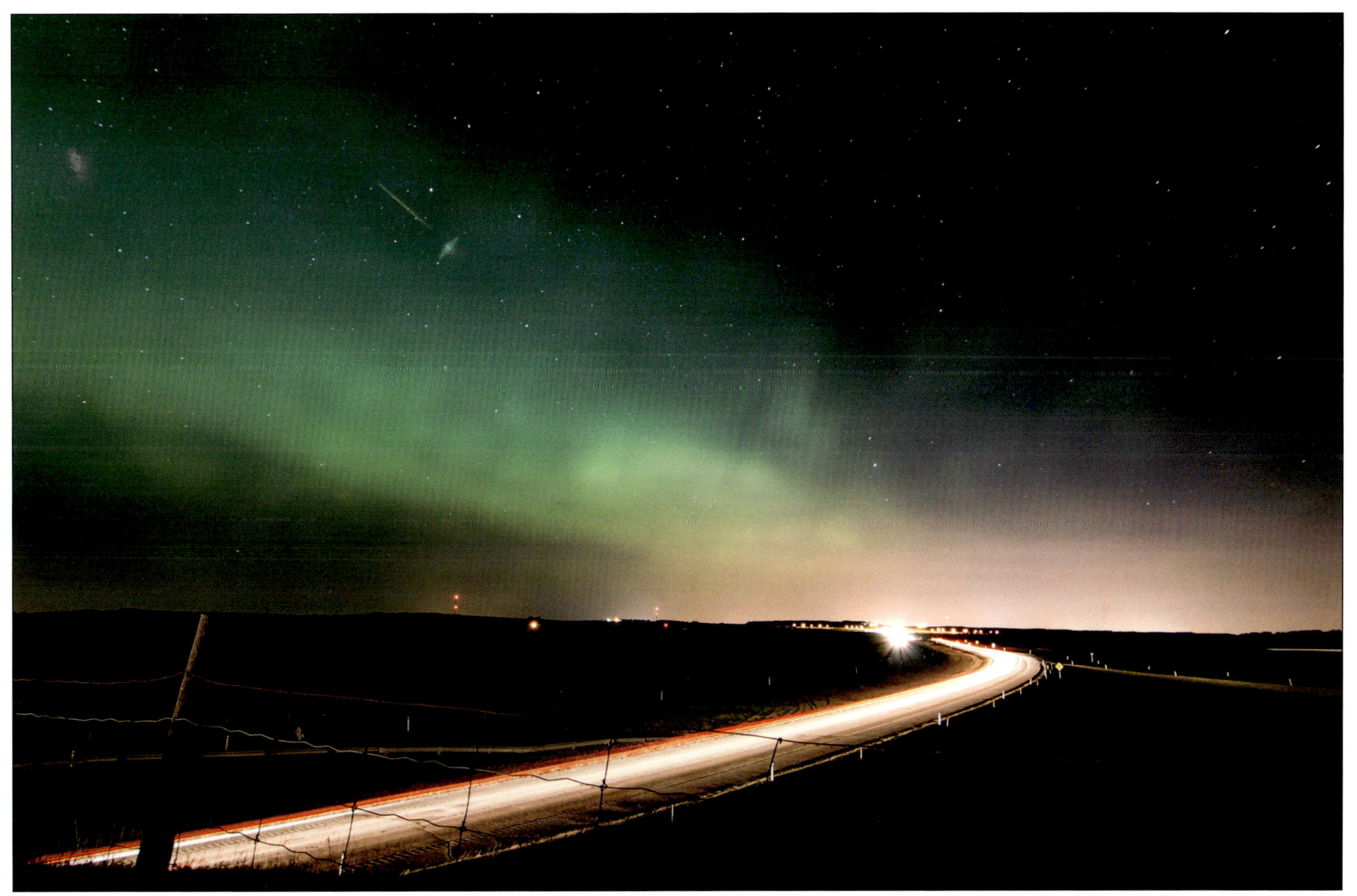

Vehicles leave light streaks on Highway 1 as the aurora borealis lights up the night west of Calgary.

SMELLS LIKE SPRING

I COULD SMELL THE RAIN FROM the day before.

Or, more accurately, I could smell the dampness left by the rain.

There's no other smell like it, that earthy smell that makes me think of green and growing things, of bird song, of water trickling.

And on Wednesday morning all those things were there.

I was not far from the city, just southwest of town out in the hills by the Cross Conservation area west of Spruce Meadows. The sun had just come up and even though it was cold – right around 0°C – and there was frost in the ditches and on roadside shrubbery, the soft, golden light made it seem warm.

It was right around 6:30 in the morning when I started through the hills and I had the world to myself. People-wise, anyway.

There were deer all over the place and I came across a group of whitetails that, for once, didn't bolt at first sight of me. There was a doe and a couple of younger deer and one little buck with the nubbins of his antlers just starting to poke up between his ears.

And about 200 metres down the road I nearly ran into an elk. Or maybe I should say it almost ran into me.

I could see the tracks of a herd in the frost coming down from the east and crossing the road in front of me, and as I was looking west at the elk in a pasture a straggler leaped the fence maybe 50 feet in front of me. Had I not been just idling along there's a good chance I would have smoked it.

The horses in the pasture seemed almost as startled by the elk as I was. They were running and jumping around the pasture as the elk trotted through and only stopped when most of the herd had passed.

There were maybe 50 elk that I could count but there were more in the trees up on the ridge. I'm always amazed to see them out there even though I know they're around and I've seen them dozens of times. Maybe it's the fact that there's a city of a million people just over the horizon that keeps the amazement factor high.

The valleys were filled with bird song. I could hear robins, the loudest of the spring singers, overpowering the chorus of less-strong voices, but there were the honks of geese echoing along as well. Driving up through the aspen forest I came out onto a hay meadow and I could see where the geese were honking from.

There was an old barn right out in the middle of the field and a bunch of Canada geese were standing on the roof. Not sure what it is about geese and roofs but I've seen them perched on buildings everywhere. They even nest on rooftops. For big water birds, they sure act a lot like pigeons.

There was mist in the valleys and sunlight bounced off every damp surface. Water dripped from fencelines and branches as the radiant heat of the sun melted the frost. Bluebirds flitted from post to post – barely pausing long enough for me to get a decent picture – and tree swallows perched on fencelines arguing and squabbling before flying off again.

I must have seen 30 hawks. Harriers, redtails, Swainson's, they were all on the hunt in the morning light. Those that had spent a semi-comfortable night, anyway. I took a picture of one redtail sitting on a fencepost looking absolutely miserable.

The mist burned off as the sun rose higher in the sky, but near ponds there were still tendrils of it hanging on so I retraced my steps from the previous day's drive down to a pond where I'd caught a fleeting glimpse of a moose the day before.

No moose but the birds were posing nicely.

A snipe stood like a statue on a post while ducks floated along half asleep on the misty water. I saw ruddy ducks and buffleheads, canvasbacks and redheads, pretty little blue-winged teal, more geese, a couple of grebes. And lots of noisy blackbirds.

Red-winged blackbirds put everything they've got into their songs. Heads twisted, wings flexed, they look like they're having a seizure. And all that effort goes into a song that sounds like somebody simultaneously hammering on and filing a steel pipe. Gotta admire that.

It was 8:30 AM by now and traffic was starting to build up. Cars were passing me every 15 minutes or so. Time to go back to town for breakfast.

I drove for a ways with the windows down to get that lovely, earthy smell into the truck. Like the scent of baking bread or of crabapples or of leaded gasoline, it triggers memories and emotions. It just plain smells good.

We're not done with the crappy weather quite yet but that smell tells it all.

It smells like spring.

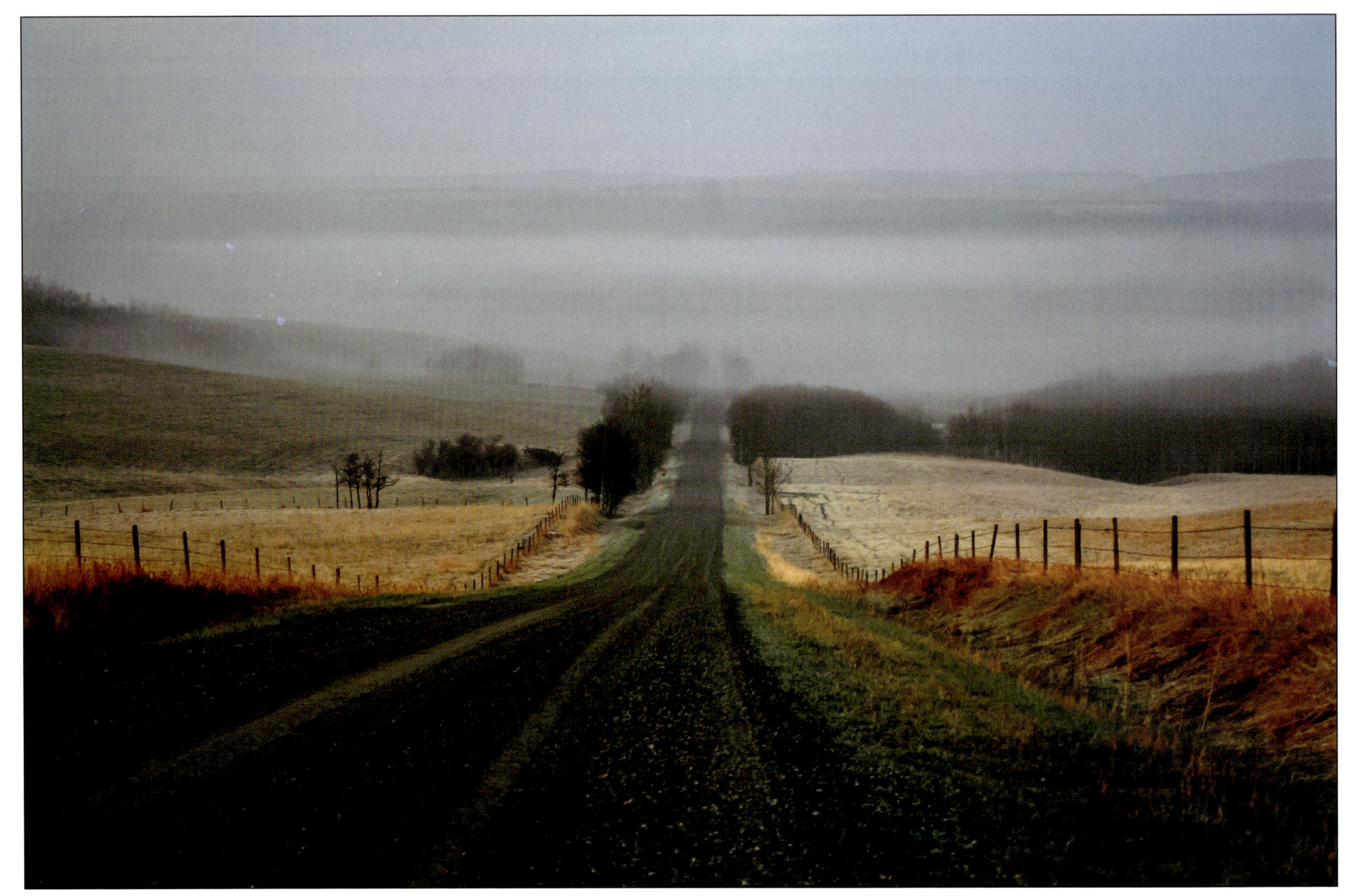

First light on a gravel road west of Spruce Meadows.

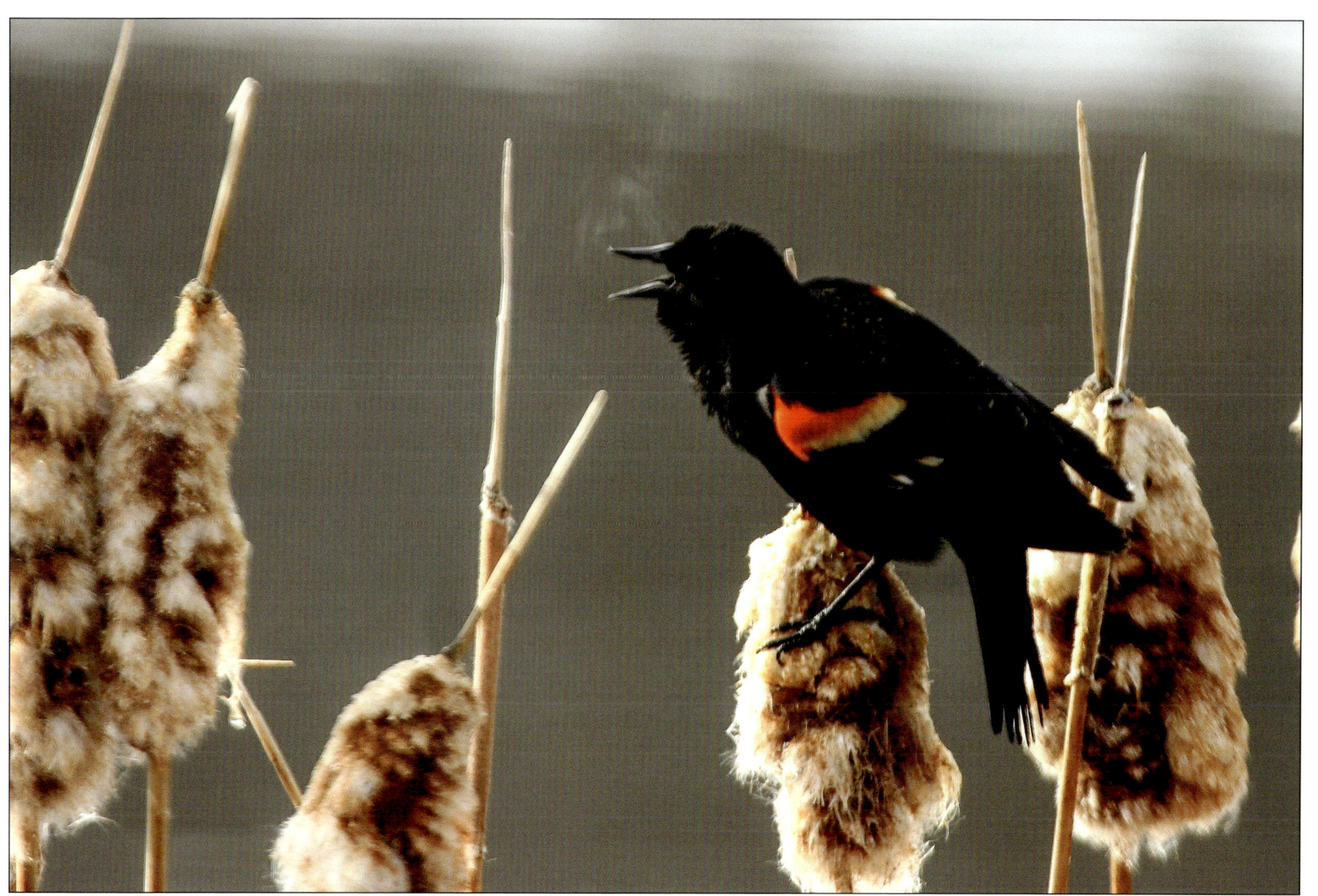

A red-winged blackbird sings in the sunrise at a pond south of the city.

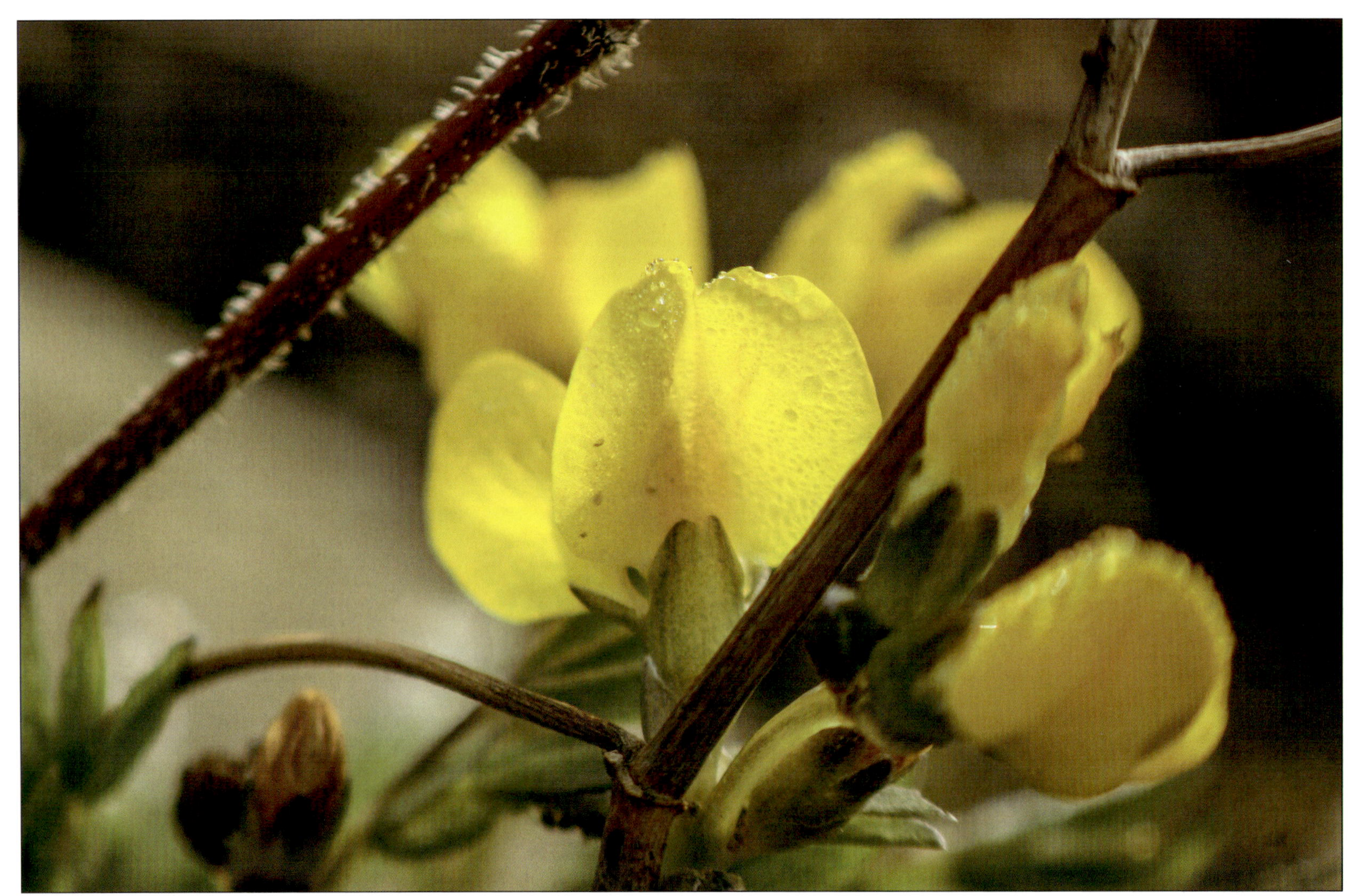

Buffalo beans starting to bloom.

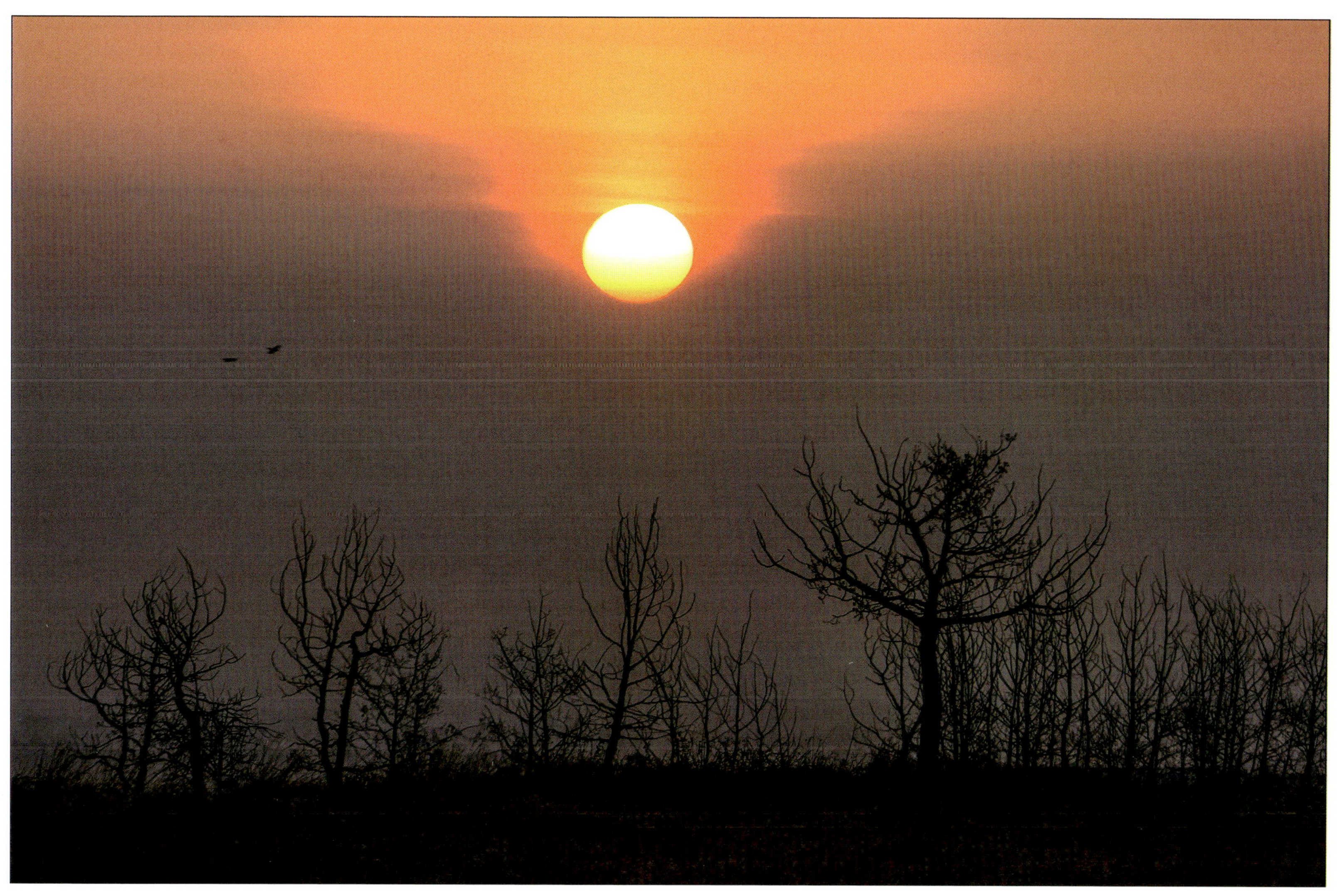

Sunrise Wednesday morning south of the city.

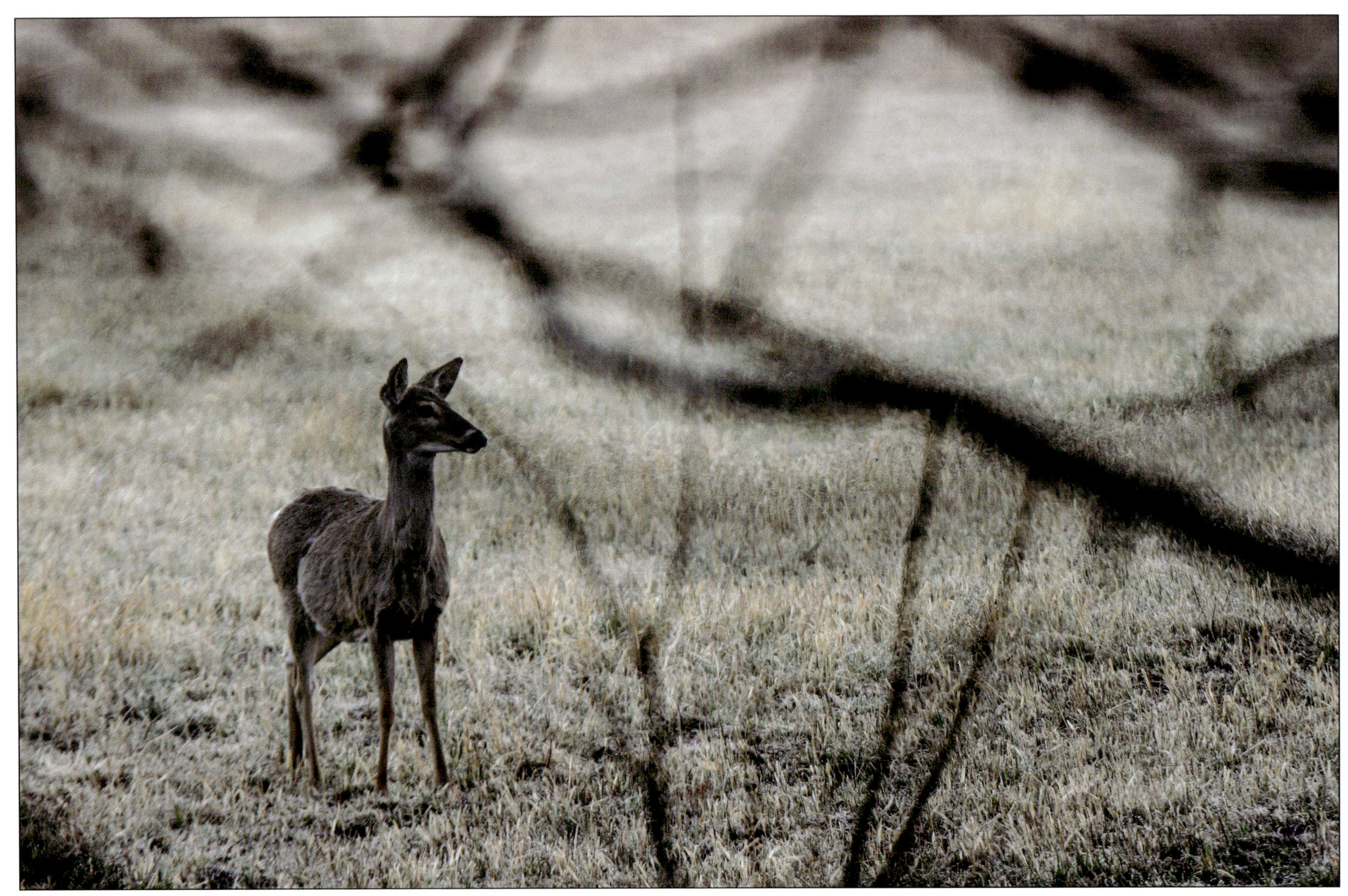

Whitetail deer in a pasture west of Spruce Meadows.

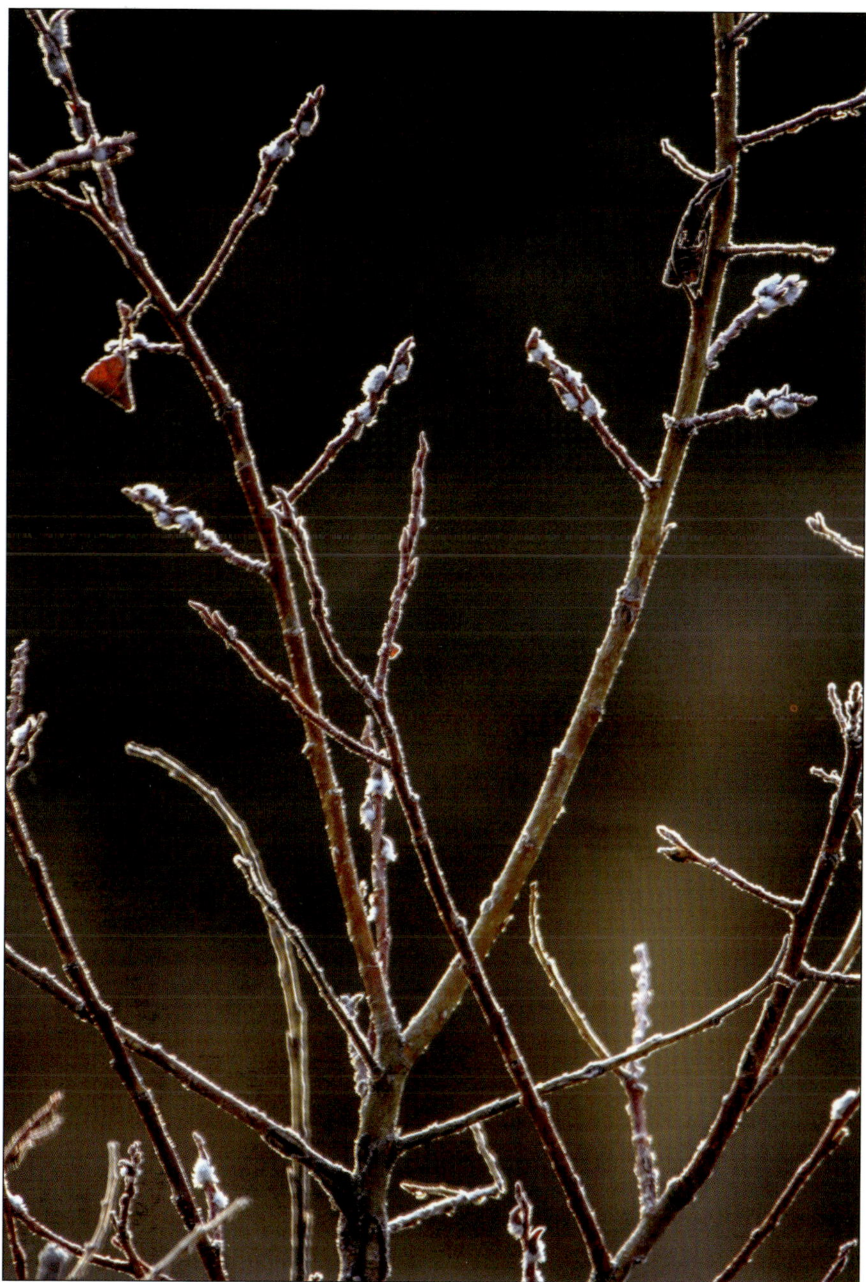

Morning frost on willow buds west of Spruce Meadows.

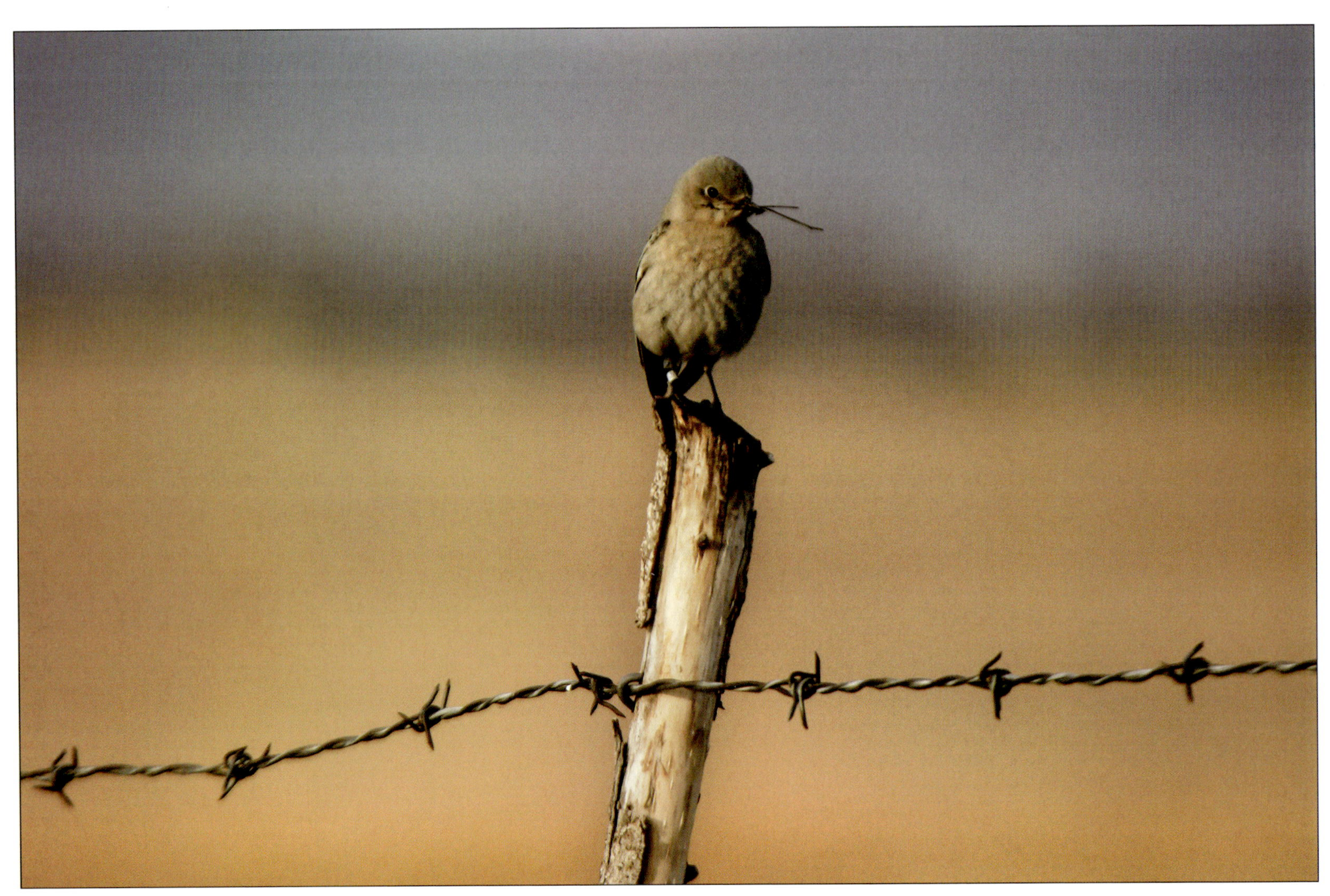

A momma bluebird gathering nesting material west of Spruce Meadows.

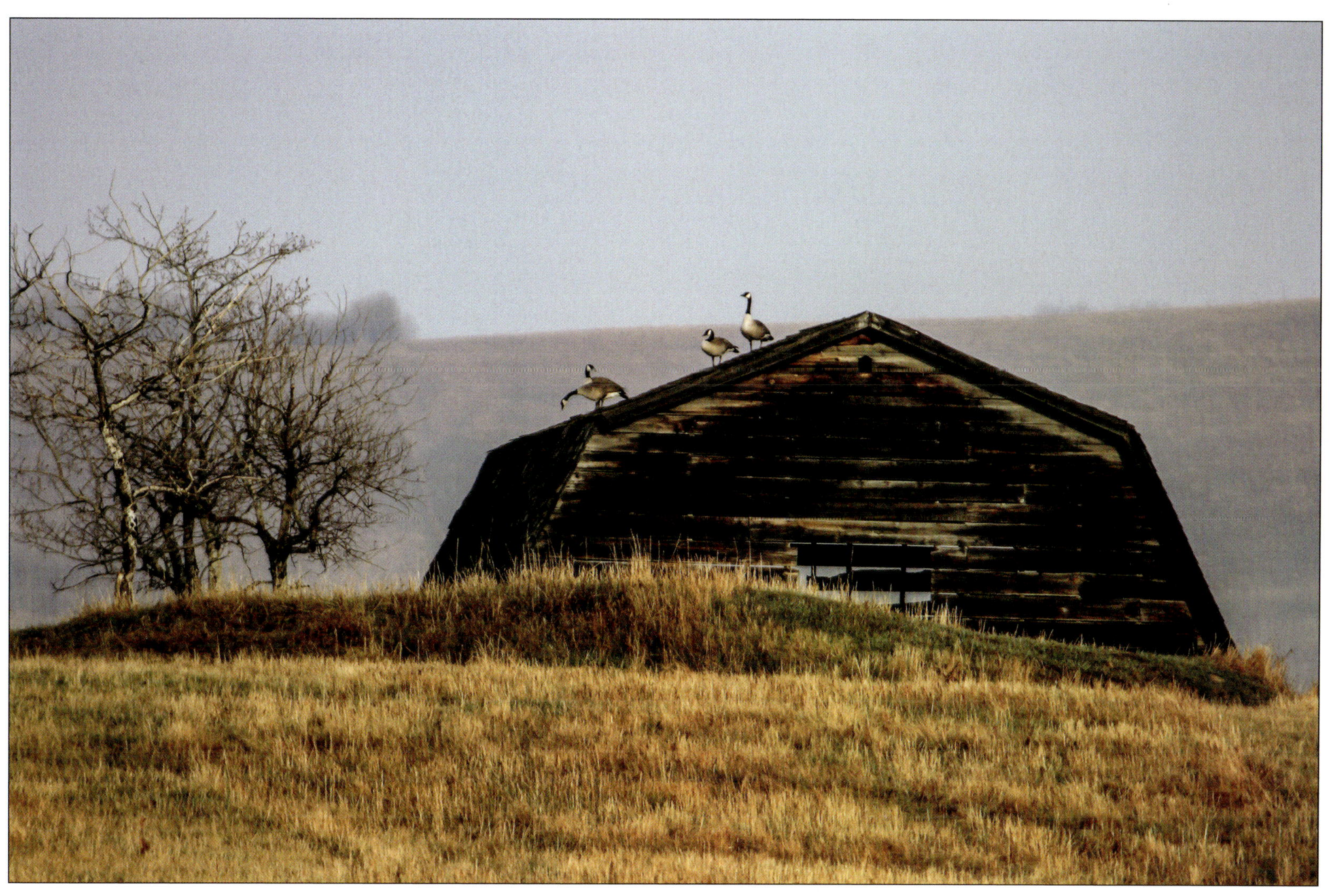

Canada geese arguing on a barn roof west of Spruce Meadows.

S U M

M E R

BOW RIVER

There were roses in bloom all around me and the scent of wolf willow filled the air.

Birds were singing in the trees and bees were buzzing from flower to flower on the wild raspberries that shared the steep hillside with the roses.

I was about 1 km upstream of the junction of the Highwood and Bow Rivers, sitting on the riverbank below a tall cliff. I'd been fishing for the last couple of hours and had just climbed and splashed my way along the river to this point, a spot where the cliff sloped out slightly and plants could take hold.

It was tough fishing, much tougher than the last time I was here more than a year ago. The flood of 2005 has changed the river a lot along here. None of it looked familiar except in a general way.

There used to be places where I could almost guarantee hooking a fish, plenty of them in fact, but now they are all gone. Sure, the river looks pretty much the same, but all that structure that used to be along the shoreline, all those little underwater nooks and crannies where I could count on the fish to be hiding, they're not where they used to be.

I'd caught a couple of fish earlier but it had been more because of the old adage that you won't catch anything if your hook ain't in the water than any knowledge of where the fish might be hiding.

And with runoff starting, the water was kind of high and dirty and I couldn't read much of the bottom structure of the newly rearranged streambed to figure out where to cast. I just plunked the flies into the water and hoped for the best.

To get to where I was now I had to cross tumbles of flood-tossed trees, slog through mud and wade through waist-deep water below sheer outcrops of sandstone. I was sore, tired and sunburned and it had been a long time since my last trout. Time for a rest.

Everything was fresh and new around me, the green grass almost glowing, the red of the rosebuds like neon. And there were insects everywhere. Stoneflies found me convenient to climb on, little yellow ones, and mayflies fluttered through the air.

There were caddis flies around, too, though not many, and a couple of mosquitoes as well. Spiders had slung webs everywhere to feed on the bounty, and the birds that were singing in the trees – along with the gulls patrolling the river – were enjoying the feast as well.

I took some pictures of stonefly exoskeletons on a blade of grass and some of the roses as I sat there resting, and I watched a couple of mule deer walk down to the opposite shore for a drink. But I really wanted to catch some more fish so I re-rigged my outfit to cast streamers – minnow imitations – and slogged back down the river.

Second place I stopped to cast I caught a lovely 18-inch rainbow that was hugging the bank behind a rock. She was skinny from her spawning run up the Highwood River but lively. I took her picture, thanked her for the tussle and put her back. Things were looking up.

Until I tore the felt sole off my left boot and couldn't wade any more. The felt on the boots lets you get a grip on slippery underwater rocks as you're wading, and with it gone from one boot, I was going to be sliding all over the place if I tried to walk out into the river.

Yeah, I could cast from shore, but to fish the river properly you really have to be able to wade. I headed back to the truck.

One of the best things about fishing the Bow River is that even if it sucks, you're still surrounded by beauty. We are so lucky to have this stream so close by. I mean, there I was maybe 20 minutes outside the city and I was walking through a riverine forest alongside the river with not another person around. Stunning.

It was snowing cottonwood fluff and birds were still singing everywhere. Wrens nattered from the low branches and tree swallows swooped through the air after bugs, stopping to perch and squabble once in a while. Along the shoreline there were spotted sandpipers peeping away and kingbirds chasing off other birds if they came too near.

But the coolest were a pair of pileated woodpeckers, big birds the size of crows. You don't see them very often so I was thrilled to get any pictures of them at all, let alone the variety of poses they gave me. Pretty nifty, I tell ya.

I made my way back up the Highwood River to where I'd parked the truck. I saw pretty little blue-eyed grass along the edge of a pasture and a blue heron hunting on the opposite bank of the river. And there was an oriole right by the truck, though it flew off in a flash of bright orange before I could get a picture.

I peeled off my waders and sat there for a minute feeling the breeze cool my sweaty legs. It had been a long eight hours of hiking and fishing. A good eight hours. The best eight hours so far this year. Next time, maybe a few more fish but, no, that doesn't really matter.

Fishing isn't all about catching. I headed on home.

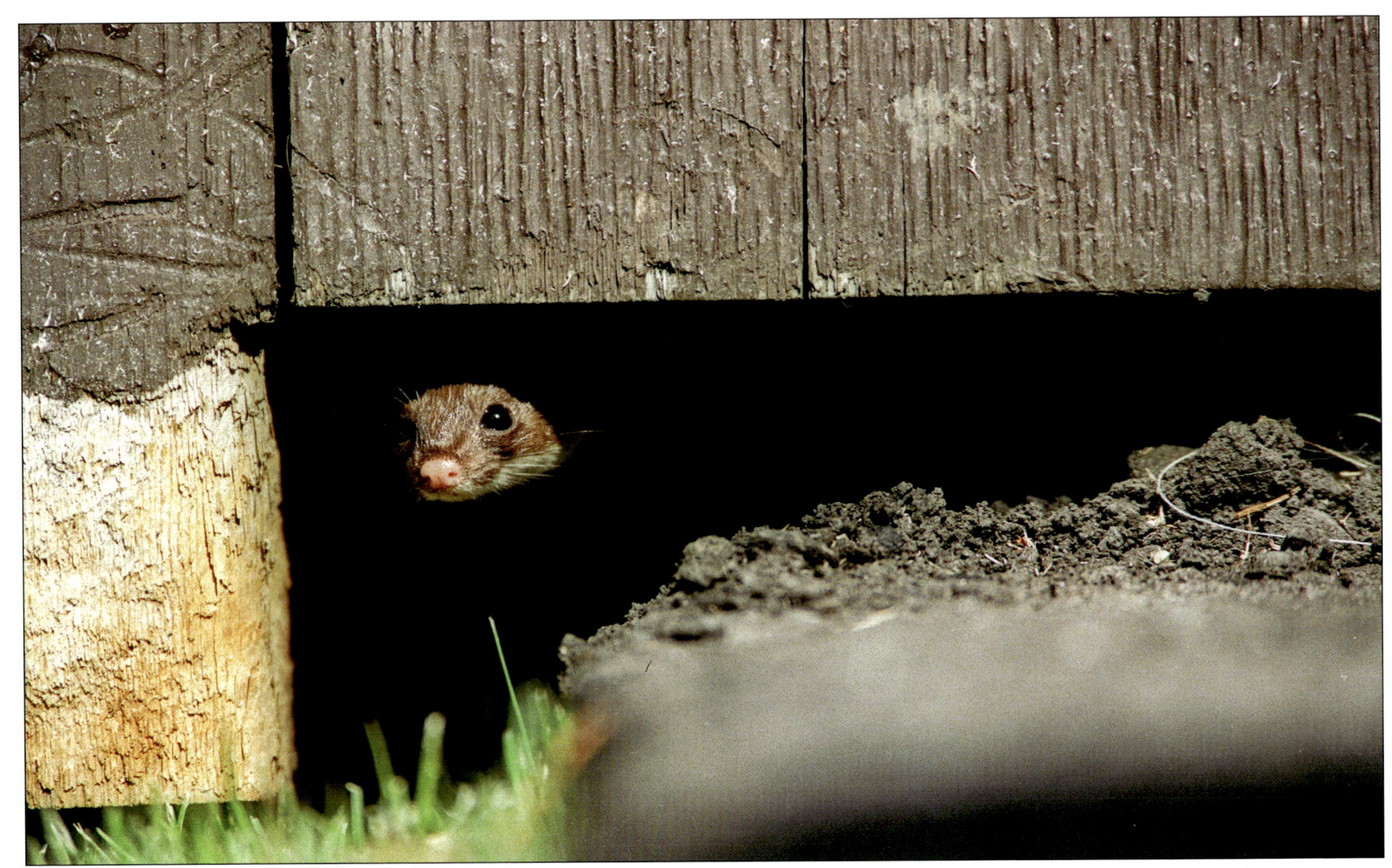

A weasel peeks out from under a shed.

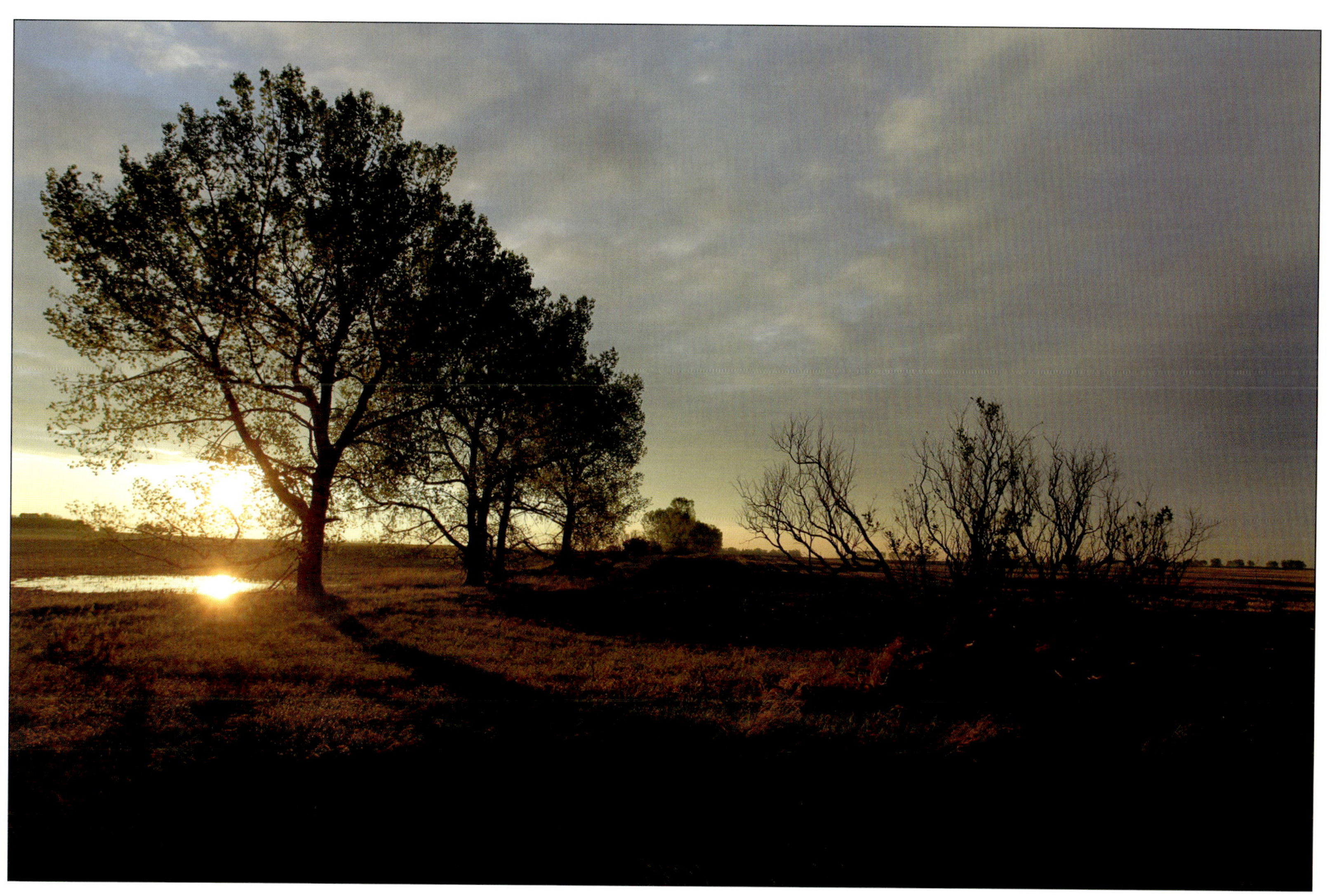

Sunrise near Indus.

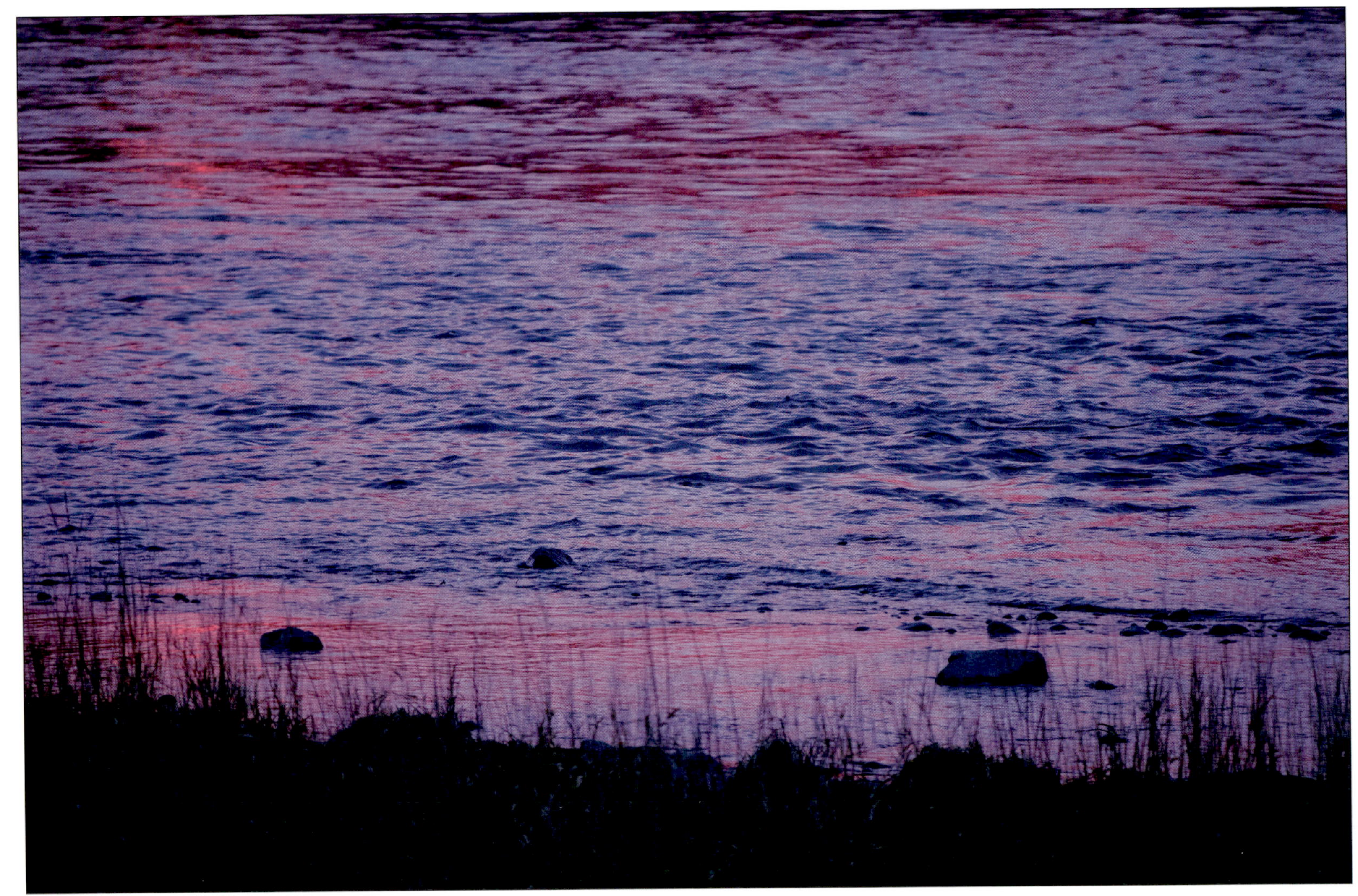

Sunrise on the Bow River at Carseland.

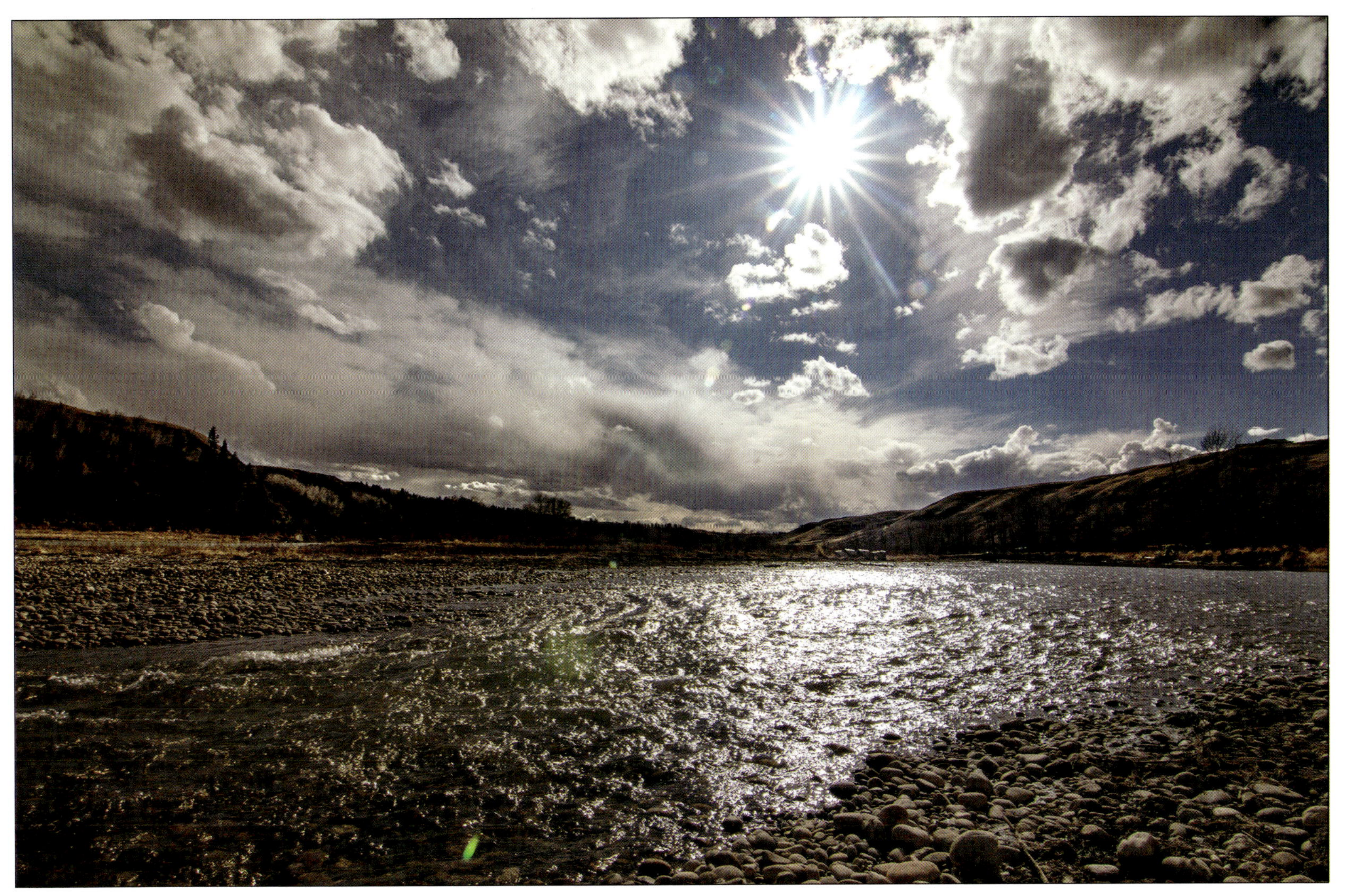

Warm sun on the Bow River near Carseland.

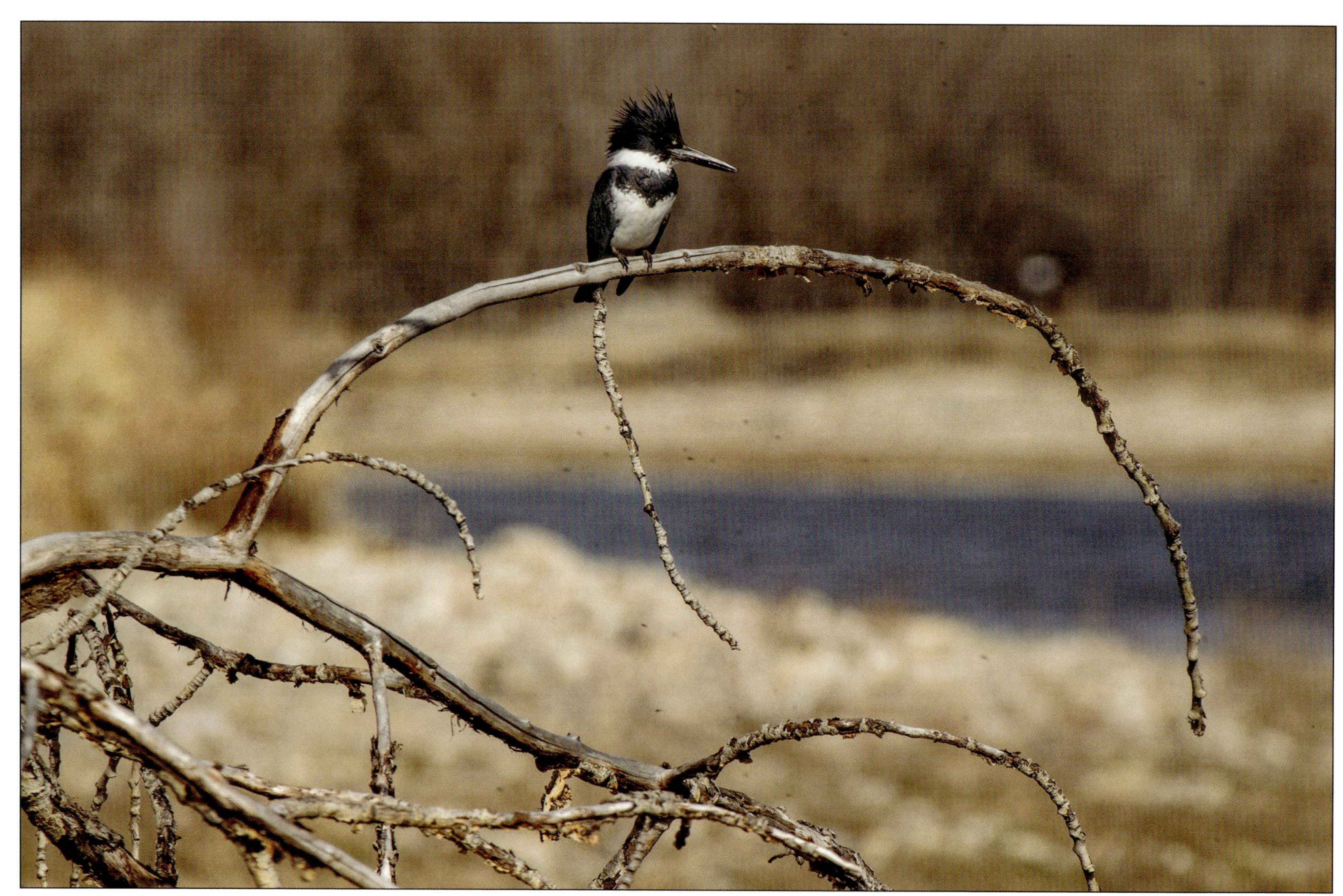

A kingfisher in the afternoon sun on the Bow River near Carseland.

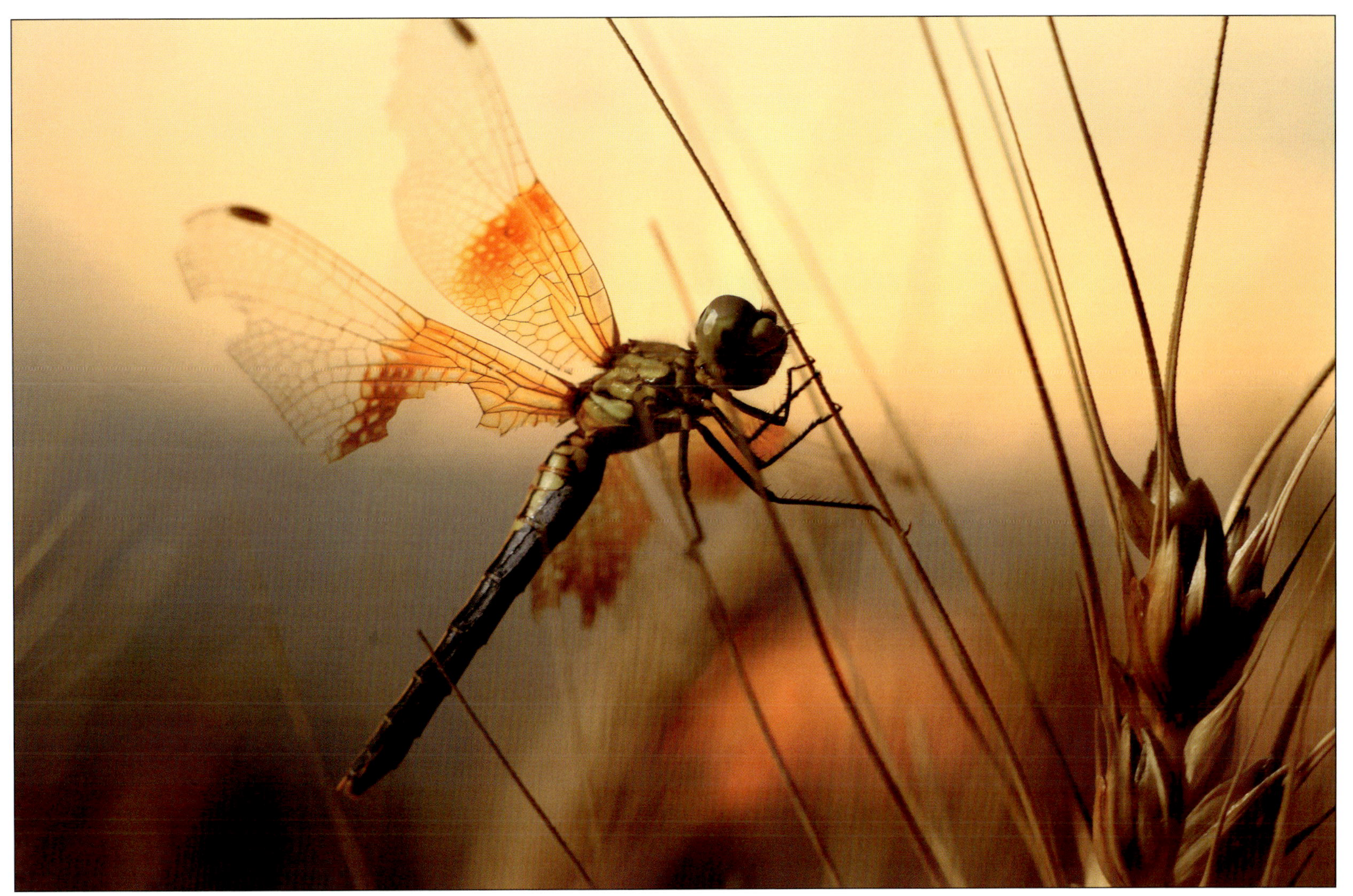

Dragonfly rests on barley near Lomond.

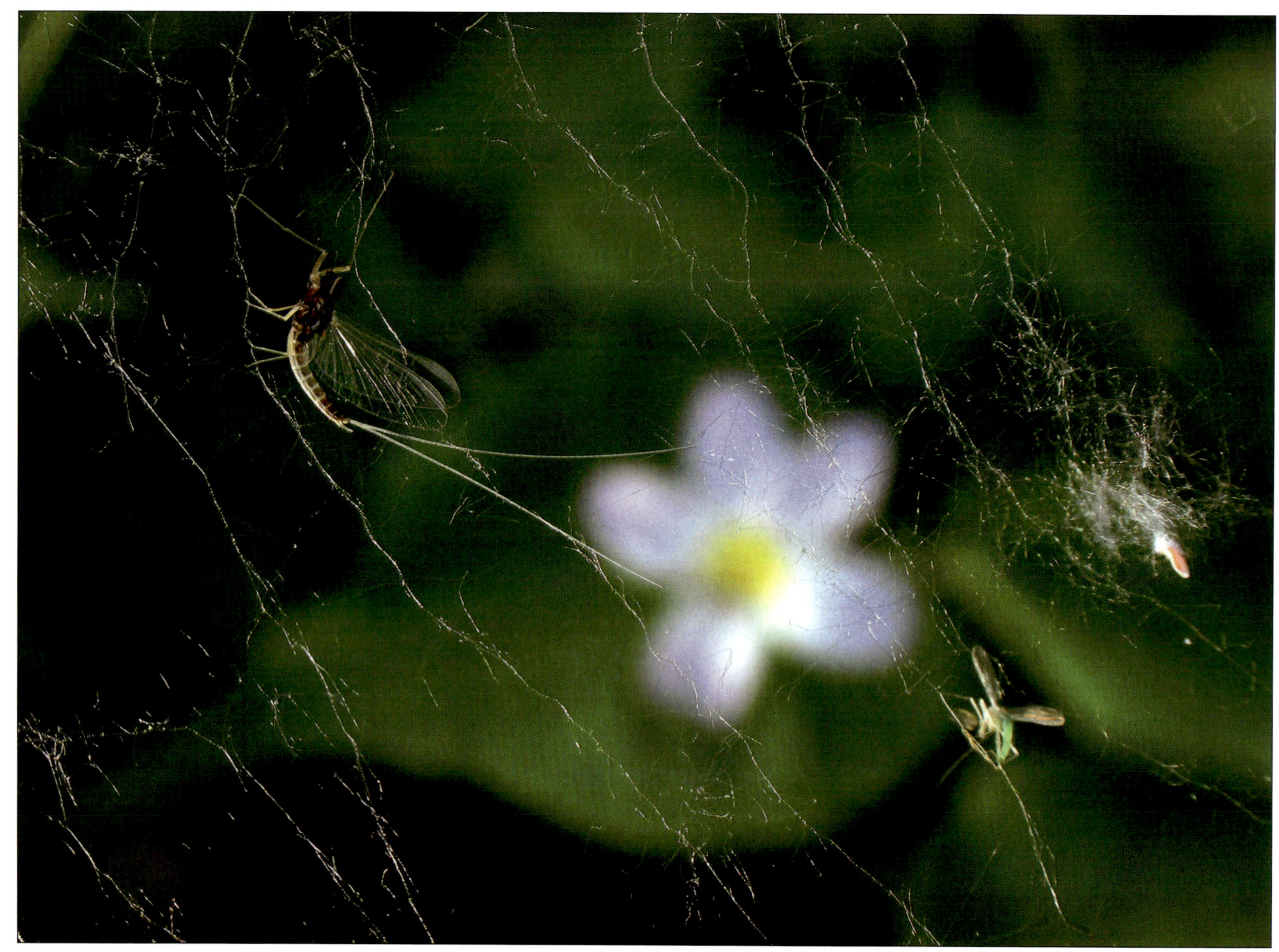

Mayflies and cottonwood fluff caught in a web along the Highwood River.

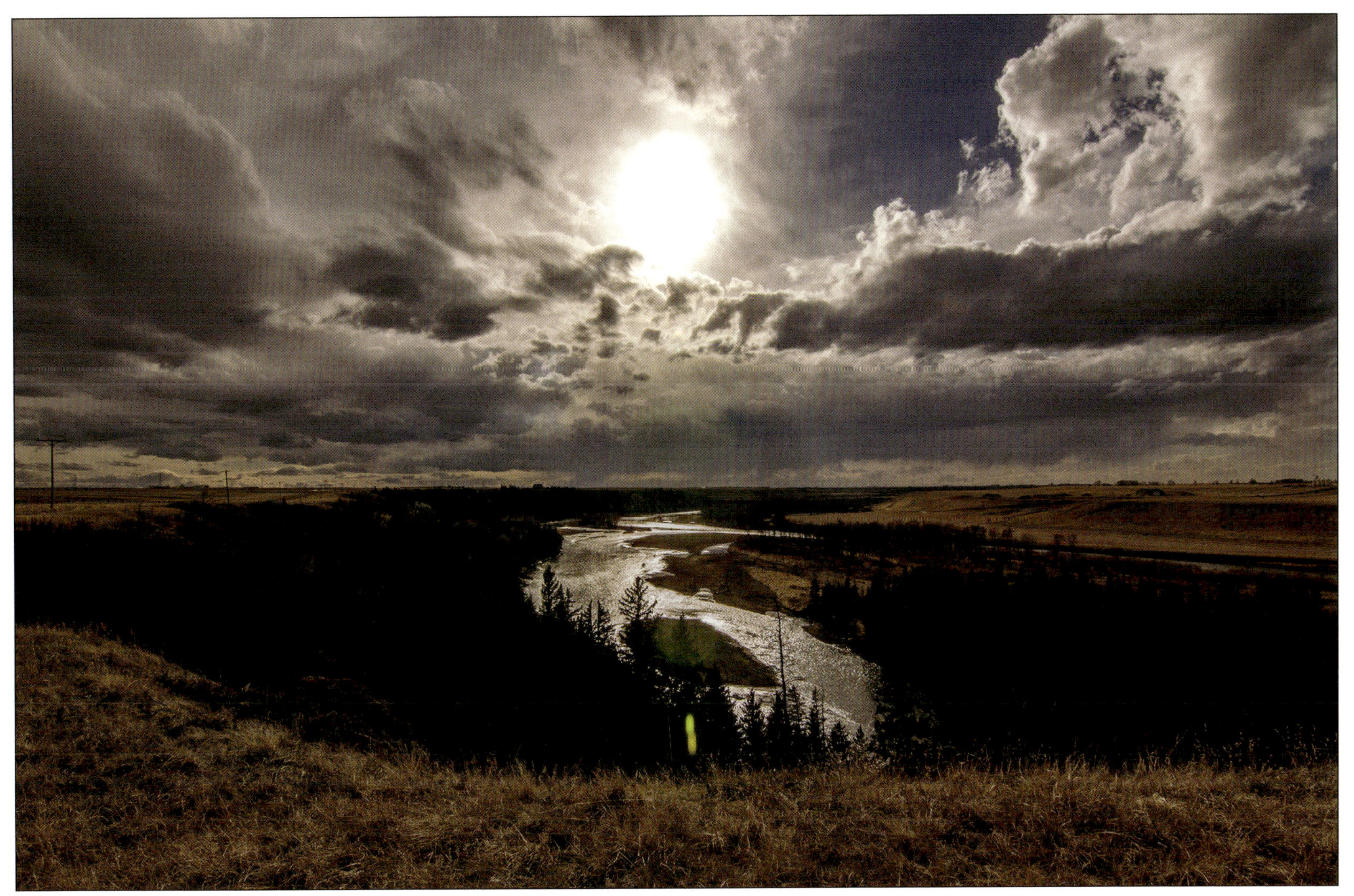

The springtime sun drops into rain clouds above the Bow River at Carseland.

CACTUS

IT LOOKED LIKE IT HAD rained on Tuesday night.

The ground was soaked, the ditches were full of brown water, mist hugged the ground above the fields and clouded the coulee bottoms.

It was just past six on Wednesday morning and I was headed east of the city. Due east through Strathmore, straight down Highway 1 to Thirteen-Mile Corner and then straight east again to Hussar.

Open country was pulling me like a nickel to a magnet. I'd just spent the better part of the last two weeks driving through trees – first to Wood Buffalo and then three days on my motorcycle on a trip through BC – and I needed to get back out onto the prairie to reset my compass.

Don't get me wrong. I enjoyed every minute of it and I'd do it all over again, given the opportunity. But spending that much time away from the sage and speargrass, the big skies and steep coulees leaves me feeling a little empty.

So I headed east just before 5 AM to look for cactus blossoms.

I was a little afraid that I was going to miss them. In a normal year the prickly pears start to bloom around the middle of June and they're pretty much done by the beginning of July. But this hasn't been a normal year.

Not that normal actually means anything in this country, but by most standards June has been wet and cool.

Just like Wednesday morning.

I drove east to Hussar and then cut north before turning east again toward Finnegan Ferry. I could have found cactus a lot closer – there's prickly pear in Fish Creek Park – but it's such a nice drive out to Finnegan I decided to go there.

The fields were all screaming green, especially in the patches of light that were sneaking through the cracks in the clouds on the eastern horizon, and I passed probably a dozen antelope nibbling on the shoots. Far off to the south I could see patches of bright yellow canola, and the native prairie pastures were knee-high with grass and blanket flowers.

The little creek that trickles down the coulee beside the road leading to the ferry crossing at Finnegan on the Red Deer River was back to normal flow, but I could see that it had burst its banks sometime recently. Mud flows on the steep coulee sides were drying in the now-strong morning sun, and I could see where one of them had taken out a length of fence.

And there were the cactus blossoms. Some had passed and the papery yellow blossoms had faded back to a pinkish shade and collapsed in on themselves, but others were freshly open and still more hung back as toe-like buds on the spiny pads.

I parked the truck and got out to walk. Mosquitoes descended on me immediately but they actually don't bother me much. I'm one of those lucky people who doesn't get itchy bumps from their bites, so I just bat them away.

The mud was worse. Sticky gumbo stuff that locked onto my shoes and wouldn't let go. When I got down in the dirt to shoot dew drops on the cactus petals my elbows and knees sank and stuck.

No problem. The air smelled of sage and wild roses and bird song echoed off the coulee walls. There was a bit of a breeze, and it carried the rumble of the turbid waters of the Red Deer River as it shoved past the ferry landing.

The mist had all burned off now and I could see far up and down the river valley. There were pelicans in the lee of an upstream island and wisps of cottonwood fluff coming off the trees on the opposite bank. The feathery tops of three-flowered avens caught the morning sun, and whole hillsides – far above a slimy wet bentonite outcrop or I would have walked up – were bright with wild sunflowers.

I spooked a mule deer out of the saskatoons when I walked over to the creek and nearly stepped on a fat brown garter snake. Big patches of cactus hung over the eroded edges of the creek bank, long roots reaching back to anchor them precariously. Long sage roots snaked among them.

There were plenty of tiny wildflowers along the creek but they had been laid flat by the flood. A couple of days and they'd bounce back up.

My shoes thick with caked-on mud, I shuffled my way back toward the truck. Just a couple of steps onto the prairie grass above the creek a frog bounced out of my way.

It was a leopard frog, a big one, the first one I've seen this year. Nice bonus. They used to be all over the place out on the prairie but in recent years they've been more and more rare. But this one was immensely healthy from the look of things. Hopefully it's a harbinger of better times for them.

I scraped off my boots and drove back up the coulee. Near the top I stopped and stepped from the truck to photograph some more flowers.

I could see probably ten kilometres in every direction, and the sky spread flagged with thin streamers of cloud in a big bowl overhead. A warming wind swept the flowers at my feet.

Wood Buffalo and the forests of British Columbia are stunning places.

But I'm a prairie boy all the way.

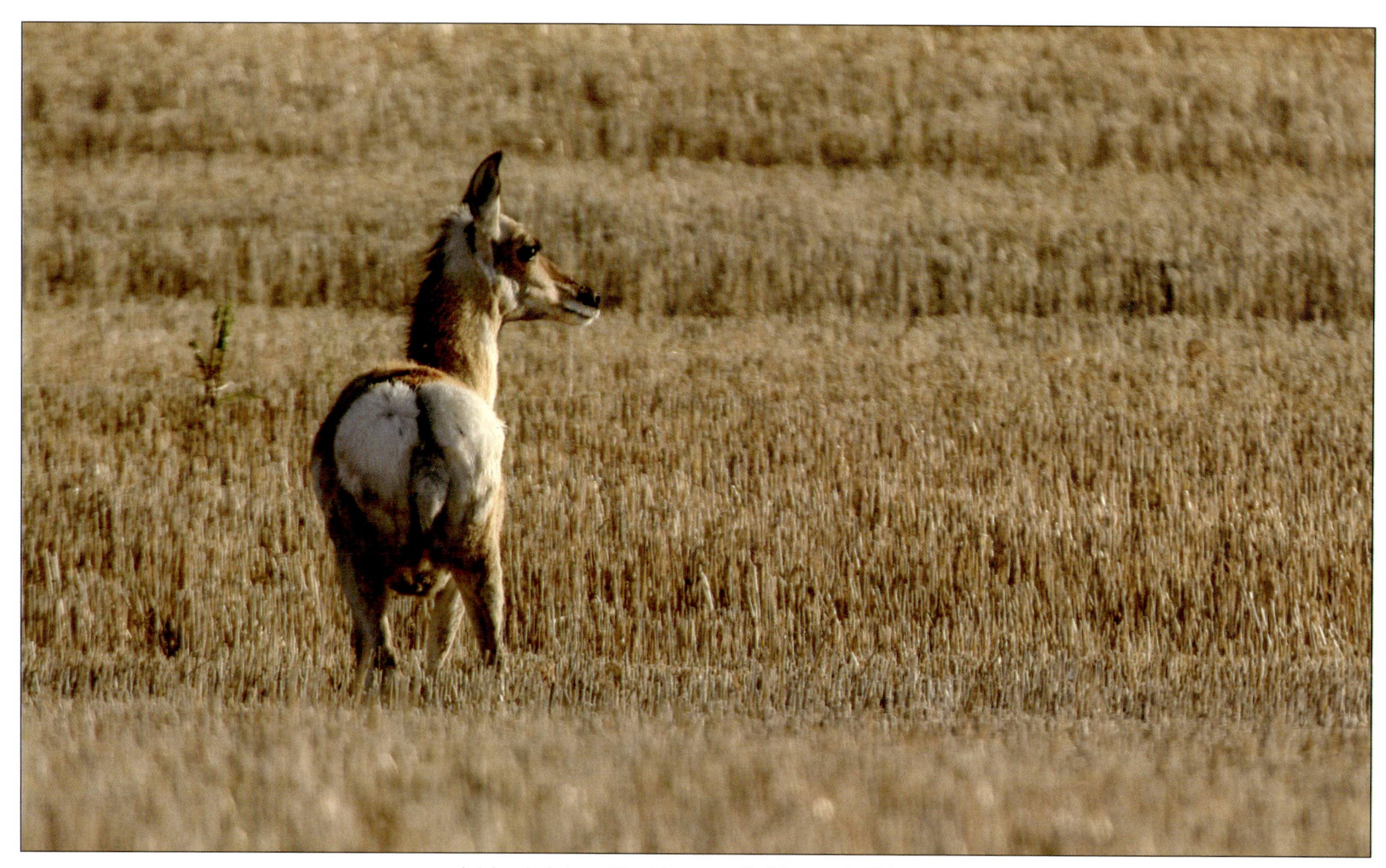

Antelope looks toward the rising sun north of Gem, east of Calgary.

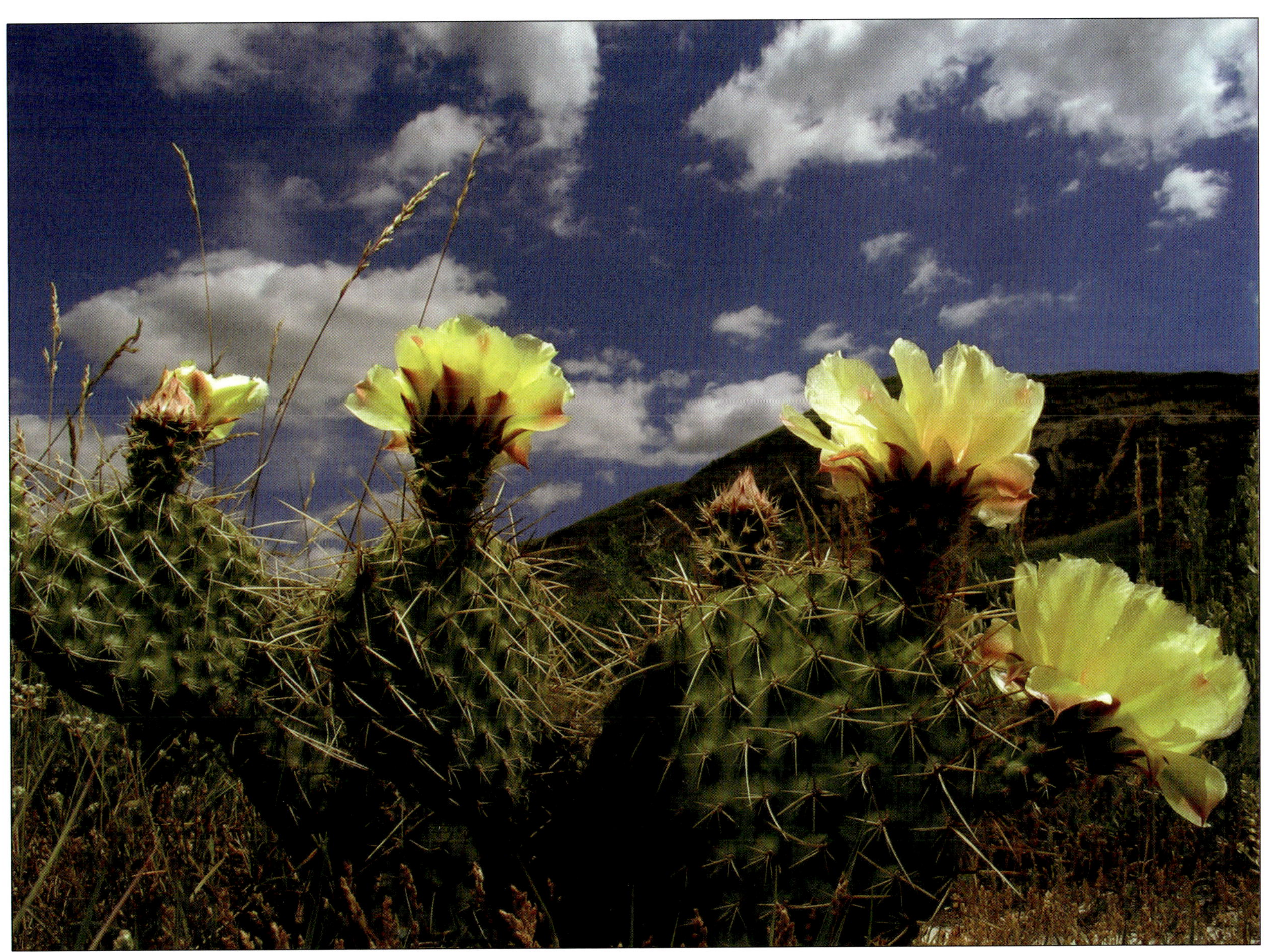

Prickly pear cactus bloom at Finnegan.

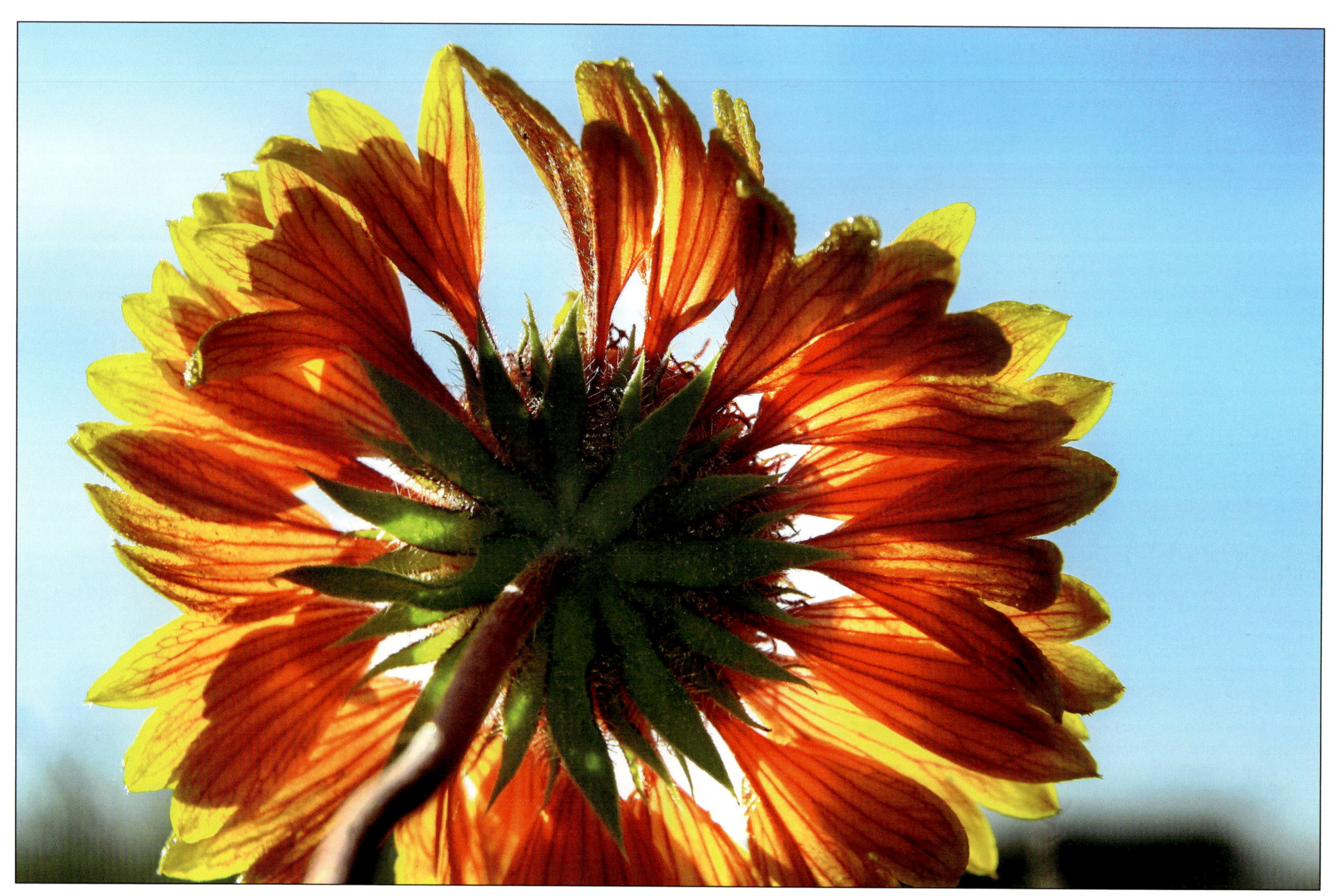

Blanket flowers brighten the green of a coulee near Finnegan Ferry on the Red Deer River east of Calgary.

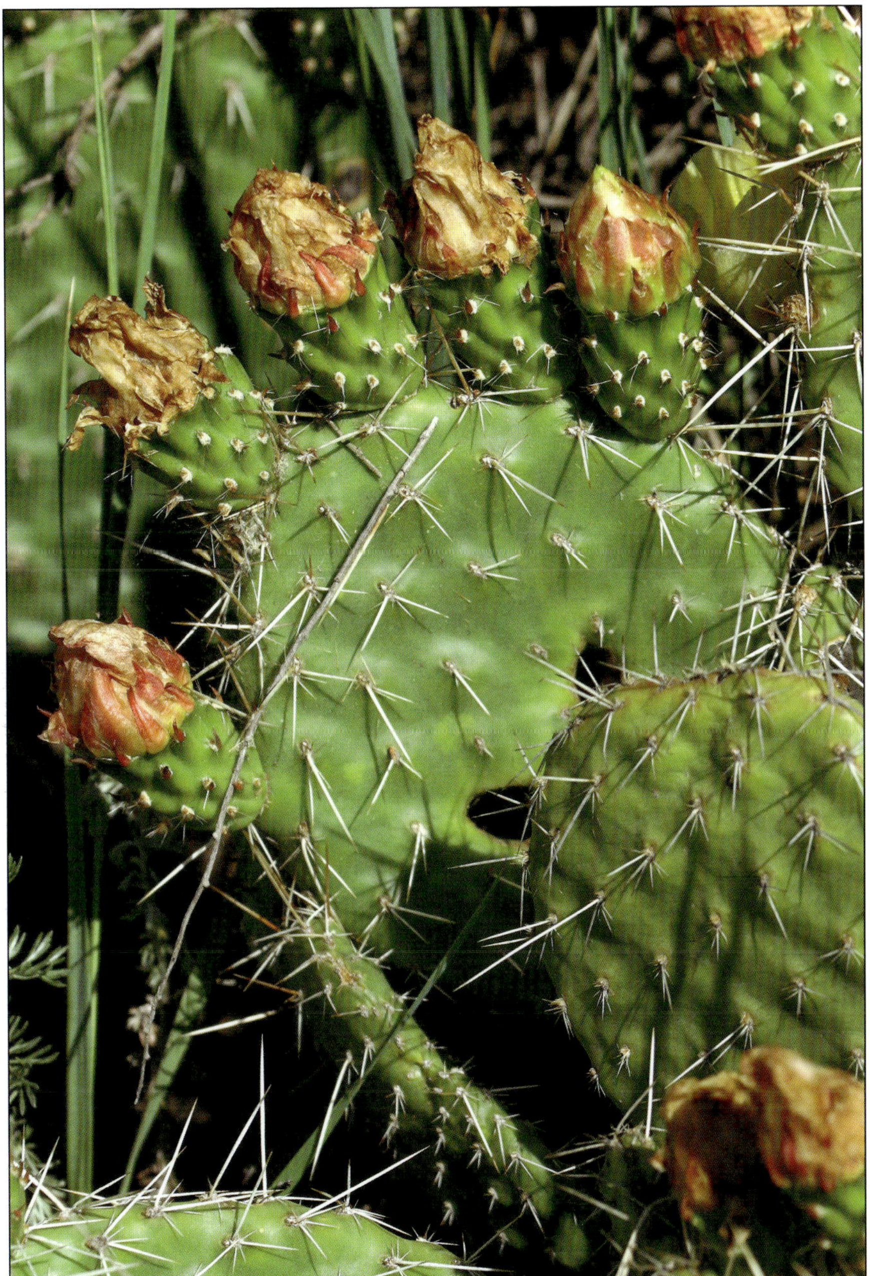

A prickly pear cactus raises its hand in greeting along a coulee near Finnegan Ferry on the Red Deer River east of Calgary. The papery yellow blossoms fade to this pinkish colour after they've set seed.

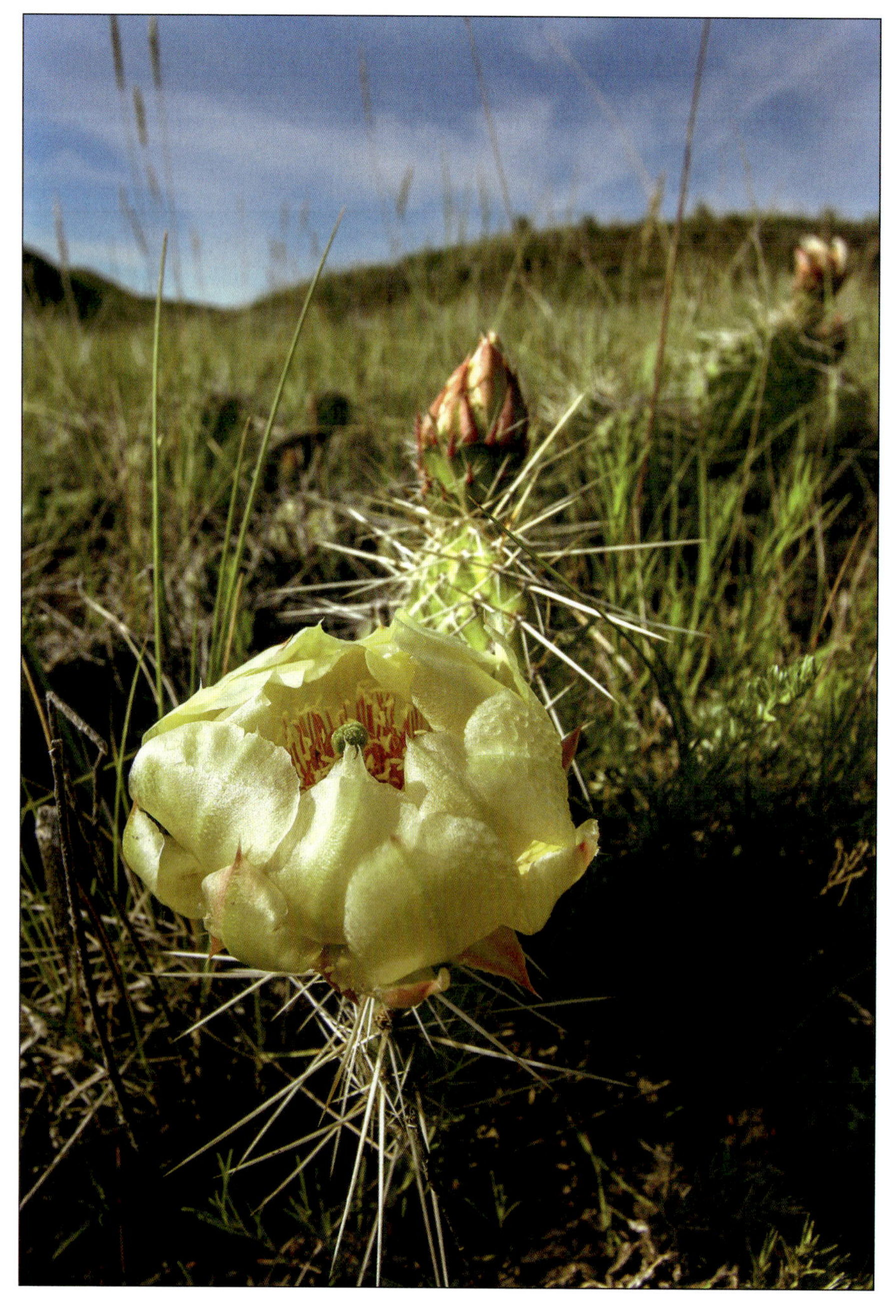

Prickly pear cactus blossoms still have a bit of dew on their petals at 8 AM in a coulee near Finnegan Ferry on the Red Deer River east of Calgary.

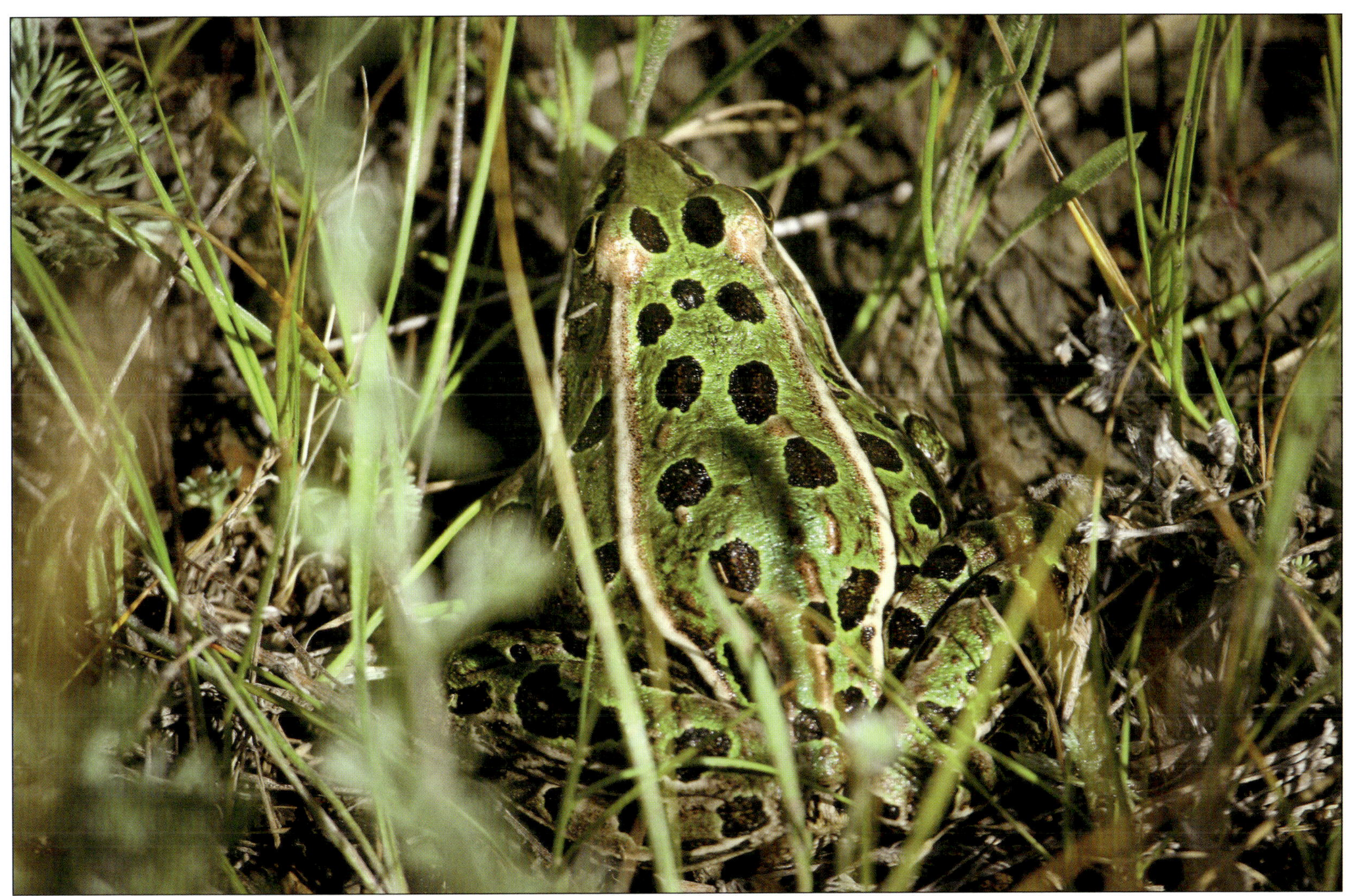

A sadly rare sight, a large leopard frog is almost invisible in the grass near a creek running through a coulee near Finnegan Ferry on the Red Deer River east of Calgary. Leopard frogs have been disappearing throughout the prairies.

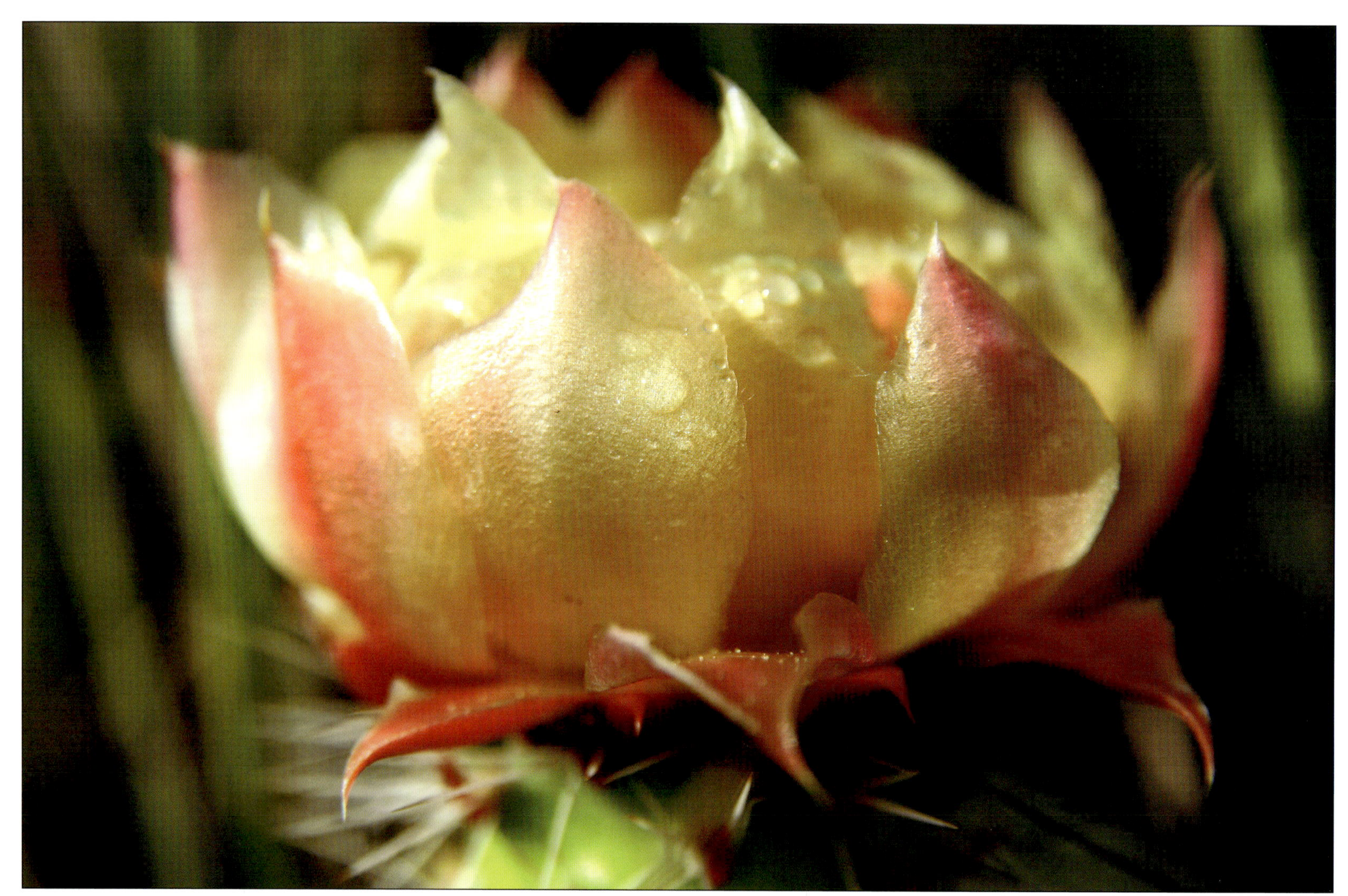

A prickly pear cactus blossom opens at Finnegan.

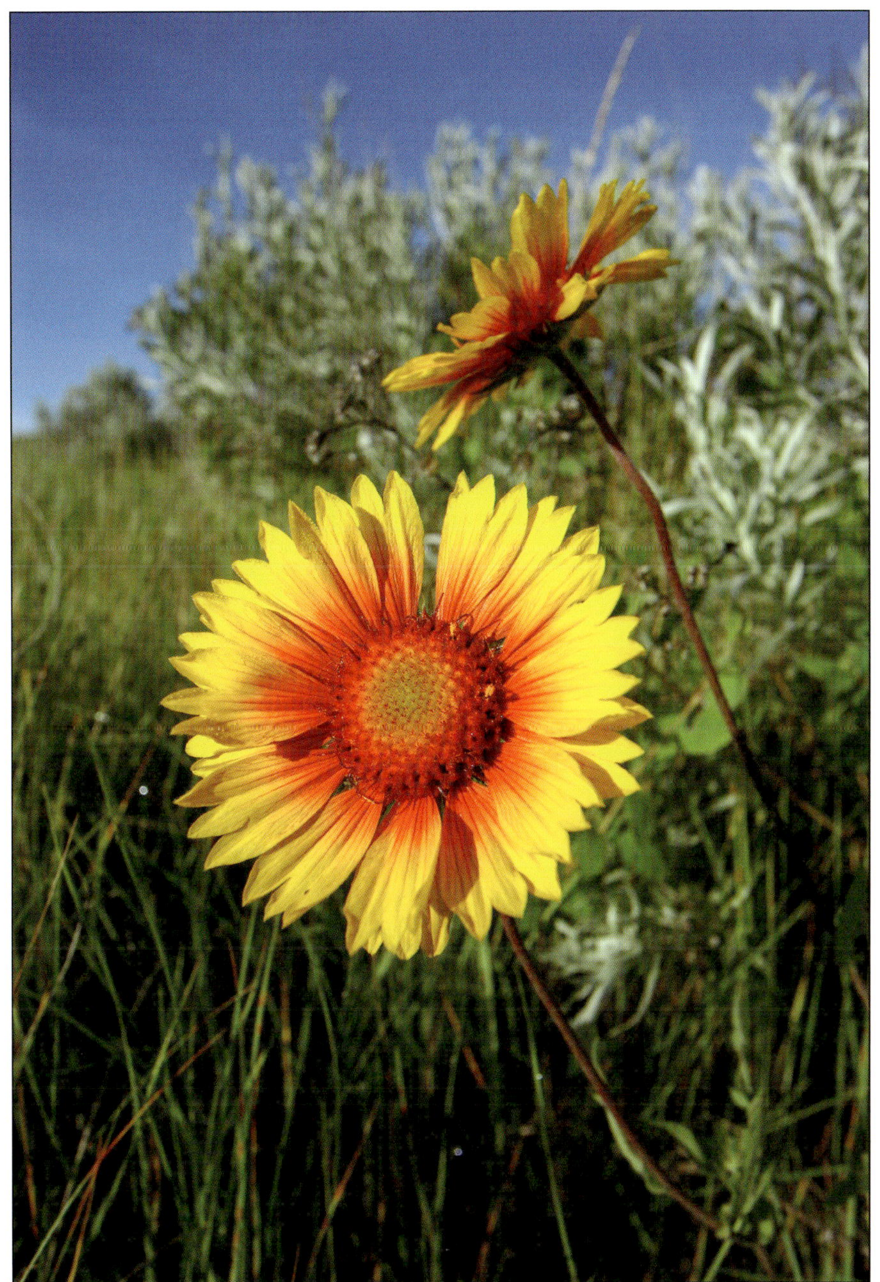

Blanket flowers brighten the green of a coulee near Finnegan Ferry on the Red Deer River east of Calgary.

JUST TOO COLOURFUL

I HEADED WEST WITH THE IDEA of shooting a bit of black and white.

The sky was full of heavy clouds, black on the bottoms and fading through silver to pure white on the top. Shafts of sunlight broke through and lit the mountains underneath.

But as I got farther west the precipitation that had held off for most of the afternoon threatened more and more, and soon I was driving through a fine drizzle and into full-on rain. I kept watching for breaks in the clouds but none were showing up. Time to change back to colour.

Funny thing, but I find bright or contrasty light more to my liking for black and white. And soft light, light that seems muted and grey, often works better for colour.

So since I was already 100 km west of the city and in the mood to rearrange some pixels, I rejigged the cameras, pulled over at the first turnoff I came to and stopped to look for a few splashes of pink.

Tiny, pretty calypso orchids bejewel the forest floor at this time of year, especially in shady groves of pine and spruce. They can be hard to find because they're so small – maybe six inches tall – but once you find one and your eye gets used to looking for them you'll often find a bunch of them.

Pretty as they are just for their colour, they're worth a close-up look. The main part of the flower is pink or magenta but the lower part is creamy white with a yellow tongue. If you have a macro lens for your camera, blow up the pictures and have a look at the tiniest parts of the flower. Those red spots are actually clusters of red growths, and there's clear growths around them that carry the colour like crystals in a chandelier. Fascinating.

The rain clouds cleared a bit so I rolled on west to the Kananaskis and on up into Peter Lougheed Provincial Park and then farther up toward Spray Lakes.

Just a couple of months ago I was up here and winter still had the whole place firmly in its grasp, but now all that snow has melted – and it was six feet deep on the flat in some places – and things are starting to get green. Not as green as at lower elevations but it's happening fast.

There was a lot of smoke in the air from a fire just over the BC border and it gave the light streaming through the still-snowy peaks an amber tint. It lit up the grass around a couple of sleepy coyotes. A tranquil scene, but when one of the coyotes got up and wandered over to nibble on the other's ear, things got a bit snarly for a couple of seconds.

Columbian ground squirrels have awakened from their winter torpor and their whistles filled the air in the meadows. Ravens croaked as they flew overhead. The Spray Lakes reservoir is very low, exposing gravel bars, submerged hillsides and tree stumps, but it won't be long before the snow melts in the high country and water tumbles down to fill it again.

I stopped to take a couple of pictures of a very ratty-looking cow elk by the side of the road and then rolled on again to find a vantage place to see the reflection of the mountains in the reservoir. The light was stunning now, golden, casting long shadows, the complete opposite of the soft light back among the orchids. I almost changed back to black and white.

But before I could I saw the bear.

He was big and chubby, one of the biggest black bears I've seen in a while. He was grazing like a cow on the green grass beside the reservoir and, except for a couple of glances, ignoring me completely as I took my pictures.

Dumb as it sounds, he just looked cuddly in that gorgeous mountain setting. Had he been disembowelling an elk calf instead of chowing down like a bovine it might have seemed a little less Winnie-the-Pooh-ish. But it would still have been an awesome scene.

The sun was behind the mountains now and the smoke haze was thinning as I turned to go down the switchbacks beside Mt. Rundle and into Canmore. Blue light filled the Bow River valley and faded to dark as I rolled back to town.

No black and white this time. It was all just too colourful.

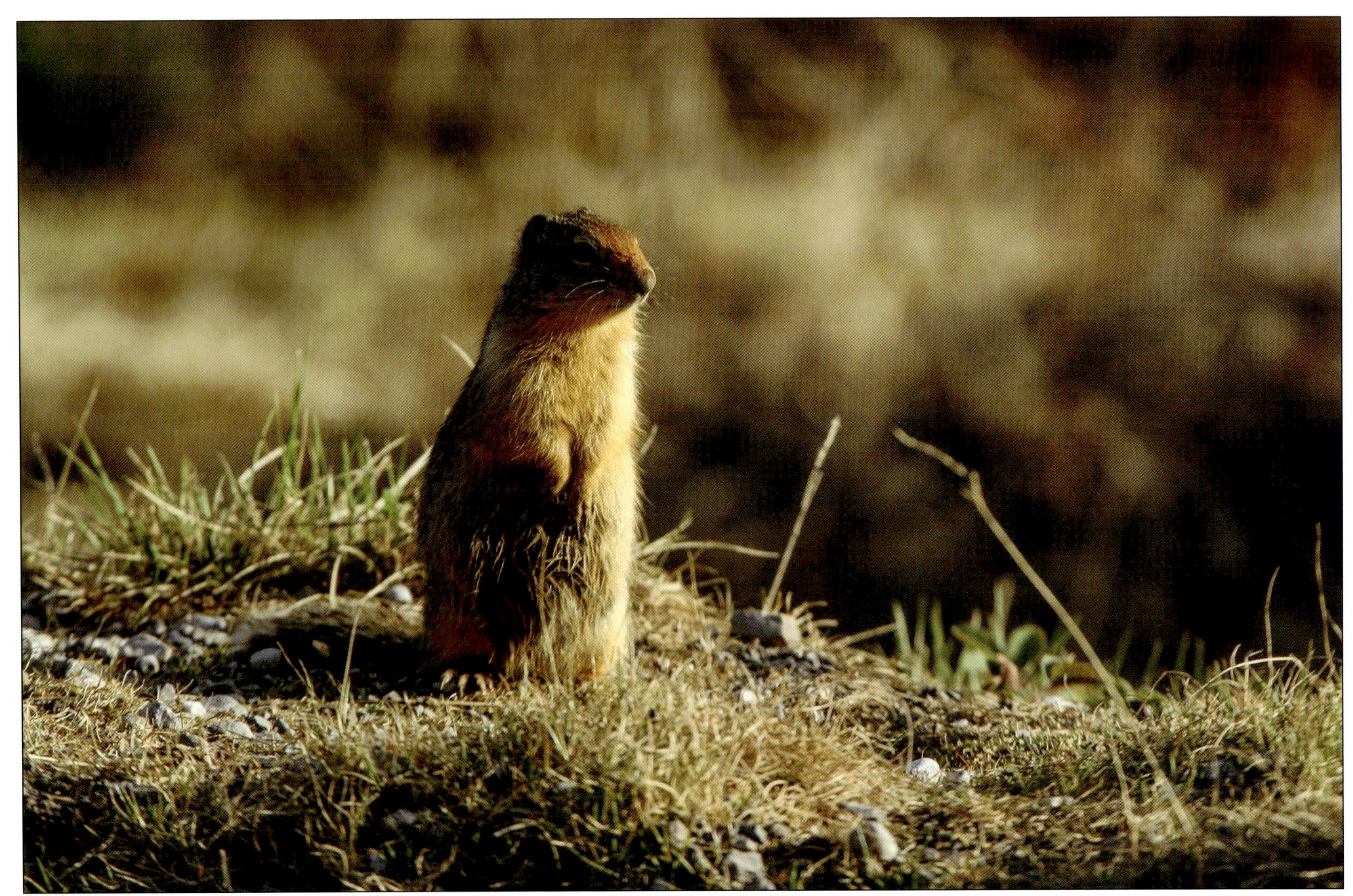

Columbian ground squirrel in Spray Valley Provincial Park.

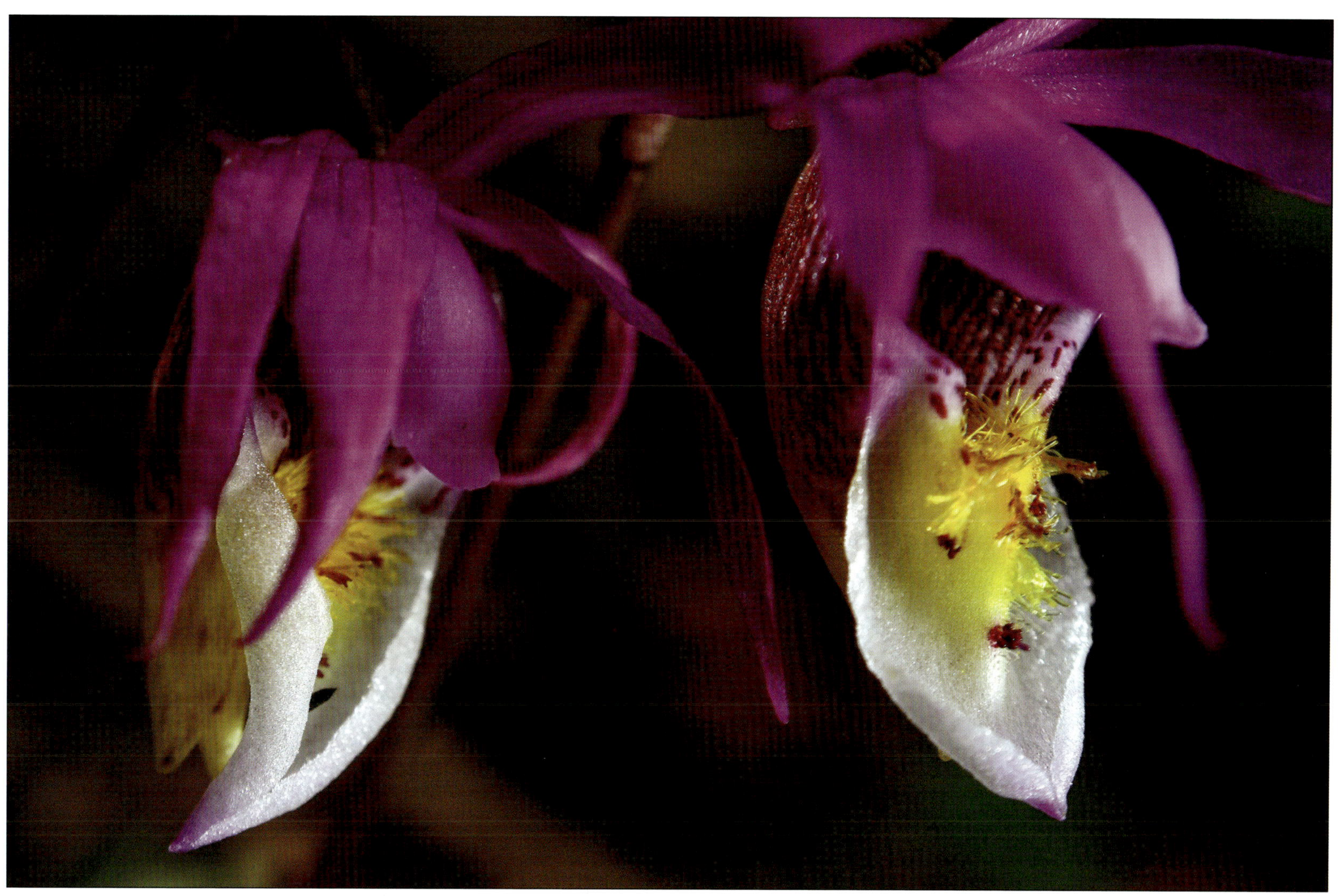

Calypso orchids on the way to Spray Valley Provincial Park.

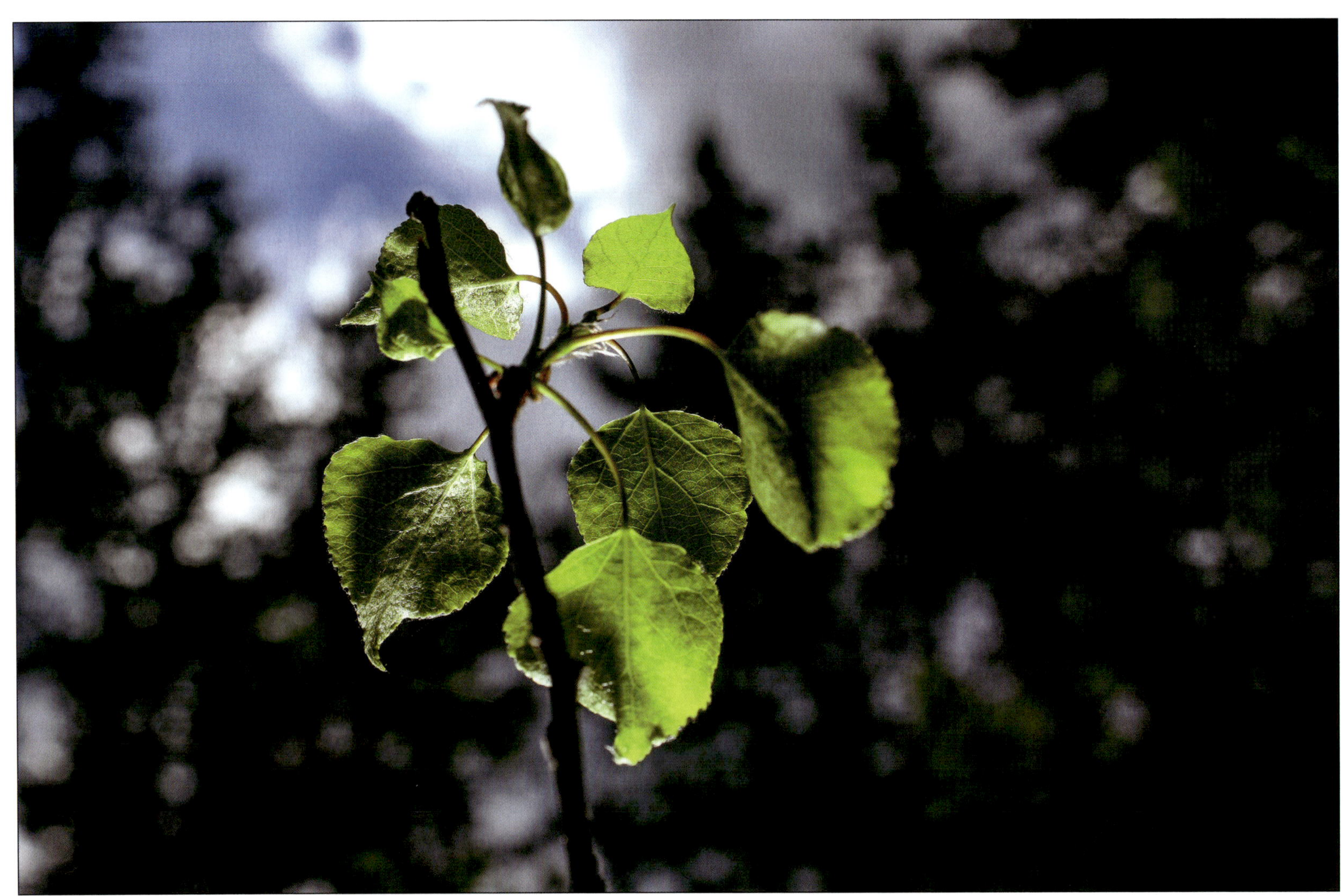

Fresh and fragrant aspen leaves in Spray Lakes in Spray Valley Provincial Park.

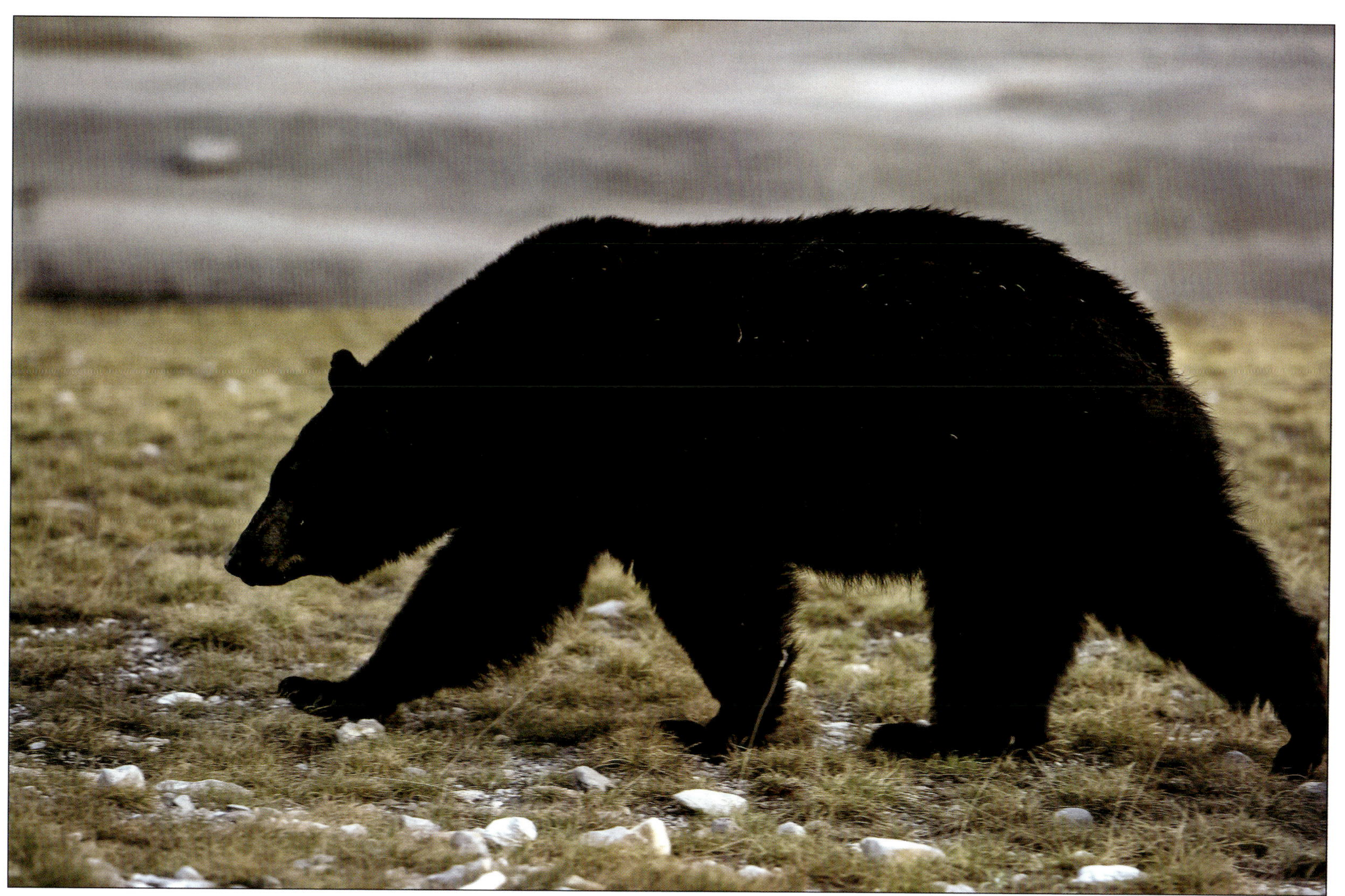

Black bear all set to graze on new green growth in Spray Lakes in Spray Valley Provincial Park.

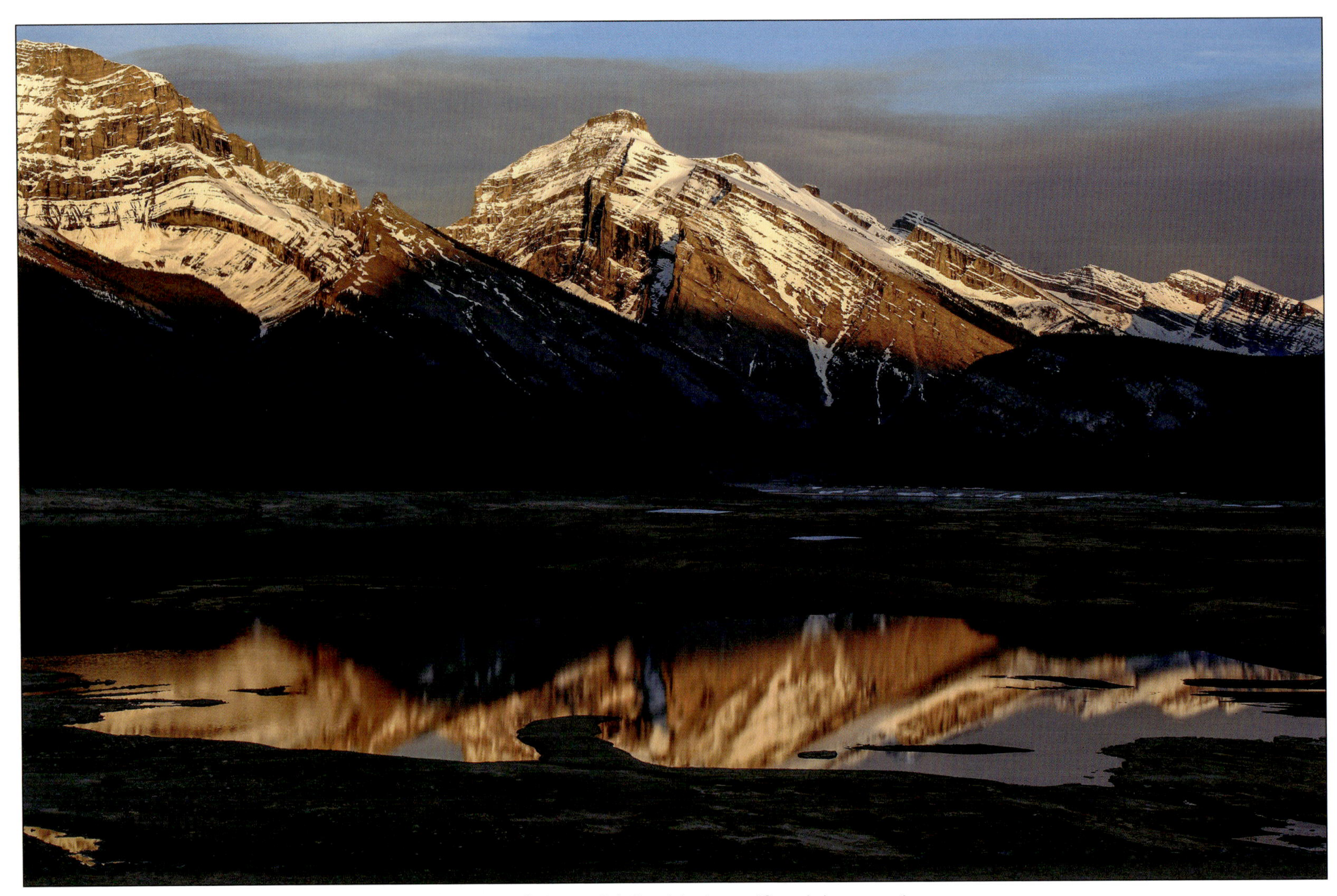

Mountains reflect on pools in the winter-lowered Spray Lakes reservoir.

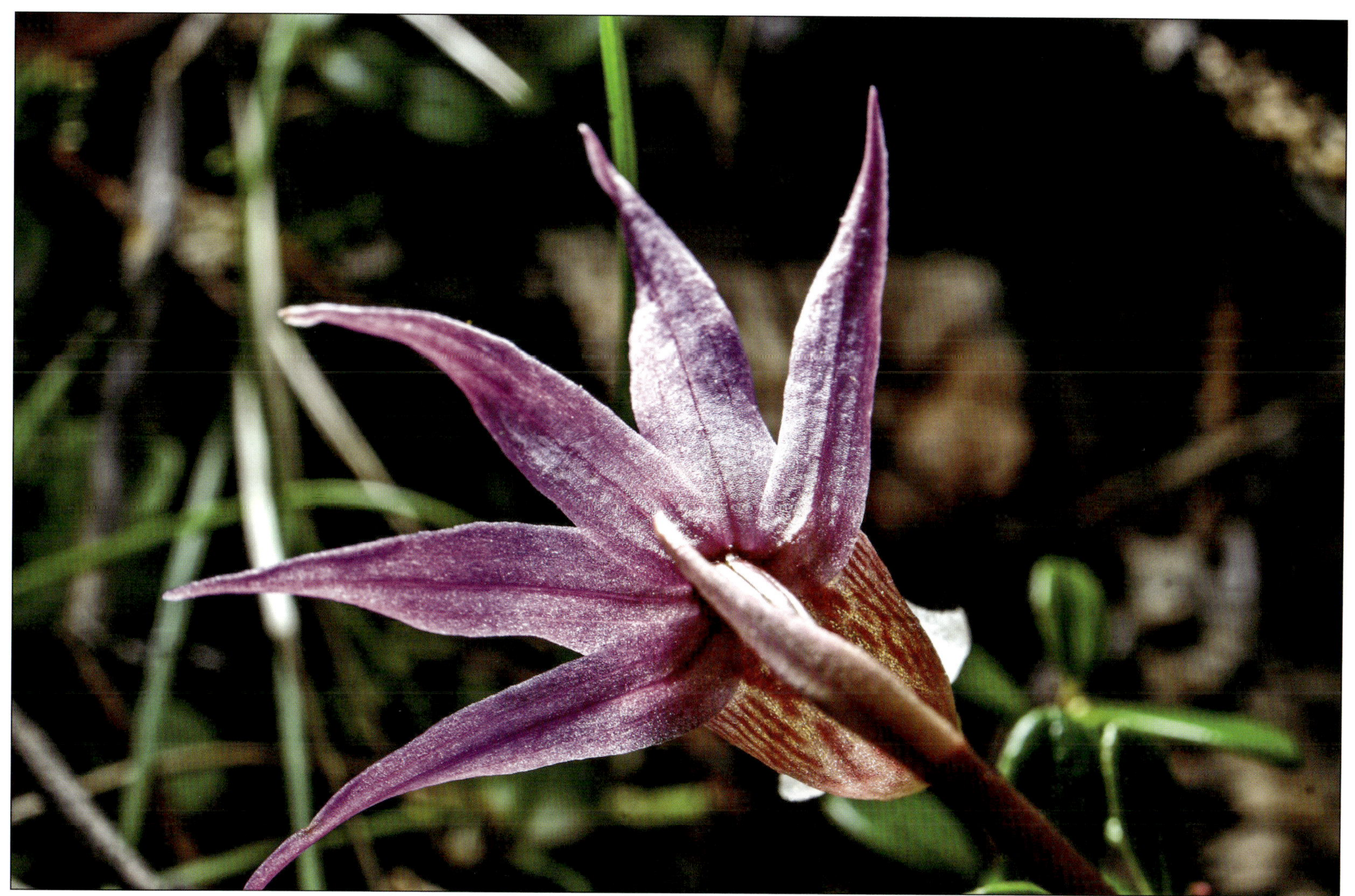

Looking down on a calypso orchid.

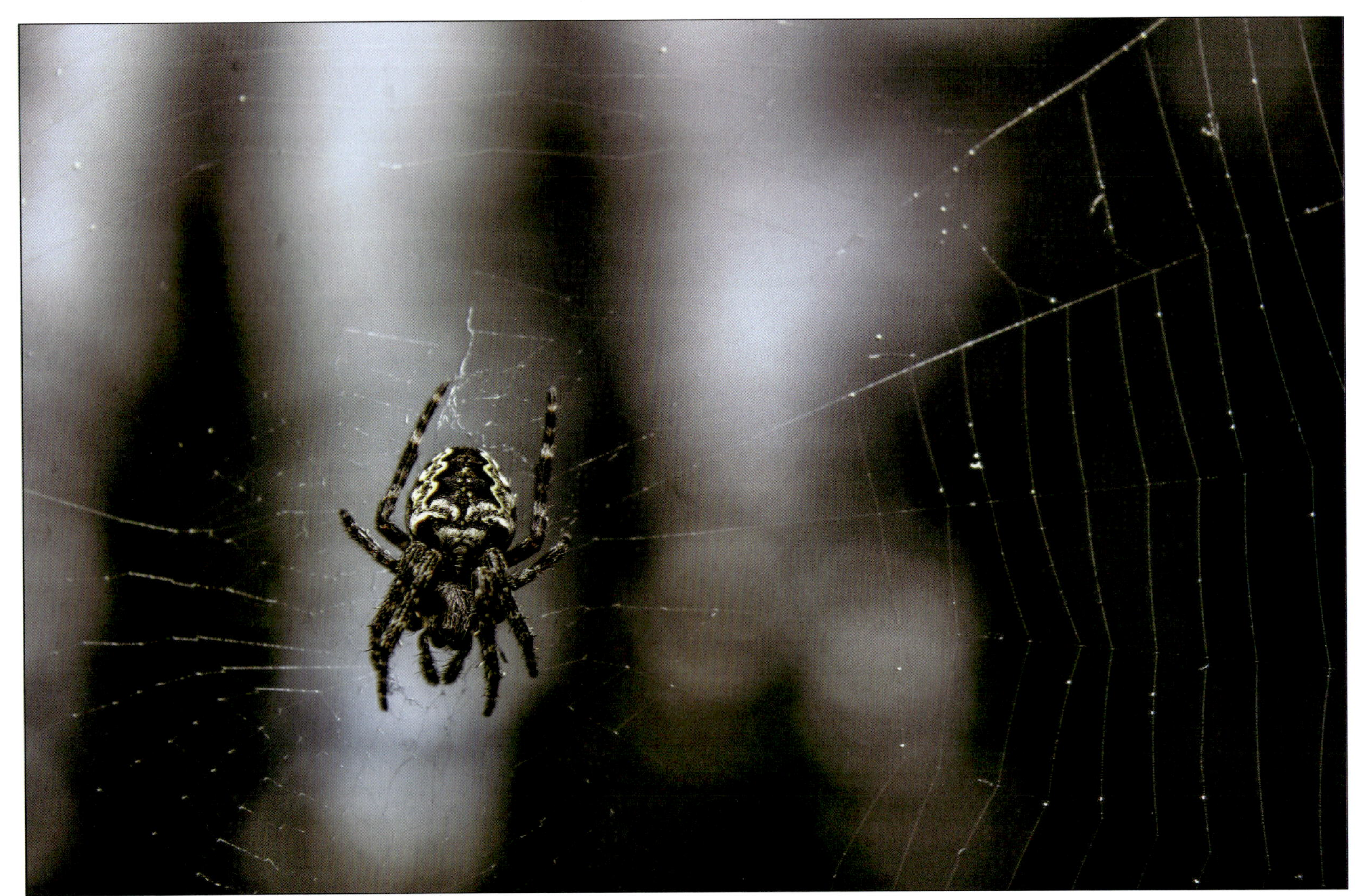

A spider hangs on a web strung between trees along Jumpingpound Creek.

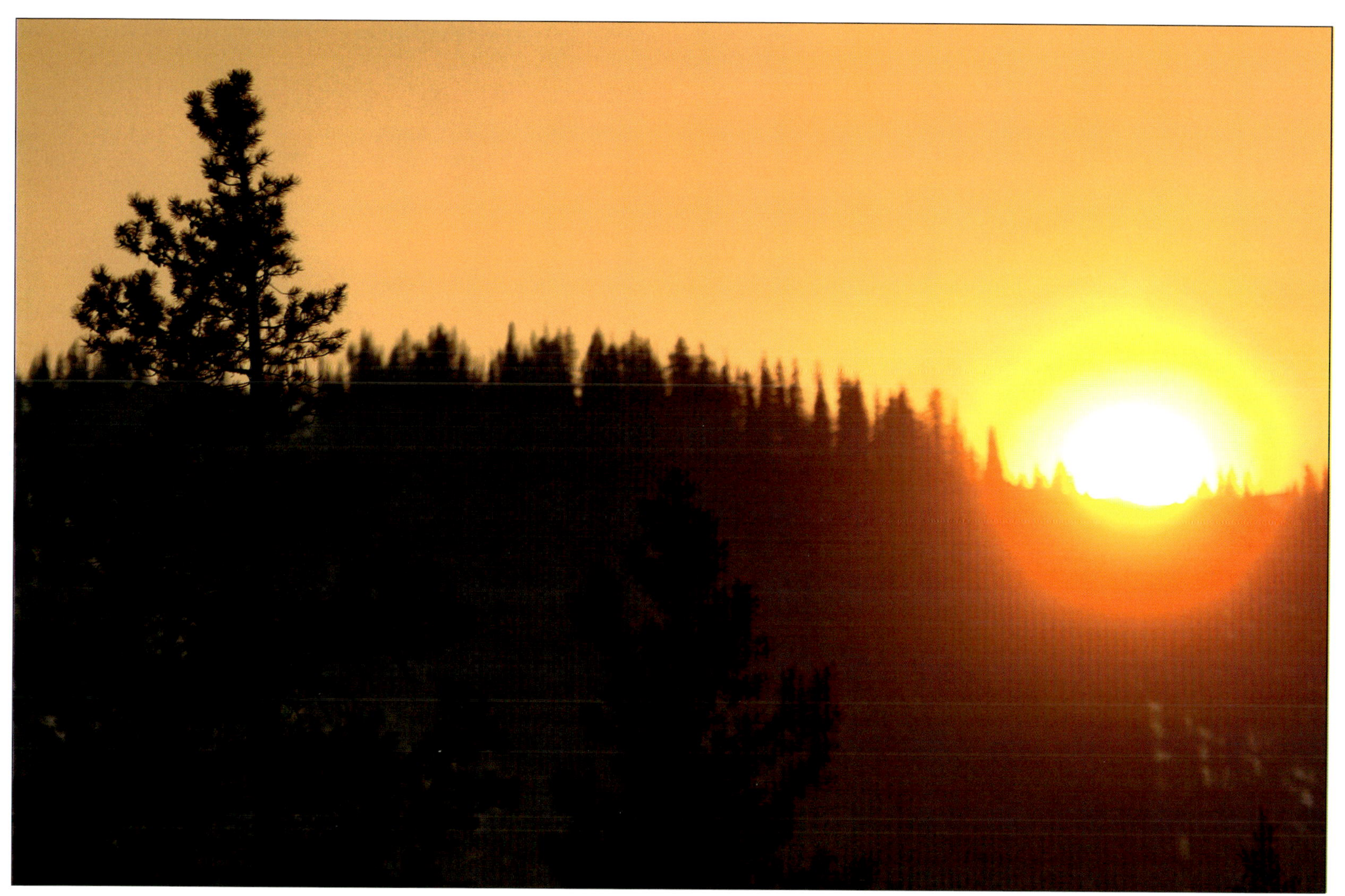

Sunset in the Grease Creek valley.

ORCHIDS

I JUST CAN'T HELP IT.

Whenever I see an orchid in the forest around here I think, this doesn't belong, it shouldn't be here.

They just look too exotic. Flowers like that belong in the tropics. They're the plant equivalent of Bohemian waxwings, birds that look like they'd be more at home in Borneo than Bowness.

But the woods are loading up with orchids right now and they are perfectly at home with their roots in half-frozen moss in the foothills of the Rockies.

And next to crocuses, they are the flowers I most look forward to seeing as the seasons change.

I found the first of the year's orchids nearly three weeks ago just peeking up from the forest floor at Sibbald Flats. It was a calypso orchid, the tiny pink downturned blossoms just starting to show.

They've always been my favorite orchid, but I really can't remember who told me they were called calypsos. Might have been Gramma, maybe mom. You might know them as Venus lady's slippers or pink lady's slippers. But no matter what you call them they are the first true jewels to appear on the forest floor.

They grow in lots of places and if you look around the foothills – and even a few places in the city – you'll find them. They seem to prefer the open, mossy ground in stands of pine or mixed pine and spruce. Like a lot of orchids, calypsos need help from fungus growing in the forest soil, so they accumulate where there's the biggest abundance of that fungus.

Just coming on now are yellow lady's slippers and they are even easier to find.

For one thing, they are much larger. And they grow in leafy clumps. But best of all, you don't even have to leave the city.

My favorite place to look for them is in the shady forest at Roxboro Park right off Mission Road. The woods there are a bit of wilderness right in the middle of the city, and this week the yellow lady's slippers were really starting to open up. You might have to do a little brush-busting but you'll find them.

And chances are you'll find another kind of orchid right close by.

These ones are called striped coral root. Now that's a name that doesn't make a whole lotta sense. Except for the striped part. They are definitely striped. Didn't check the roots. There's a kind of logic to the names of the yellow lady's slippers and the so-called pink lady's slippers but I guess the coral root flowers don't look much like shoes.

Striped coral root has no chlorophyll and doesn't put out any leaves. It lives as a parasite on the fungus that grows in the soil, taking full advantage of the nutrients the fungus frees up while its cousins like calypsos and yellow lady's slippers only use part of it.

The plants really stick out, looking like red candy among all the green grass and shrubs.

And there's other flowers taking off now, too. Clematis is starting to trail its vines and spread its papery blue flowers and there's violets everywhere. It won't be very long until they're joined by wood lilies and paintbrush and soon the woods will be a riot of colour.

But it's the orchids that I really like. There's just something exotic about them.

If you've ever been to the tropics, you know what I mean. There are orchids in every ecological niche down there. Our local ones would fit right in.

Their waxy flowers and lack of scent give them a kind of unreal appearance that adds to their uniqueness, too. Try to take a close look at the coral root blossoms if you get a chance. They look made up, like cake decorations. Even the yellow lady's slippers, flamboyant as they are, look like add-ons.

But the calypsos are just pretty. They don't look strange or unreal – well, maybe that bright colour – and their low flat leaves fit right in with the other plants on the forest floor.

They're probably the easiest ones to find as well. Just keep your eyes cast downward as you walk among the pines out by Sibbald Flats and you'll soon pick out the tiny splashes of pink.

They are a little touch of the tropics right here at home.

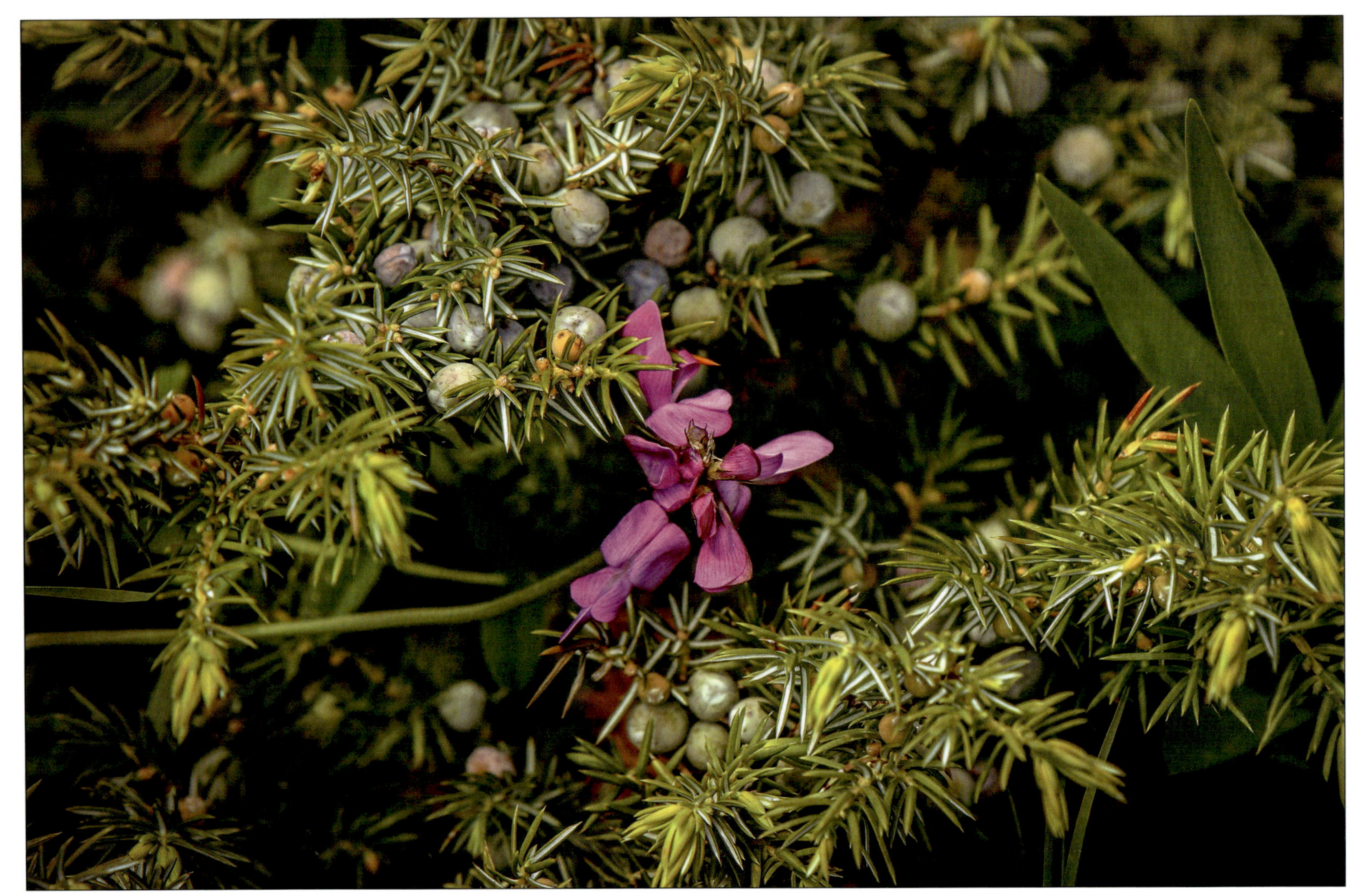

Hedysarum and ground juniper.

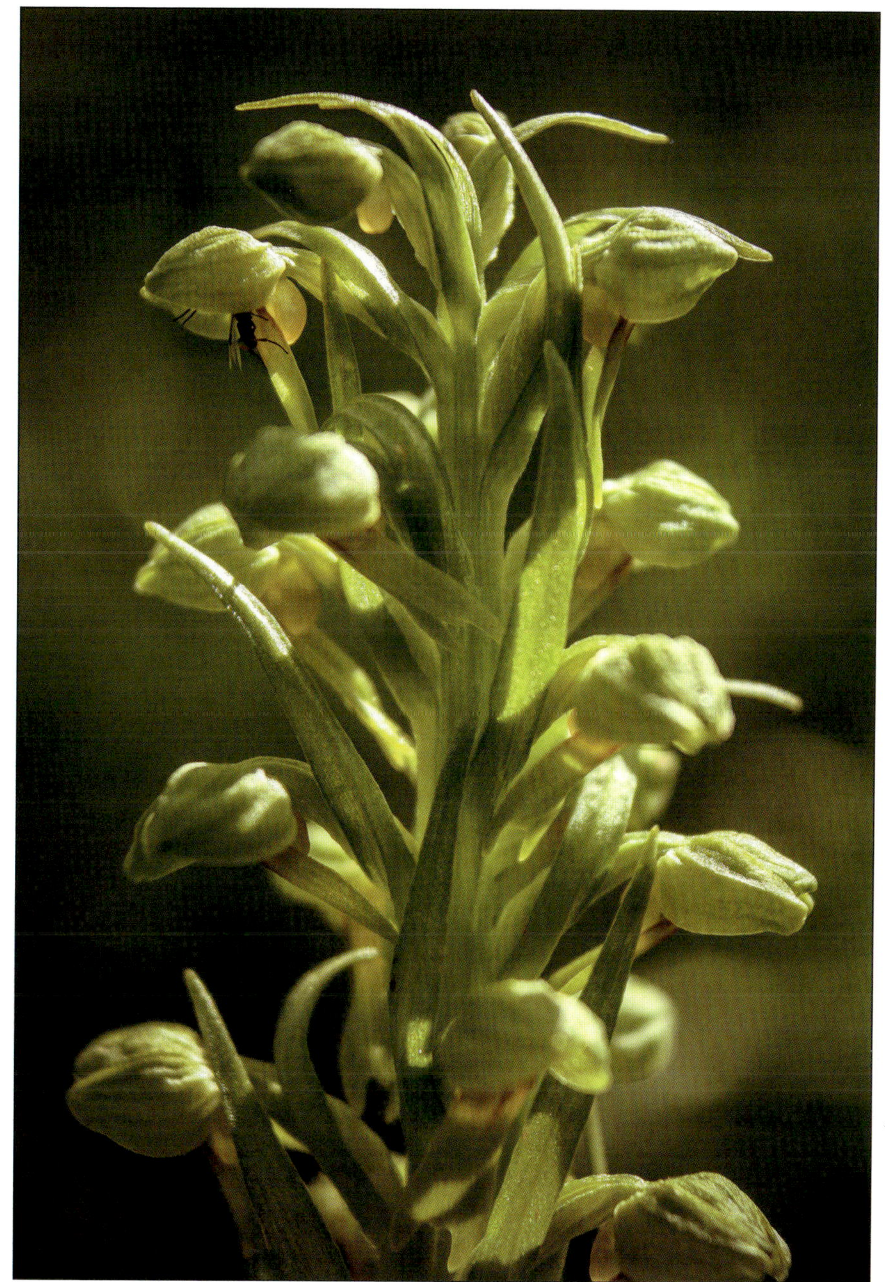

Green bog orchid.

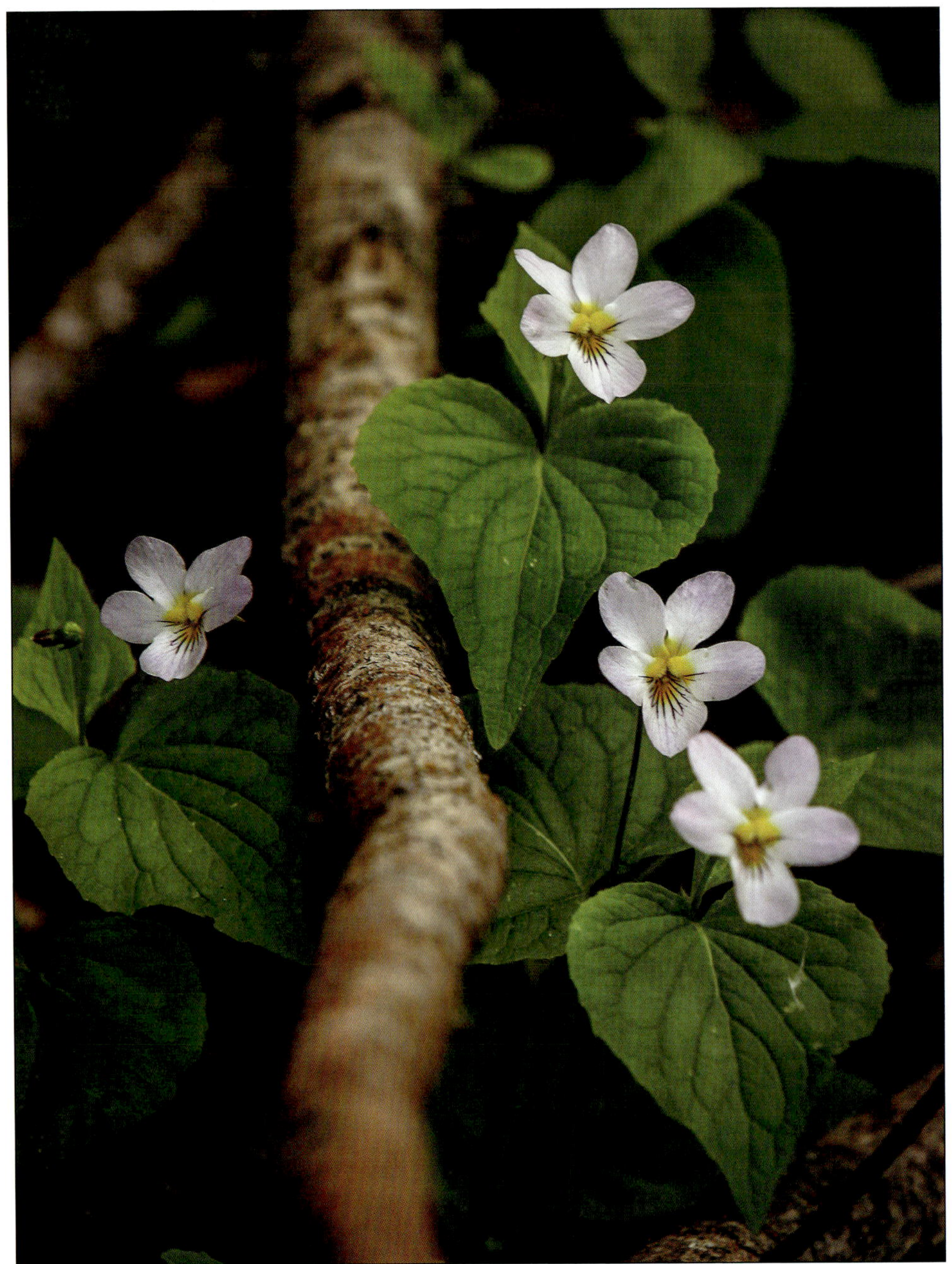

Wood violets.

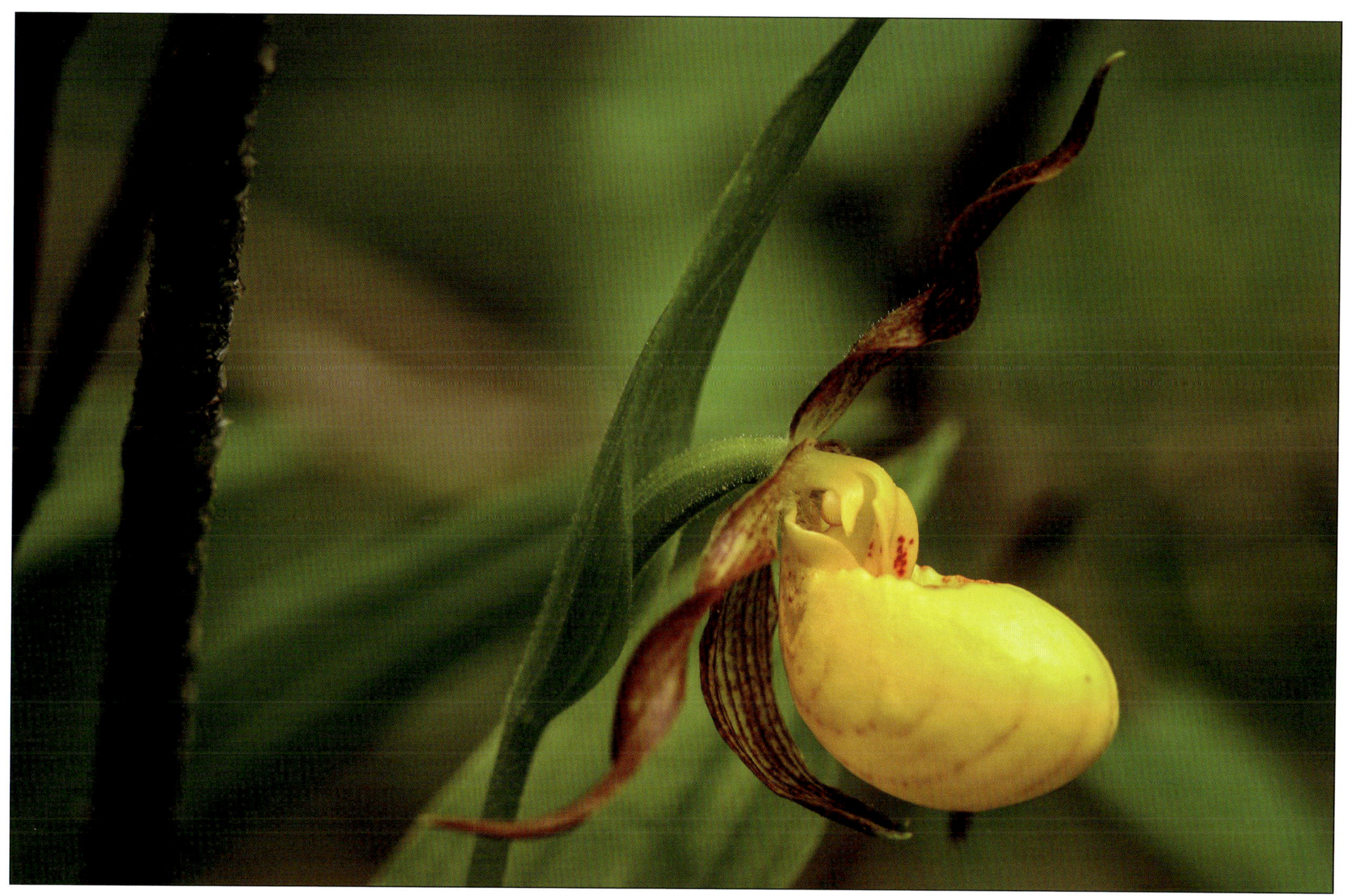

Yellow lady's slipper.

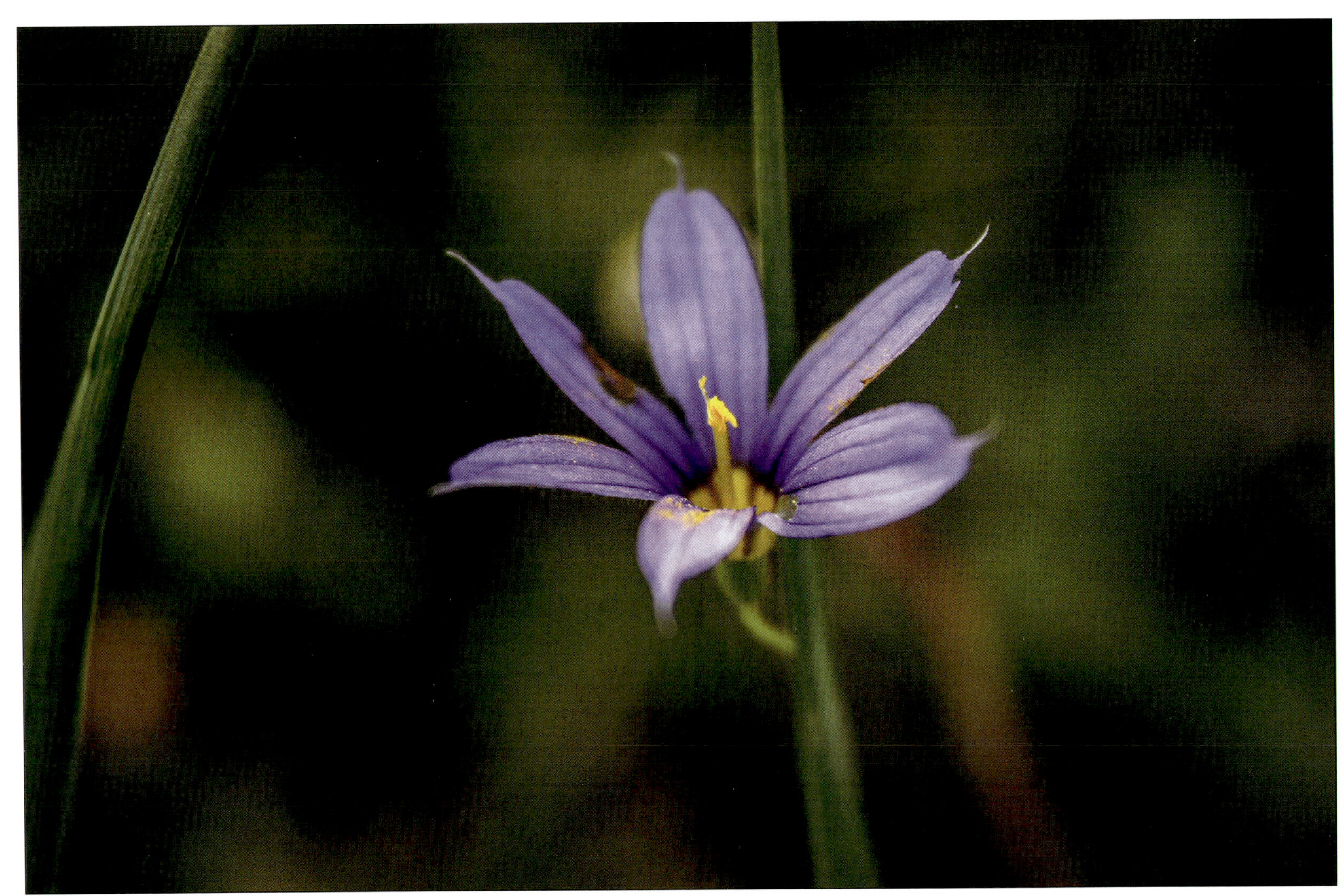

Blue-eyed grass.

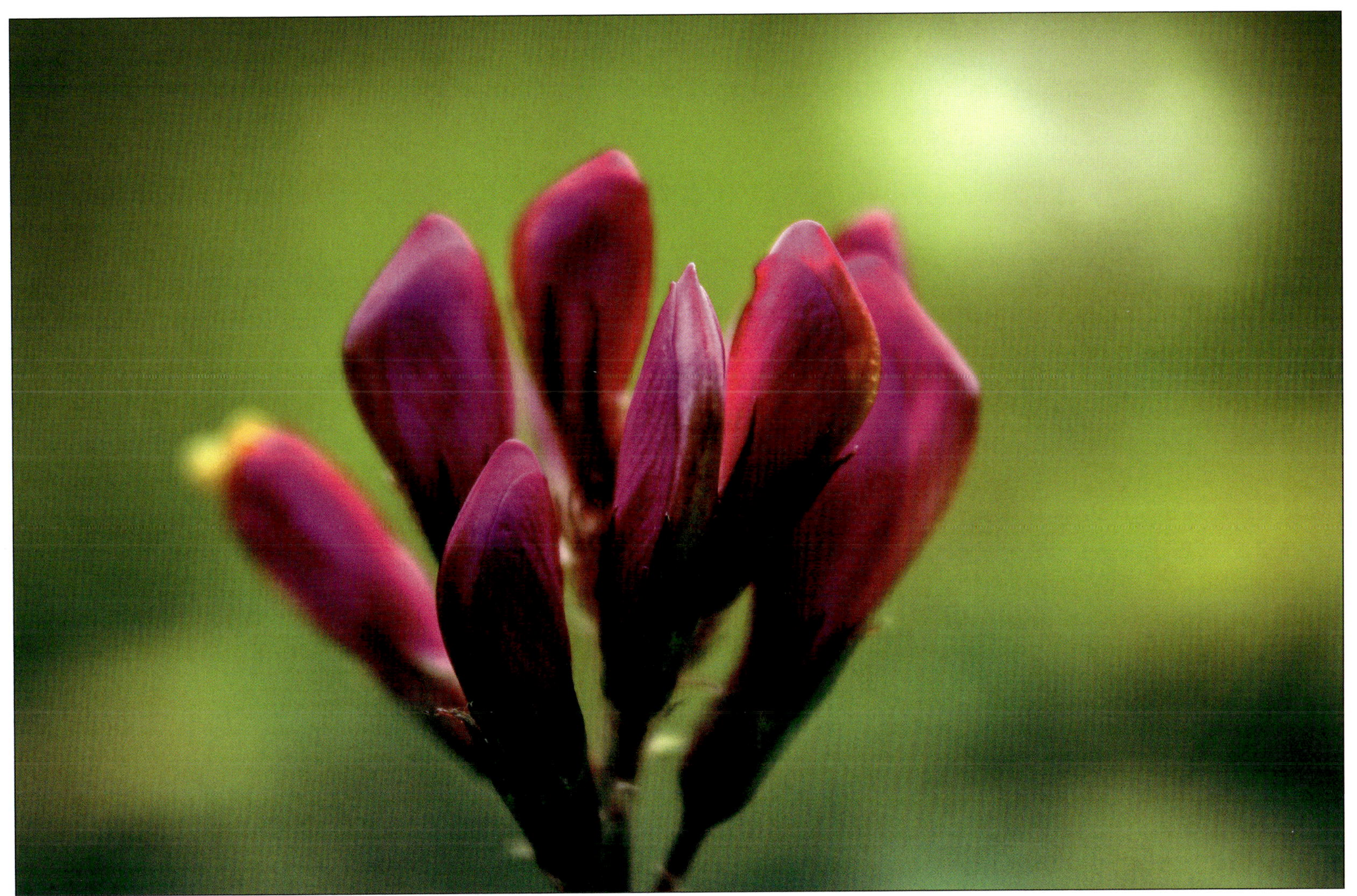

Hedysarum.

STORM CLOUDS

YOU CAN SEE STORMS COMING from a long way off when you're out on the prairie.

Drive a gravel road for a hundred kilometres or so and you can watch the clouds form on the horizon, puff out, grow and spread in the high-altitude wind.

It's really pretty cool to watch one of the storms form up. They start off about midday when the heat of the sun gets the air above the ground moving. As it rises, full of moisture from the soil, it eventually hits cooler air, and just like from a drier vent on a winter morning, the warm, wet air condenses into a cloud.

They start off as little cotton balls, bright white against the dark blue sky, but soon they start to run together and congeal, forming thicker and thicker masses as the day gets hotter and more moist air rises into the sky.

Eventually the clouds start to create their own updrafts and down-drafts as the shadow of the cloud cools the air both within and beneath it. Turbulence forms inside the cloud mass and makes the bottoms bulge and the sides puff out.

The clouds are full of moisture drawn up from the land and the surrounding air. And the more the moisture accumulates the more dense the clouds become. Seen from far off on the horizon, the storm clouds look soft and bright. Seen from underneath where their sometimes 50,000-foot thickness blocks the sun, they look evil.

At some point the weight of the water becomes too much for the air currents in the clouds to keep juggling, and rain starts to fall. And sometimes the rain doesn't quite make it out of the bottom of the cloud before it is sucked back up into the heights by more updrafts. If it goes high enough to reach the chilly air of the upper atmosphere it freezes.

If you were in the city this past week you likely saw the results of that. Rain and hail that turned the Stampede rodeo into a mud pit and flooded parts of the city. These summer storms can get pretty intense.

But they can also get just downright pretty. Especially when seen from a bit of distance.

I shot these pictures over the last couple of weeks, mostly out east near the Saskatchewan border and down by the Cypress Hills. This time of year you can almost always find a storm brewing somewhere out there.

Out toward Castor and Coronation and south around Oyen, Empress and Buffalo, the prairies get a lot of sun in the summer, and almost every day from mid-June on into August there'll be big billowy clouds somewhere on the horizon.

And the Cypress Hills are just as good for storm watching, maybe even better.

With our normal westerly winds blowing nearly every day, storms that form to the west get pushed toward the heights of the hills, and the cloud tops soar so high they almost seem like they'll topple over on themselves.

It's a great place just to sit and watch the clouds come sailing along. Just find a spot somewhere out near the edge of the escarpment and watch the skies. And if the storm gets a little electrical – as they most often do – you'll get a fireworks show almost as good as the one at the Stampede.

If you happen to come upon a place where a storm has just passed, you'll be in for even more of a treat. I tell ya, I could retire if I could figure out how to bottle the smell of sage after a thunderstorm has passed. It's indescribable.

But for now I'll just have to be content with driving out east and watching the skies. Like I needed another excuse to go drive around on the prairie.

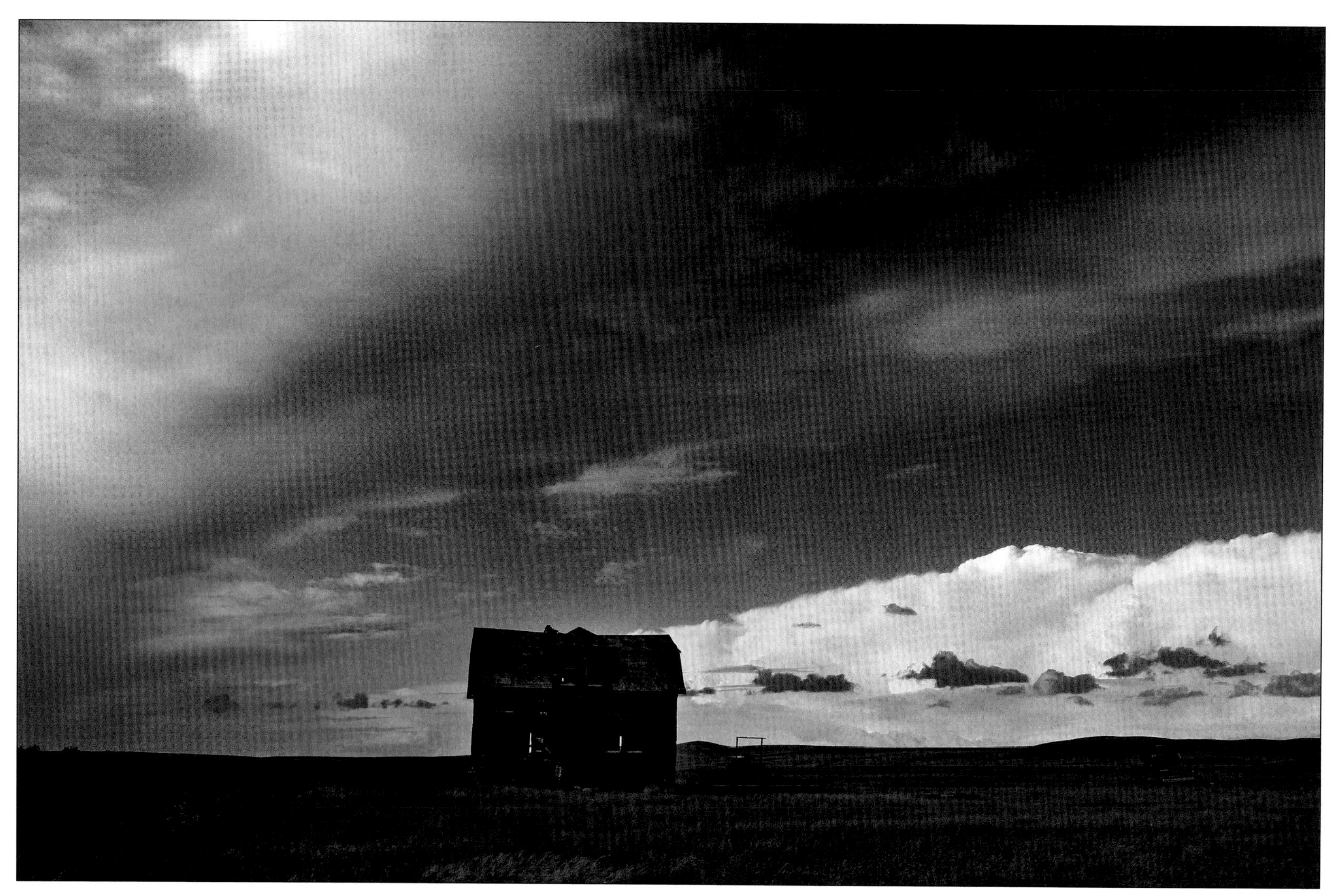

Farmstead along the Red Deer River near Buffalo.

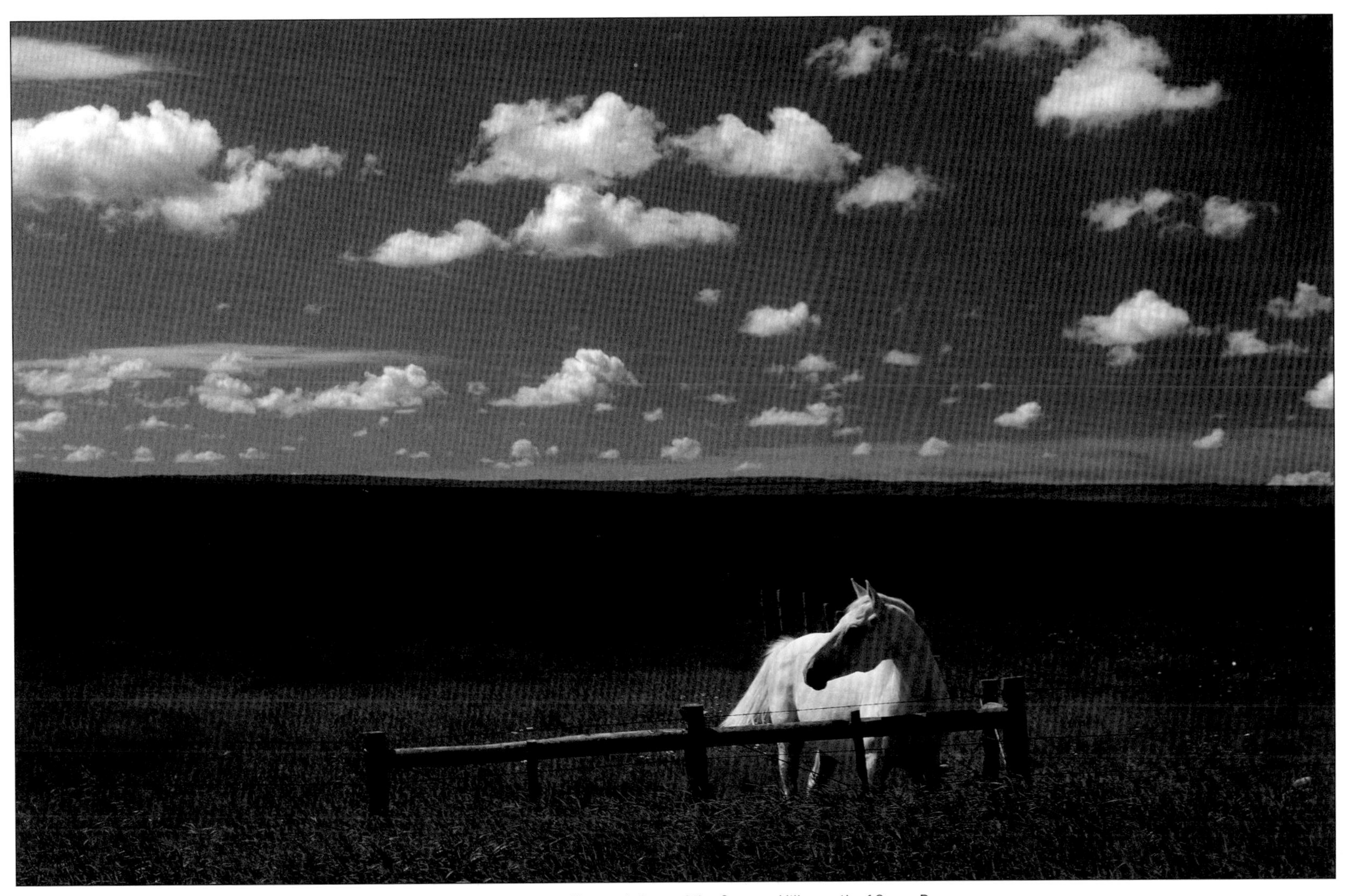

White horse in a pasture on the west slope of the Cypress Hills, south of Seven Persons.

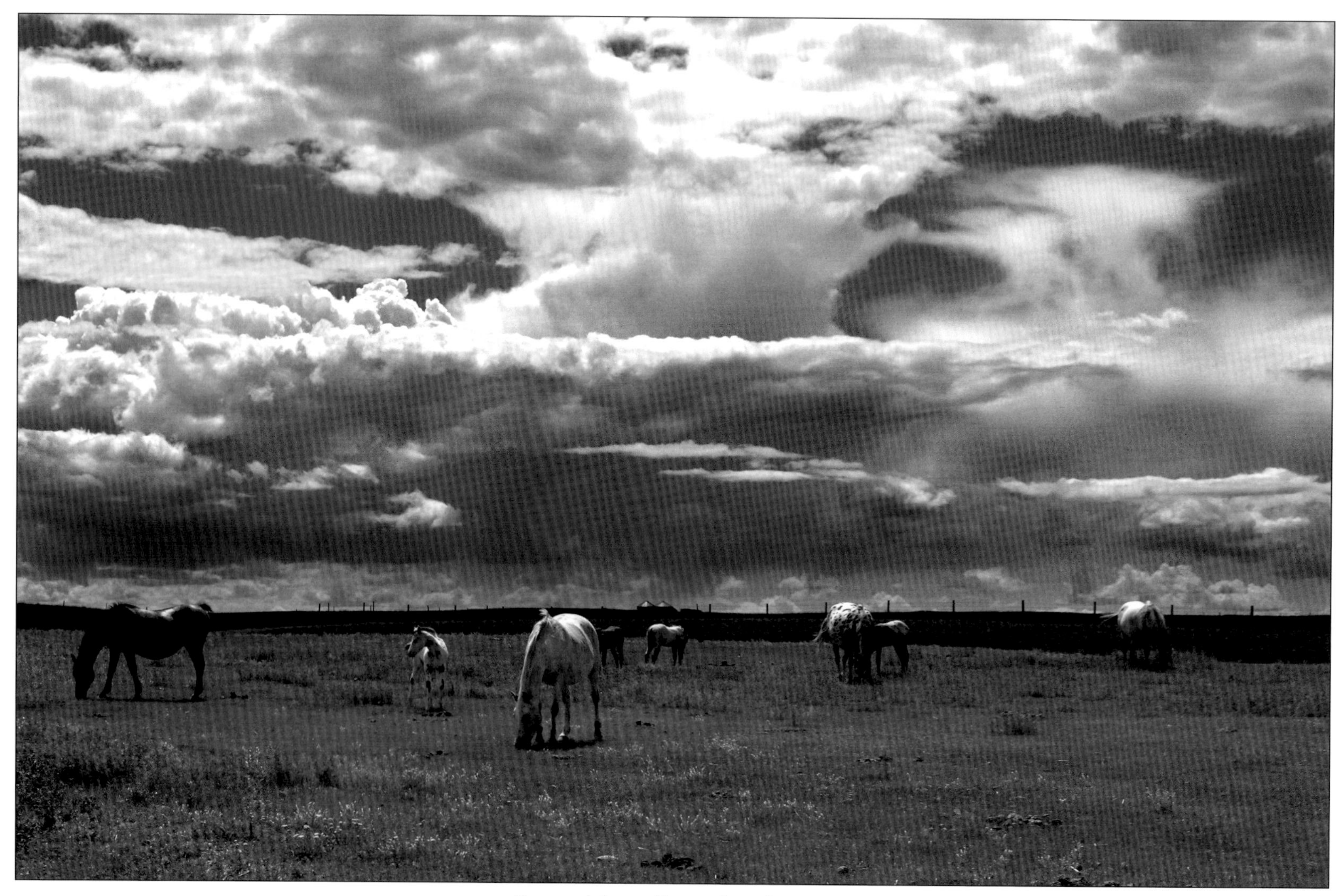

Horses and stormy skies near Seven Persons.

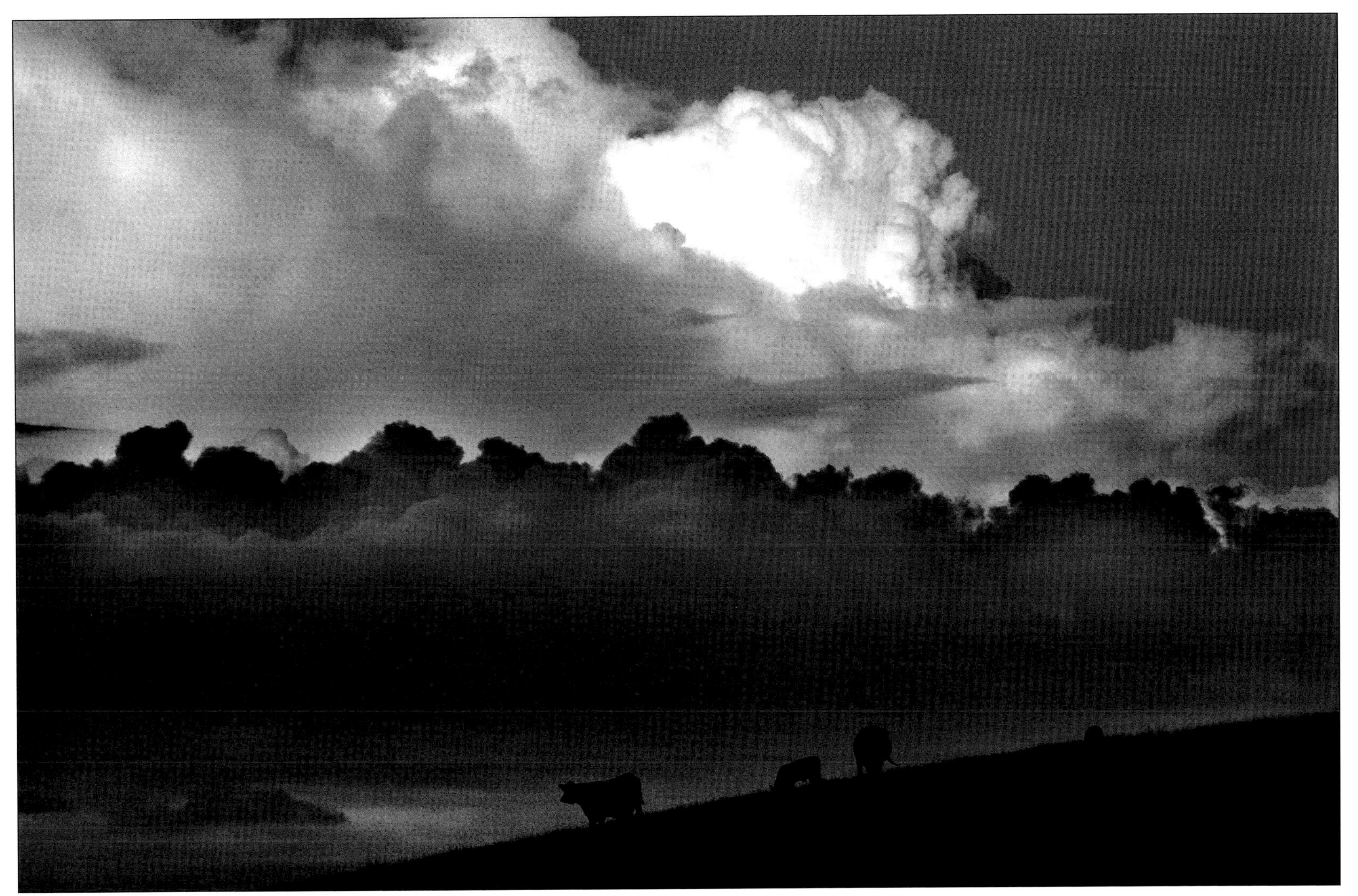

Storm coming in near Bindloss.

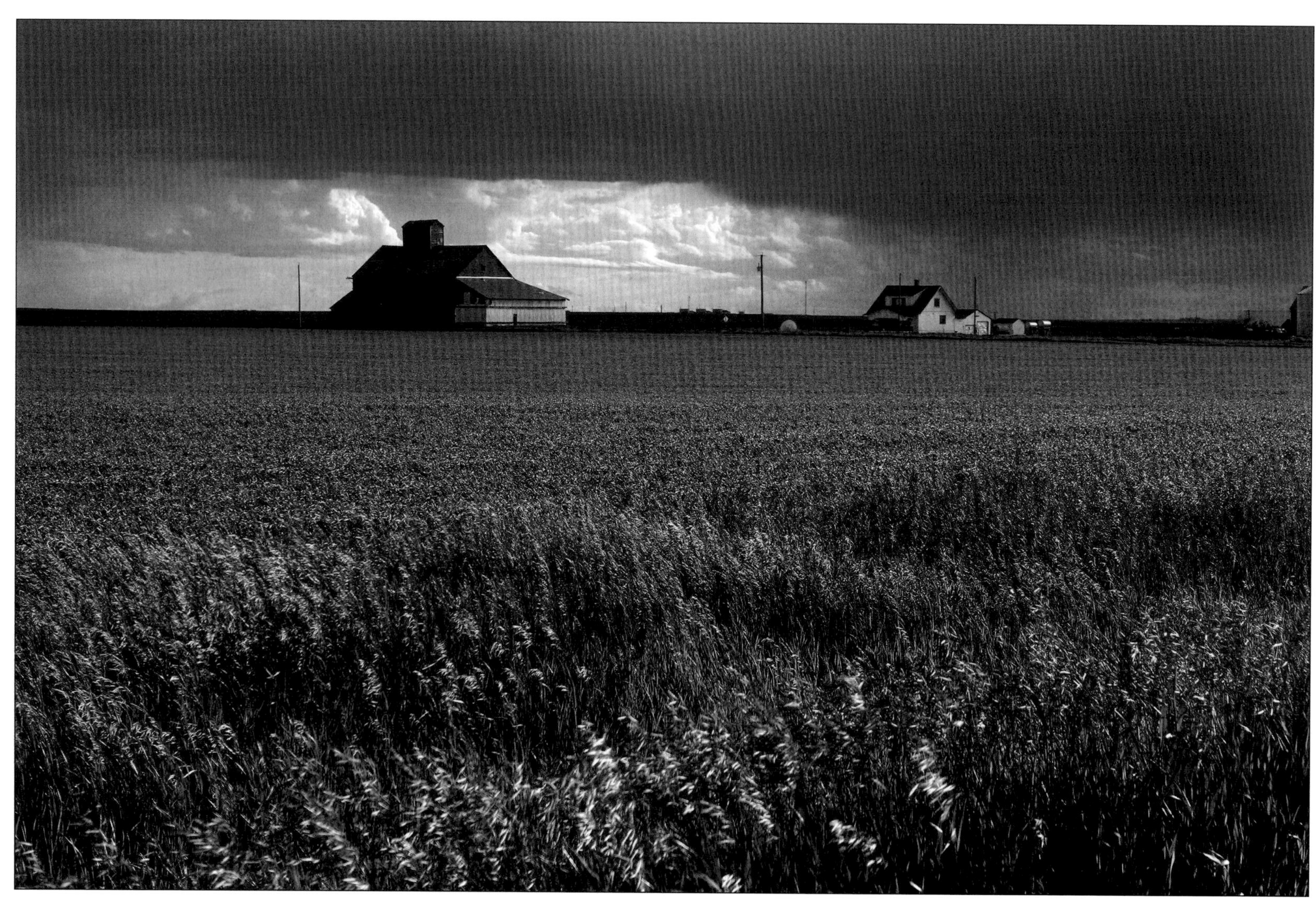

Stormy weather north of Cluny.

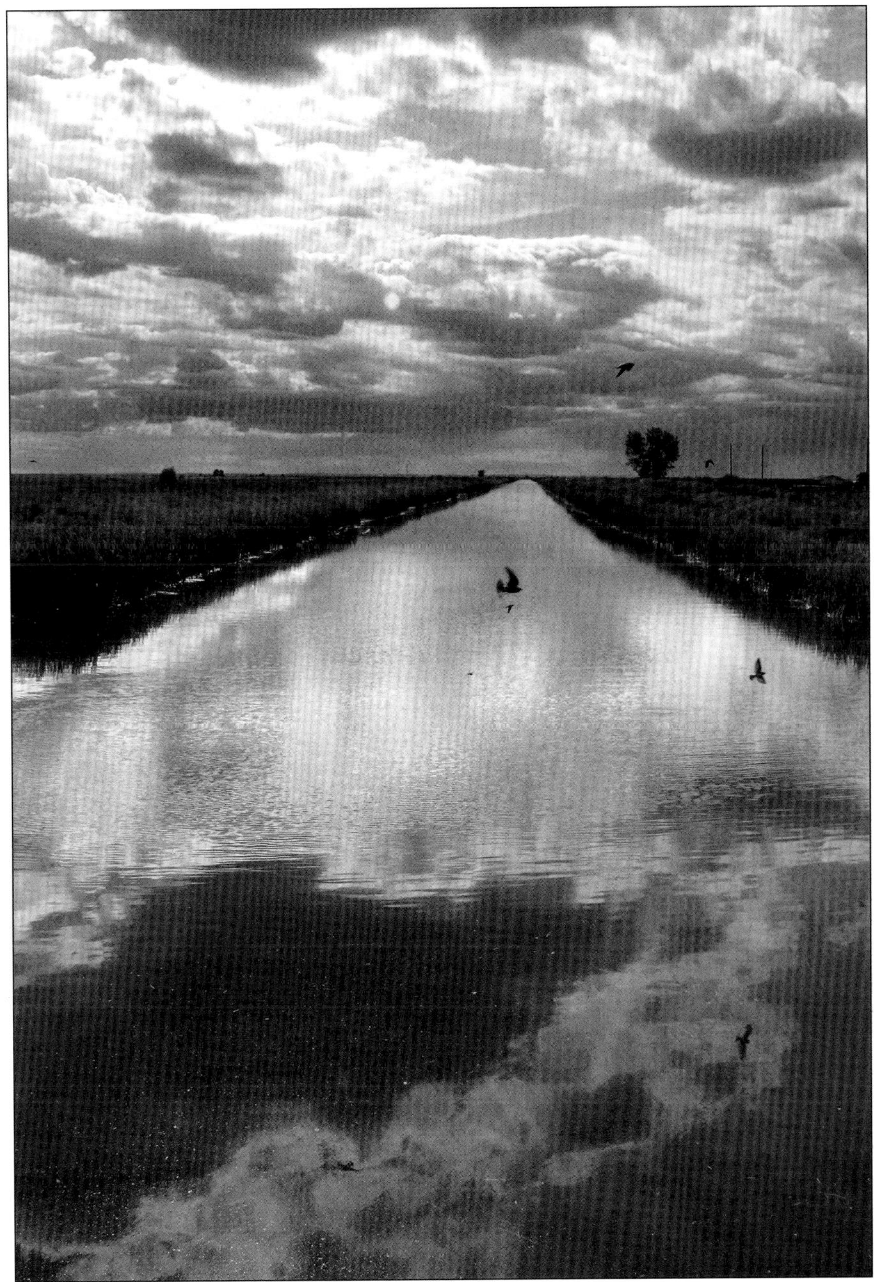

Swallows swoop above an irrigation canal near Rosemary.

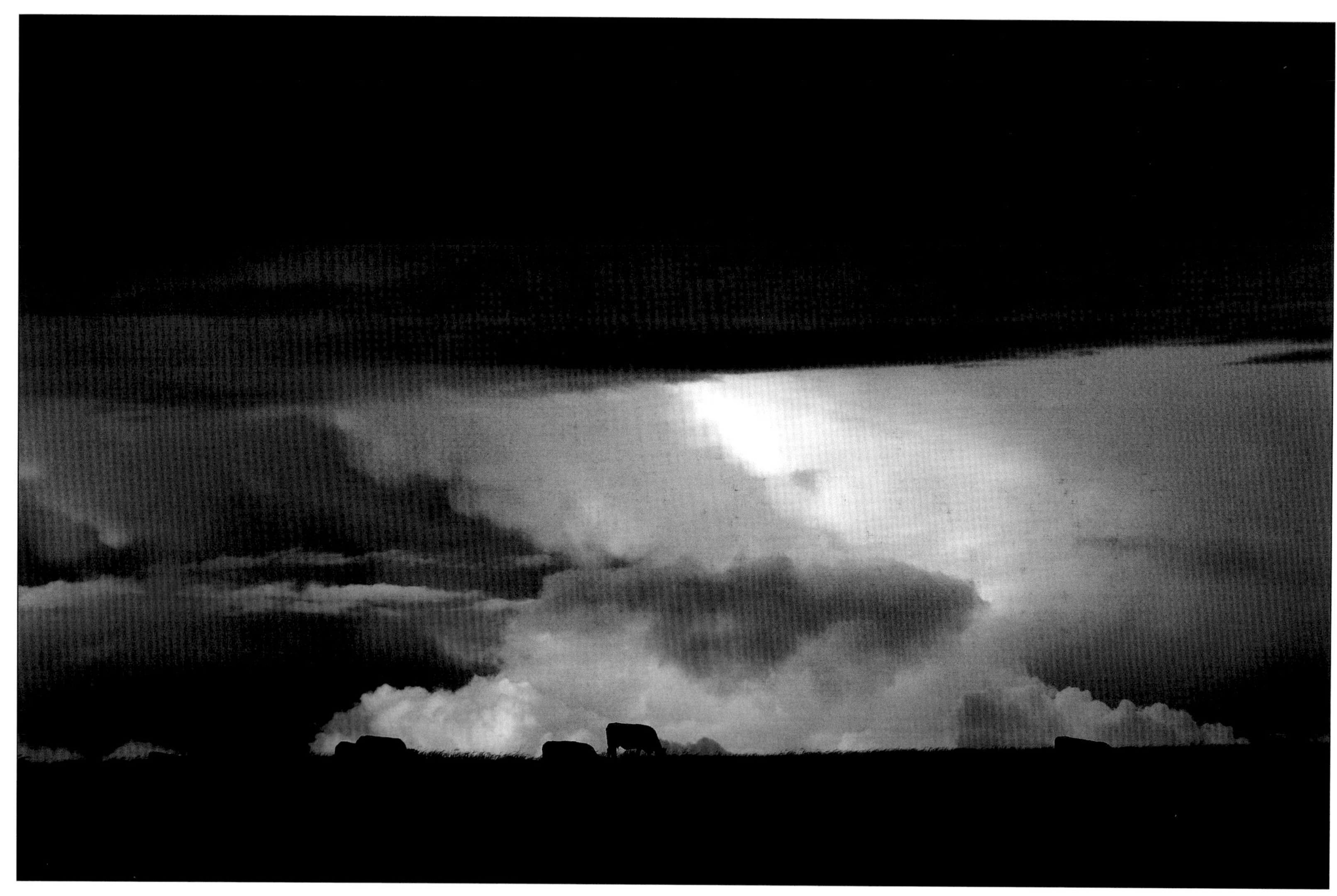

Storm clouds along the Red Deer River east of Jenner.

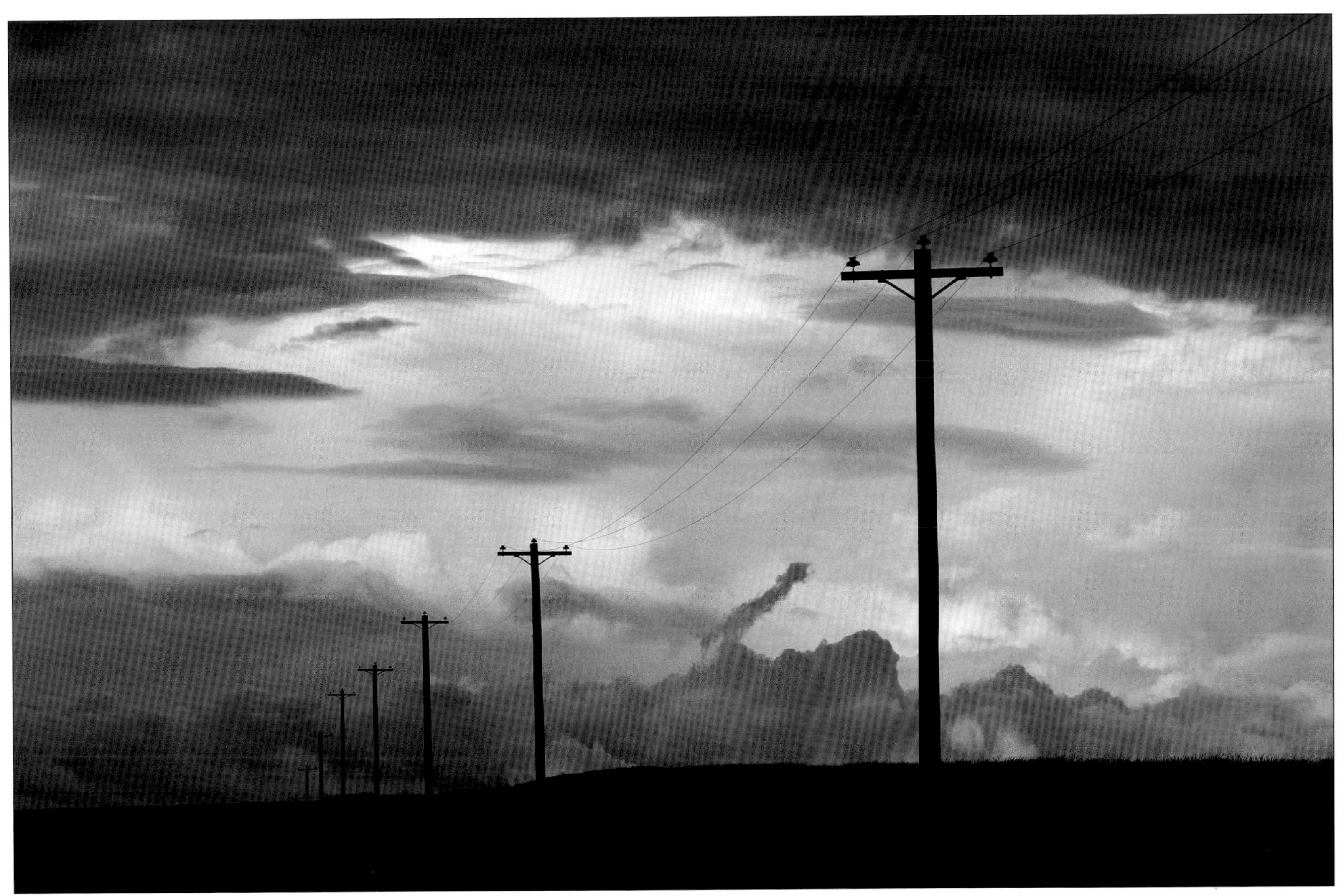

Thunder coming east of Jenner.

STORMY

THE COLOUR OF CANOLA REALLY plays tricks with my vision.

Not so much the acuity or the ability to discern motion. But the way all that bright yellow affects the rest of the colours in the scene you're looking at really shifts my interpretation of the spectrum.

In this case, I was looking across a sunlit field backdropped by towering, tumbling storm clouds with the sun shining through a rent in the cumulus wall and hitting the 300-and-some acres of yellow blossoms in front of me. The lower half of the scene was nearly solid yellow. The top half was blue.

At least, that's how my brain interpreted the scene. My camera showed something different.

It wasn't a radical difference. Certainly not as strong as when you, say, walk out from under a blue tarp at a campsite and the world turns orange for a couple of seconds. No, it was more subtle than that.

The camera was set to record the scene in daylight – the colours produced by the sun at mid-afternoon – so it saw the scene as a mixture of green, greenish-yellow and grey.

Me, I saw it as bright green, even brighter yellow and dark blue. My brain said that the camera was wrong. My camera thought my brain was being unduly influenced by emotional chemistry and an imperfect light-interpretation system.

It was, for the moment, an unwinnable argument. And one that was to be left un-debated as the storm closed the gap in the clouds and sloshed the entire scene with blue-grey light.

Rolling on, I headed into the parade of storms that were marching across the countryside east of Airdrie. The seemingly unending sweep of towering clouds that form in the foothills and spread out across the plains to the east was on its way again. I'd already been out chasing them a couple of times in the last week or so but I'd always started too late and the storms had always been moving too quickly for me to get very many pictures of them.

Today, though, I'd managed an earlier start. And the storms seemed to be co-operating.

I rolled east from Airdrie and then headed north toward Acme. I'd hoped that the rise of land around the valley of Kneehills Creek might slow the northeastward progress of the storm fronts so that I could get more or less in front of them. So far, the plan seemed to be working.

The sun was shining over the tops of the clouds as I crossed a valley just north of Beiseker and lighting up a pasture with lazing cattle. Behind them the sky was nearly black, the shadow of the clouds so deep that it looked more like I was gazing into the heavy blue of deep water than across the prairie.

This time, without the canola, the camera and my eyes agreed.

I crossed Kneehills Creek west of Linden and paused there to watch the storms swirl. It looked like there were three separate systems at work, one to the north of me, a second to the south and a third nearly directly overhead. Curtains of rain fell from the two on the flanks but it was dry where I had stopped.

There was no point staying where I was. The storm would be on me in a few minutes and picture-taking would be done. The one to the north looked okay but it was a ways off. I turned south.

The rain started to fall within minutes and I tried to stay ahead of it. I paused to quickly photograph a Swainson's hawk shaking off the drops and, a little farther down the road, I watched a whitetail buck nibbling on leaves as he stood close to a clump of willows for protection from the freshening wind and rain.

Now I was headed toward Carbon but the rain was really starting to come on strong. I crossed the Rosebud River and dropped into the Serviceberry Creek valley by Rockyford just ahead of the rain.

My cloud problem popped up again.

Looking south across the valley I could see the gigantic foot of the southern storm looming on the far horizon. Below it were fields of grain and canola. All of it was softened by a combination of light rain and soft mist.

Was it blue or was it grey? And was the camera's version right or was my brain's? I fired off a few frames and moved on just as the rain and wind caught up.

I crossed the valley and drove through the lovely little town of Rockyford. The storm was angling northeast so I got out of its grip as I crossed the valley and stopped again to photograph the big reflections in a big puddle left by a storm that had passed maybe a few hours before.

The sky looked properly grey, much as it had in pictures I'd shot near Carbon and Hesketh and coming pictures I'd shoot north of Hussar. But canola tricked me again as I headed south. But in at least one picture I had a slight rainbow as a point of reference.

The day was winding down, and with it, the storms were starting to dissipate. I passed Severn Dam and rolled east toward Hussar and then turned south again to Chancellor. It was calm enough to shoot reflections of the sky on roadside sloughs, and the silver grain elevator – so grateful that one has been left standing – at Chancellor glowed bright against the bluish grey of the evening sky.

There was nothing left but wispy clouds off to the north, and they caught a bit of orange and pink as the sun set. Driving past canola fields near Standard, my eye perceived them as shades of cerulean and grey.

As they perceived everything else. Naturally, the camera disagreed. With the cameras still set to record daylight colours, I took a picture. It was entirely shades of blue.

Okay, so now which one was correct, my brain or the camera's? And does it matter? I think not. Beauty truly is in the eye of the beholder. And really, it doesn't matter whether that eye is organic or electro-mechanical.

The fact is that – stormy or not – we live in an undeniably beautiful place. No matter how the light is interpreted.

Driving on into the blue – or was it grey? – I headed on home.

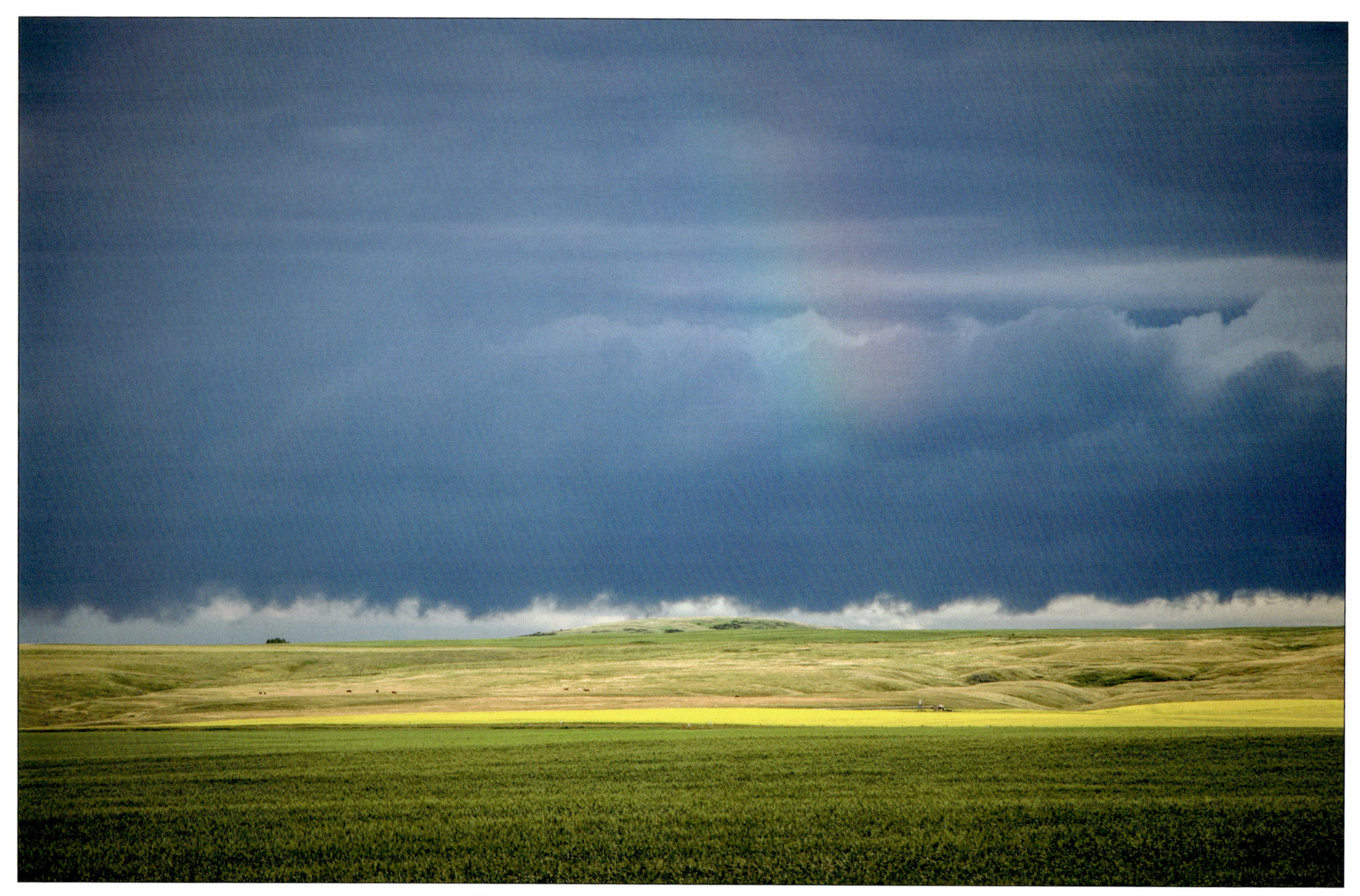

Slight hint of a rainbow against the dark sky near Rockyford.

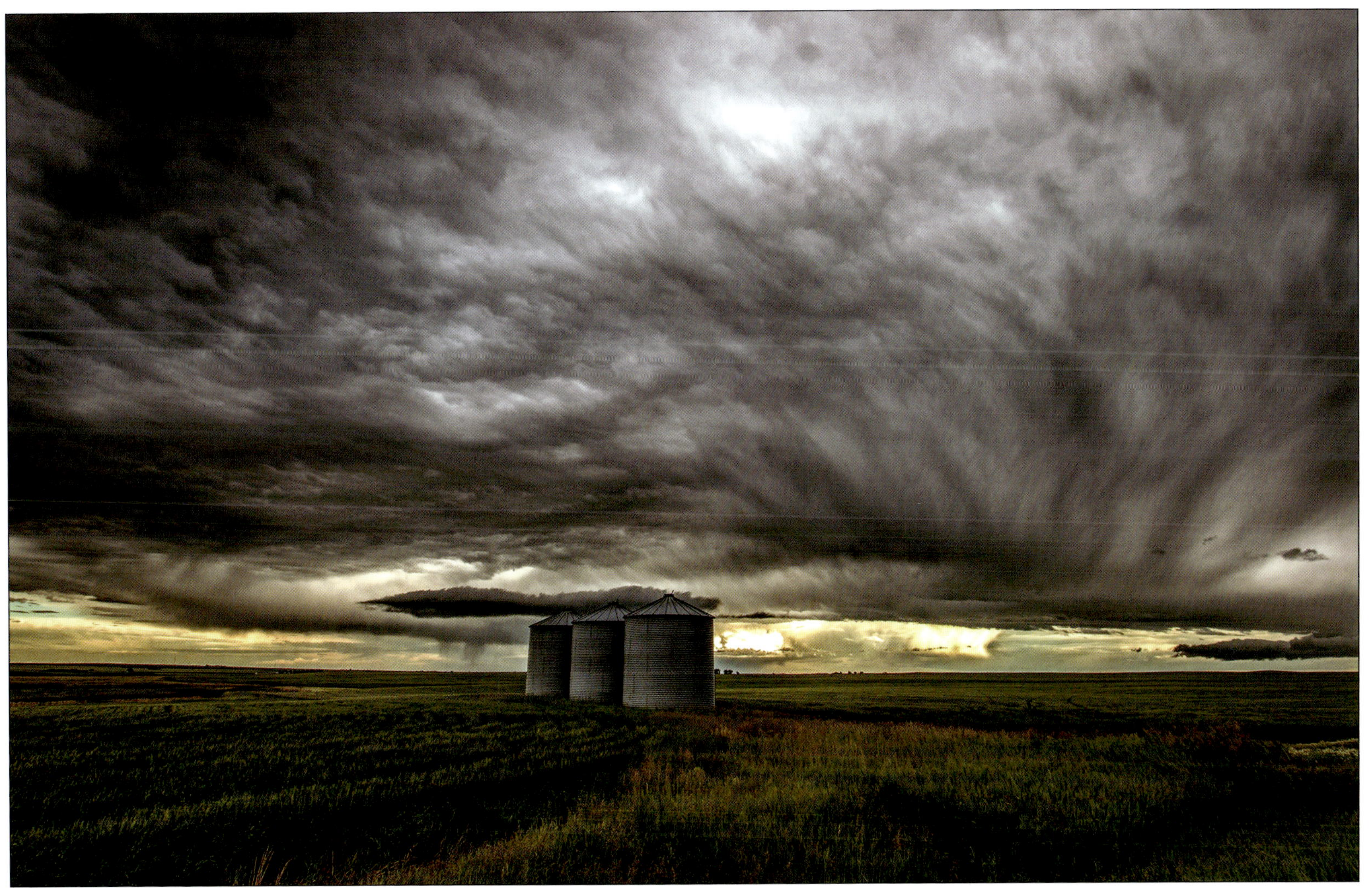

The underside of a thunderstorm east of Beiseker.

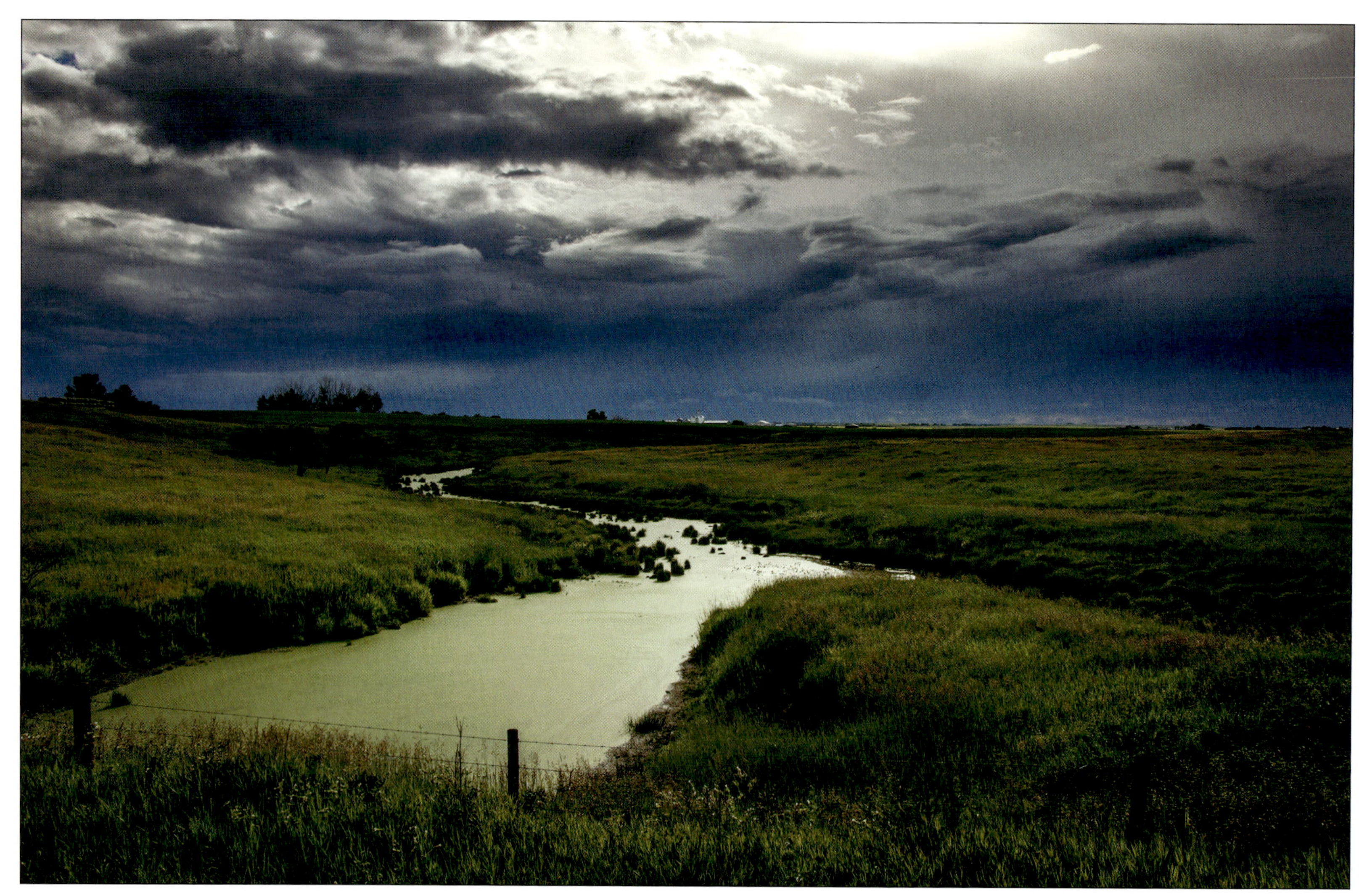

Storm clouds near Linden.

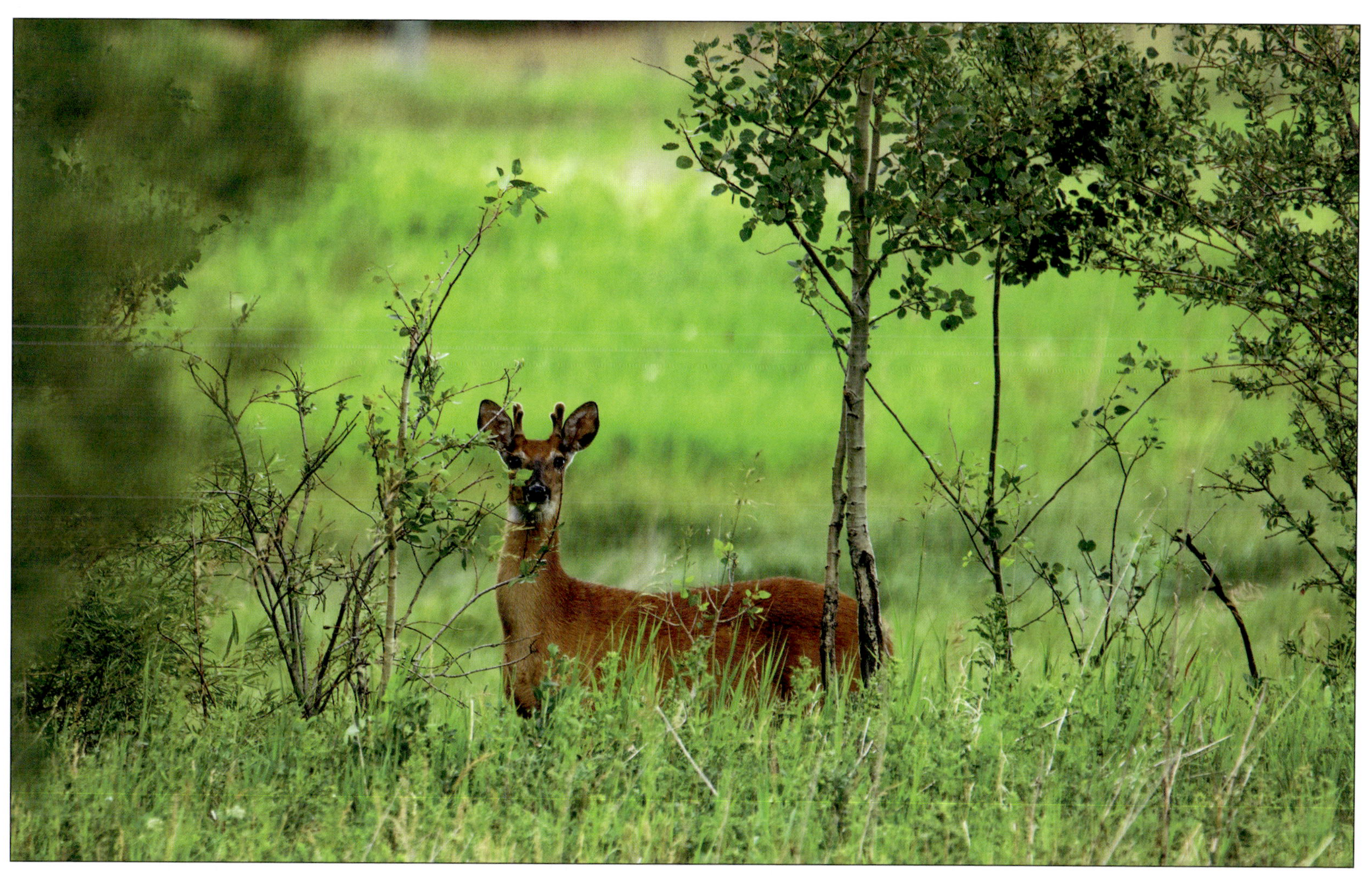

A whitetail buck looks up from cover north of Acme.

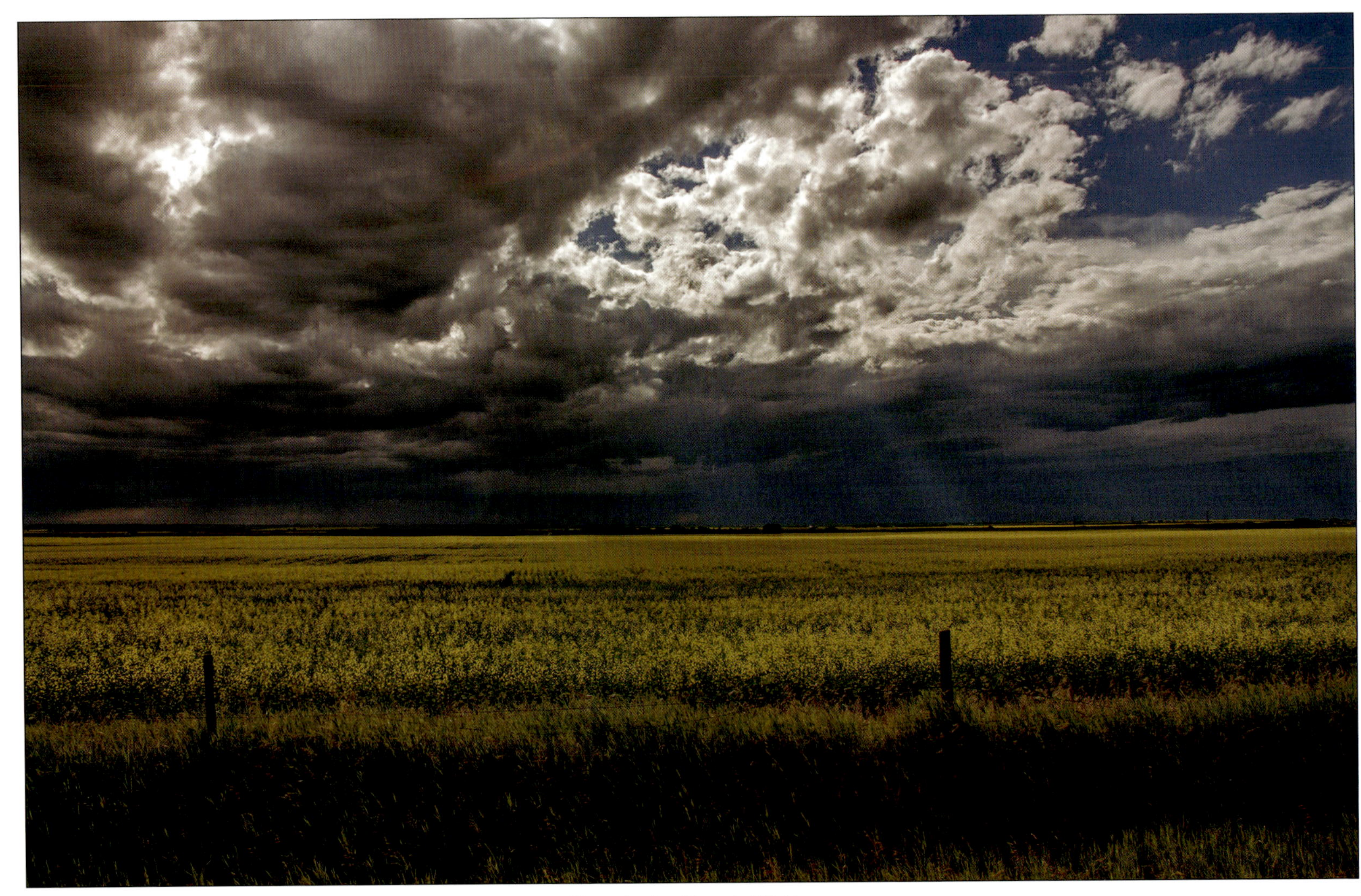

Storm clouds roll in east of Airdrie.

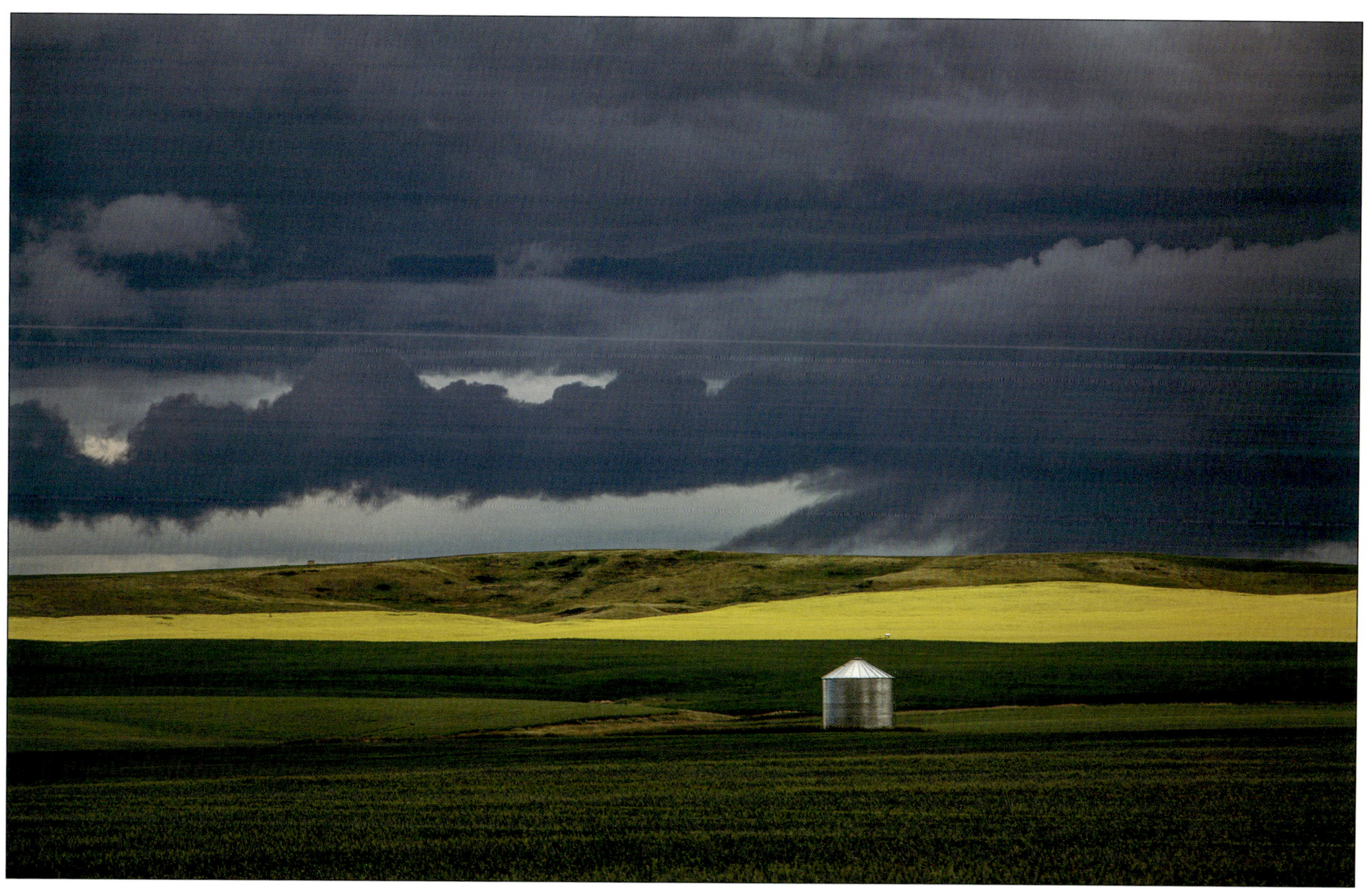

Dark sky over fields of canola, peas and wheat near Rockyford.

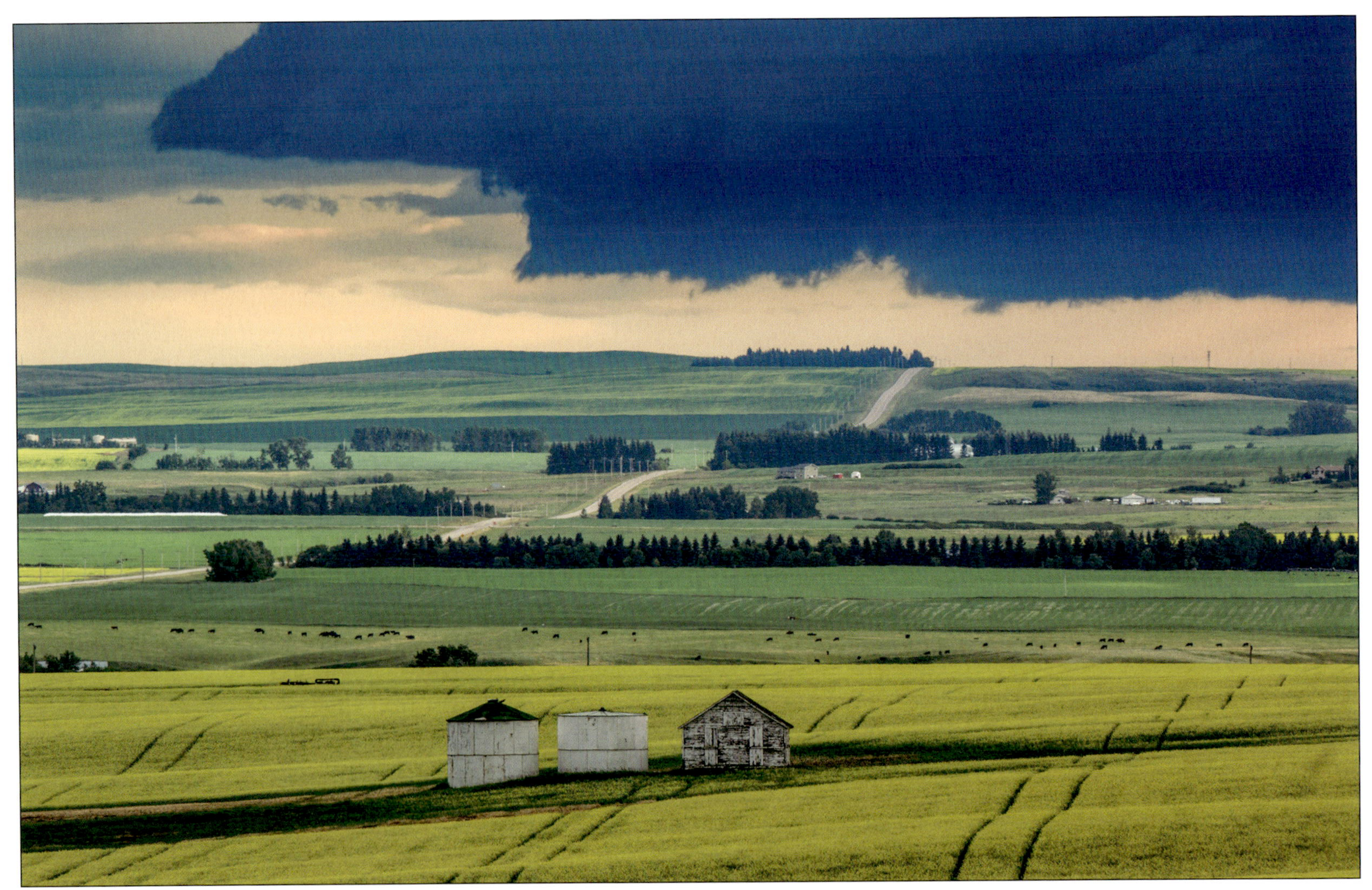

Storm clouds and haze over the Serviceberry Creek valley near Rockyford.

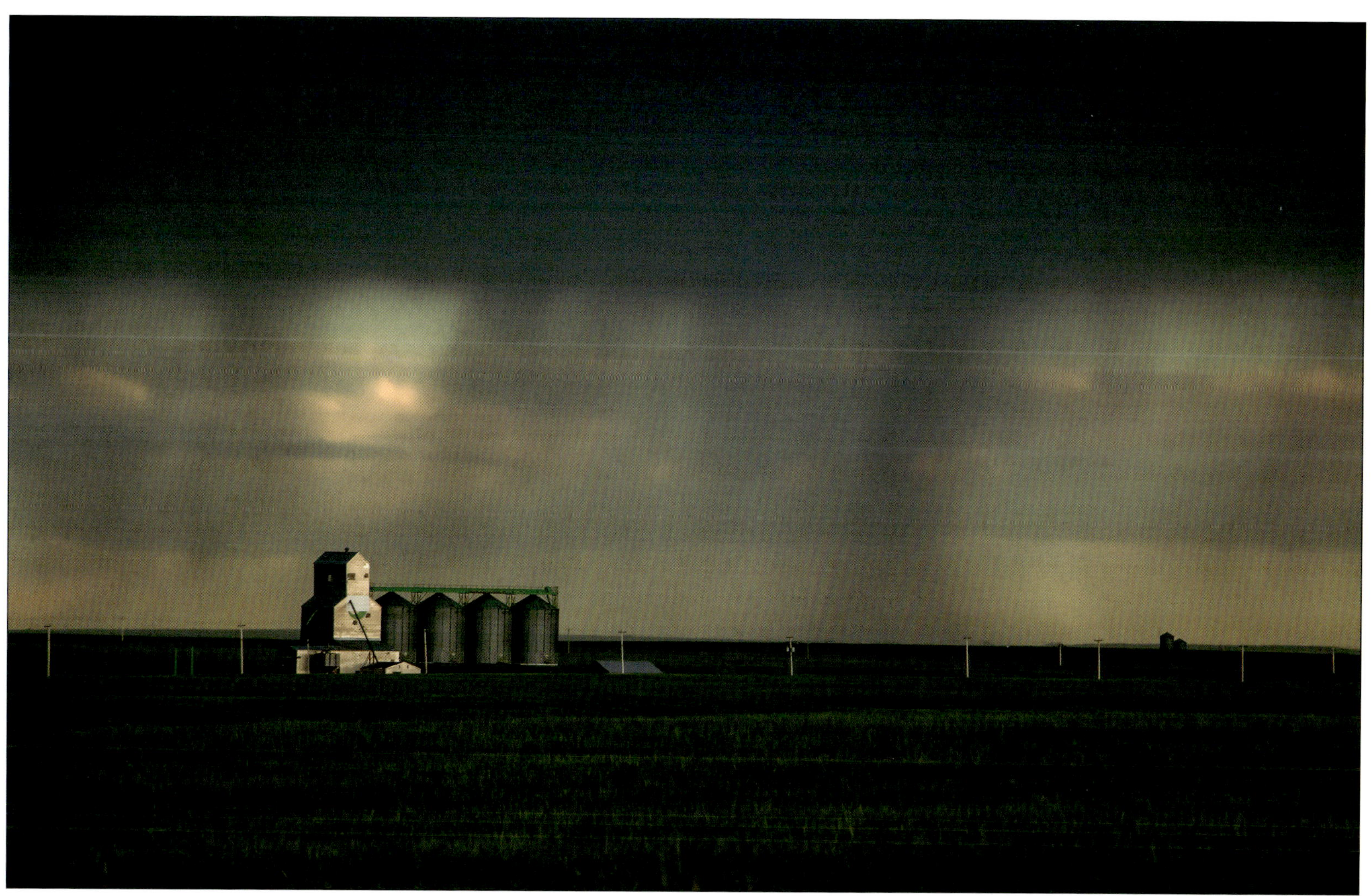

The sky begins to clear behind the grain elevator at Chancellor.

WRITING-ON-STONE RODEO

The rodeo grounds were strangely quiet as I came over the hill.

There were very few vehicles parked there, no horses, no bulls, only a few steers in the corrals. There was nobody taking money at the gate.

I thought, no, I couldn't be that dumb. I couldn't have mixed up the dates of the one rodeo I try to get to every year. But as I drove into the grounds and looked at the sign I saw that, yes, apparently I could.

Every year I whine about getting a day off to go to the Writing-On-Stone Rodeo. It's an important event to me, a chance to relive a bit of my misspent youth back in my favourite part of the world. But because I work every weekend, it's tough to arrange.

Sometimes, though, it happens, and this year, because I work with a great bunch of guys, we managed to do it.

So you can imagine the churning of my stomach as I pulled into the rodeo grounds and saw the sign saying that the rodeo runs August 2 and 3, 2015.

I'd pulled into the grounds just after 3 PM on August 1.

With trepidation, I made a phone call. Yeah, I work with a great bunch of guys.

With an entire day to kill before getting back to the rodeo – thanks again, gentlemen – I headed out to poke around my old stomping grounds along the Milk River by Writing-On-Stone Provincial Park. It was hot – 37°C – and smoky from fires in Montana but still stunningly beautiful.

The grass has gone to seed now, the green of early summer replaced with brown, and the antelope babies are speeding across the prairie as fast or faster than their mothers even though they're only a few months old. The velvet on the mule deer bucks is getting shaggy as the antlers near maturity. The rattlesnakes are fat from a summer of hunting, ready to fast through fall and winter before summer arrives again.

I walked among the sandstone outcrops looking for carvings, climbing and sliding on their gritty slopes. Tore the back pocket out of my jeans doing it but found a few old cowboy names from a century ago, a few of which still show up at the Writing-On-Stone Rodeo today.

I poked around for the rest of the afternoon and as dusk descended I headed back to the grounds to camp for the night. Some Australian bull riders were there with friends and I shot pictures of them playing cards in the moonlight before hitting the sack.

Next morning I climbed out of the truck, grabbed my jeans. And immediately put my foot right through the seat of them. One too many slides down the sandstone slopes.

Five hours later I was back at the rodeo after a trip to Lethbridge to get new jeans.

I don't know why I never pack a change of clothes when I'm on the road. But, well, I refer you back to the third paragraph.

As 5 PM approached, the rodeo was about to start. It was cooler than the day before – only 34°C – and the smoke had backed off just enough to give the light a soft bronze colour. The flags were paraded around the arena, the anthem played, the broncs clanged their hooves against the metal chutes.

The 50th Anniversary Writing-On-Stone Rodeo began.

It was like watching a movie as I aimed my camera. The light was stunning, the action sometimes just inches away from my lens. The sights, the sounds, the smells were all so vivid. I have been coming to this rodeo as often as I can since 1968 and it never gets old, never gets dull.

For one thing, the setting looks like it was built to be photographed. Honey-coloured sandstone cliffs and hoodoos surround it on one side, while a bend of the silty Milk River caresses the other. The chutes and announcer's stand face southwest, so the sun is always shining on the action.

And, as if it were designed from a photographer's dream, the Sunday performance begins at 5 PM. The light starts out perfect and just gets better.

And unlike, say, the Stampede, the action is right there. Close enough to get you covered with dust, close enough to smell it. And it all feels so authentic. The Stampede rodeo feels kind of like a staged show, a performance more than a competition. Not that the participants aren't top quality athletes and giving it their all. No, far from it.

But at Writing-On-Stone, in that setting far from any population area – the town of Milk River is 60 km away – and with a crowd of mostly local folks, it feels like what I imagine the first rodeos must have been like, just a gathering of wranglers showing off their skills.

And with an organizing committee of nearby farmers and ranchers putting it together, with corporate sponsors like implement dealers and trucking companies, it has a glow of community pride that the big events like the Stampede just can't compete with.

As Writing-On-Stone veteran Les O'Hara says, "What you see is what you get."

And man, how I love what I see.

The sun heads westward as the rodeo rolls on. My cameras are covered with dust from shooting barrel racers flying by and calf roper horses kicking clods at my lenses. The kids along the rails have to be retrieved as the bulls buck out of the chutes, and the line at the burger shack grows as the band warms up for the after-rodeo dance. Down at the river, girls ride their horses through the warm silty water, the animals having as much fun as their riders.

The last bull bucked, the pickup men turn the bucking horses into the corral and lead them galloping out of the gate and into the big pasture that abuts the grounds. I've climbed up onto a sandstone perch – being careful of my new jeans – and now I can hear the rumble of the hooves as the horses charge by and thunder along the Milk River, the water sparkling with amber highlights as the sun settles in the west.

I sit there on the warm sandstone looking around at it all and I think, my God, how I love this place. There is just nowhere like it. For 50 years, they've been riding and roping here at the Writing-On-Stone Rodeo.

May they keep on riding and roping forever.

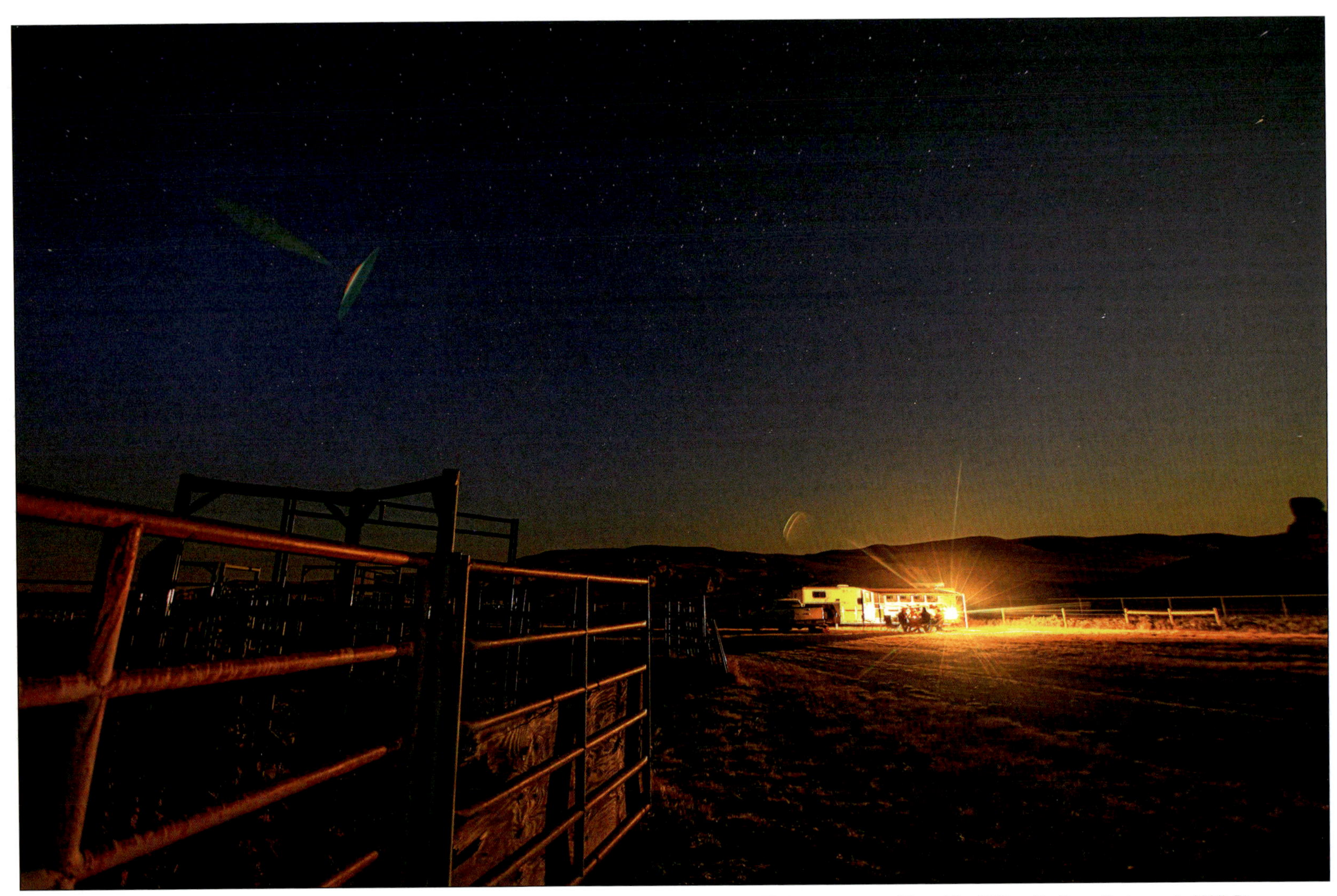

First rodeo cowboys on the grounds play cards in the moonlight under the stars the night before the 50th anniversary edition of the Writing-On-Stone Rodeo east of Milk River.

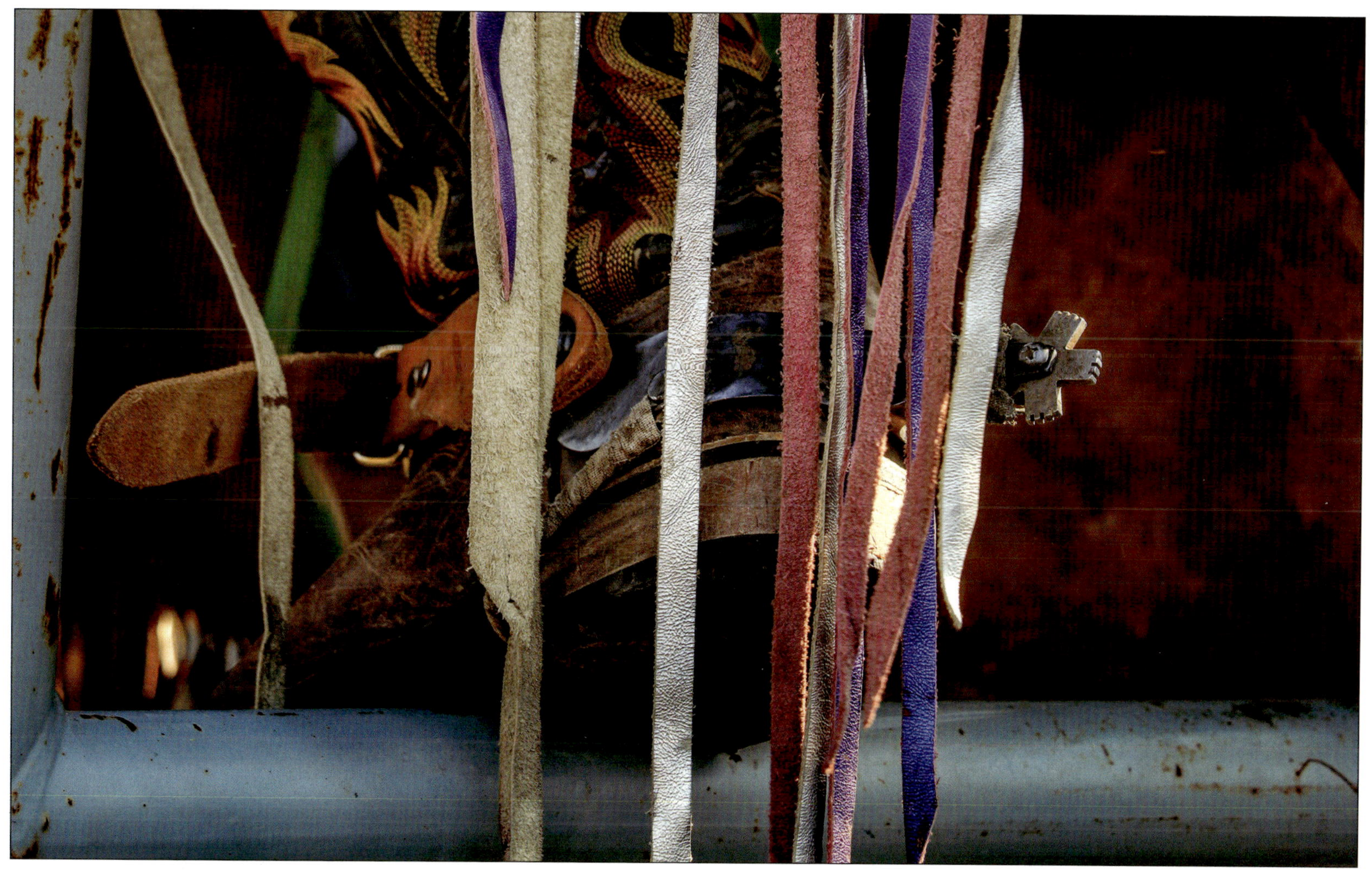

Bucking spurs and chap fringes behind the chutes at the 50th anniversary edition of the Writing-On-Stone Rodeo east of the town of Milk River.

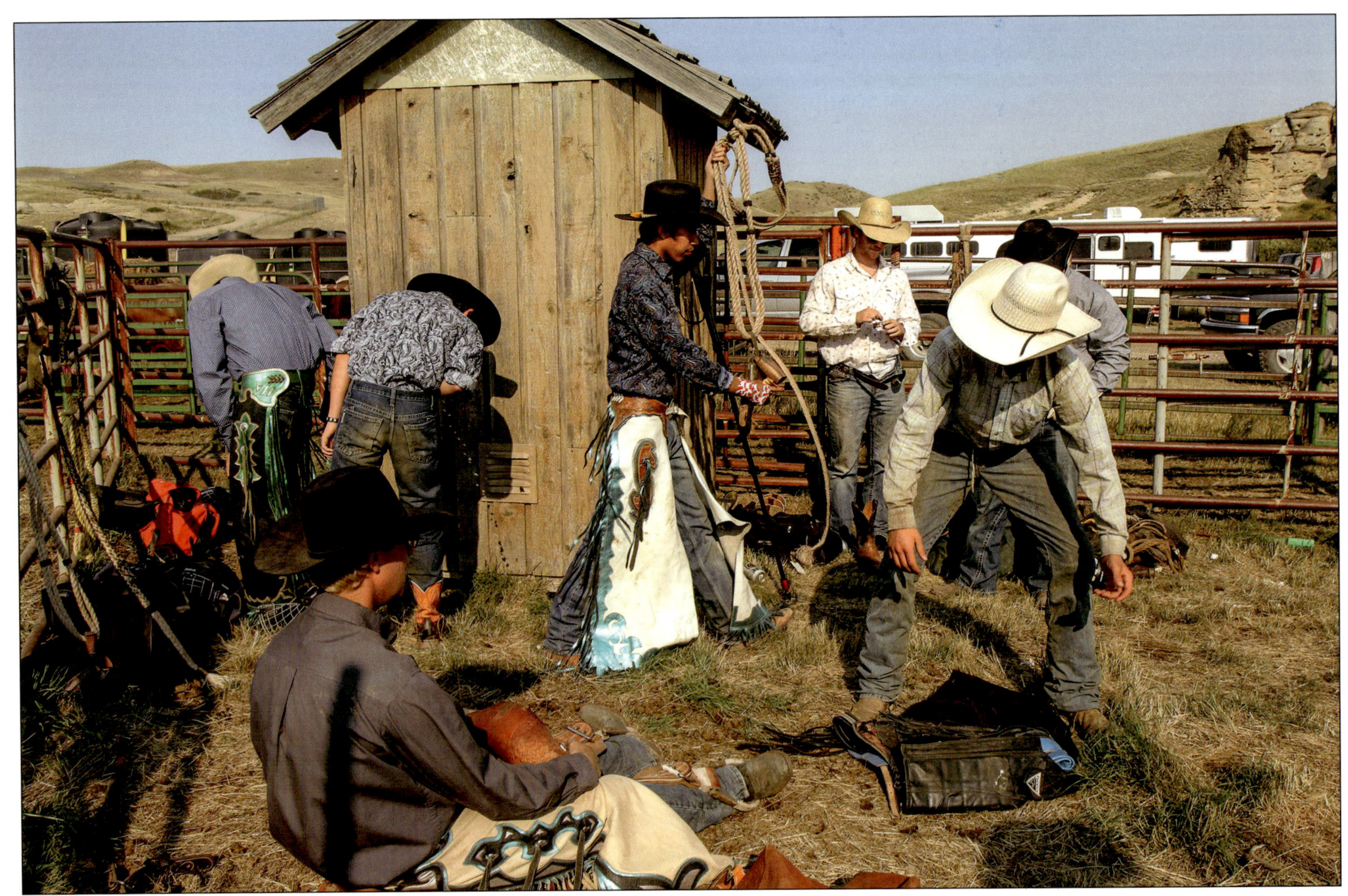

Getting ready to ride behind the chutes at the 50th anniversary edition of the Writing-On-Stone Rodeo east of the town of Milk River.

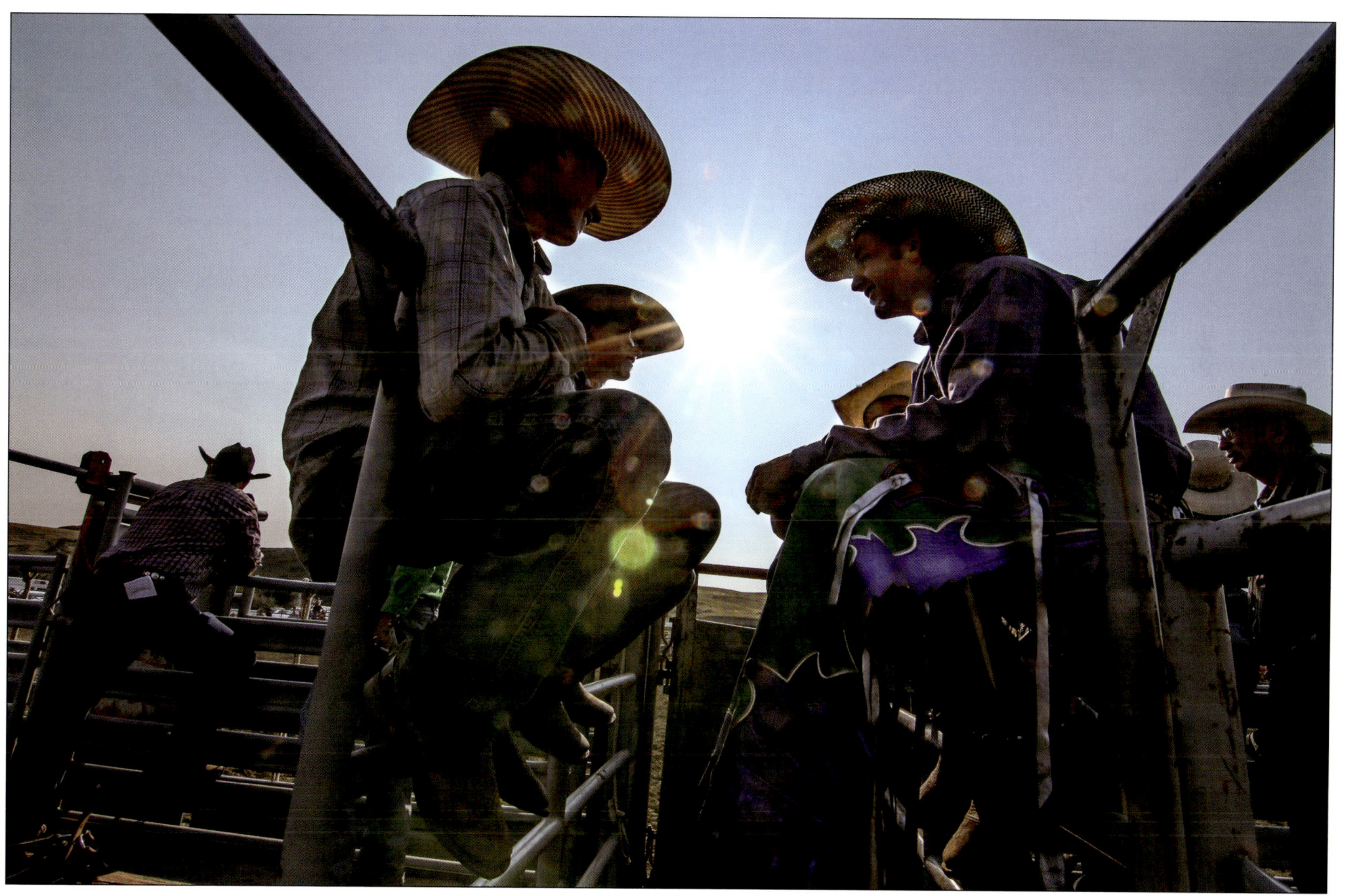

Ready to ride behind the chutes at the 50th anniversary edition of the Writing-On-Stone Rodeo east of the town of Milk River.

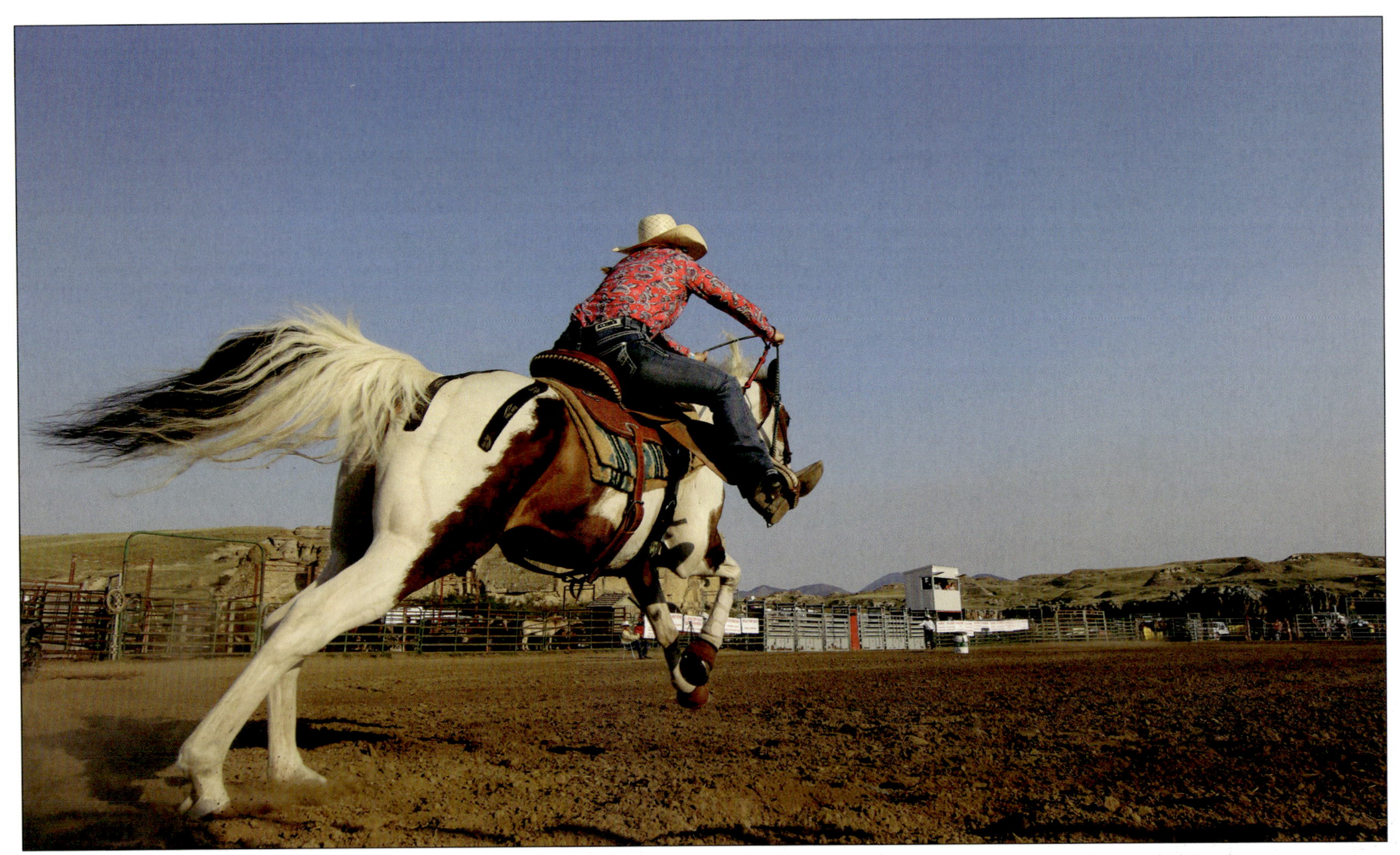

A barrel racer flies out of the gate at the Writing-On-Stone Rodeo.

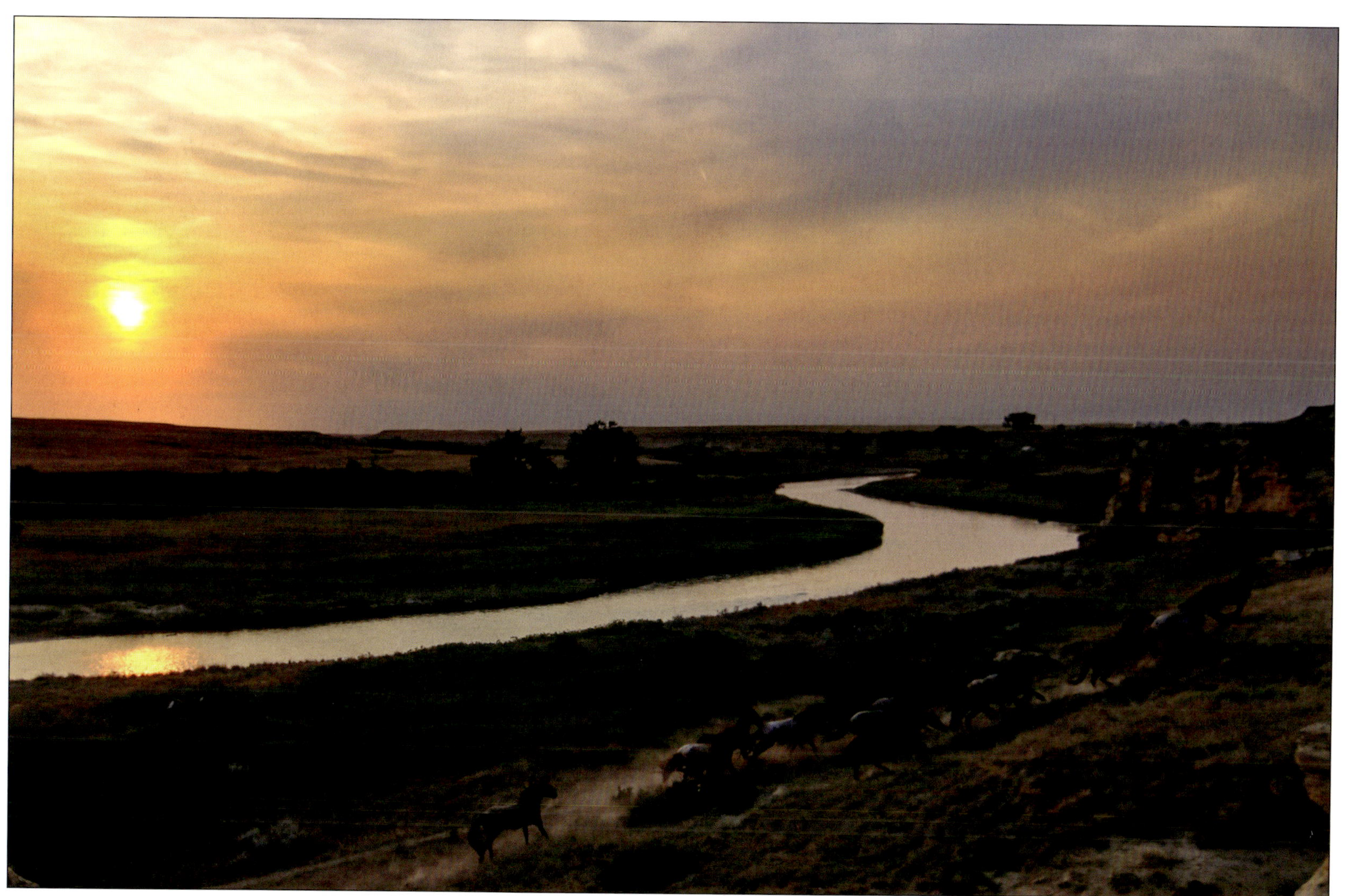

Bucking horses sent out to relax for the night after the Writing-On-Stone Rodeo.

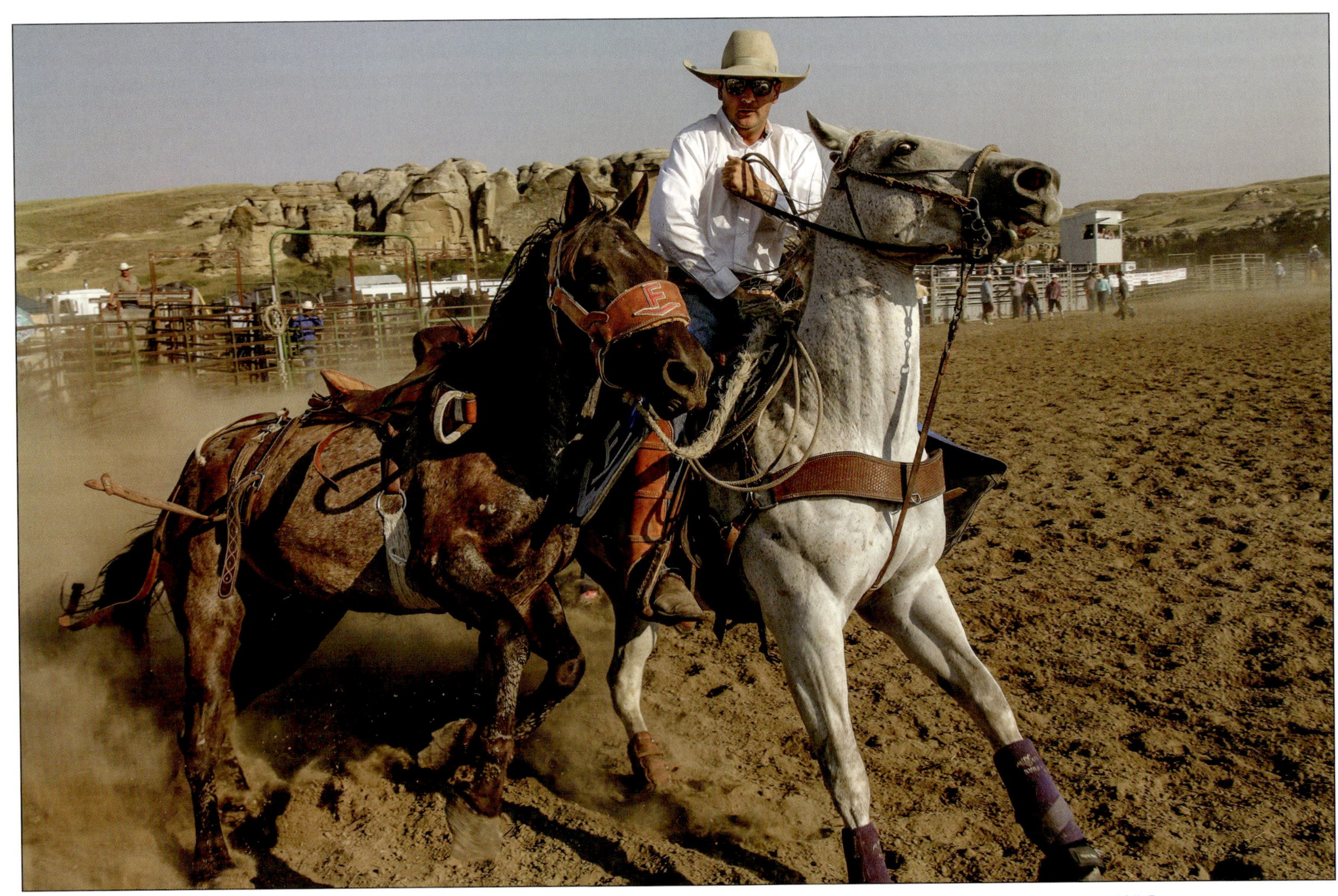

Pickup men gather the cowboys and horses after the ride at the 50th anniversary edition of the Writing-On-Stone Rodeo east of the town of Milk River.

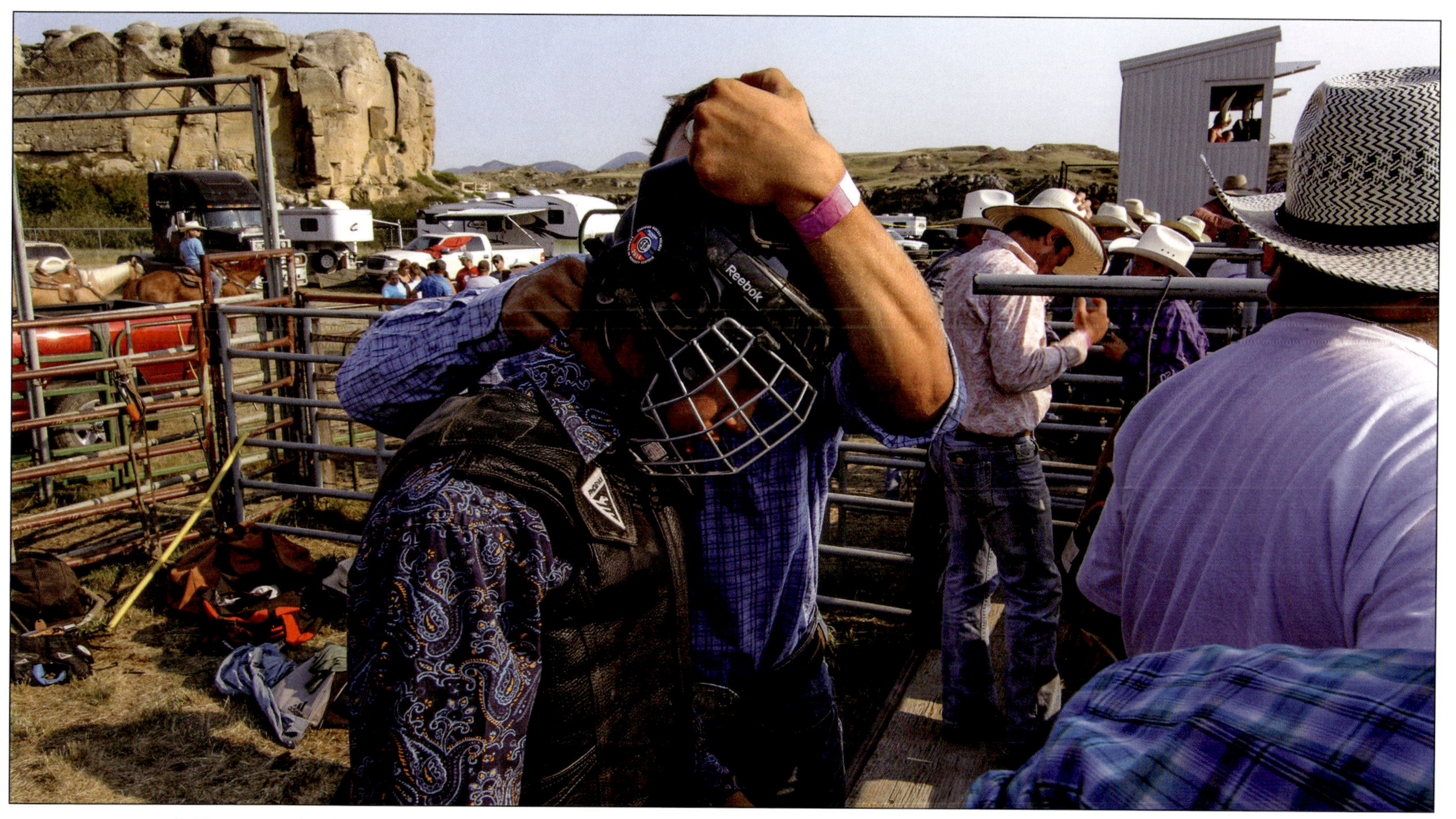

Getting armoured up before a bull ride behind the chutes at the 50th anniversary edition of the Writing-On-Stone Rodeo east of the town of Milk River.

A U T

U M N

ANTELOPE

I AM VERY LUCKY TO HAVE such understanding friends.

Friends who, when I call them on the phone to tell them about something interesting that I've just seen, don't just say, sure Mike, that's nice, okay I'm kinda busy, I'll get back to you.

I wouldn't blame them if they did. I even bore myself sometimes. I catch myself thinking, now Mike, who else but you could be interested in the fact that white-faced ibises wander around sloughs near Nobleford or that a thirteen-lined ground squirrel will just sit still and rely on its camouflage to hide it instead of running for its burrow like its cousin, a Richardson's ground squirrel?

I tell my friends these things and they are kind enough to indulge me or even, occasionally, feign interest. Great people, I tell ya.

But I think I was testing the bonds when I started making calls about the antelope I saw on Tuesday.

They were all polite enough but I could sense the hope that another call would beep in and give them the excuse to hang up – even a reminder that their videos are past due – and they could get on with their day.

Now I've seen a lot of antelope. They're fairly common out east and I almost always see them near Brooks and beyond. But the antelope I saw on Tuesday was different.

This one was just a couple of kilometres east of the city limits, along Highway 22X near Indus.

Wait, wait, don't turn the page yet. Your videos are already late, another couple of minutes won't matter.

I was headed out to do a bit of fishing on the Bow, maybe check out the crops a bit, look for a nice field of canola to photograph, when I saw an animal wandering down a gravel road leading to a gas well site. There's lots of deer out this way but I knew at first glance that it wasn't a deer. It was the wrong shape, the wrong height, it had the wrong head.

I knew right away what it was but it took my brain a second or two to realize how unusual it was. I managed to make the anti-lock brakes stutter on dry pavement as I stopped and turned around.

Had I seen an antelope on this piece of ground 150 years ago it would have been no big deal. For one thing, Calgary wasn't here. For another, neither were the farms.

A century and a half ago there were nearly as many antelope on the plains of North America as there were buffalo. Literally millions of them roamed from Mexico to central Alberta. But their numbers declined as the buffalo – with whom they were symbiotic – were nearly wiped out toward the end of the 19th century.

And when their native prairie started getting turned grass-side down and planted to things like wheat and barley, the range for the remaining few thousand of them forced them onto what was left of the original grassland east of here in the land of scant rainfall and big blue skies.

They are perfectly adapted to that kind of land. They eat the toughest prairie grasses, they almost never need to drink and they cover open ground like a rocket. In fact, next to cheetahs, they are the fastest land animal on earth. The parched, cactus-studded open prairie is their home and has been for thousands of years. We're lucky it's so dry out in eastern Alberta and western Saskatchewan or we wouldn't have antelope at all.

But they are so adapted to that native prairie that they have a hard time with farmland. They don't generally eat grain crops and their feet can't find comfortable purchase in soft fields.

They have evolved in open country where they could run around anything in their path so they have never really learned to jump. Faced with a fence an antelope will go under instead of over.

They don't like farmland.

So seeing one right next to a city of a million people standing in a field of grain and surrounded by treed farmsteads and acreages was pretty darned unusual. True, this is their ancestral land. But any resemblance to that long-ago landscape has been erased for the better part of a century.

I pulled the truck into the ditch and stepped out to take some pictures. There was no way I was going to try to drive closer for fear of scaring the antelope off. It was obviously a long way from home and unsure of its surroundings so I didn't want to add to its confusion.

But I needed to get closer so I took advantage of one of the antelope's quirks. They are very curious animals.

I laid down in the grass and started to crawl closer, knowing that if I raised my hand once in a while the antelope would see it and move closer to investigate.

Yep, it did exactly that, and I raised up to take a series of pictures as it came closer. It got so close that I could see its eye teeth when it gave a little buzzy bark and turned away with rump hair flashing a warning to other antelope. That weren't there. It was all alone.

I walked back to the truck and started phoning my friends about this amazing, rare sighting. They all listened politely and undoubtedly shook their heads in indulgent good humour when I hung up.

Maybe just like you are right now. Okay, go on, take back your videos.

Thanks for listening so politely. You're all great friends.

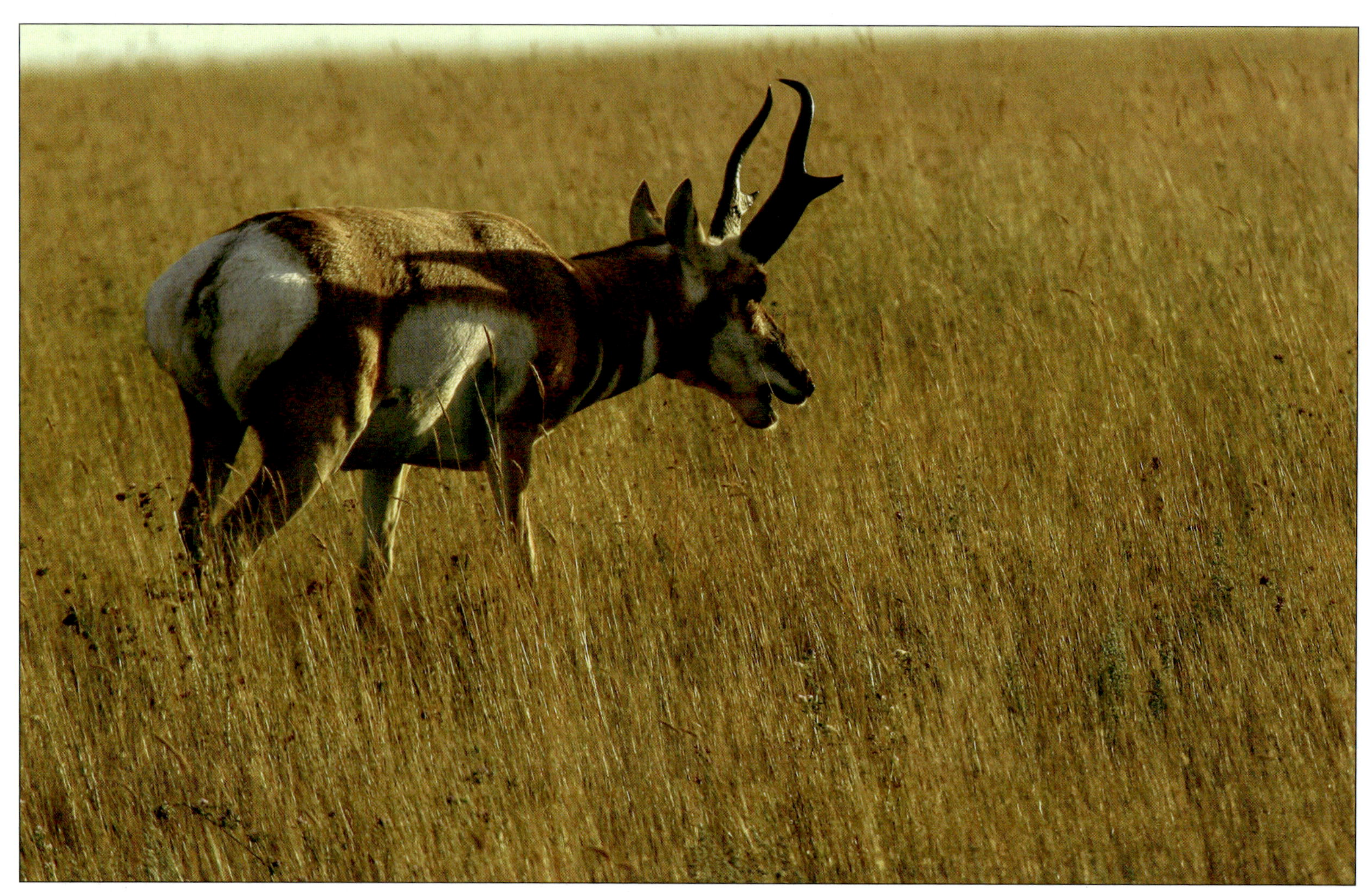

A buck antelope grazes on prairie grass near Finnegan Ferry.

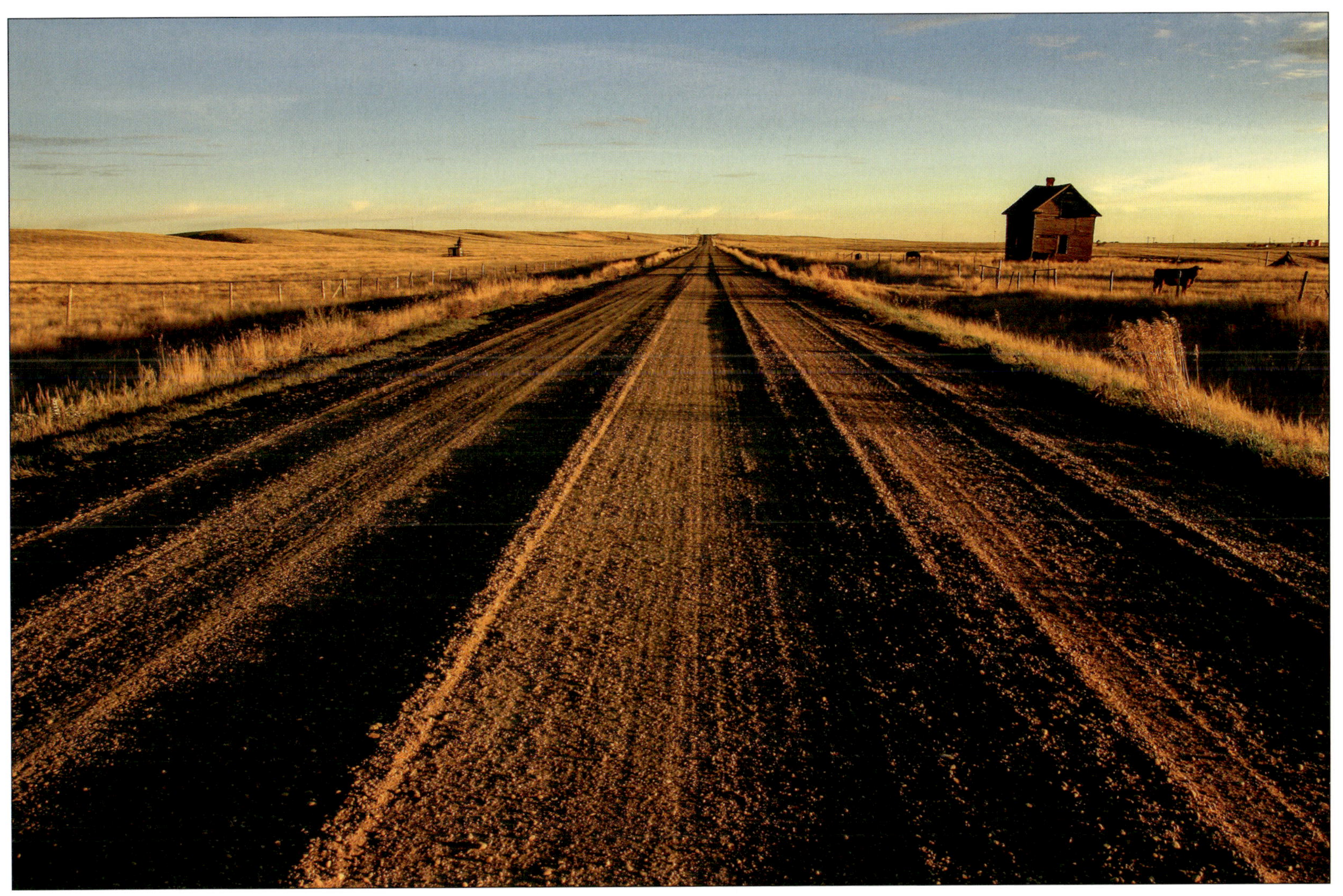

Lines of gravel leading to Wardlow.

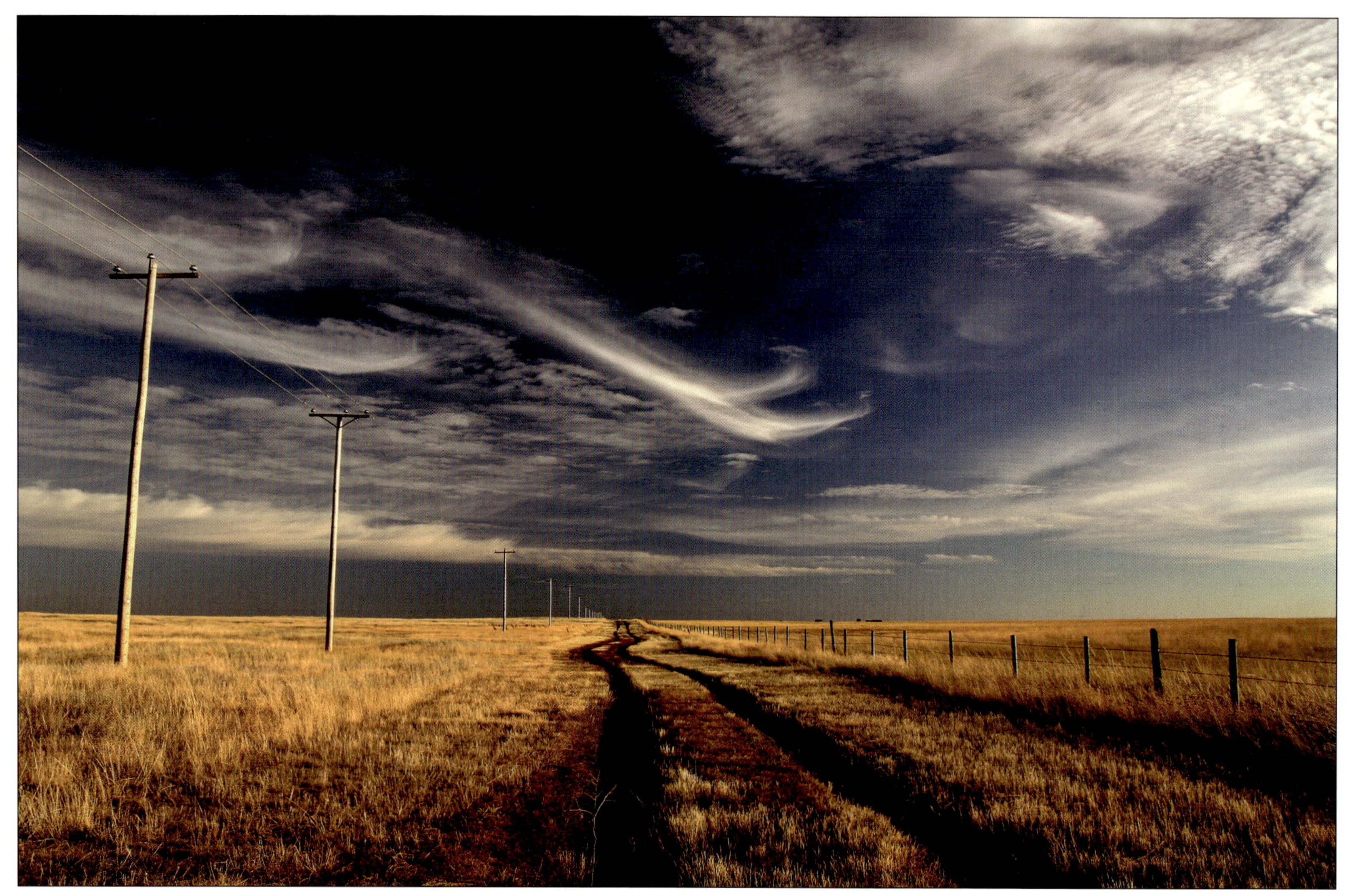

An oilfield trail through the prairie grass on the flatlands west of Pollockville.

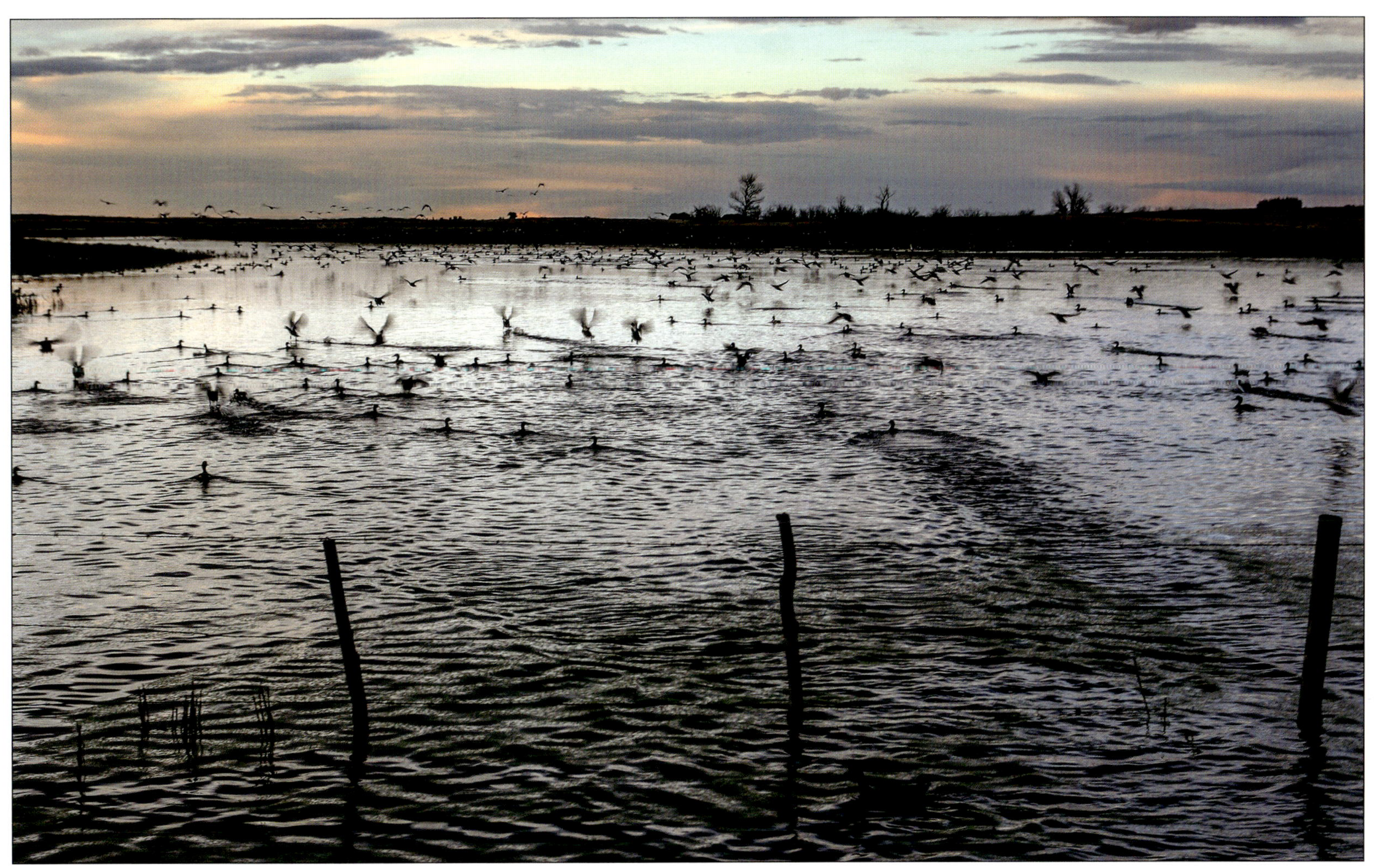

Ducks and coots take off from a slough near Gem.

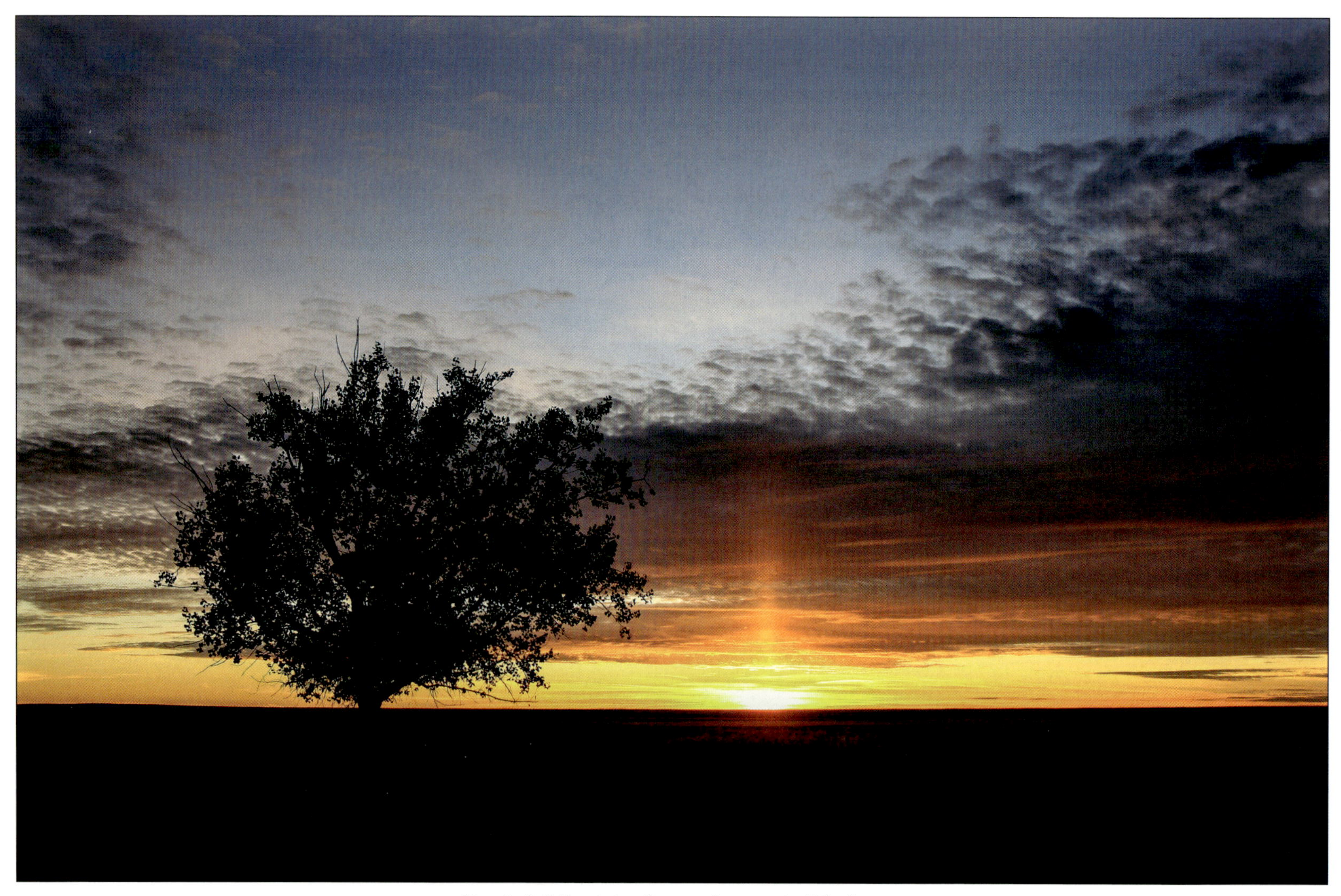

Okay, that's it, time to head home as the sun sets at Wardlow.

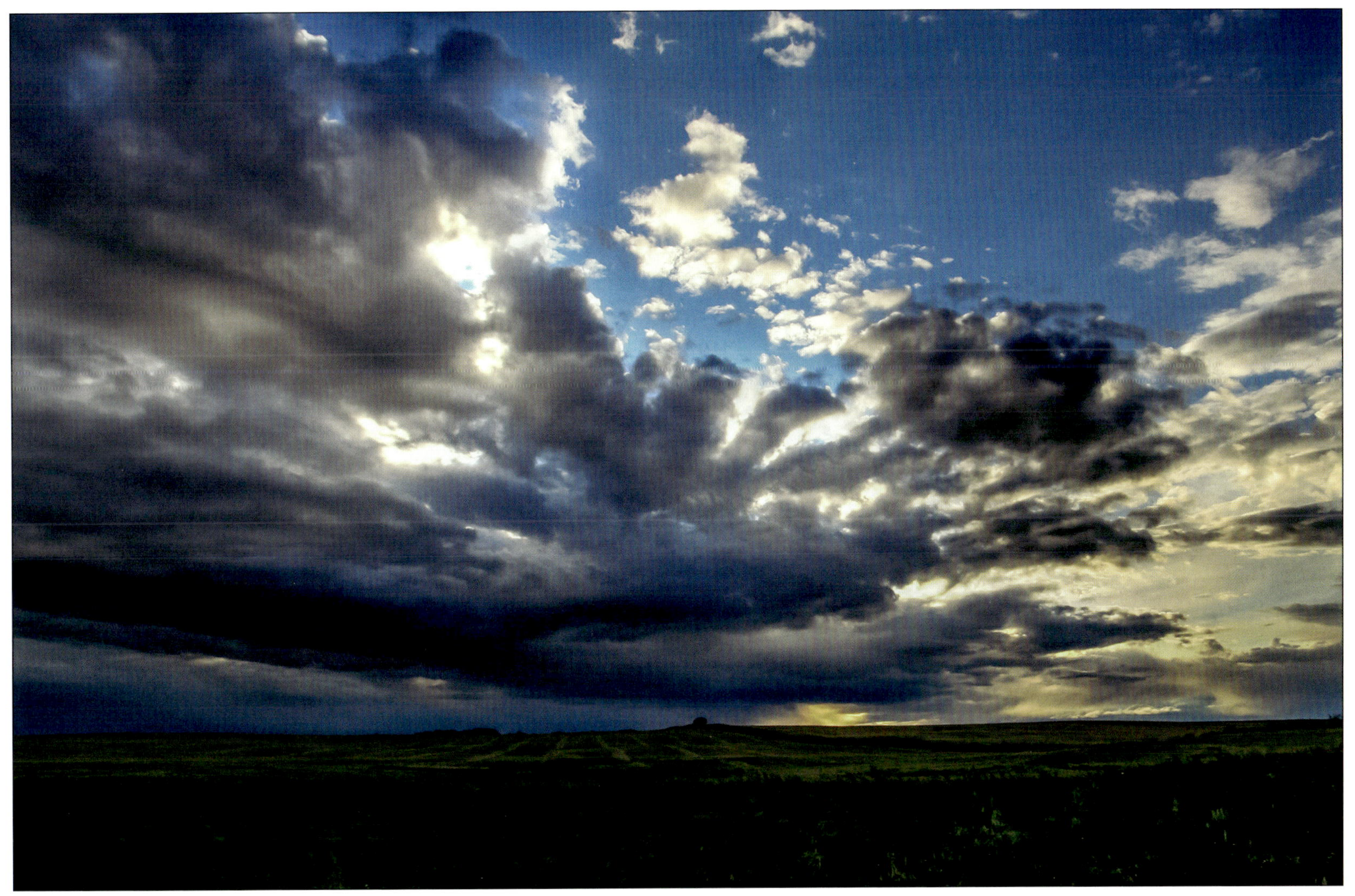

Sunset at Cessford.

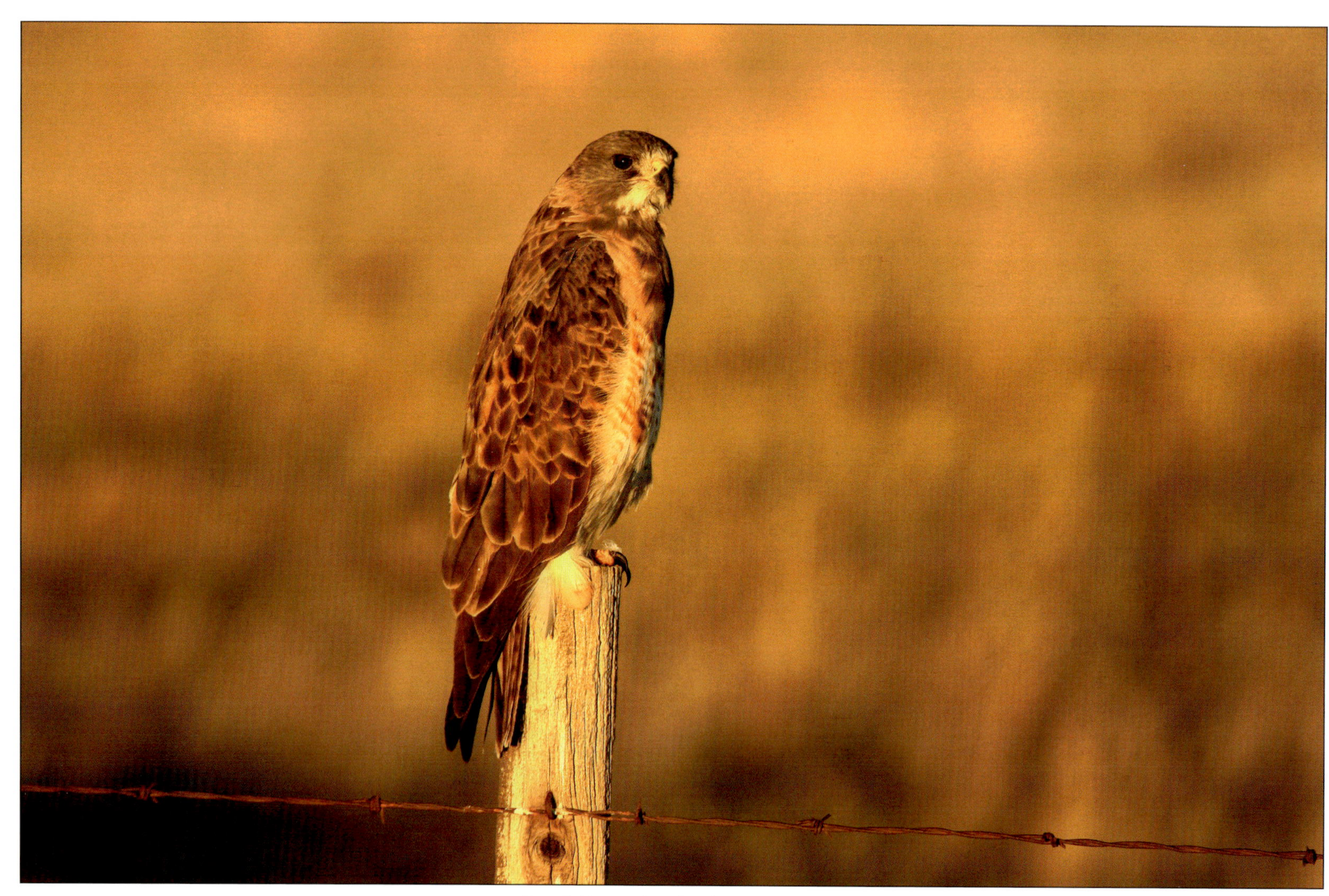

Warm light on a relaxed hawk near Wardlow.

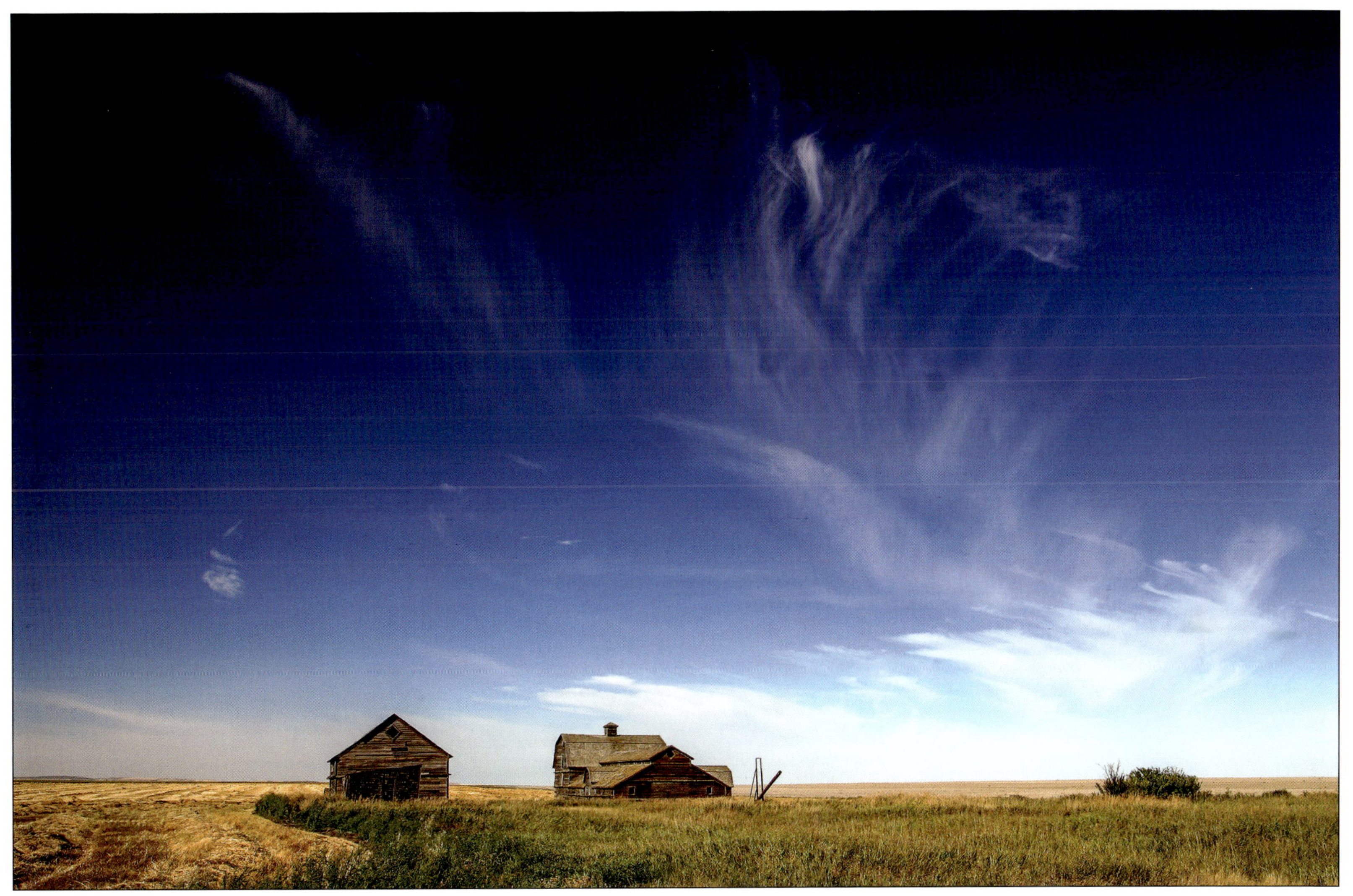

Prairie sky north of Steveville.

HARVEST

SINCE I WAS FLAT ON the ground anyway, I thought I might as well take some pictures.

I mean, I was lying on the edge of a wheat field with a camera in my hand so I figured as long as I was down there, I might as well try to salvage something from the situation.

I'd been driving around for most of the afternoon out among the fields between Lomond and Enchant checking out the crops. I'd come east past Arrowwood and cut down through Milo, passing the dryland crops – most of which were already harvested out that way – and rolling on into irrigation country as I edged closer to Vauxhall and Taber.

The sky was cloudless as I drove along, the day hot and dry. Clouds of dust rose from combines in the fields. Fields of wheat and barley gave way to tracts of corn, canola and sugar beets.

Crops must be great this year. A wet spring – oh my, what a wet spring – followed by a hot summer had to have been good for growing. Everything I saw sure looked healthy. Although since most of them had already been harvested, it's pretty much impossible to guess what the dryland crops were like – and I'm a long way from being an expert anyway – all the stuff under irrigation looked heavy and healthy.

Combines were chewing through the grain crops quickly, but I found a field of corn still standing so I decided to explore a bit around its edges.

This field clearly wasn't intended for on-the-cob type corn, the stuff sold from the backs of trucks for the last month or so. Those fields, the famous Taber corn fields, are all pretty much done now. I'm going to guess that this particular one was feed corn, the cobs left to fully ripen before they're cut down.

I've always found corn fields fascinating, those tall, thick stalks growing so close together, the sound of the leaves rattling in the breeze, the damp heat that blows between the rows. And I love the way light moves through them.

Dragonflies were everywhere – cherry-faced meadowhawks, mostly – and the clatter of the cellophane wings combined with the rattle of the corn. Ladybugs crawled on the stalks and cast their shadows on the backlit leaves.

There was starting to be a bit of colour in there as well, some of the leaves turning brown, others edged with yellow and orange. Varying shades of green coloured the ripening ears and contrasted with the dangling black tassels protruding from their ends.

But there were very few birds. A few sparrows were around, a couple of blackbirds and the usual cadres of magpies. That was it, though. I had figured there would be more.

Down the road there were. Still not in the numbers from a month ago but more than in the corn field. The most common were mourning doves. They thronged the fences and powerlines, their soft grey-brown feathers catching the sun and kicking back their underlying blues and purples. Such lovely birds.

The big flocks of water birds haven't come in from the north yet, though, but they ought to be along shortly. They'd better hurry if they want any grain to eat.

As the afternoon rolled on I saw more and more combines, sometimes rows of four or five of them rumbling through the fields reducing the standing grain to acres of stubble in a single pass. Trucks and tractors pulling grain trailers pulled up beside the combines as their augers swung out like they were saluting to disgorge their hoppers full of grain.

The smell of the dust was intoxicating. In small doses anyway. It's one of the scents that brings back a lot of memories, but it also brings on fits of psychosomatic itching as thoughts of shovelling barley come to mind. Nasty stuff.

I paused to take pictures of an old threshing machine by the edge of field as I searched the roads for fields of standing grain. There's still lots close by the city but down here they were hard to find.

But finally, just beyond the edge of the irrigated lands I found a field of black-bearded wheat. I pulled the truck into the ditch to be out of the way of grain trucks, grabbed my camera and stepped out.

Straight into a badger hole. I went down fast but I managed to turn as I fell so I didn't crush the camera. And when I rolled over to get up, I was face to face with the wheat.

Well, as long as I was there anyway . . .

The buzz of crickets and the clatter of grasshoppers filled the air around me as I shot close-up pictures of the heads of wheat and the delicate shells of wind-shucked wild oats along the margins of the field. Once again I was transported by the smell of soil and grain. A family of meadowlarks zoomed by overhead.

I straightened up and got back in the truck. The sun was on the horizon now and combines churned on through the orange light into the blueness of dusk and on to the light of the crescent moon.

I rolled on back to the city under that same moon, taking pictures of the modern grain elevators at Vulcan and the antiques at Mossleigh. At Carseland I paused to watch combines working a field under their powerful lights.

As the dust from their chaff wafted over me I headed back home, memories of harvests past bouncing in my head.

Harvest time. It might mean summer is nearly gone but it is most definitely a wonderful time of year.

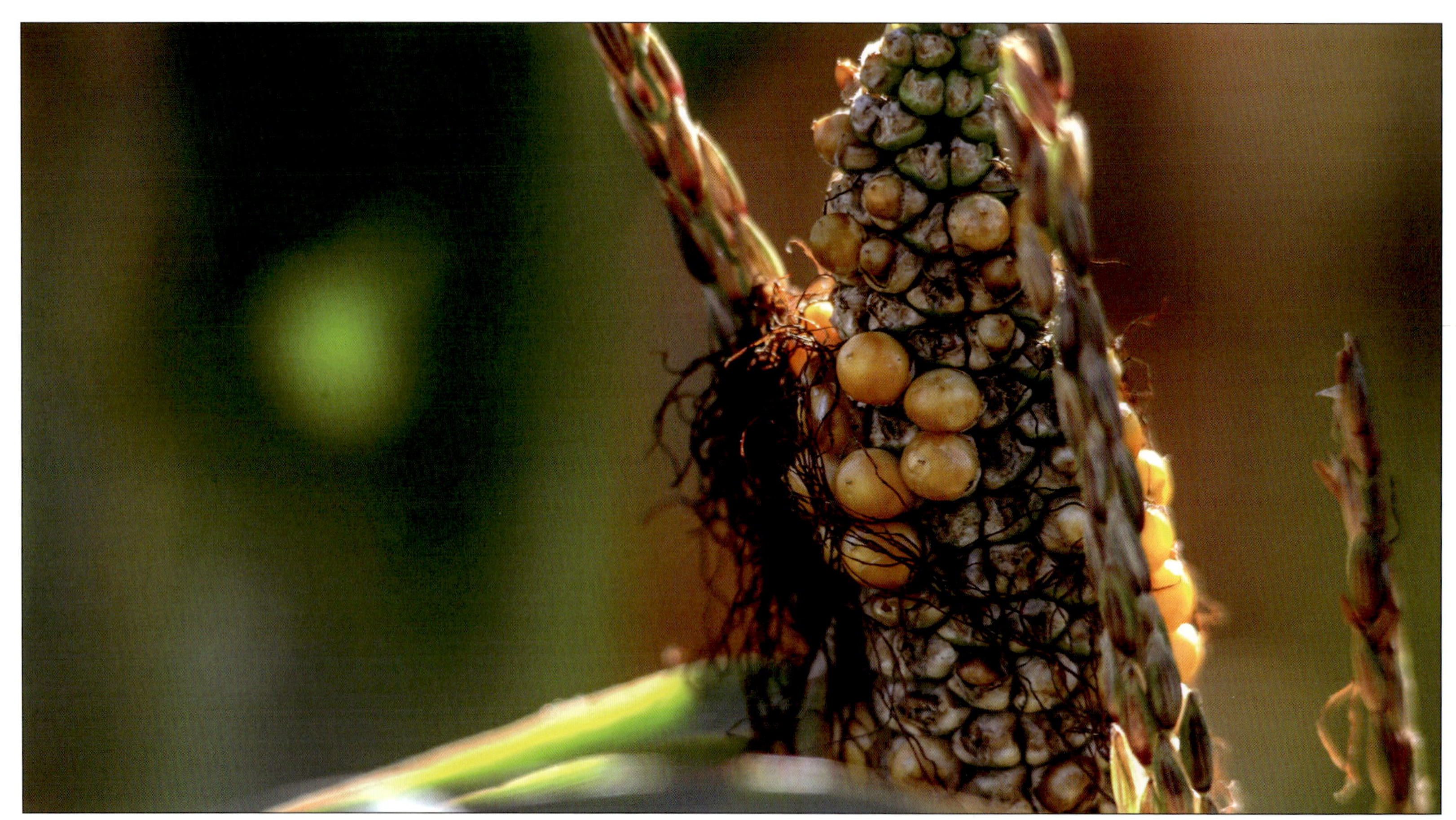

A not very pretty ear of corn in a field near Enchant.

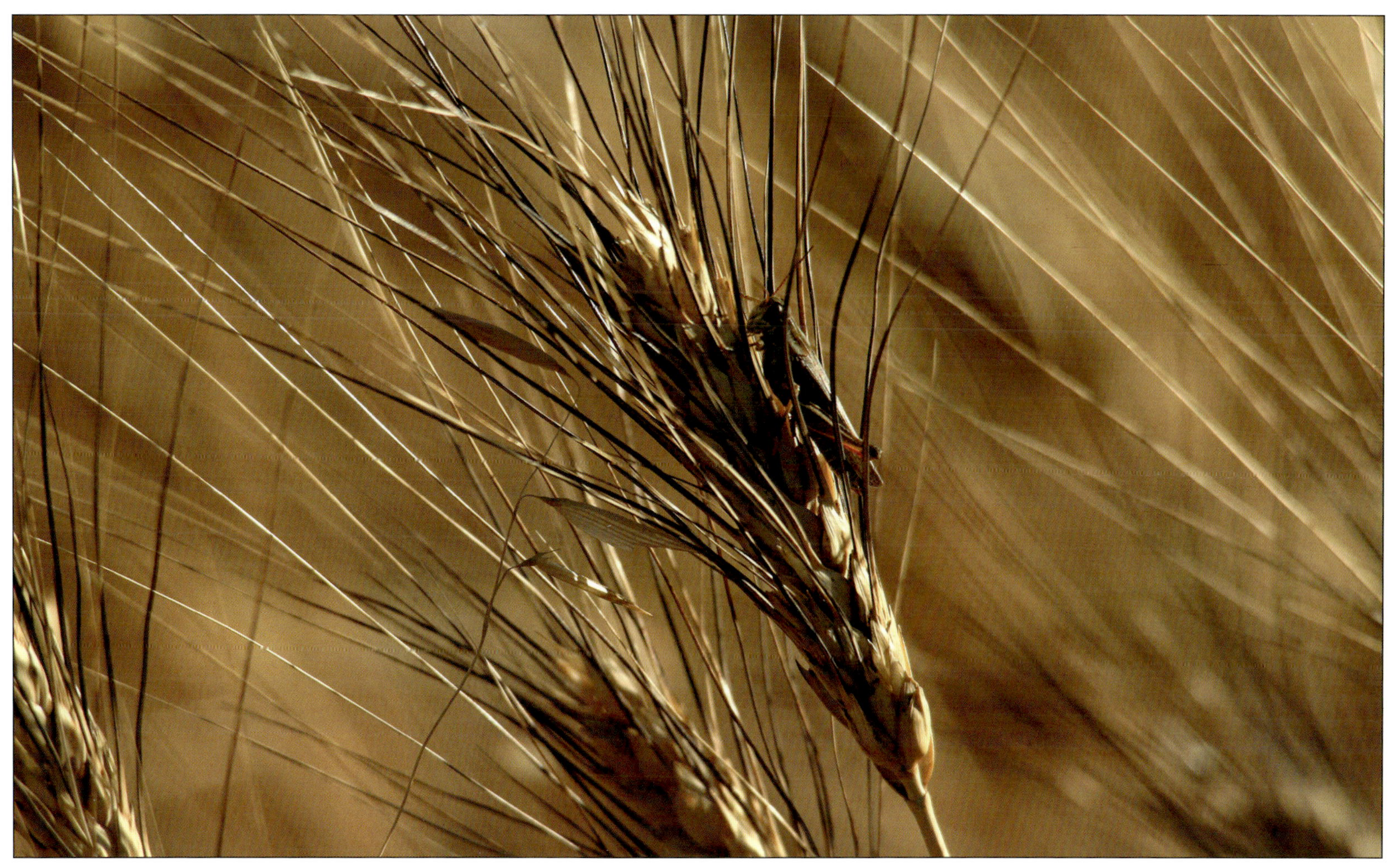

A grasshopper perches on wheat ready to harvest near Enchant.

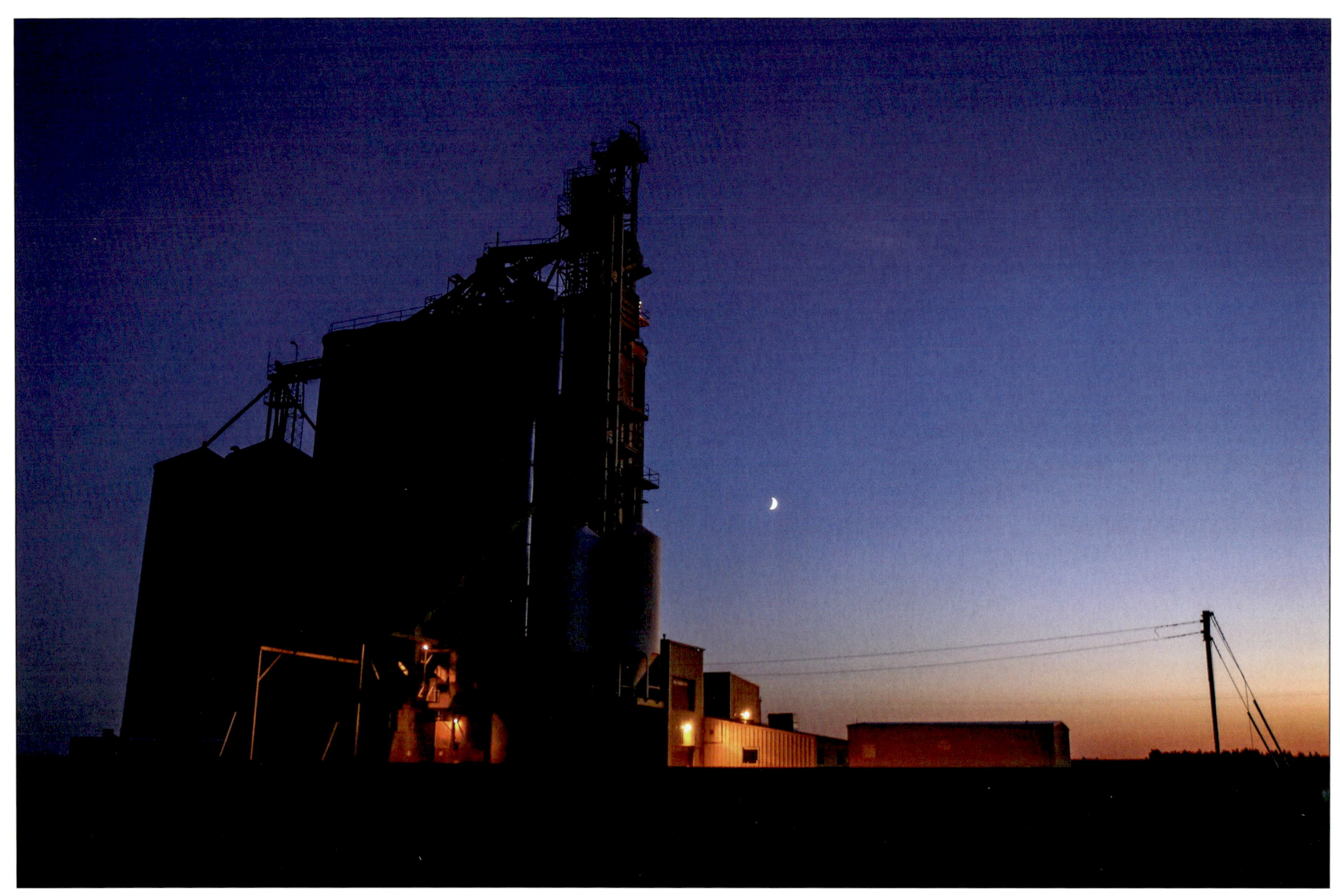

The crescent moon and a modern grain elevator near Vulcan.

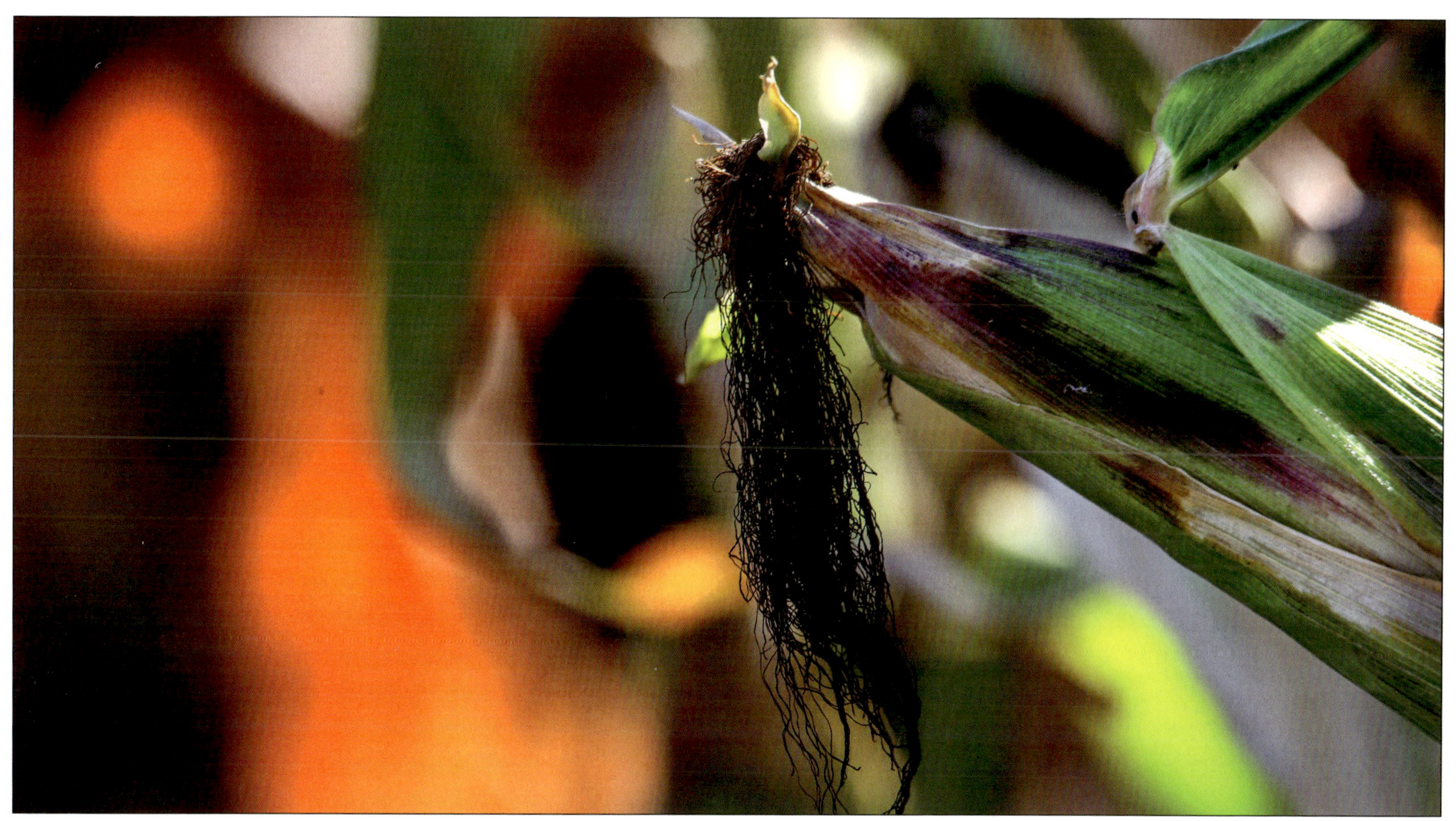

Sunlight and shadow in a corn field near Enchant.

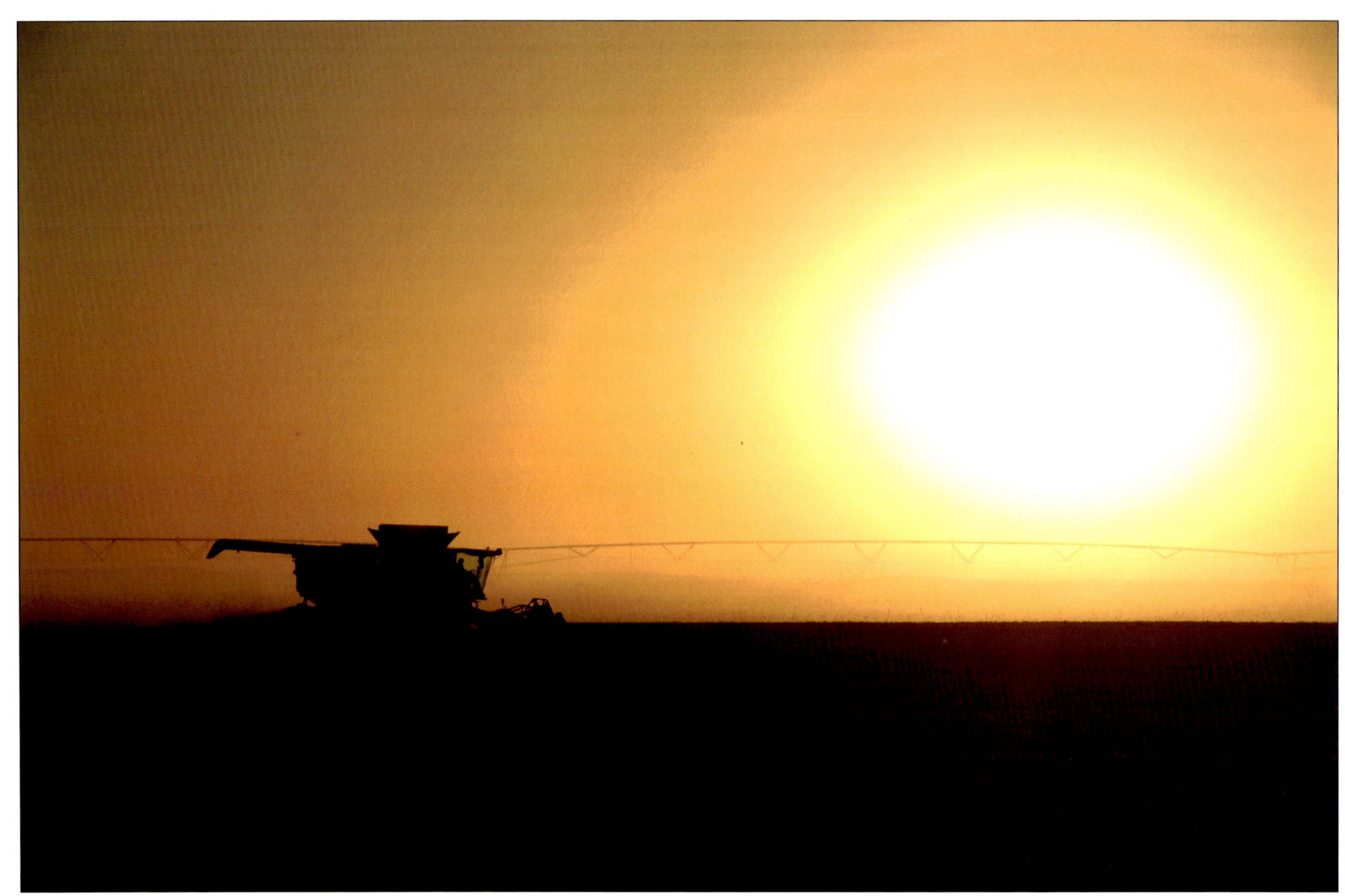

The sun goes down and the combines keep going near Lomond.

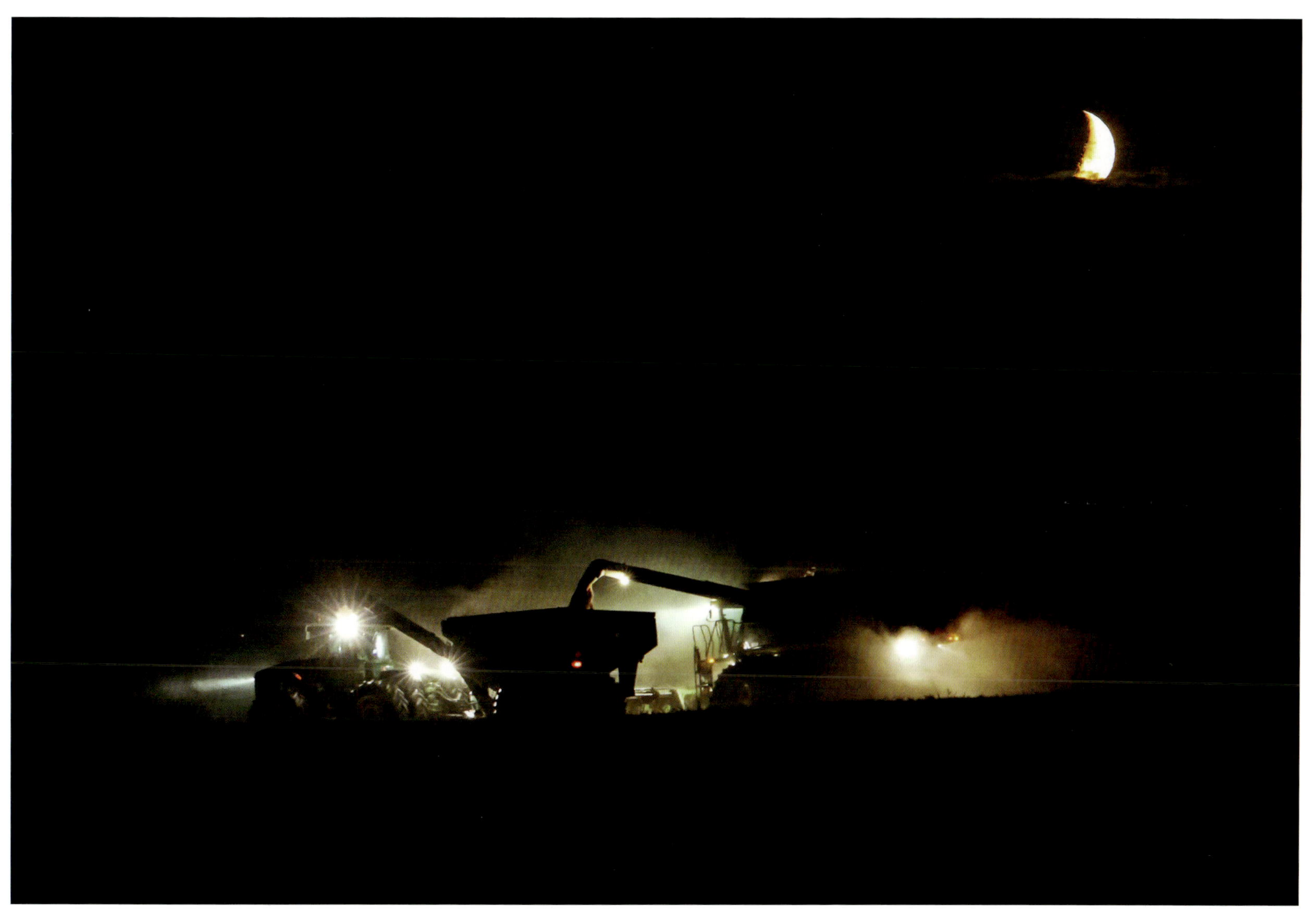

Harvesting train at night near Carseland.

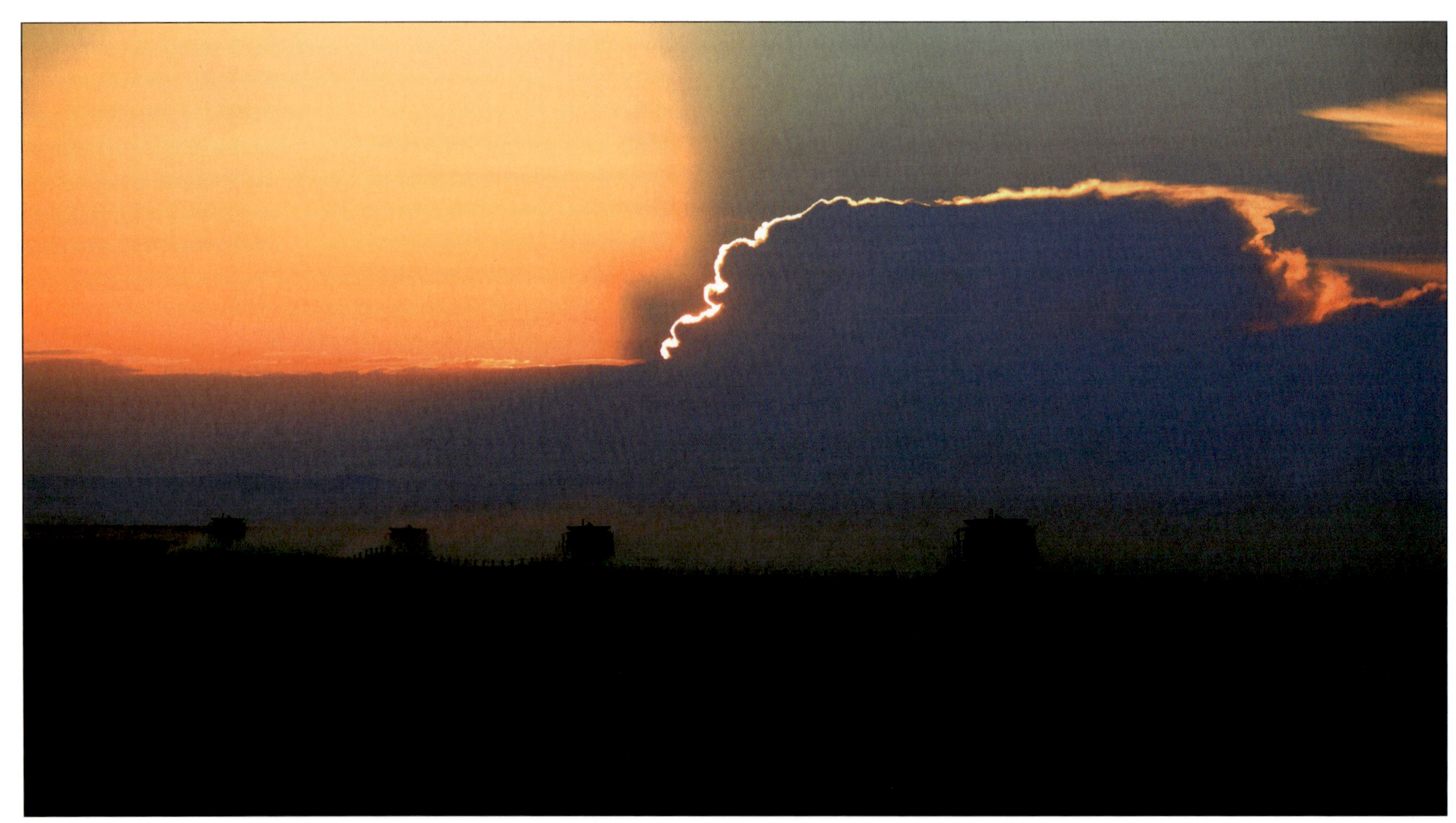

Getting the crop off before the rain hits near Granum.

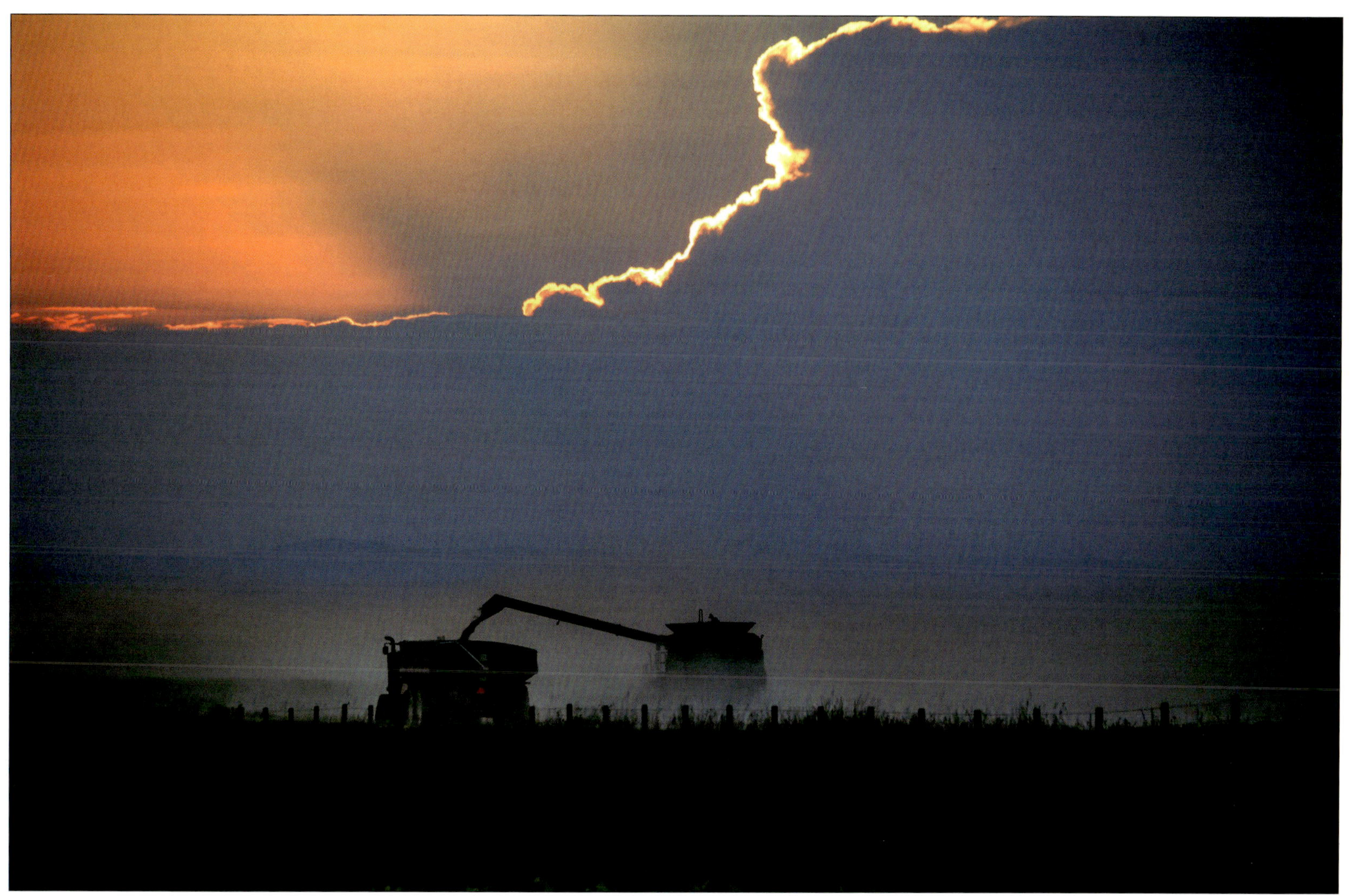

Emptying the hopper before the rain hits near Granum.

IAN TYSON

I WAS SITTING IN THE NAVAJO Mug in Longview when the rain started to fall.

One of Ian Tyson's songs – he owns the place – was playing in the background as I was editing these pictures, and he was singing about a drought.

I had just driven a couple of hundred kilometres of dusty road, thinking the whole time about how little rain we've had since June and there was Ian crooning a tune about it.

I'd driven out of the city early Wednesday morning trying to get to the mountains ahead of the coming storm. I made it to the southern city limits just as the first drops started to fall, but before I'd gone even a few kilometres more I was out of it again.

It was cloudy and cool but dry as I headed southwest through Okotoks. To the north an ominous bank of clouds lurked on the horizon but to the south I could see morning sunlight hitting the Porcupine Hills. Above me and to the west there were thin grey clouds and the peaks of the mountains were shrouded in mist.

I headed for Highwood Pass, thinking that maybe I'd find some of the larches that grace the high country cloaked in golden needles, but as I drove west past Longview and on through Eden Valley, the clouds got lower and thicker and darker. I wouldn't see anything on Highwood Pass. I turned south at Highwood House junction instead.

I'd headed this way in the first place because I wanted to see how the leaves were doing. It's that time of year, the time when all those colours hidden under the green of spring and summer start to show through and the leaves drop off for the year.

I didn't have much hope for a spectacular show. For one thing, it's a bit early – something I thought to circumvent by heading to higher altitude – and for another, we've had almost unrelenting hot and dry weather for the past two months. Can't say I didn't enjoy it.

No, I didn't expect to see much for autumn leaves but I hoped at least to see some animals. Disappointing both ways.

There's a lot of logging going on in the country south of the Highwood River and during the day the trucks thunder down that skinny gravel road constantly. The noise keeps the animals away and the dust thrown up by the tires coats everything along the road with a powdery grey jacket. Even if there had been lovely roadside leaves to shoot I wouldn't have stopped for fear of being crushed by a truck.

So I kept going south past the logging area and then cut back east again hoping to find some pictures in the mist on Hailstone Butte.

Yeah, there was mist, but it was so thick I couldn't see anything but the shadows of cattle crossing the road in front of me as I crept along.

But then I started descending down the twisty road toward Willow Creek and the skies opened up. Sort of.

There was still a lot of smoke in the air so everything had a kind of amber tinge as I rolled down into the valley, but I could see again and that lovely panorama spread out before me with the tiny creek sparkling on the valley floor and the Porcupine Hills misty on the eastern horizon. I parked and got out for a walk.

Yeah, there's a drought going on. Everything crunched under foot as I walked, and the leaves on the trees and the shrubs all seemed worn out, dry, ready to just give up and fall to the ground.

Can't blame them. They've had a long season since they first appeared in mid-April. Some forester counting tree rings a century or so from now will come to the one for 2006 and remark on how thick it is. And it's all thanks to these now-weary leaves.

Yeah, there was a bit of colour but mostly it was subtle bits here and there on individual leaves, not the vast hillsides of yellow that we commonly see. True, it's still a bit early but I just don't think it's going to happen on any big scale.

I photographed the worn-out aspens and balsam poplars and then crawled around for a bit among the geraniums, mountain ash, saskatoons, fireweed and the plants along the creek, but all I saw were tired leaves with lots of blighting and subtle colour. They needed rain a month ago.

And now here it was, pelting down on the deck of the Navajo Mug, threatening snow, even. Too little, too late.

But maybe not, maybe it'll help keep what little colour we have bright. I can't complain though. Summer was wonderful so I don't mind a brown fall.

Maybe Ian can write a song about that, too.

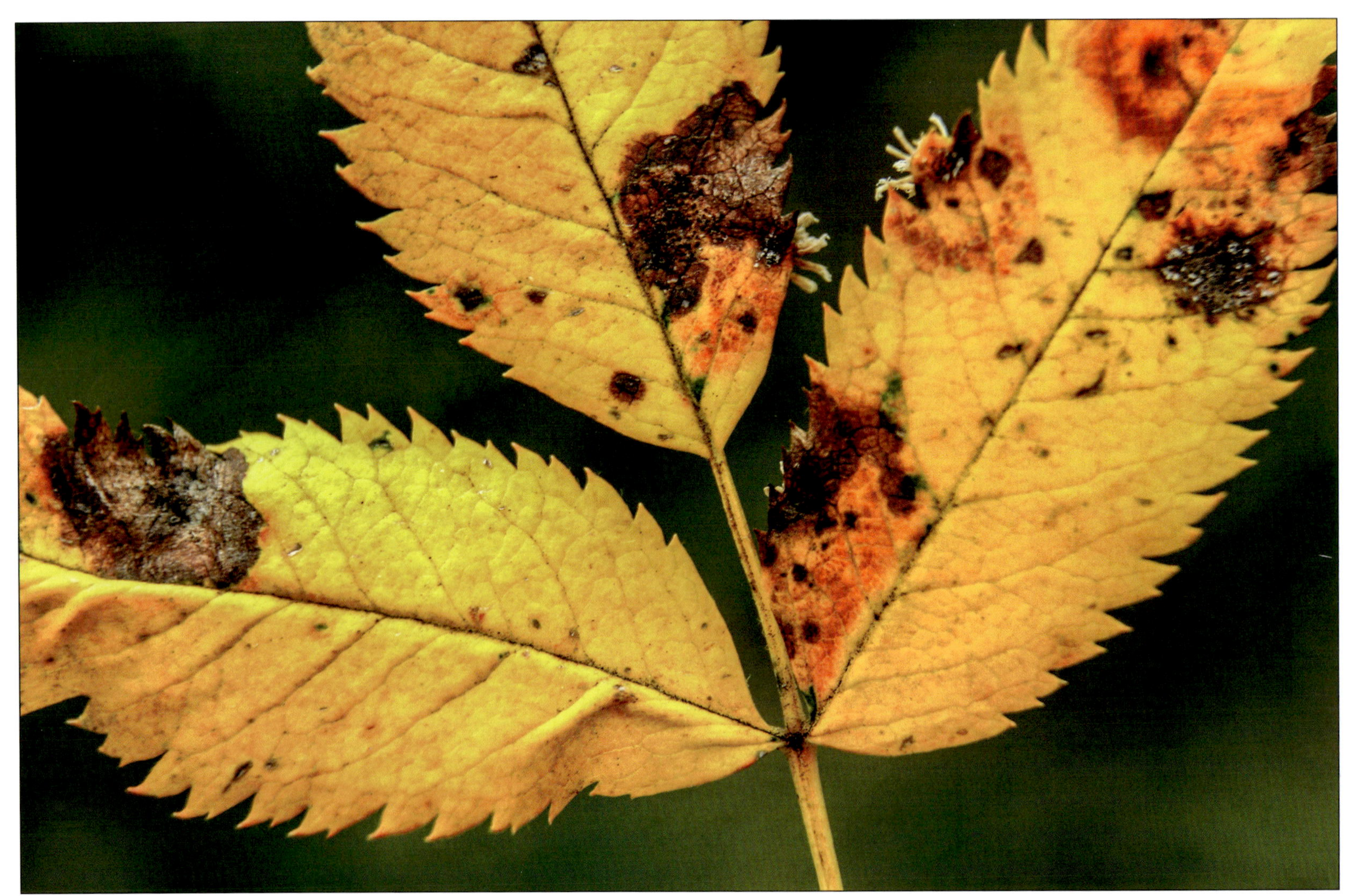

Worn-out mountain ash leaves south of Longview.

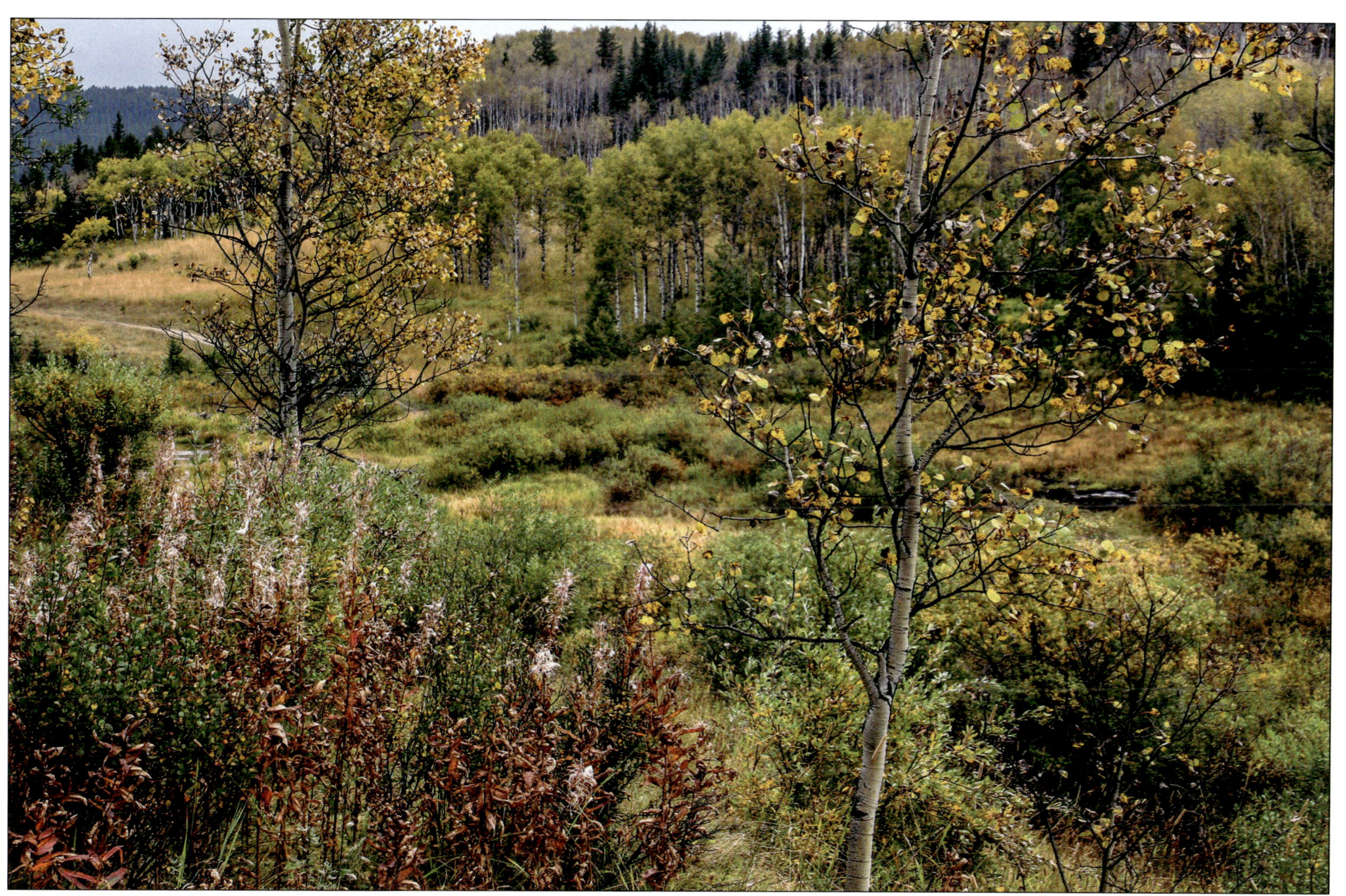

Aspens, poplars, willows and fireweed south of Longview.

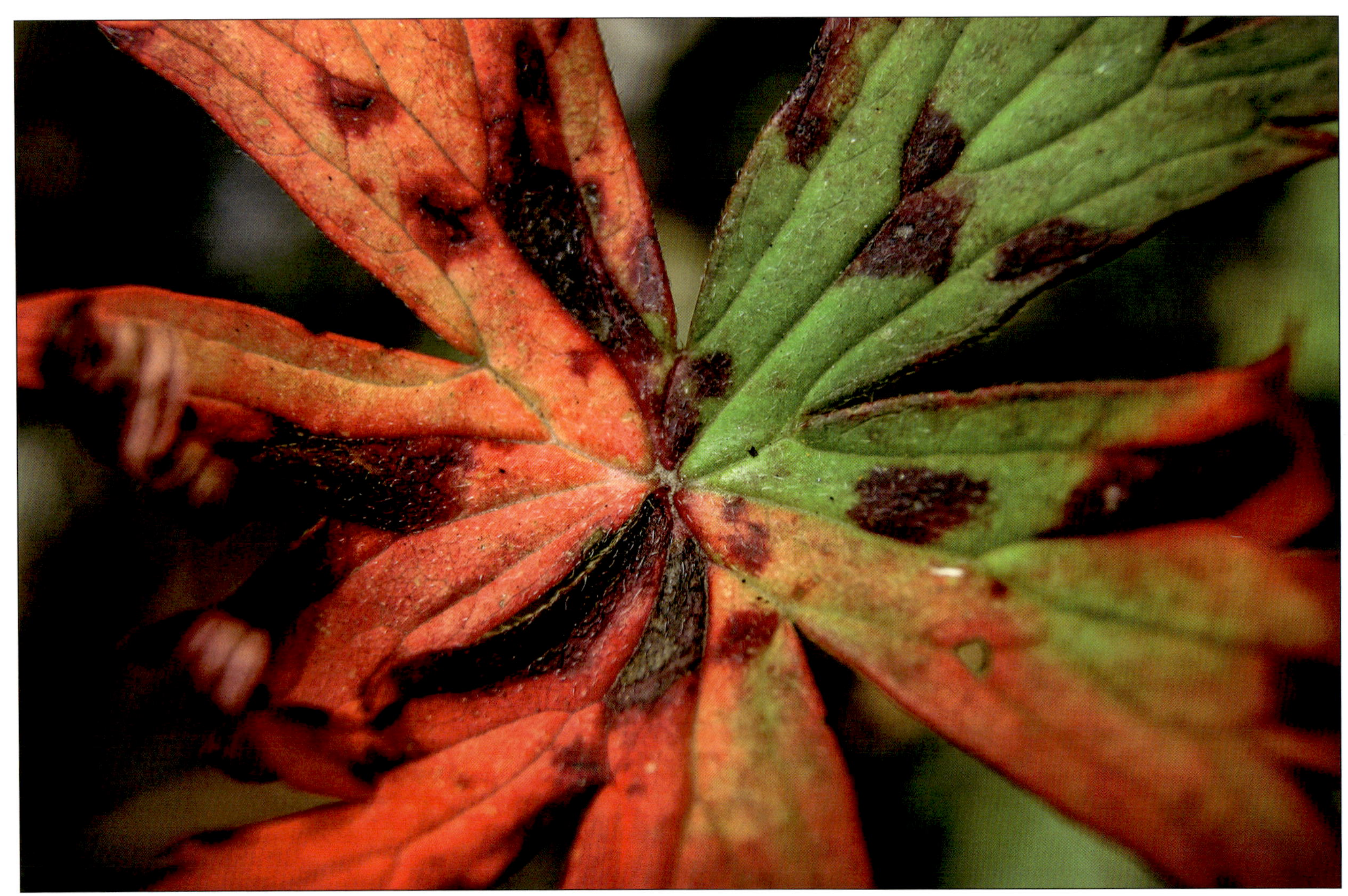

Worn-out geranium leaves south of Longview.

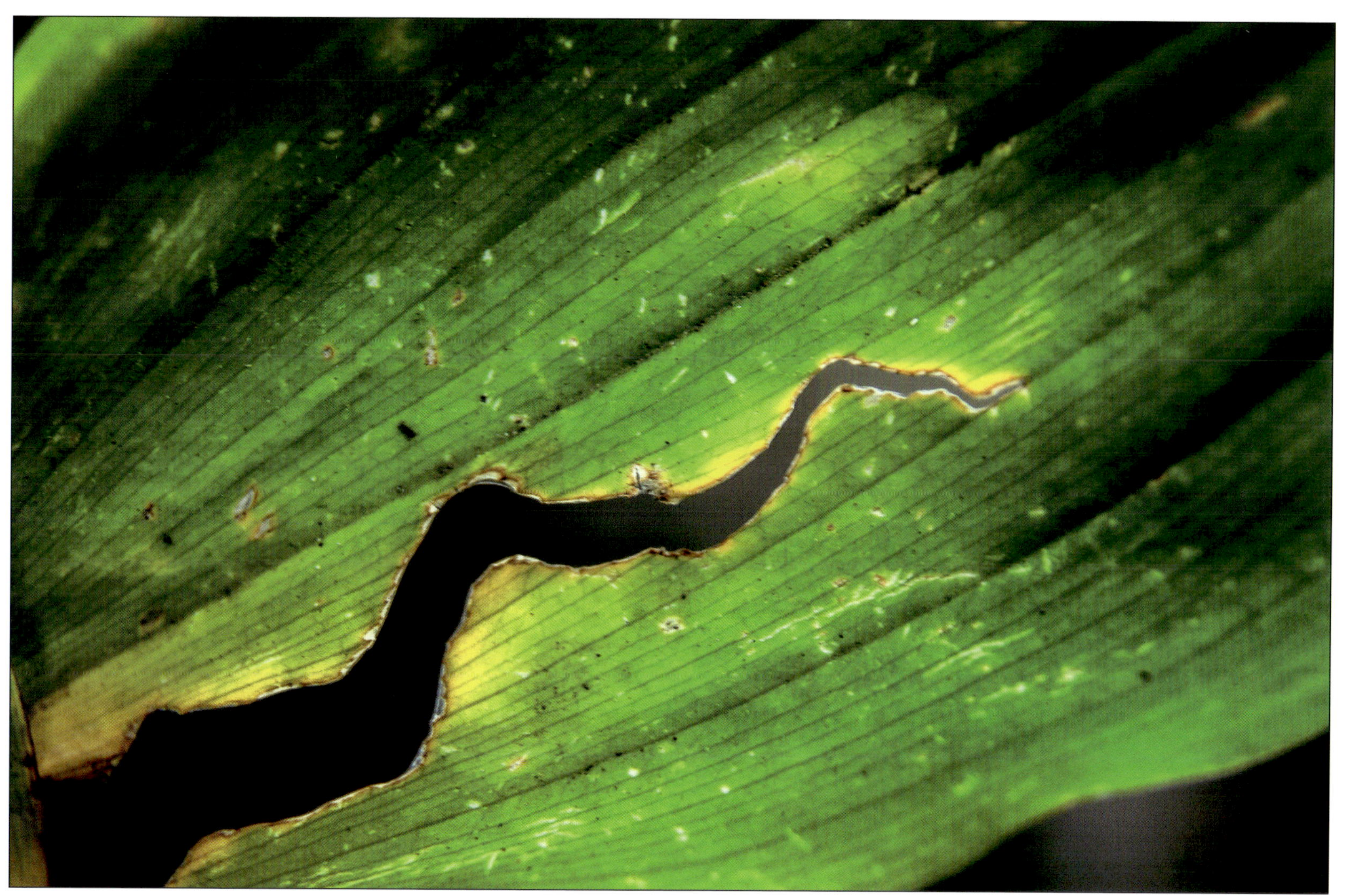

Worn-out twin flower leaves south of Longview.

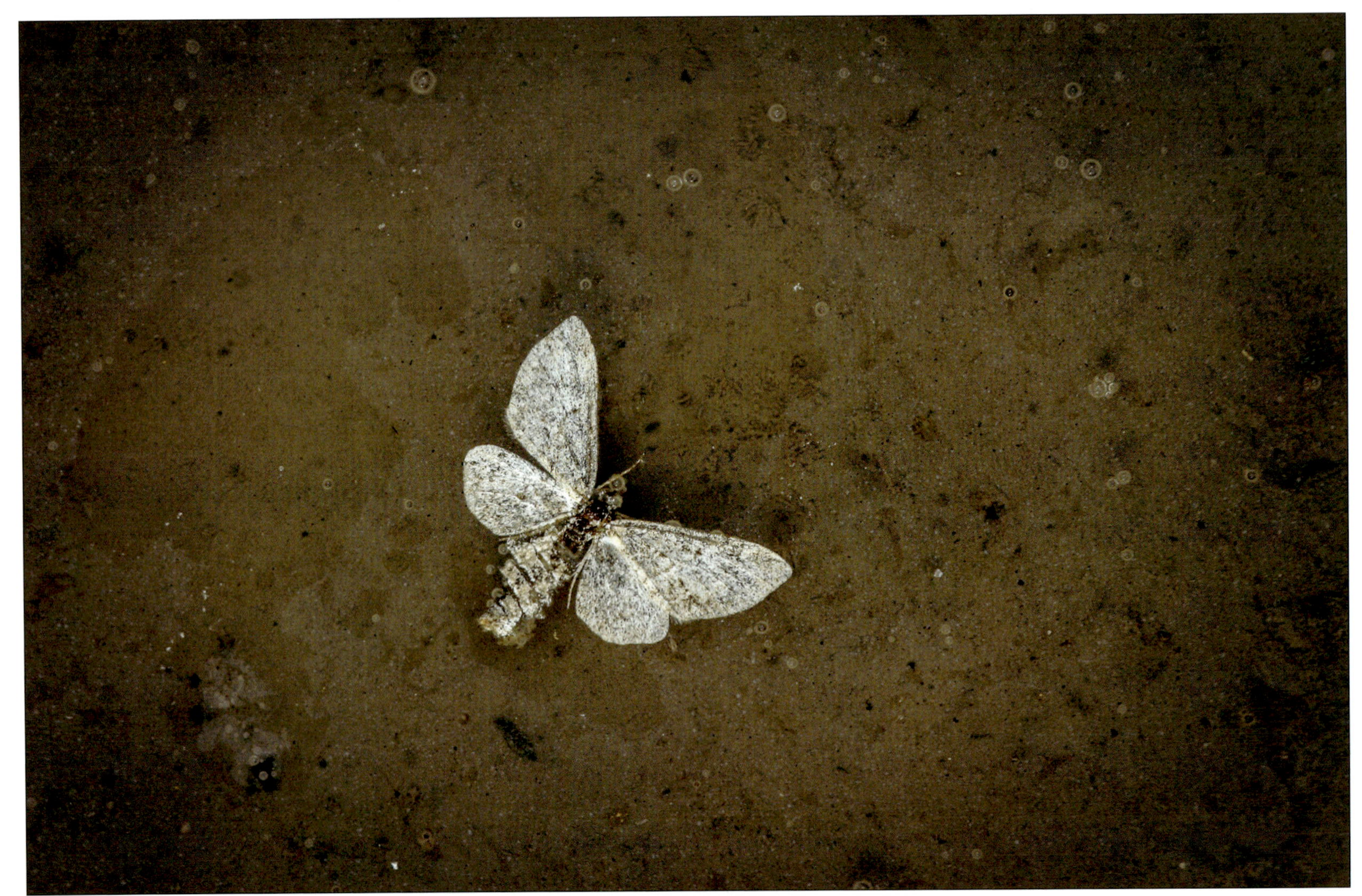

A worn-out butterfly floats in a puddle.

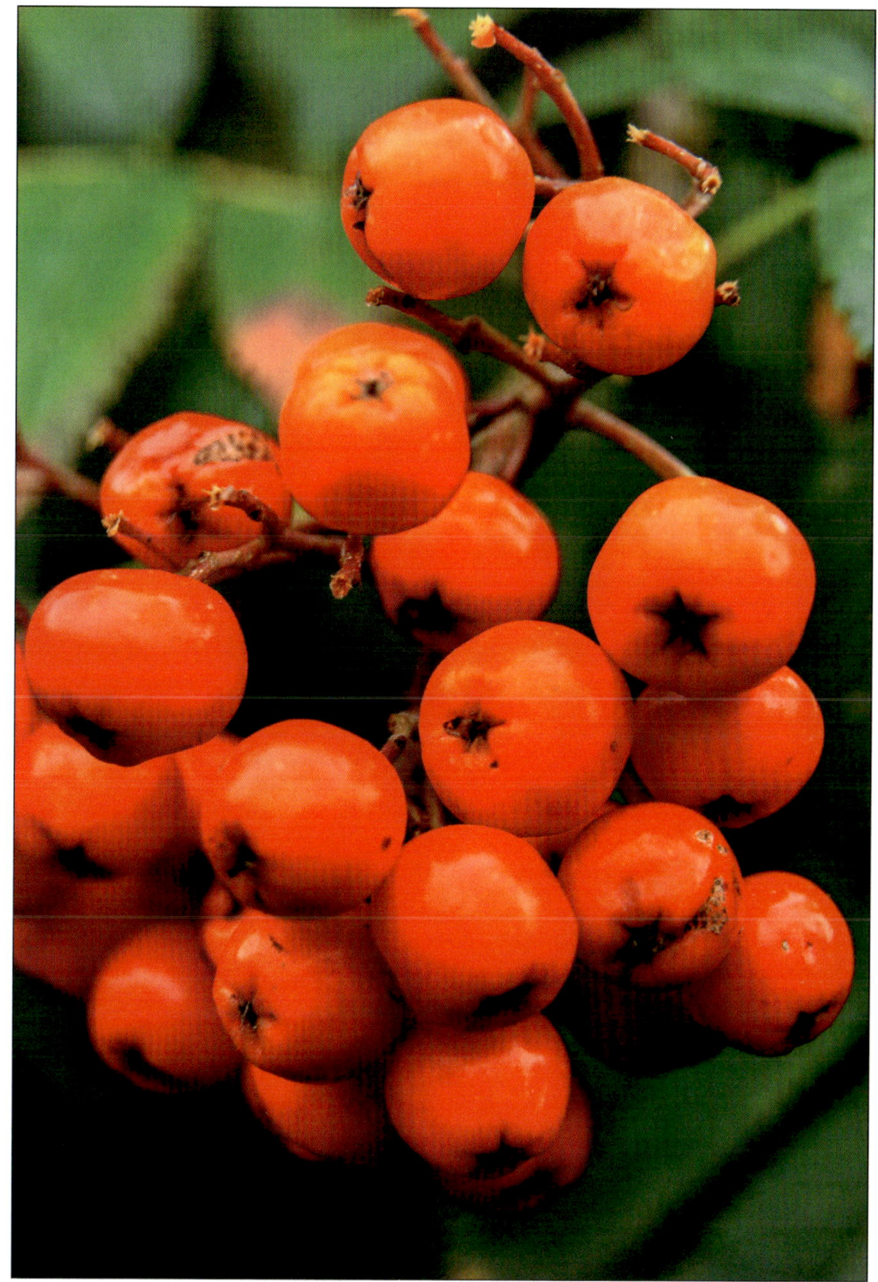

Screaming bright mountain ash berries.

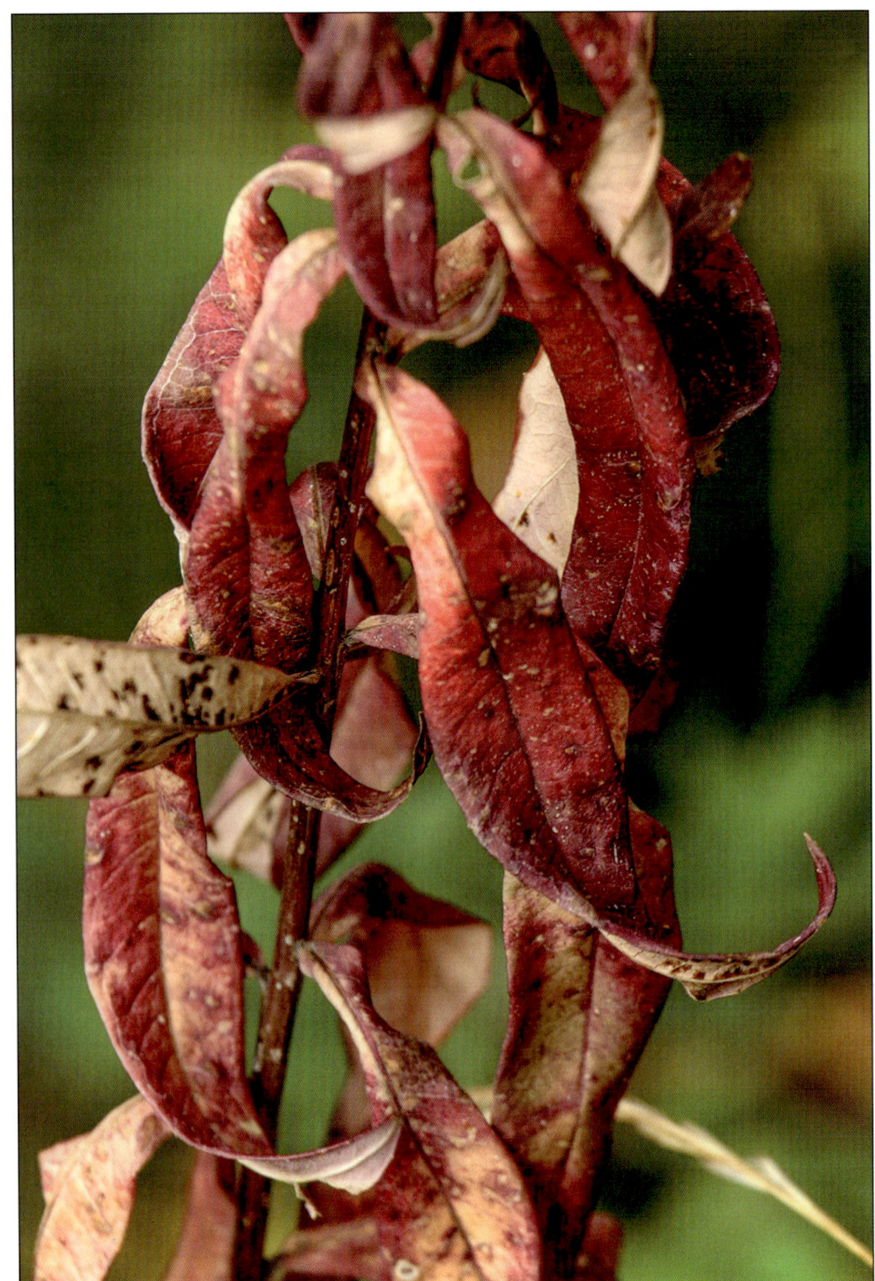

Flamed-out fireweed.

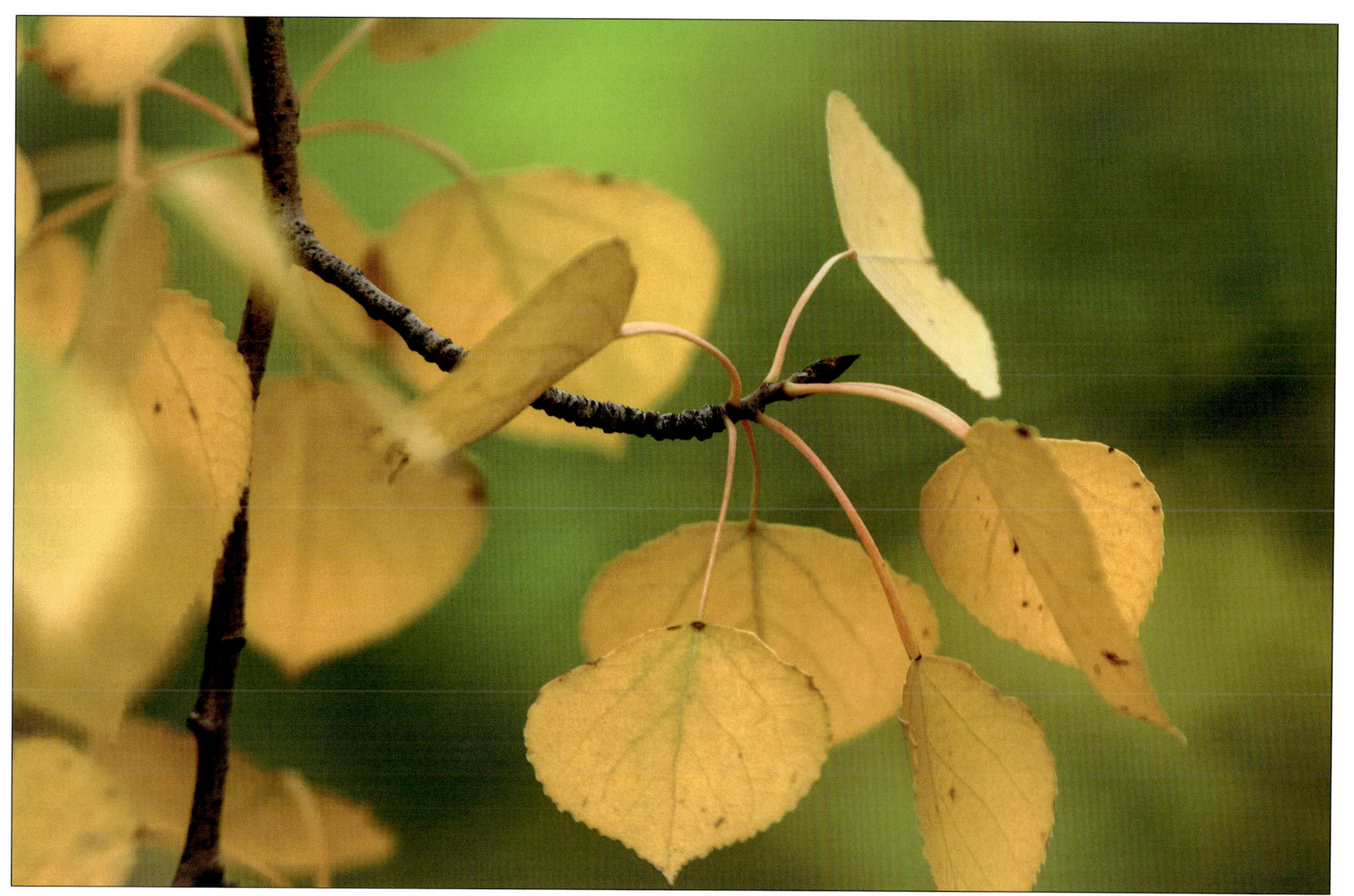

Aspen leaves quiver in the breeze.

WOLVES

CAMERA IN HAND, MY ENTIRE body shaking in anticipation, I edged my way through the trees.

The wolves were just in front of me, slipping among the aspens like ghosts. Silently as a ghost myself, the light breeze in my face to mask my scent, I walked as quietly as I could on the frosty forest floor.

Suddenly the alpha female turned. Her ears flattened against her head. She looked right into my eyes and her lips pulled back to reveal . . .

Sorry. I'd love to tell you that I was stealthily making my way through the mountain-shadowed forest to sneak up on these wolves, but the truth is that I was driving along the Banff Parkway looking for bugling bull elk when I came around the corner at the Muleshoe Picnic area and the wolves were standing in the middle of the road.

Don't get me wrong. It was amazingly exciting. I have driven this road for years and never before seen a wolf, let alone a whole pack of them.

But it wasn't exactly a National Geographic/Farley Mowat moment when the big male lifted his leg to mark the rock by the No Parking sign in the picnic area. In fact, I didn't even fully realize they were wolves until I saw the black ones.

The first wolf I saw was a young one, much smaller than the rest of the pack, and it looked at first glance like a particularly well-fed coyote.

But as soon as I saw the big male – black with a frosting of grey – I knew they were wolves and I started grabbing for the cameras.

I've only seen wolves in the wild a couple of times before – once from a helicopter not very far from where these ones were and once far off across a meadow in Yellowstone. I wrestled with a young human-raised wolf pup a decade or more ago in Montana. There was liquor involved. But other than that the closest encounter I've had is hearing their howls echoing off valley walls.

I don't know that I'll ever get this close again. The wolves were so oblivious to my presence that I was able to drive right beside them as they trotted along the road. I had to back off on my 70–200 mm zoom to get more than just their head in the photo.

The only real indication that any of them were paying any attention to me was when the alpha female turned her head, flattened her ears and pulled back her lips to reveal . . .

A mouthful of huge teeth as she uncorked a very large yawn. Then she sat down on the side of the road, scratched the back of a foreleg with a back paw and walked up into the trees.

All this about 30 feet away from the truck. Of course it would have been a different story had I been on foot. Most wild animals don't find vehicles threatening. I'm sure they'd have melted into the woods immediately had I been hoofing it.

But they didn't. They wandered around through the forest along the road – although I also saw one far below Muleshoe following the railroad tracks – and paused to sniff around the brush and test the air. The young ones were a bit more cautious but even they moved along without any obvious hurry.

I hung out with them for maybe half an hour, shooting photos and video along with a few other lucky folks who happened along, but the wolves were slowly edging their way from the highway down to the railway and most of them had moved in that direction when a train came rumbling by.

Two of the youngsters were still up by the highway and one of them started to howl. It stood right out in the open and tilted its head back and was answered immediately by the rest of the pack. Their ululations even overpowered the rumble of the train. Absolutely magical.

And then they were gone. I talked to photographer John Marriott, a Canmore shooter who knows the pack well. He told me there are ten wolves in the pack and they roam the Bow River valley from Minnewanka to Lake Louise. The alpha female is black with a grizzled jawline while the alpha male is all black, frosted with grey. The rest are a mixture of adolescents and pups.

Thanks, John.

I rolled on up the Parkway to Castle Junction and then headed back down the highway toward Banff. It was just shy of 8:30 in the morning. Sun was pushing through the clouds over the mountains, hitting the new snow on the peaks and setting the autumn leaves aglow. Somewhere down in the valley the wolves were on the move.

No, it hadn't been a National Geographic moment. I didn't have to pull a Farley Mowat and drink enough tea to mark my territory. But I'd had my first close encounter with wolves, and the fact that it was from the driver's seat of my truck didn't diminish the experience in the slightest.

In fact, it might have made it even better. I was barely 150 km from my front door, not on the Arctic tundra or freezing my butt off in wintry Minnesota. And I still had plenty of time for a leisurely, scenic drive back to the city to start work at noon.

Ah, the joy of dumb luck. And living in southern Alberta.

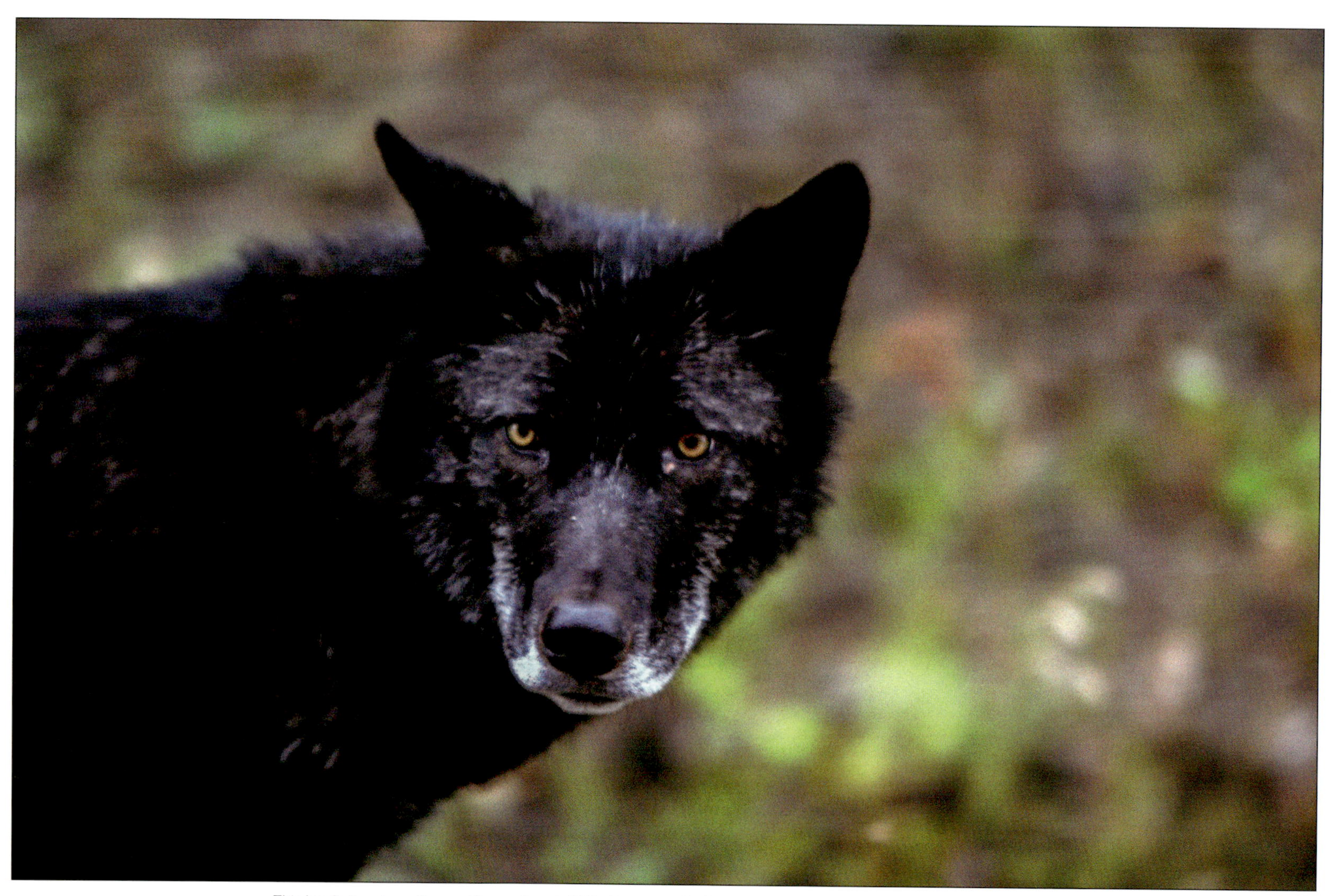

This lovely female wolf posed for me barely 20 feet away on the Banff Parkway just after 7 AM on Monday morning.

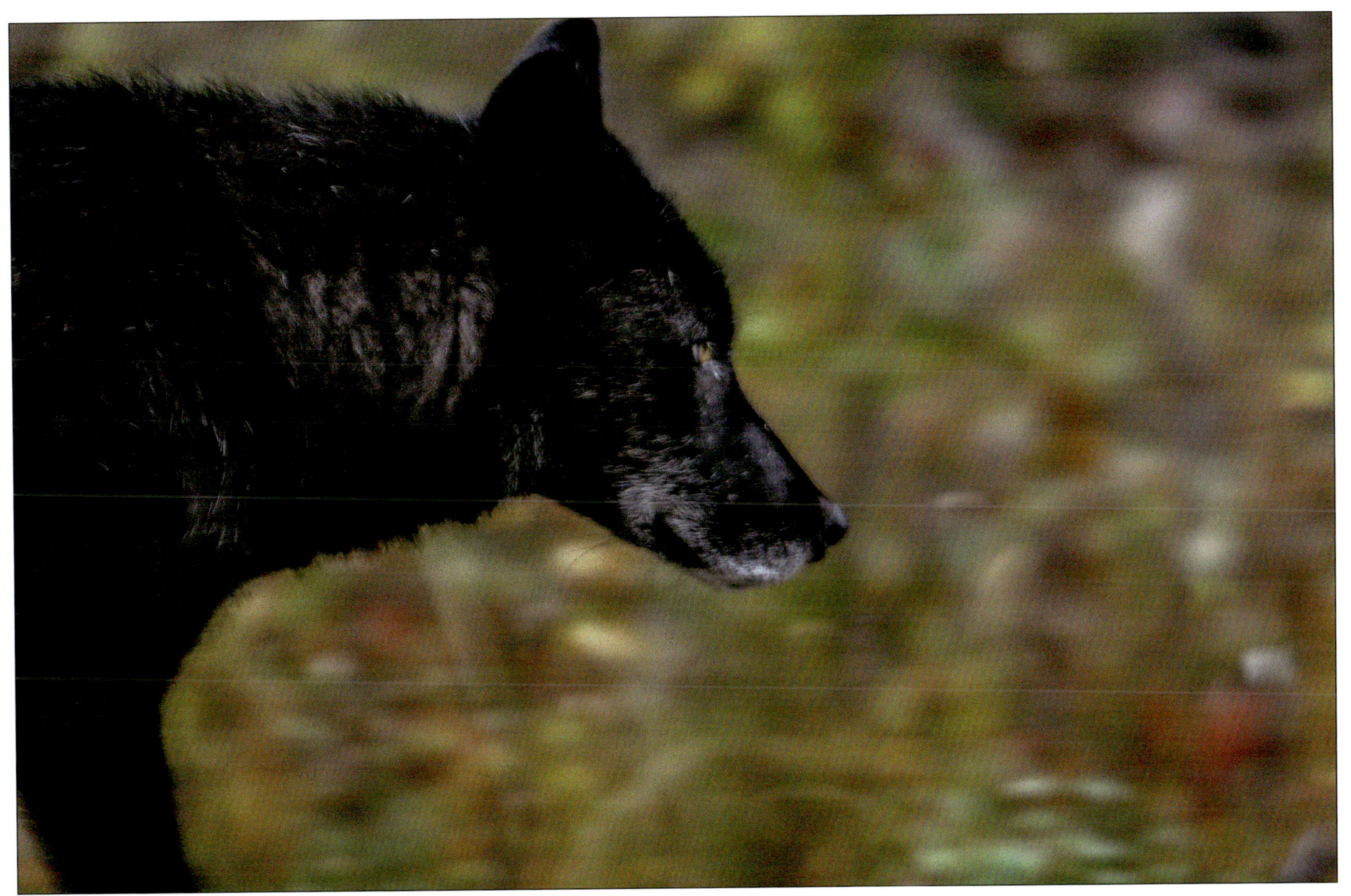

It was an indescribable thrill to have this female wolf trot beside my truck on the Banff Parkway just after 7 AM on Monday morning.

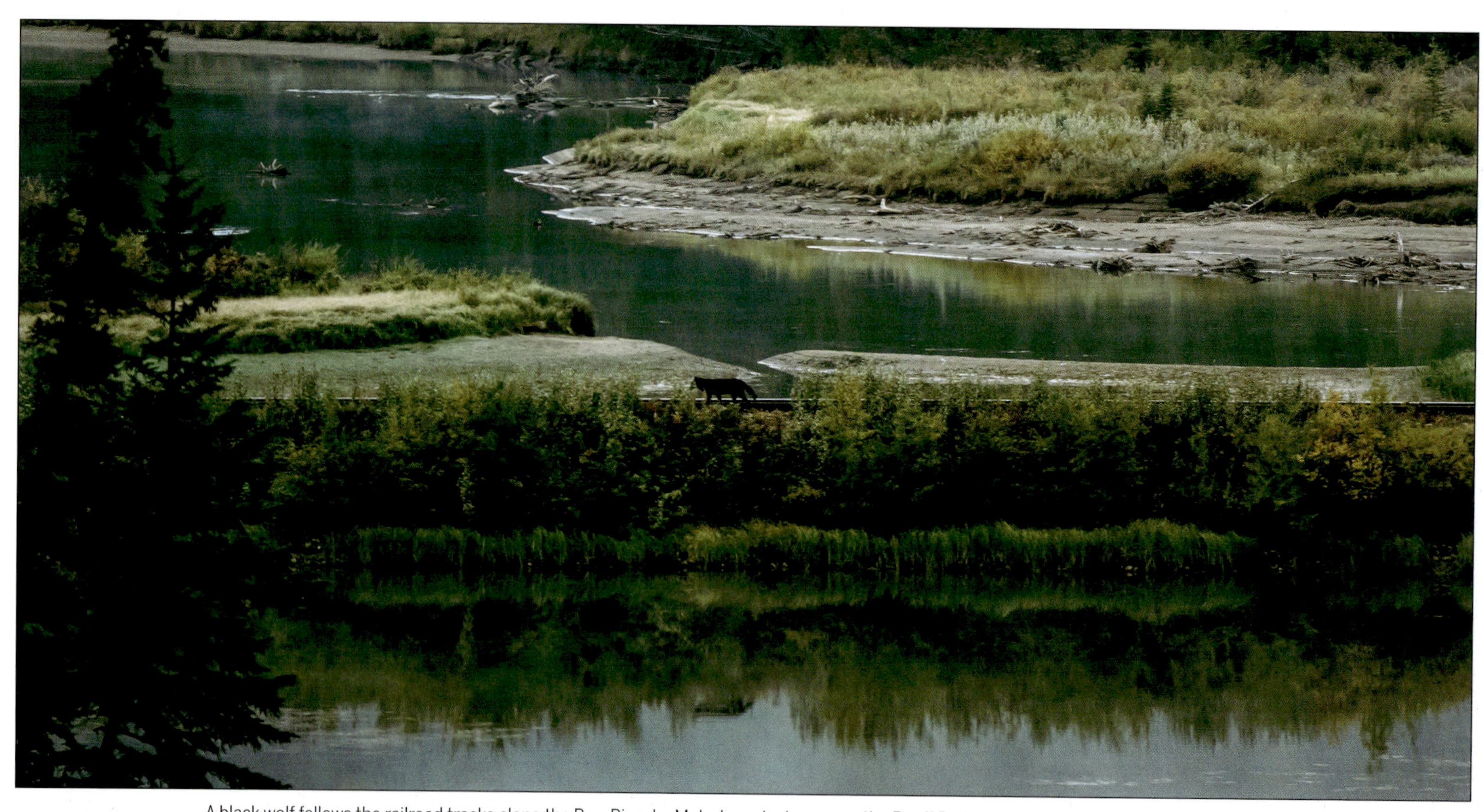

A black wolf follows the railroad tracks along the Bow River by Muleshoe picnic area on the Banff Parkway just after 7 AM on Monday morning.

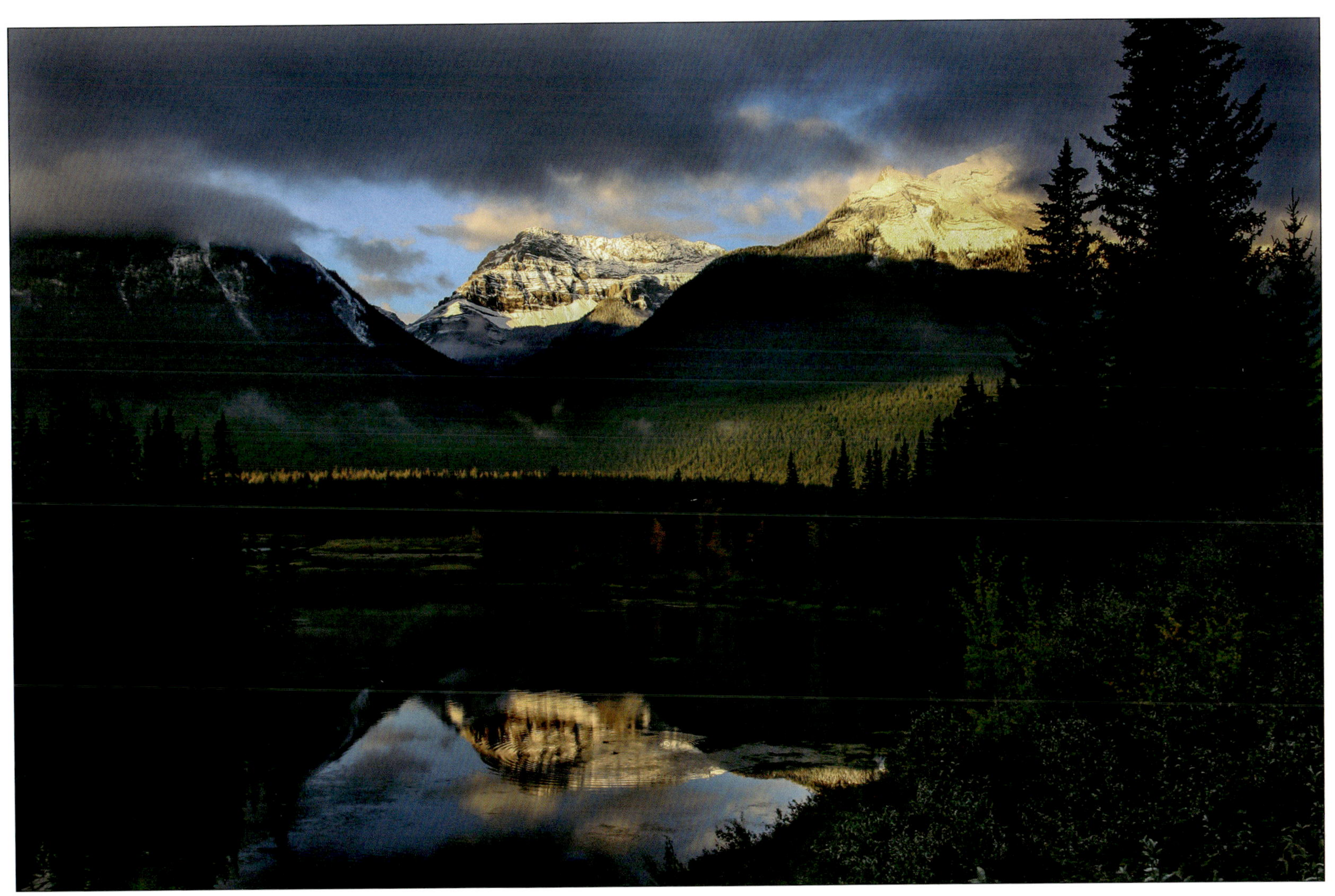

Morning light on the mountains near the Muleshoe picnic area on the Banff Parkway just after 8 AM on Monday morning.

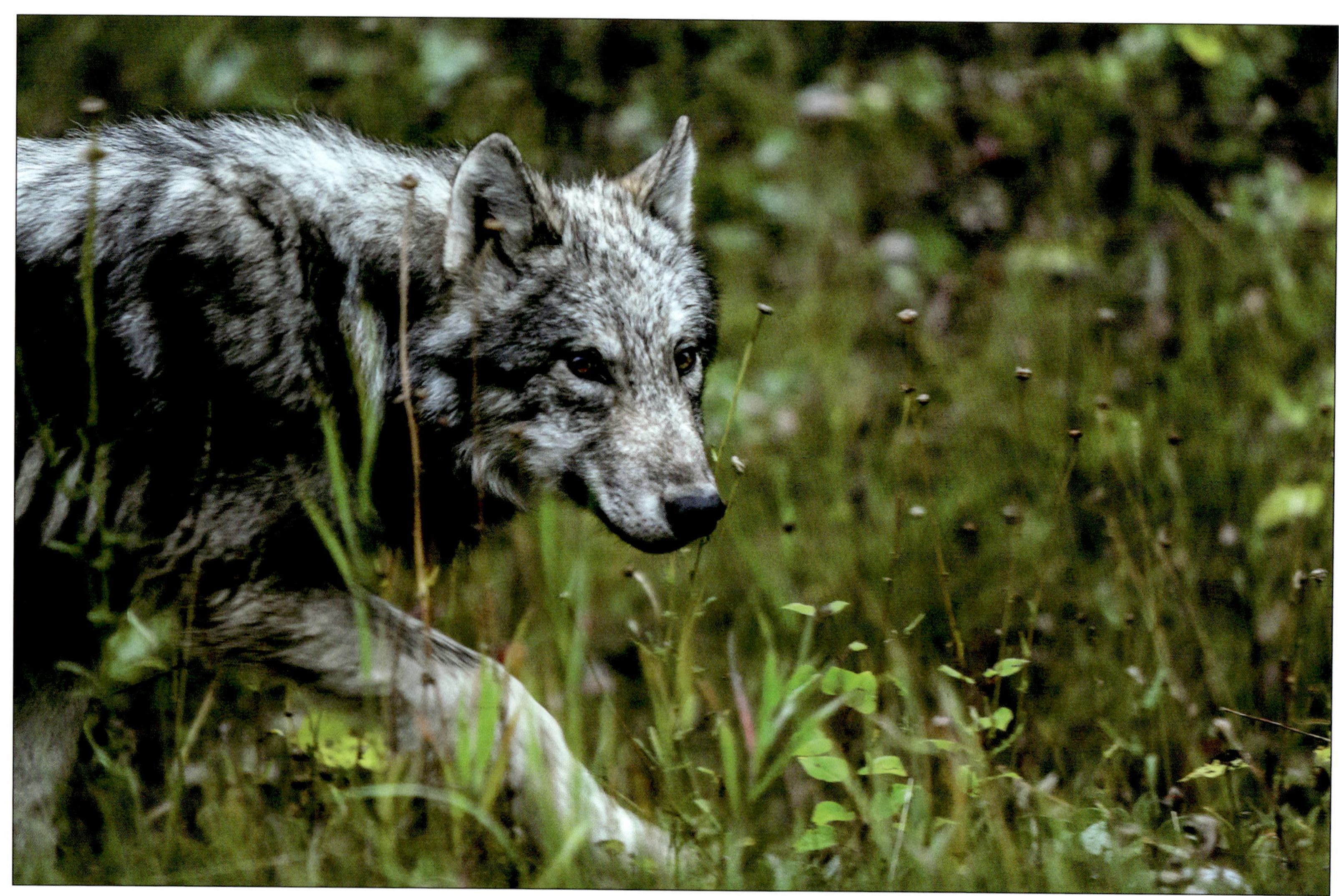

A young wolf trots among the trees near the Muleshoe picnic area on the Banff Parkway just after 7 AM on Monday morning.

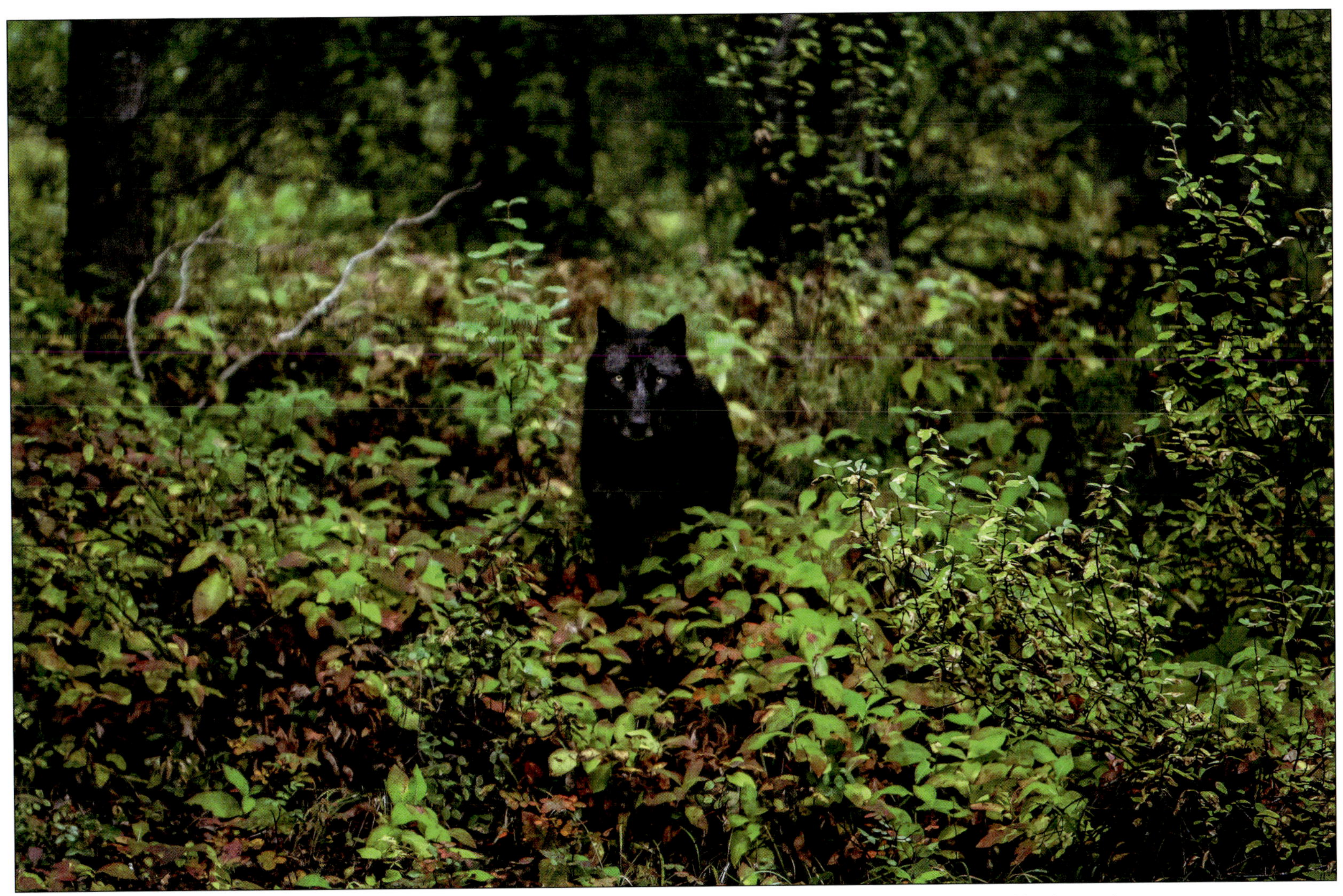

The alpha male wolf pauses among the trees near the Muleshoe picnic area on the Banff Parkway just after 7 AM on Monday morning.

LARCH YARN

THE WIND TORE THE CLOUDS to shreds as they flew over the mountains.

But the larches were unperturbed. Right at treeline, among the spruce and low-lying alpine plants, they glowed golden in the alternating patterns of bright light and near dark as cloud shadows sped over them.

White flags of snow streamed from the mountain tops on the approach to Highwood Pass. A chinook was roaring in from the west and the previous week's snow was being redistributed by the wind.

Down in the valley where I was, the wind was strong but coming in gusts. It shook the branches on the pine and spruce trees and sent aspen and poplar leaves skittering down the road. But up high it was really hammering along.

I was on my way to Highwood Pass to visit the larches. Alpine larches, to be more precise. Shaped like their spruce and pine cousins, tall and conical, they look like evergreens, right down to the cones they produce.

But this time of year their needles turn yellow and begin to fall. Another week or so and they'll be skeletal for the winter. Come springtime there'll be a new crop of needles, soft and lime green, and the cycle will begin again.

Larches are the only deciduous evergreen we have, and I love the way they reveal their presence in the fall. They run along ridgelines and cluster in some of the last soil before altitude makes growth impossible. In summer they blend in with the rest of the trees, but when the needles turn to gold you can see where they live and begin to appreciate just how hardy these guys are.

I rolled on up the Highwood River valley, passing cattle in the lowlands and a pair of whitetail bucks among the aspens farther up. It was warm down low but the higher I climbed the colder it got. The bighorn sheep I saw were walking in snow near the summit, and ice covered the spring seeps.

I would have thought that the wind would have stripped every needle from the larches, but no, they were hanging tough.

The ones among the spruces at the summit were protected a bit by the surrounding trees, but they were being hammered back and forth by the gusts just the same. Aspens would have been stripped bare. The larch needles hung on. How they managed it out on the rocky ridges, I can't imagine.

But maybe that's why I like them so much. Tough trees that have chosen a tough place to live.

Three days later I headed out to look for more larches up by Caroline. The land here is 1200 m lower in elevation than Highwood Pass but there are larches here as well. A lot more of them, in fact. These are kissin' cousins of the alpine larches but every bit as tough and pretty.

These are the larches my Gramma used to call tamaracks. The names larch and tamarack both refer to the same family of trees, members of which live around the entire northern hemisphere. Gramma called the lowland trees tamaracks because that was the name she'd learned for them growing up in Quebec. She called the alpine version larch because after moving west she learned that that's what westerners call the ones at treeline in the mountains.

Call them what you want, they're still a stunning sight.

I pulled up near a stand of them about an hour before the sun went down and went for a walk. The first thing I noticed was that these larches like wet feet. The ground around them was saturated with water and the soil was spongy.

The needles were hanging on a bit more tenuously, too. There was barely a breath of wind, but the next time a storm rattles through needles will be flying. I gave a low branch a shake just to see what would happen and the needles showered down.

But on this day it was warm and quiet. Insects flew in the shafts of sunlight coming through the branches and a bit of fireweed fluff found a perch among the needles. A mule deer buck stood stock still in a hay field near by. The only sounds were coming from a couple of ravens croaking from the shadows.

The setting sun turned the yellow needles a deep amber before touching the clouds above with salmon and then sinking behind the mountains. The colour of the larches slowly faded with the light.

Not long from now their colour will be gone for another year. But it's nice while it lasts. No matter where you find them, on high rocky ridges or brightening muskeggy land, autumn larches enliven the landscape.

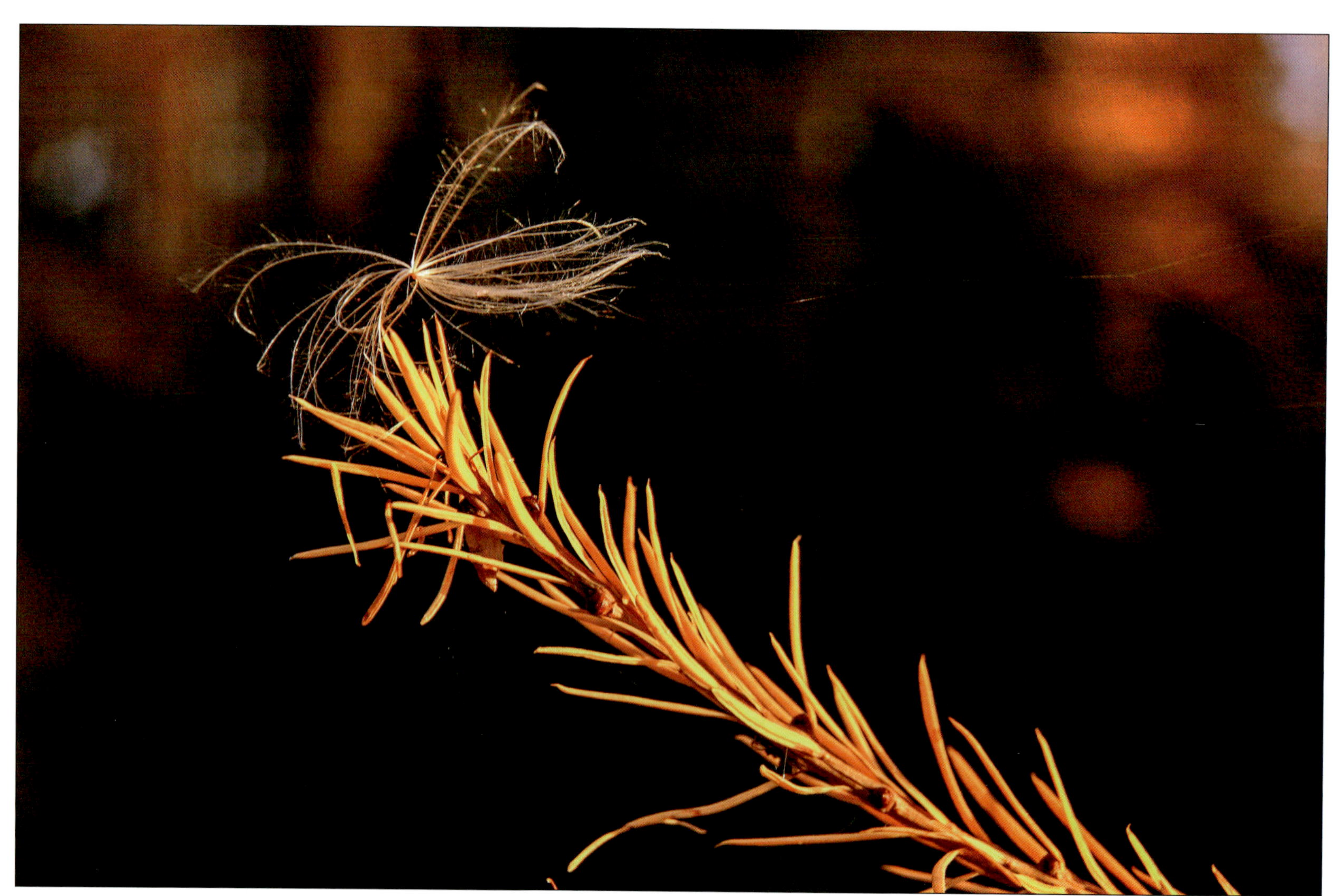

A bit of fireweed fluff snags on a larch branch near Caroline.

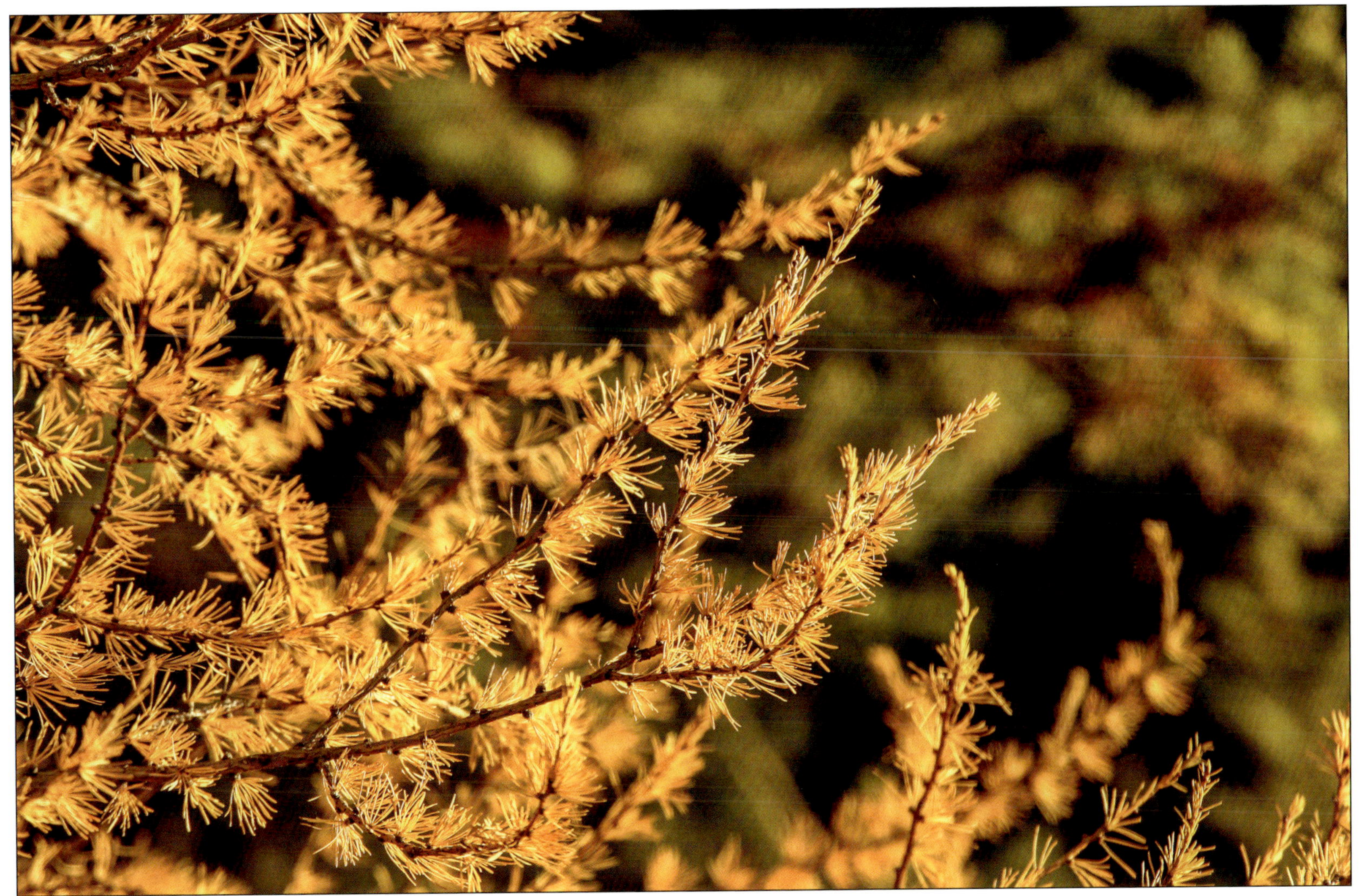

Larch branches about to drop their needles near Caroline.

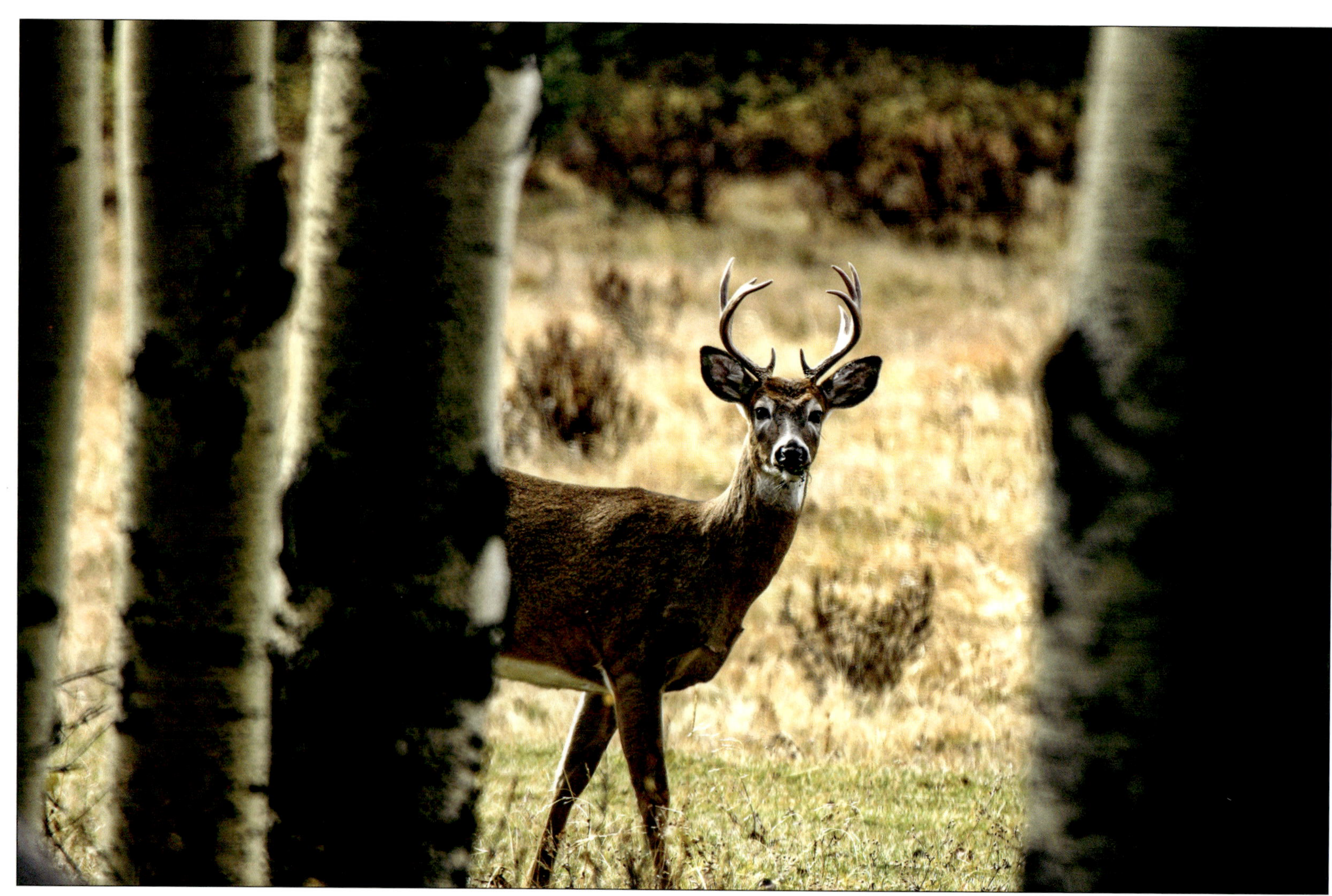

A whitetail buck peeks between some aspens on the way to larch country at Highwood Pass.

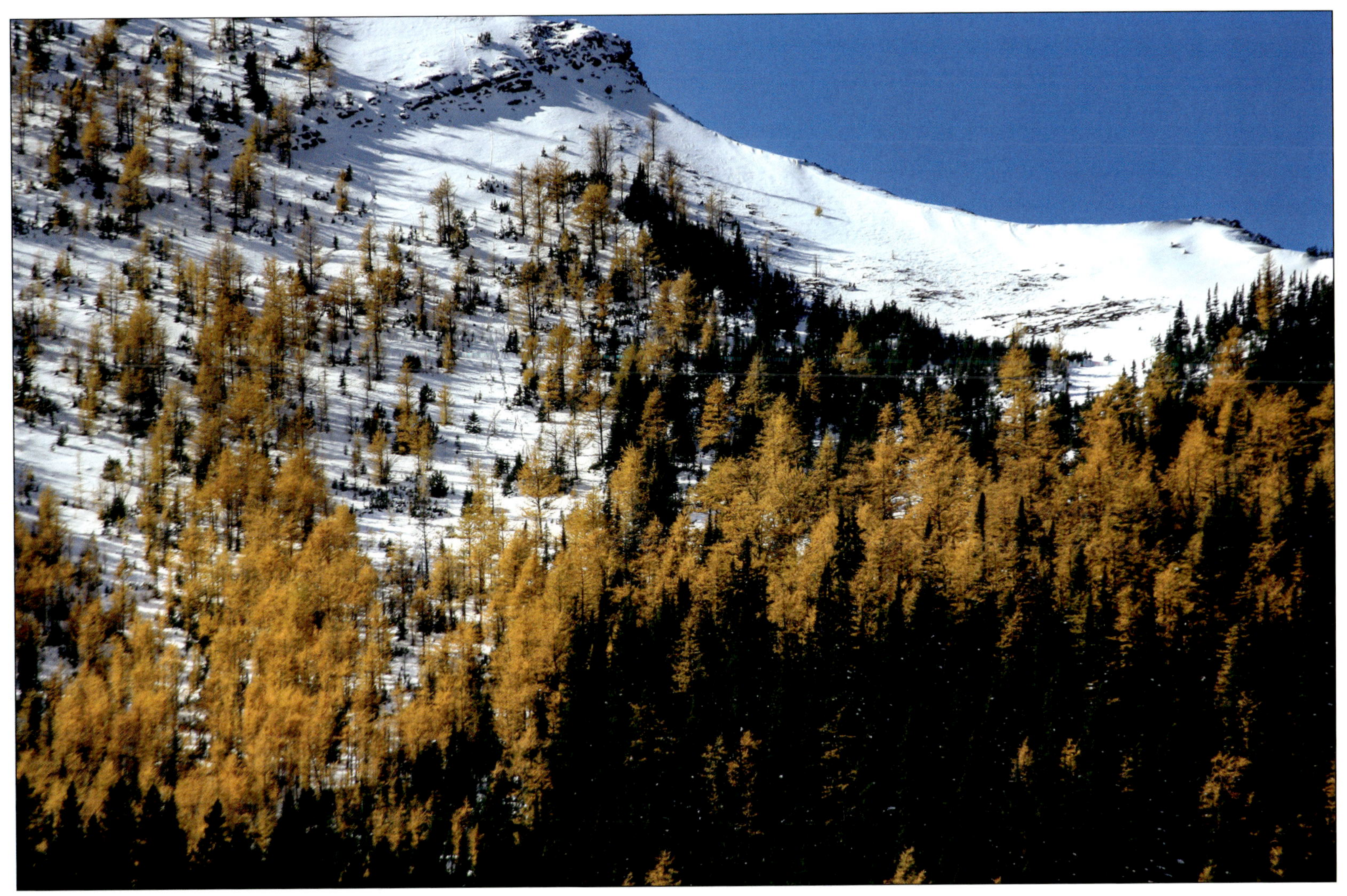

Golden larches at treeline near Highwood Pass.

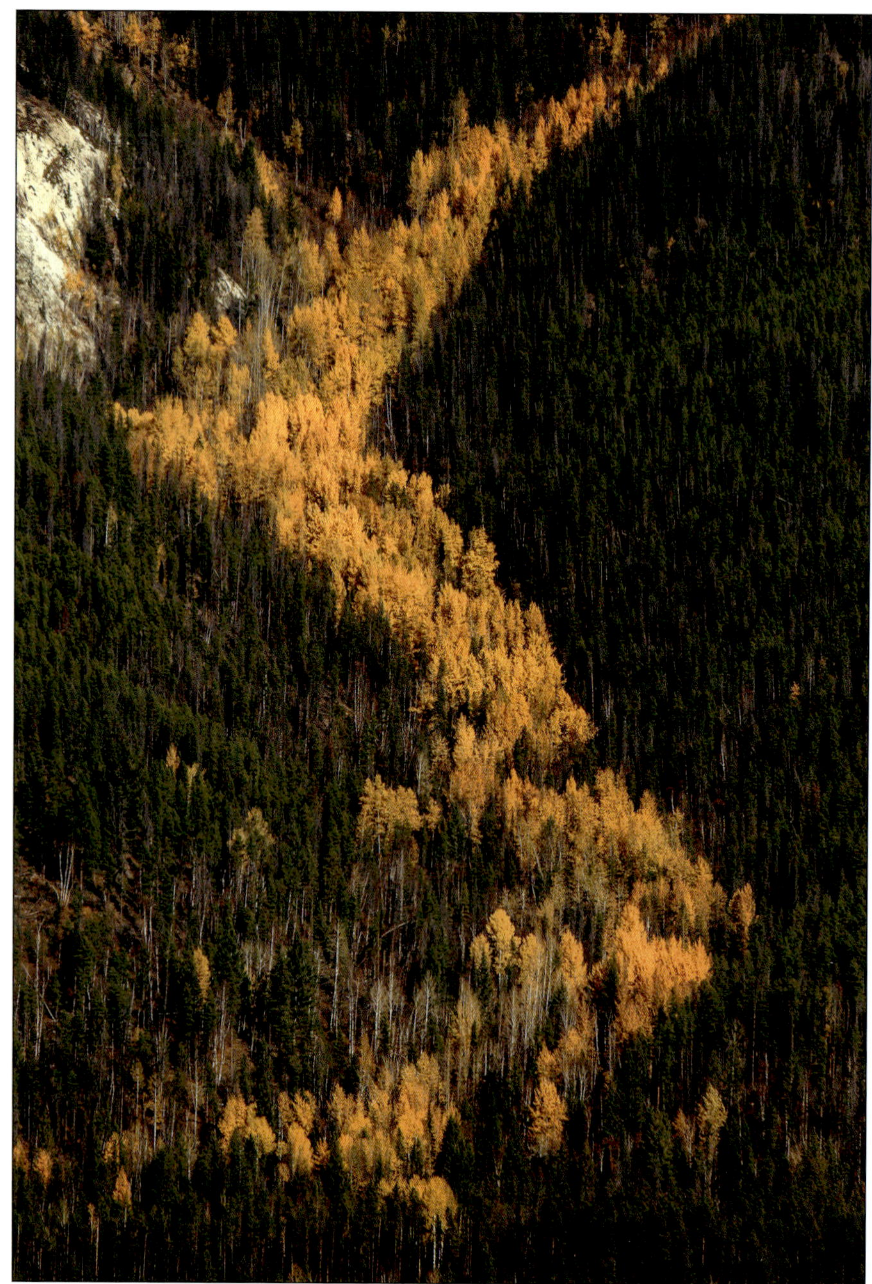

Aspens and balsam poplar brighten a ravine in the mountains.

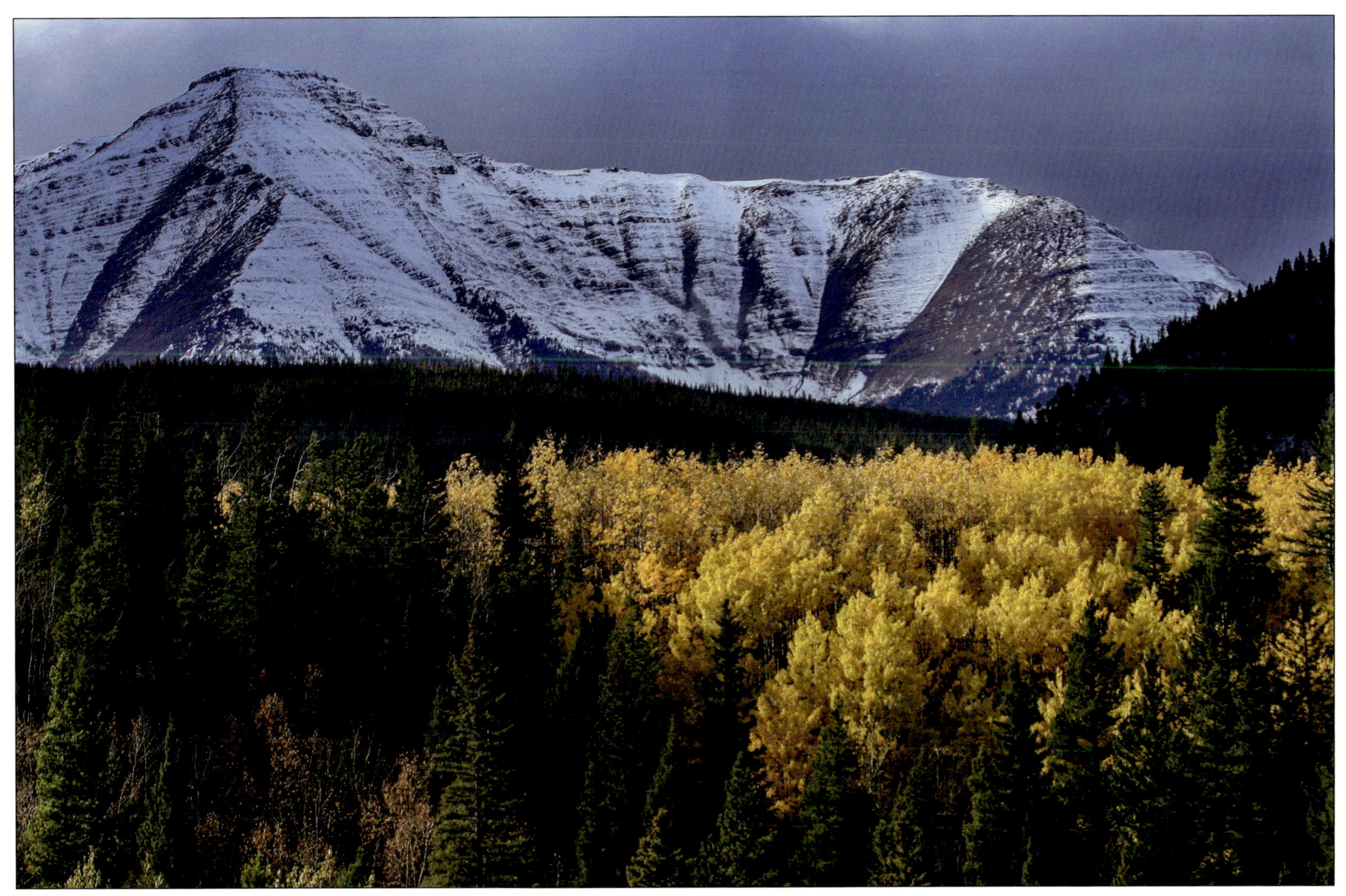

Autumn colour west of Turner Valley.

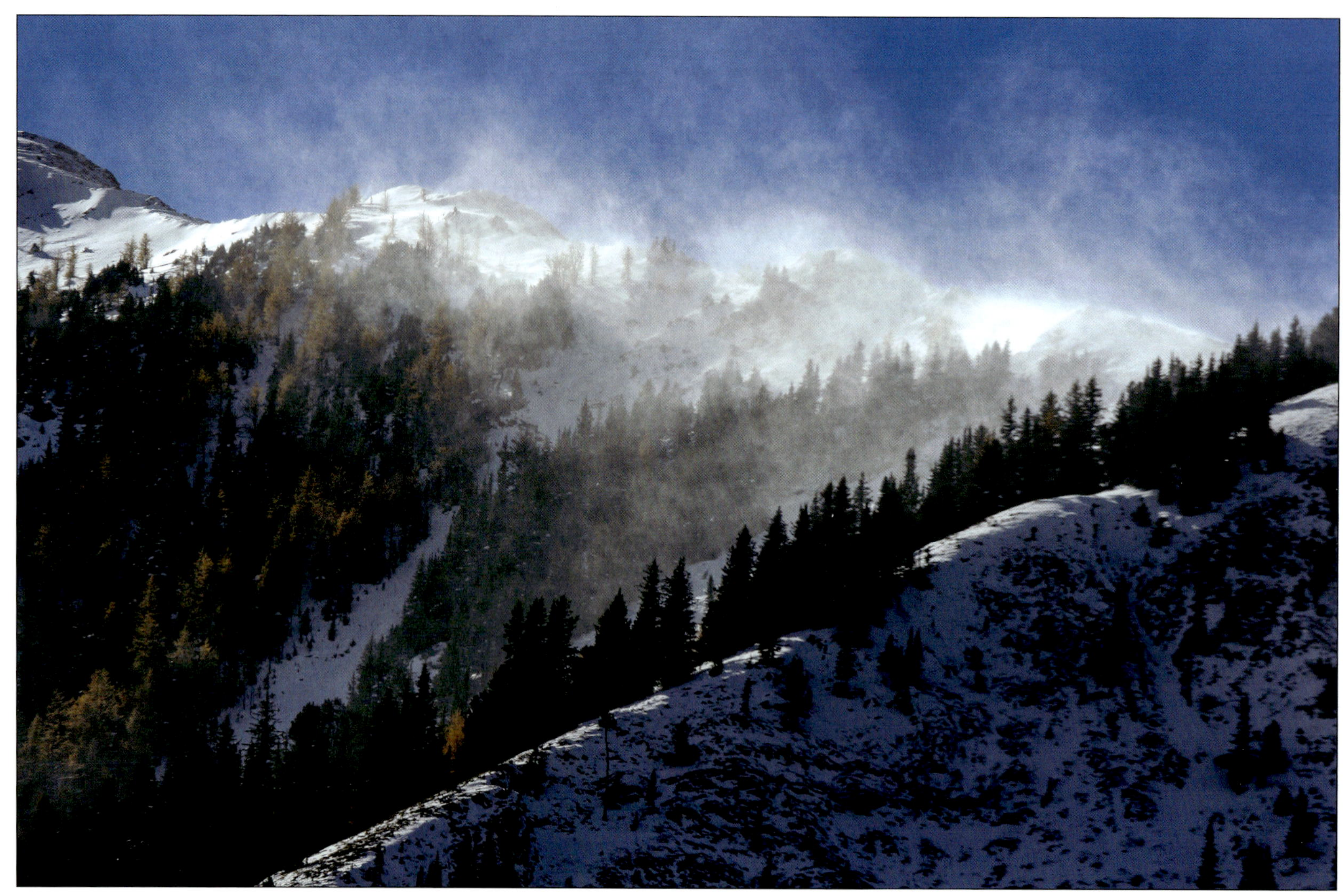

Early snow blows around on Highwood Pass.

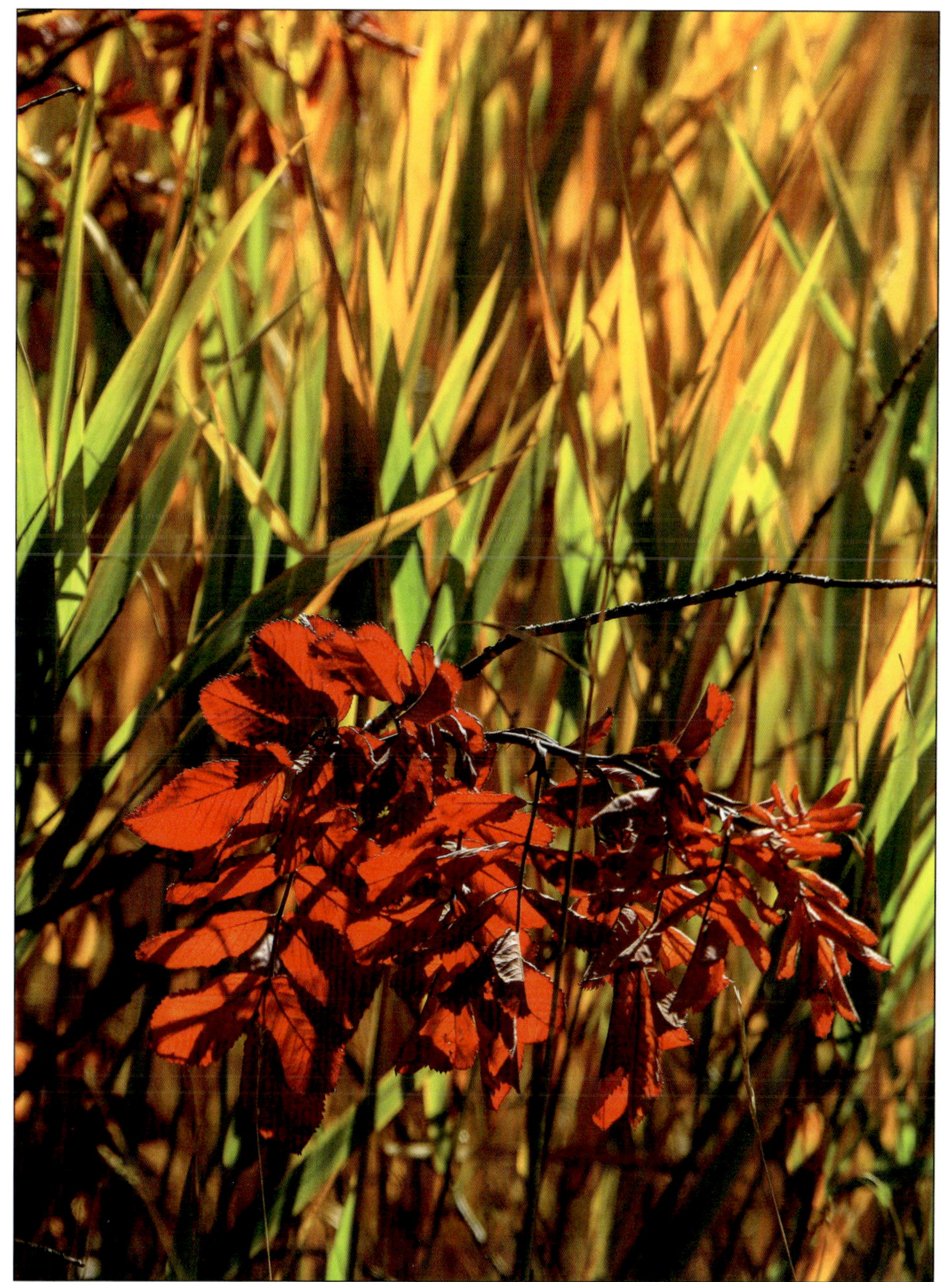

Roses and roadside grass glow near Highwood Pass.

SNOW

THAT LITTLE SKIFF OF SNOW we had mid-week?

It ain't nothing compared to snow country.

Out west, up in the mountains the snow piles up and it stays. Down here we get a little dusting and suddenly everybody's annoyed and driving as if the snow has somehow offended them. Doesn't matter that the sun will melt most of it off before midday. How dare it fall.

But up in the high country the snow comes early and stays late. And the citizens of the slopes don't seem to mind at all.

I headed west early, long before dawn, and turned onto the Banff Parkway not long after sunrise. First thing I saw was a couple of bighorn rams happily snorfing road salt off the pavement. They sure do love that stuff. I see them out gravel-grazing almost every time I head west.

And then, not a couple of kilometres down the road, I saw a pine marten bouncing through the snow looking for squirrels and mice. They're not exactly uncommon but they are forest animals so they're hard to see most of the time. But with all the snow and their contrasting red coats they become a little more visible.

I pushed on up over the pass and into BC past Lake Louise. There was a bit of sun shining through the clouds over the mountains and it lit up the snowy peaks above the Kicking Horse River. Normally I find the mountains a bit monotonous, but with lovely light I have to admit they look kinda nice.

There was a herd of elk lazing on the snow along the river near Field and I caught one big bull in mid-yawn. Then I turned up toward Emerald Lake.

The snow was piled like pillows among the trees. Soft and welcoming, it covered the fallen logs and draped across the branches. I paused at a little creek to shoot a couple of pictures but I couldn't linger. There were a lot of vehicles on that little road for a Tuesday.

I rolled on past Golden into the Columbia Valley. And out of snow country.

Maybe later in the year there'll be a blanket of white but this last week it was bare. I crossed over to the west side of the valley to look for a little more snow.

In the trees there was snow, but until I got up a little higher in the hills it was still pretty bare. Lots of deer, though. One little whitetail posed nicely for me in a patch of sunlight.

I didn't hit much snow again until I was past Radium and headed into Kootenay National Park. The river was lovely flowing through the snowy countryside, and it was just warm enough that the snow on the spruce boughs was melting.

Even though it was barely two in the afternoon, the sun was already dipping behind the mountain range to the west. But as it swept between the peaks it lit up the far side of the valley. A fire had roared through here a couple of years ago and the bare standing trees stood stark against the bright white.

Wildlife was a little more sparse through the valley but I came across a bull moose licking up salt just as I'd seen the sheep doing, and for some reason there were ravens everywhere.

Clouds snagging on the peaks dropped fitful little swirls of snow, but as I crossed back into Alberta the sun was shining again. I didn't really think I'd see any more wildlife, given the sun's position over the western horizon, but I hit the Banff Parkway again anyway.

And then I saw the elk.

It was a big bull and he was eating osier dogwood berries. There were a half-dozen cars parked on the road watching him nibble but he couldn't have cared less. Up to his hocks in snow, he licked out his long tongue to grab the branches and pulled off the berries with his lips.

Clearly, he wasn't bothered by the snow. It was just another day to him, snow or not. But then, he lives up in snow country, just like the bighorns, the marten, the moose and the ravens and all the other critters who manage to make their way through the snow seasons.

So next time we get a skiff of snow and every driver around us is doing something annoying, just remember that up in snow country, they don't gripe, they cope.

And anyway, there's always a chinook around the corner to melt it all away.

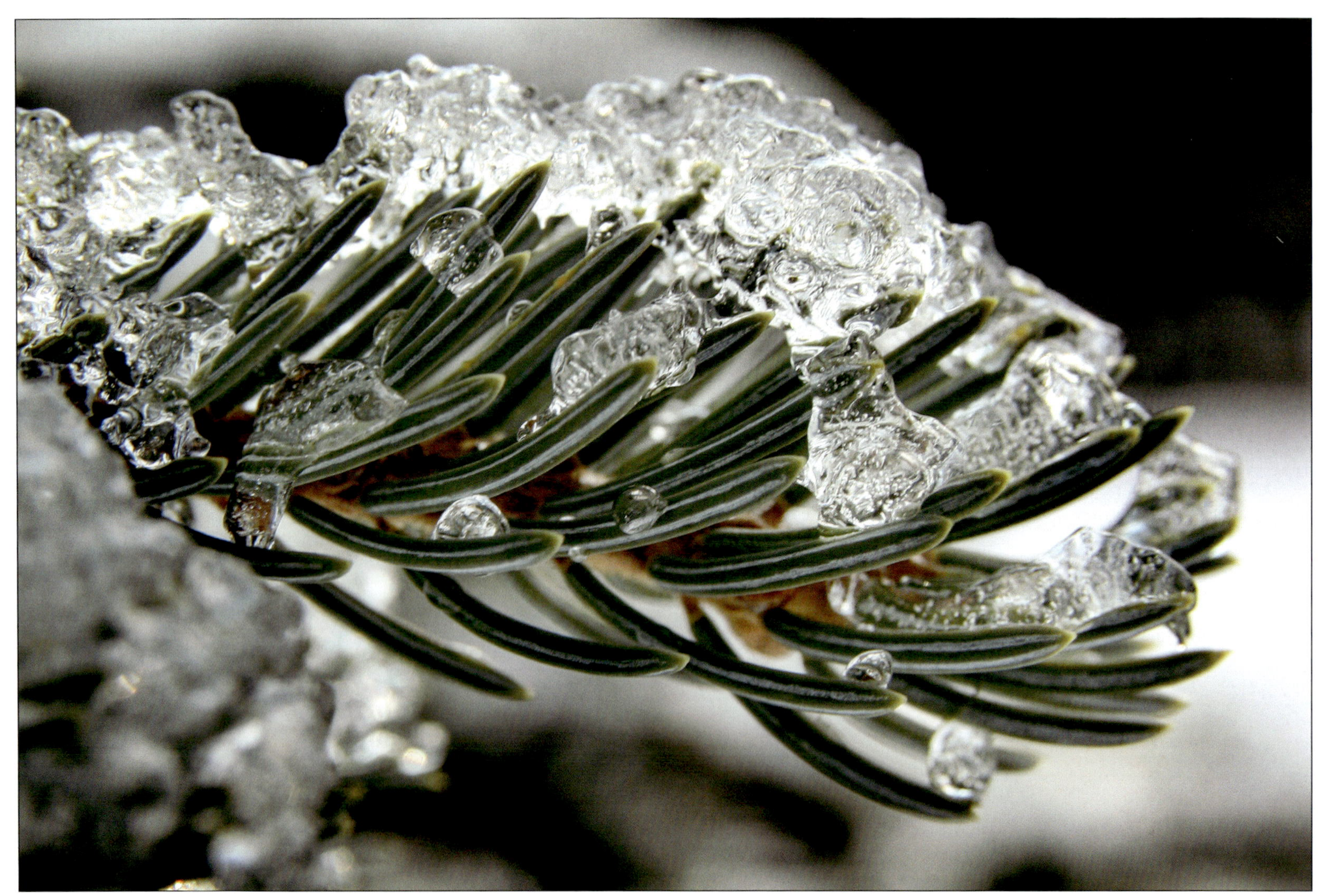

Snow melts just a little bit on a spruce bough along the Kootenay River in Kootenay National Park in BC.

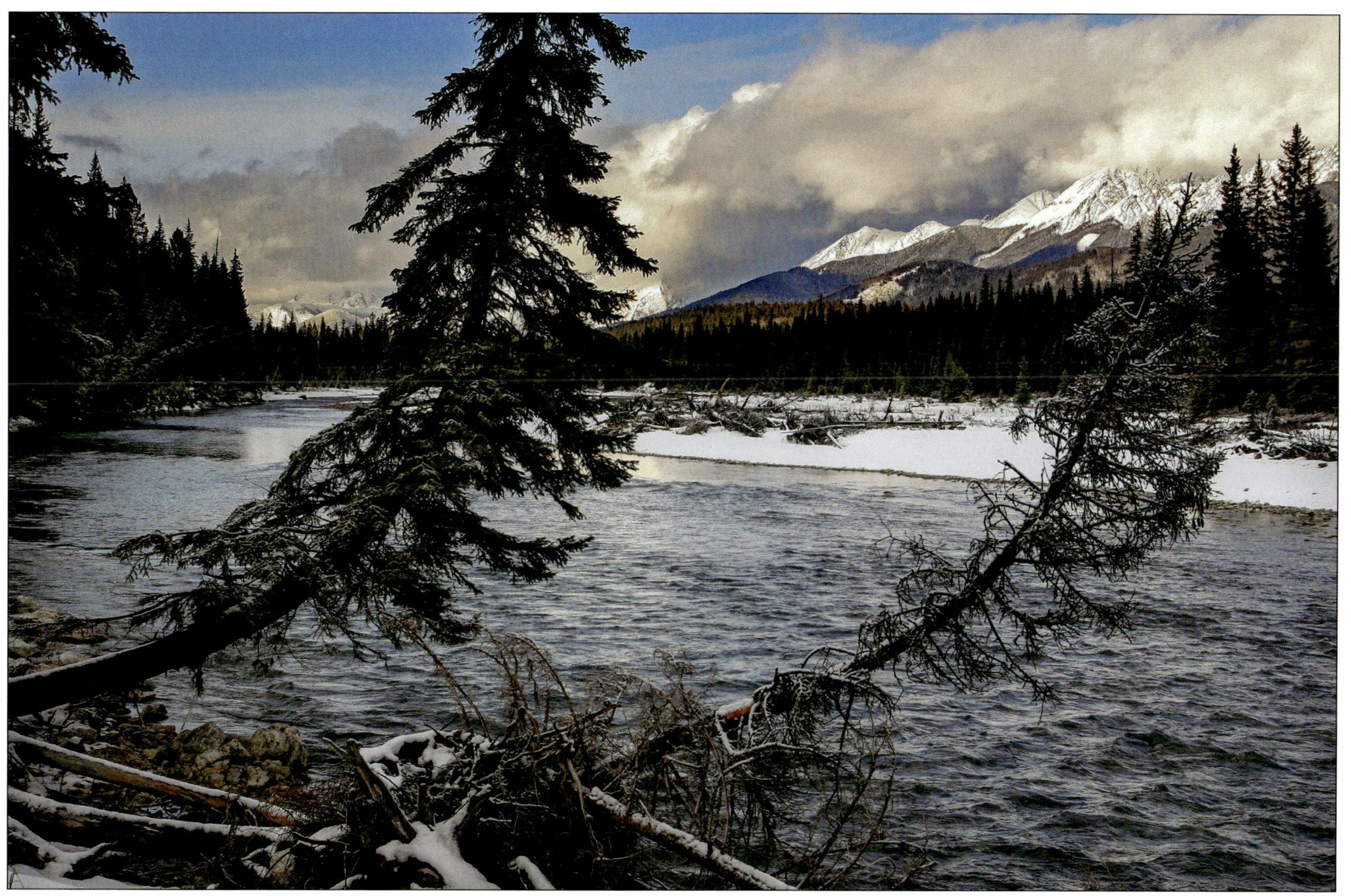

Clouds pushed by west winds snag on the mountains above the Kootenay River in Kootenay National Park in BC.

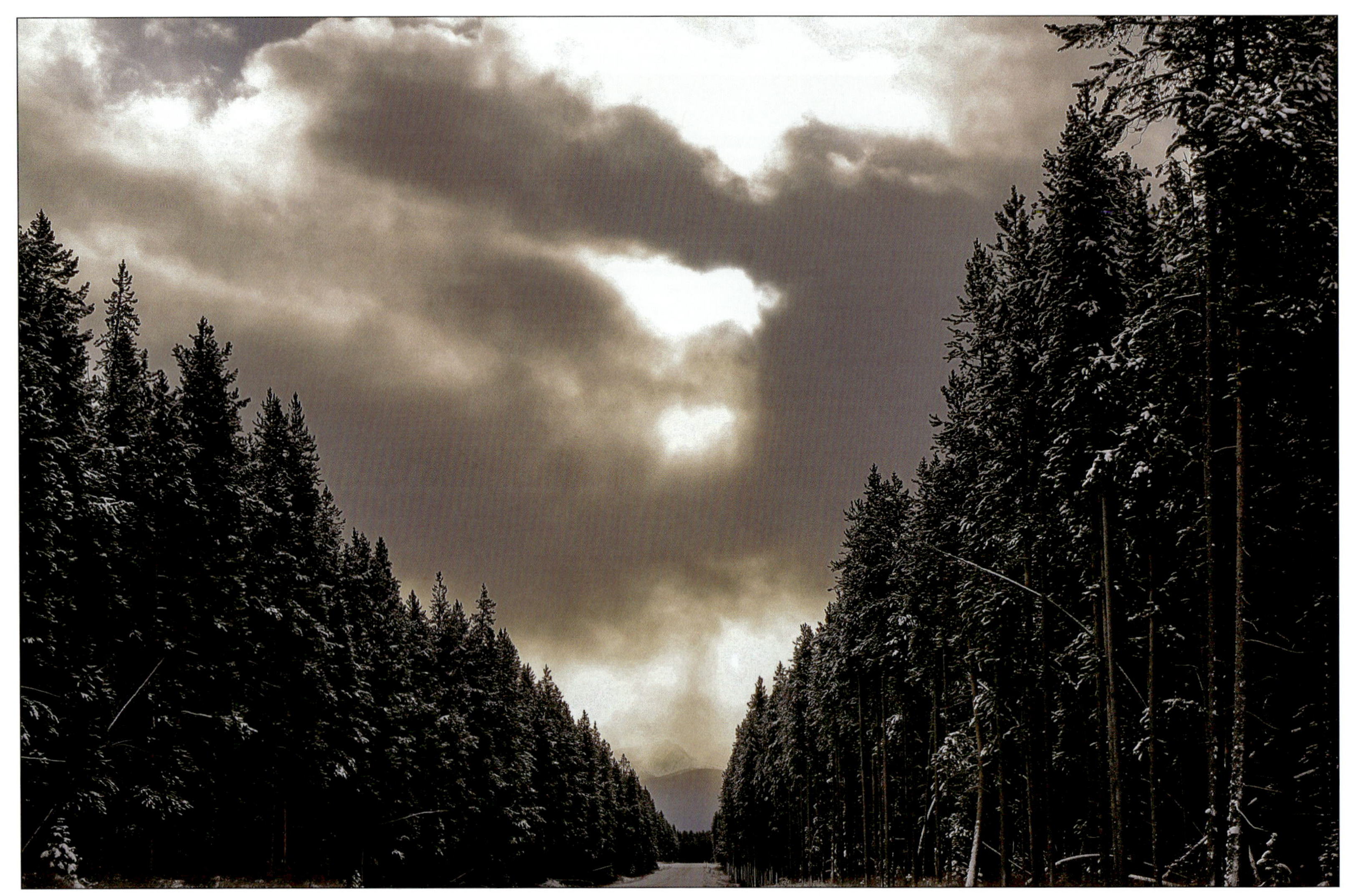

Clouds pushed by west winds stream over the Bow River valley near Castle Junction.

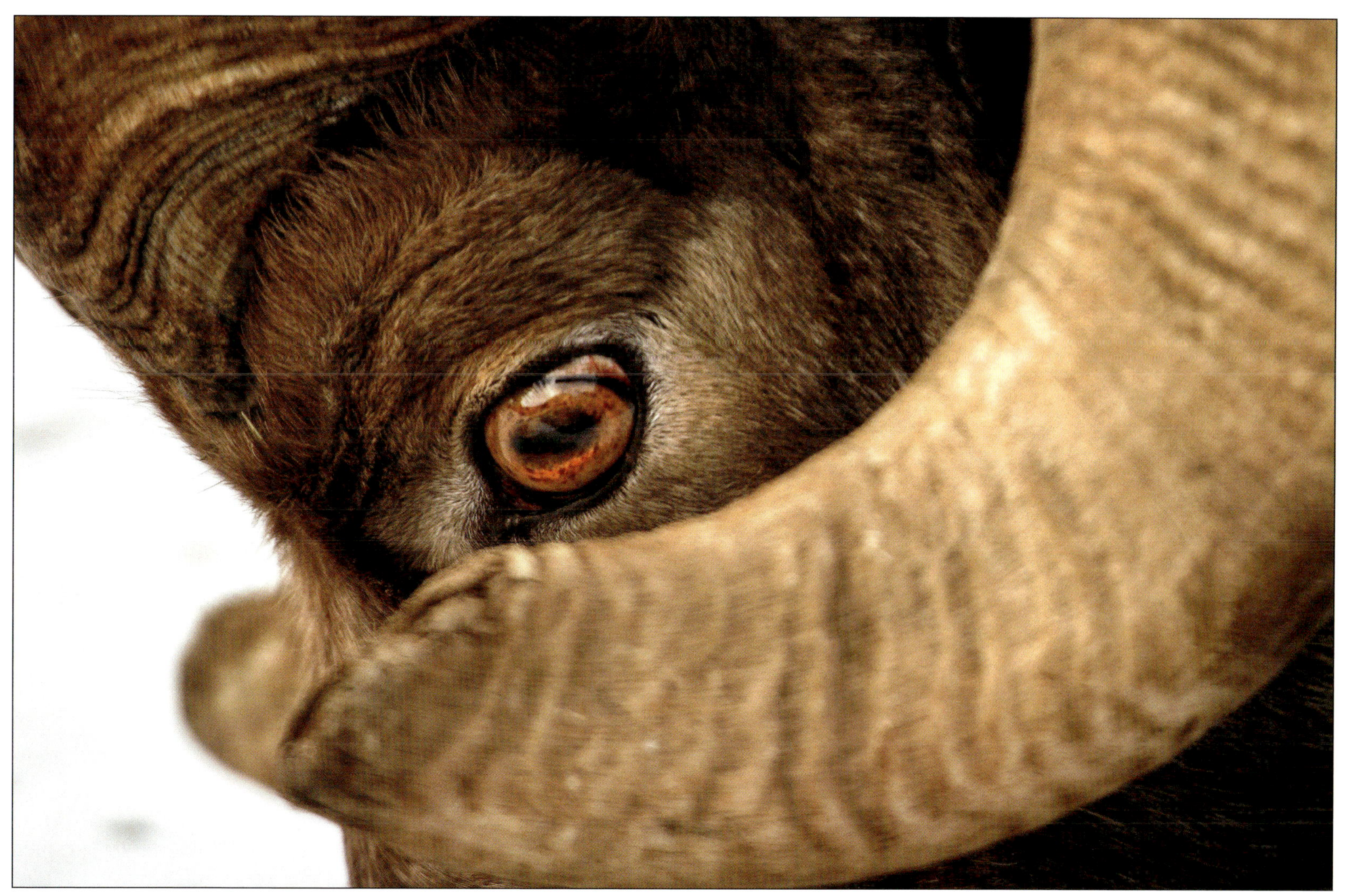

A bighorn ram slurps up road salt along the Banff Parkway.

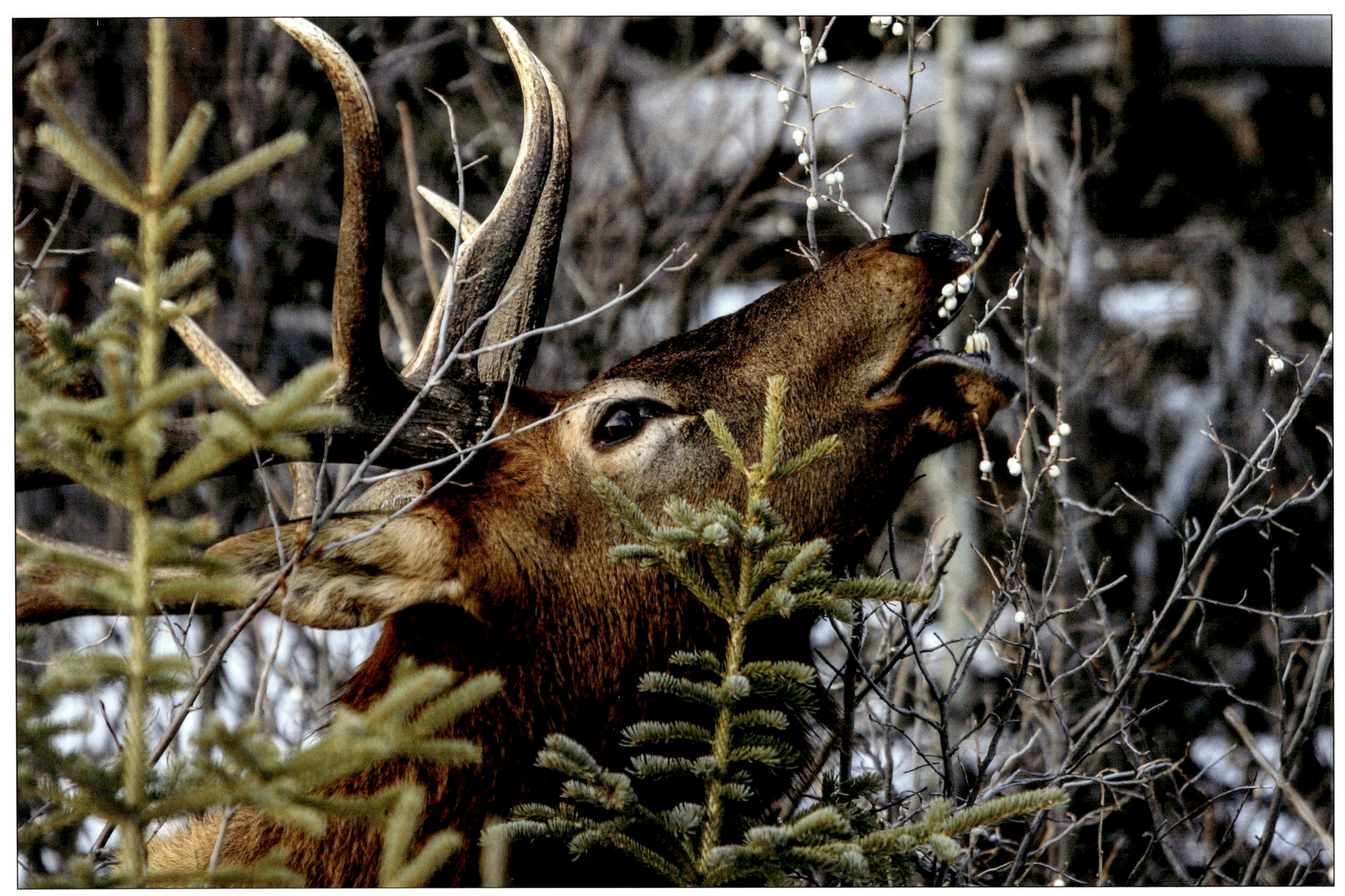

Those osier dogwood berries must have been mighty tasty. This bull elk barely noticed all the people who stopped to watch him nibble along the Banff Parkway.

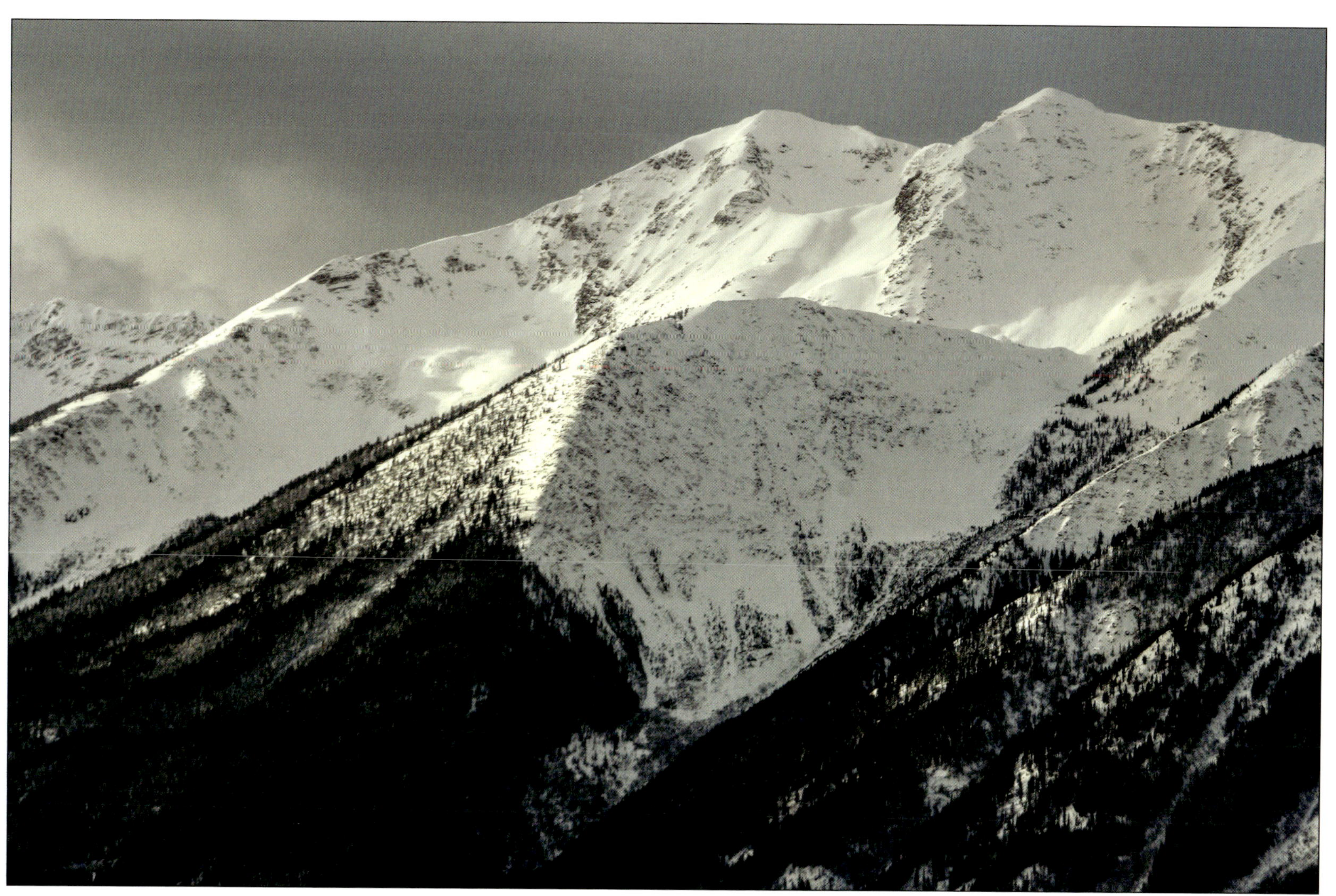

Snow in the high country above the Kicking Horse River.

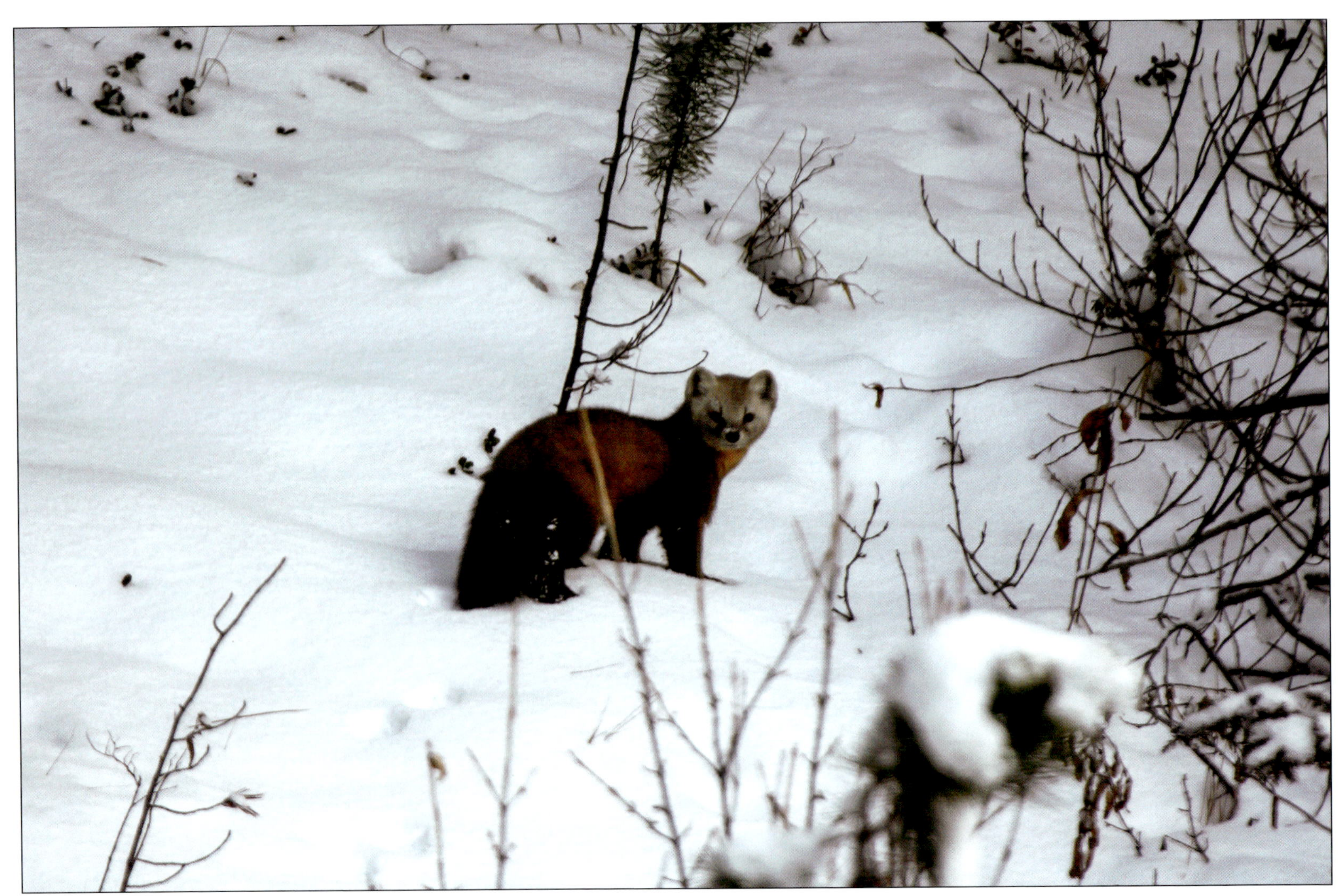

This pine marten paused in his hunt to pose along the Banff Parkway.

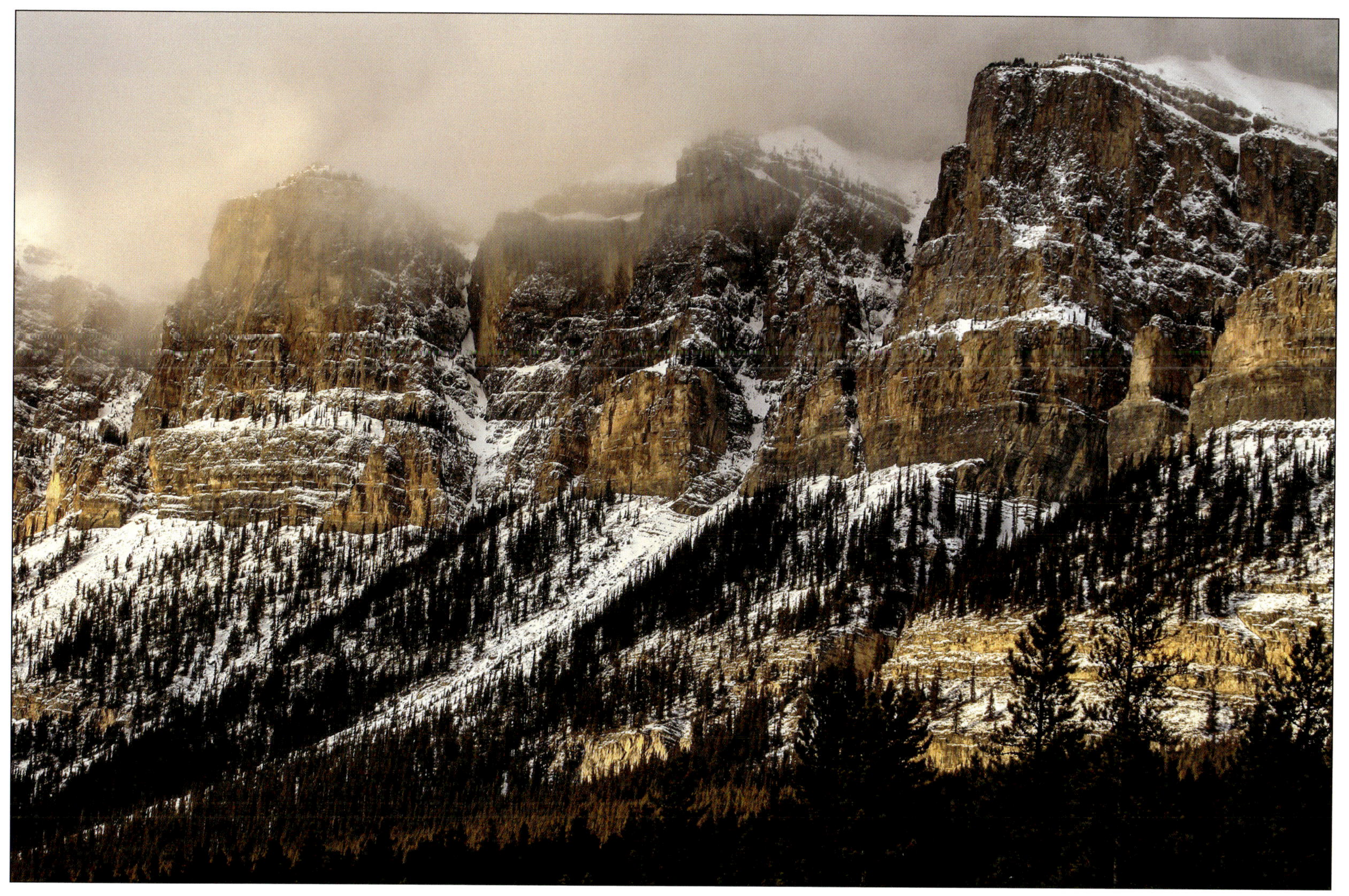

Castle Mountain in the Bow Valley.

W I N

T E R

MOON

THE AIR WAS CLEAR AND the sky was blue and the moon shone with a silver glow over Mossleigh.

Framed by the three elevators lined up along the town's main street, it looked like a point of light. Through my long lens I could see craters and what looked like vast dusty plains on its surface. As the sun set and the brightness of the day drained from the sky I could see it even more clearly. A bit longer lens and it seemed I might be able to see the Apollo astronauts' footprints.

I drove on into the gathering dusk to try to take some pictures by moonlight.

The sun had set and a long twilight began as I drove east through Arrowwood and on past Shouldice and Queenstown. I saw deer out on the fields in the deepening blue light and came across a rubbish fire burning behind an old farmhouse. It was kinda pretty, the orange glow of the flames rising behind the smoke into the indigo sky.

I hit fog patches at Milo but I could see the glow of the moon through the mist so I headed back north again toward Cluny, and just before Blackfoot Crossing the sky cleared again.

But it had turned cold. Not that it was exactly balmy back in the city, but the fog had marked a demarcation between warmer air to the west and a band of cold to the east. My mirrors fogged and I had to crank the heater a couple more notches to keep comfortable.

Bands of cloud covered swatches of the sky now but the moon still shone through and lit the countryside with a soft glow. The whiteness of the snow kicked the light around and here and there were the coloured specks of Christmas lights on farmhouses. I turned off the highway at Bassano to check out Bassano Dam by moonlight.

I drove slowly along the snow-covered roads leading to the dam and watched the countryside slide by in the silvery light. A couple of times I stopped and shut off the truck just to listen. A train was coming from somewhere to the west and I could hear the rumble of the engines long before I heard it sound its horn at a crossing. A dog barked somewhere off in the distance.

There was probably a 20 degree difference between here and the city, and the cold filled the truck as I drove along with the heater off to avoid warm air ripples when I stopped to take photos.

By the way, if you decide to drive in the country by yourself on a dark, cold winter night, don't listen to any audiobooks of Stephen King stories while you're doing it. I had *Salem's Lot* going and there were a couple of times when I could have sworn I saw something move just on the edge of the headlight's reach.

Mist was rising from the open water below the dam and swirling in the yellow sodium lights of the spillway. Frost covered everything. The moon had gone behind a band of thin cloud but most of its light still made it through, and the combination of moonlight and sodium vapour lamps gave the frosty cottonwoods and sagebrush a lovely glow.

I could hear geese down on the river calling up from the dark, and a light wind generated by the moving water shook the frosty sage. But it was cold standing there waiting for the camera to finish its long exposures. I headed back west again.

I passed back through the fogbank near Crowfoot Creek – another Stephen King shiver at that – and was back into warmer air by Gleichen. I paused for more pictures on Hammer Hill.

This time the moonlight was undiminished by clouds and the long exposures rendered an almost daytime look to the scene. Had the horses I was shooting known to stay perfectly still for 15 seconds it would have looked like mid-afternoon. Well, except for the stars in the sky. Moonlight is just reflected sunlight so even though it looks bluish, it actually has the same colour spectrum as daylight.

I drove on toward the city under the light of the last waxing moon of the year. It would be in its full glory on New Year's Eve just a couple of days later, but the forecast called for clouds and snow. This would be the last moonlight of 2009.

Not a bad way to end the year, driving in the country with the moonlight's silver sheen. But what's that just on the edge of the headlights? Something moving. Something with very sharp teeth.

Just a coyote trying to outrun me. I slowed until it turned off into a field. Maybe next time I do this I'd better listen to a Christopher Moore audio book. *Coyote Blue*, maybe?

Welcome to 2010.

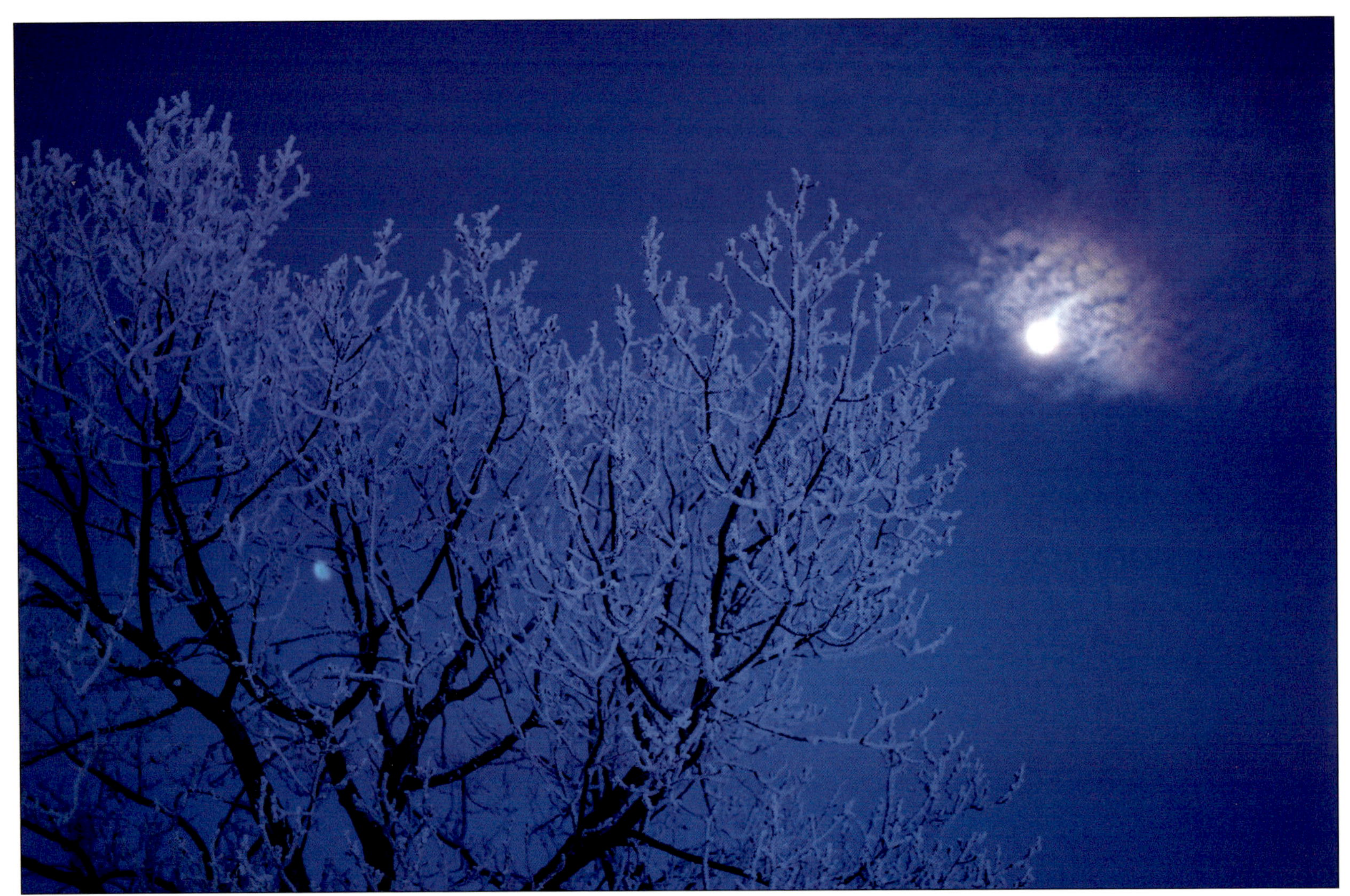

The moon already high in the sky an hour after sunset near Queenstown.

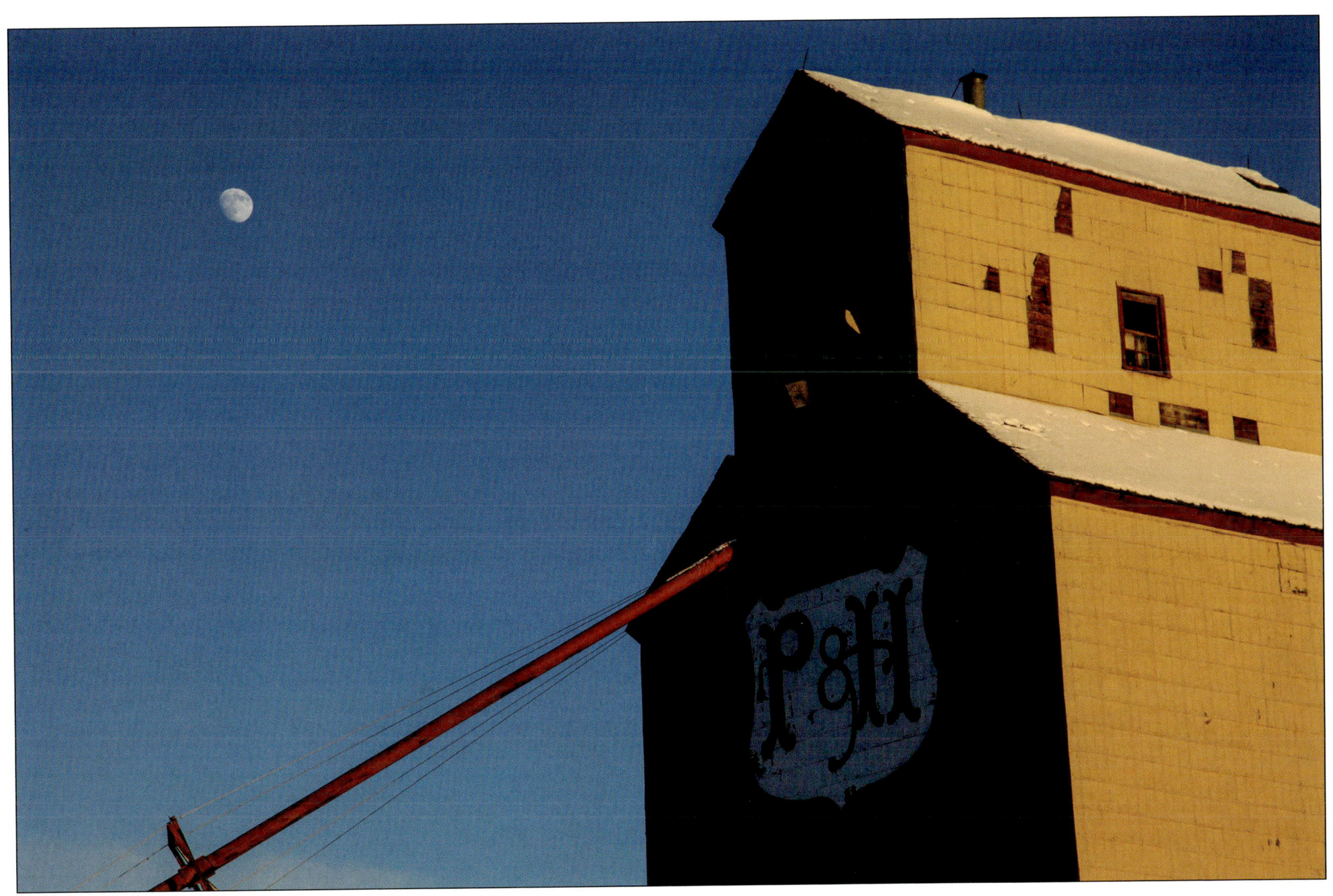

A nearly full moon hangs in the sky over the elevators at Mossleigh.

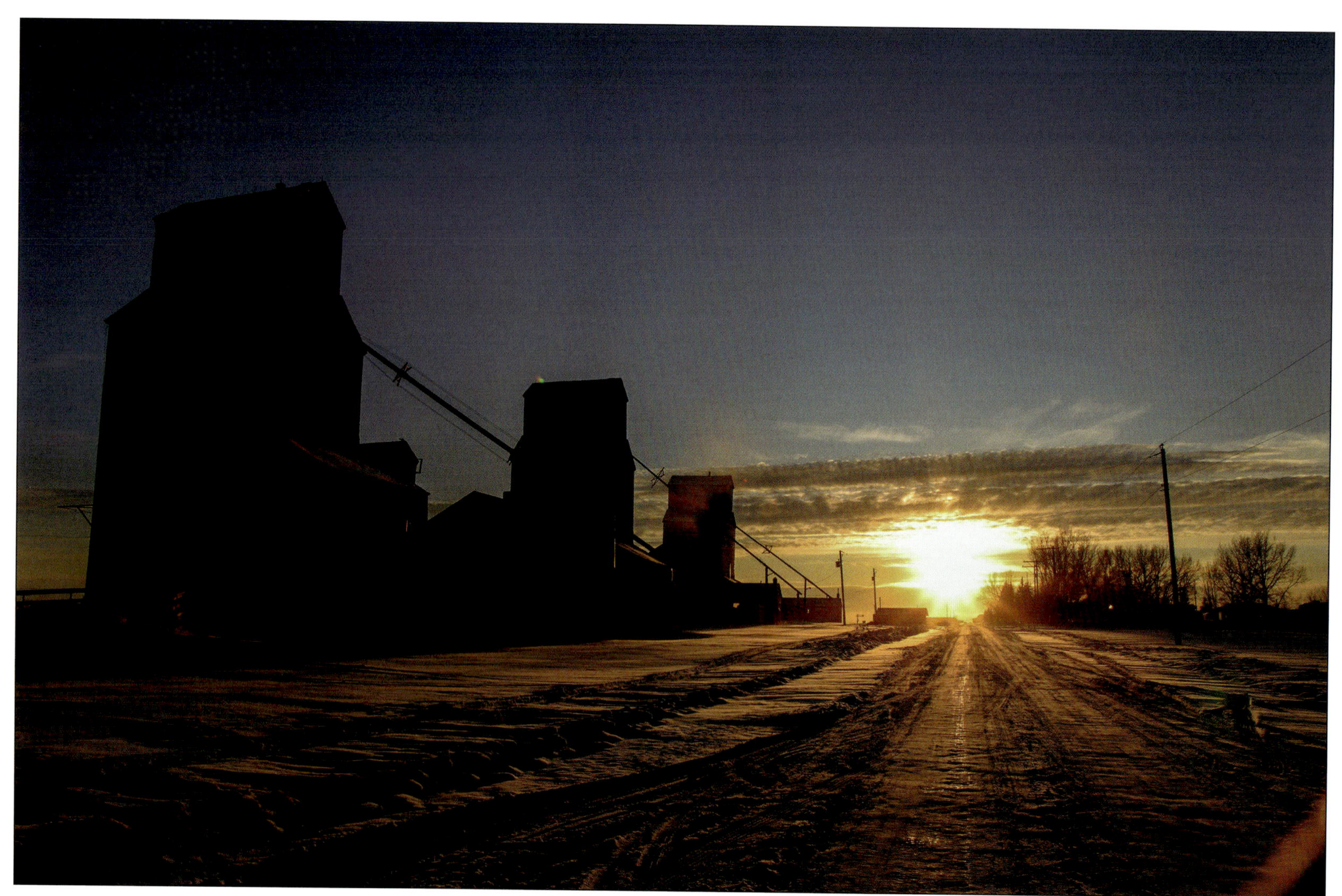

The sun sets at the end of the main street at Mossleigh.

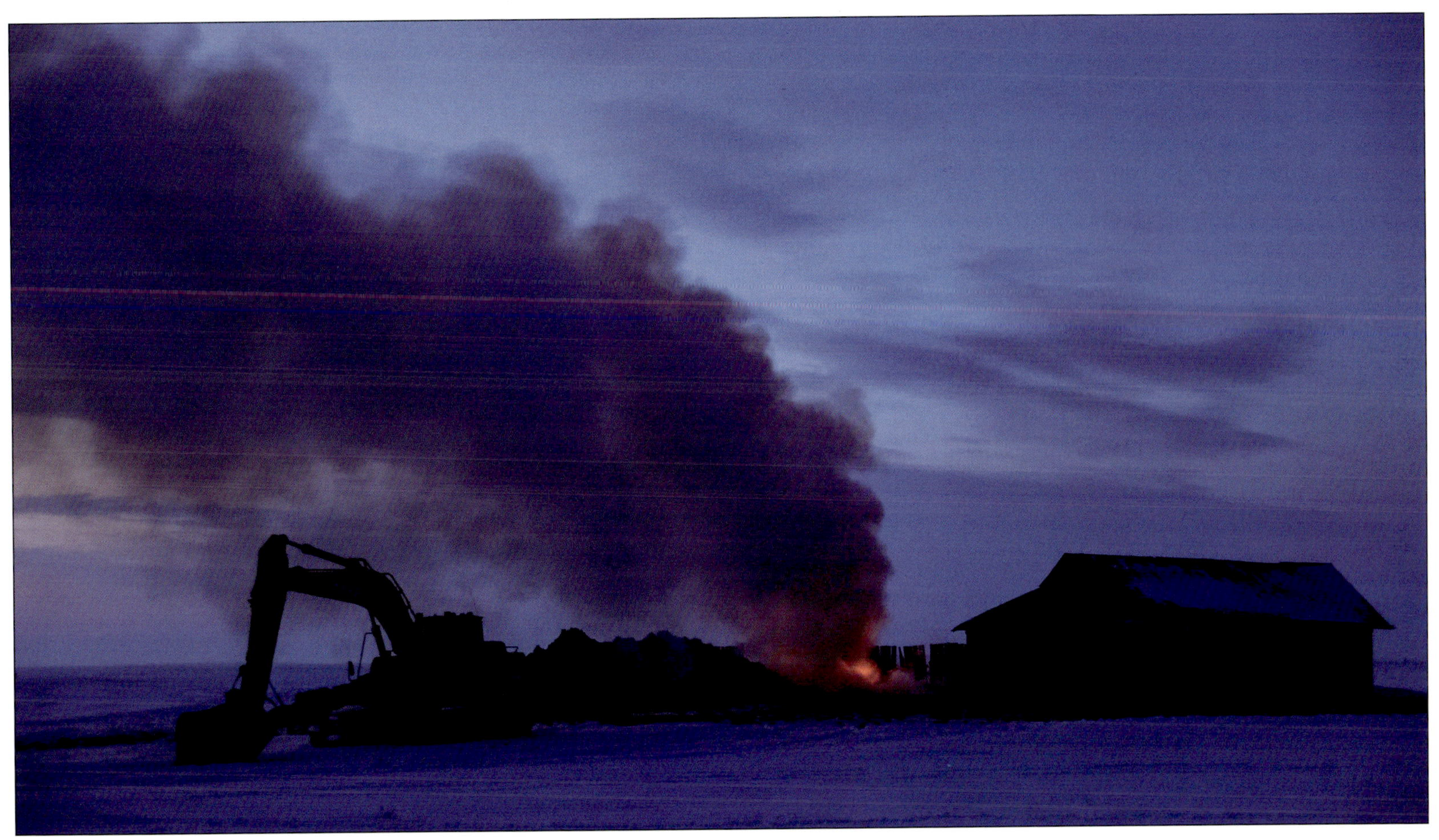

A rubbish fire adds a slight orange glow to the blue dusk near Queenstown.

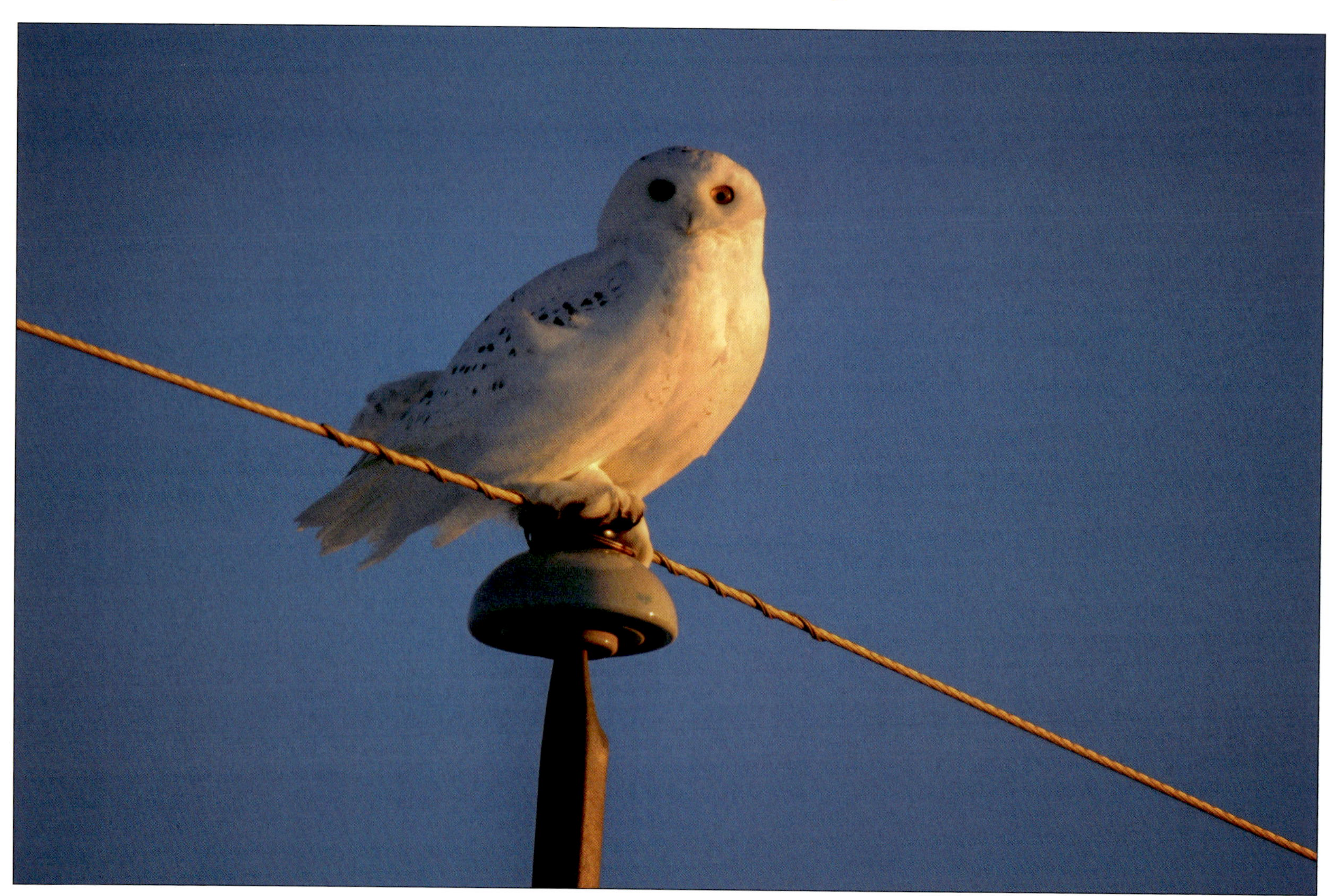

A snowy owl stares back at the camera.

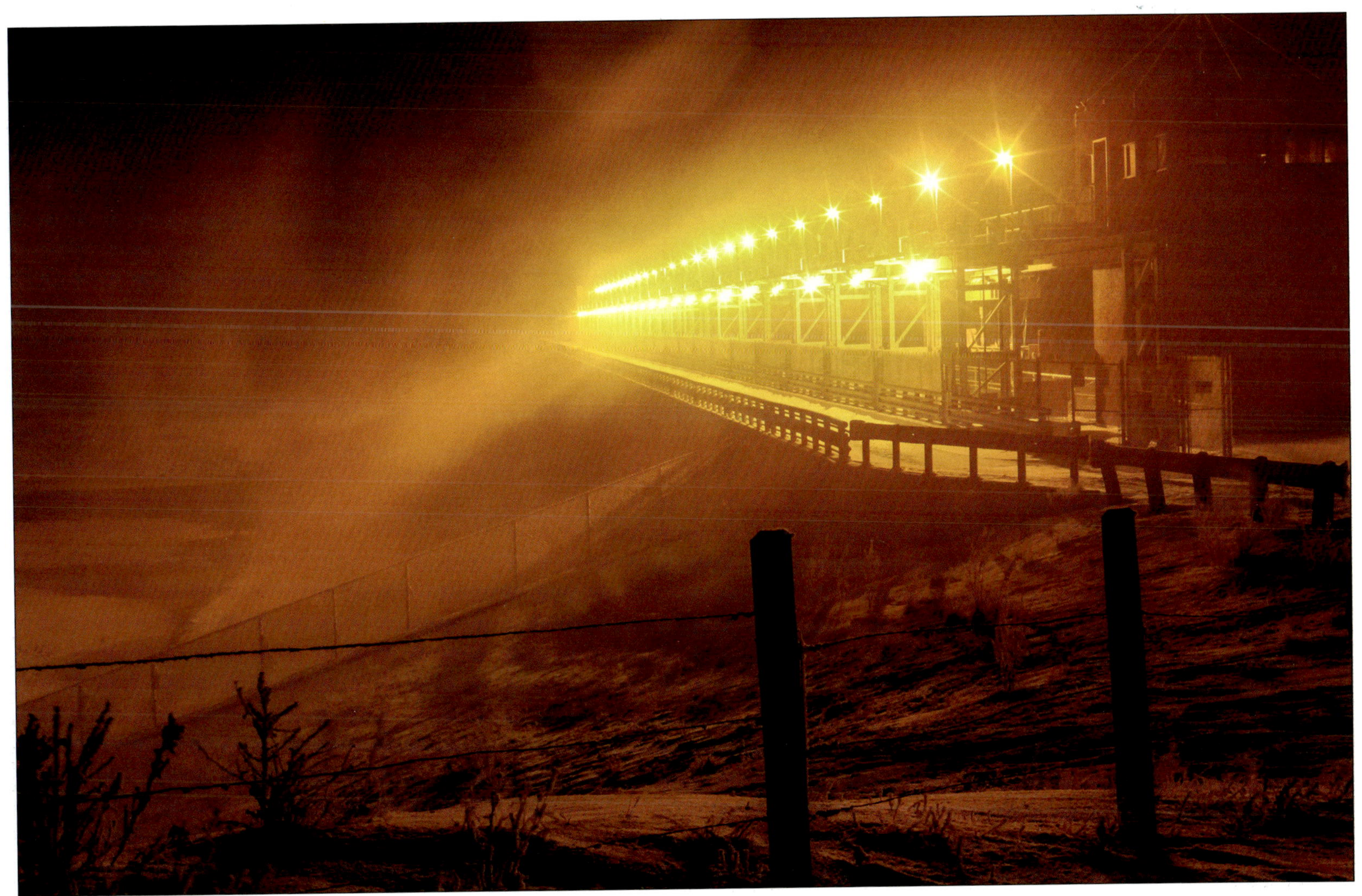

Cold mist rises from the spillway of Bassano Dam.

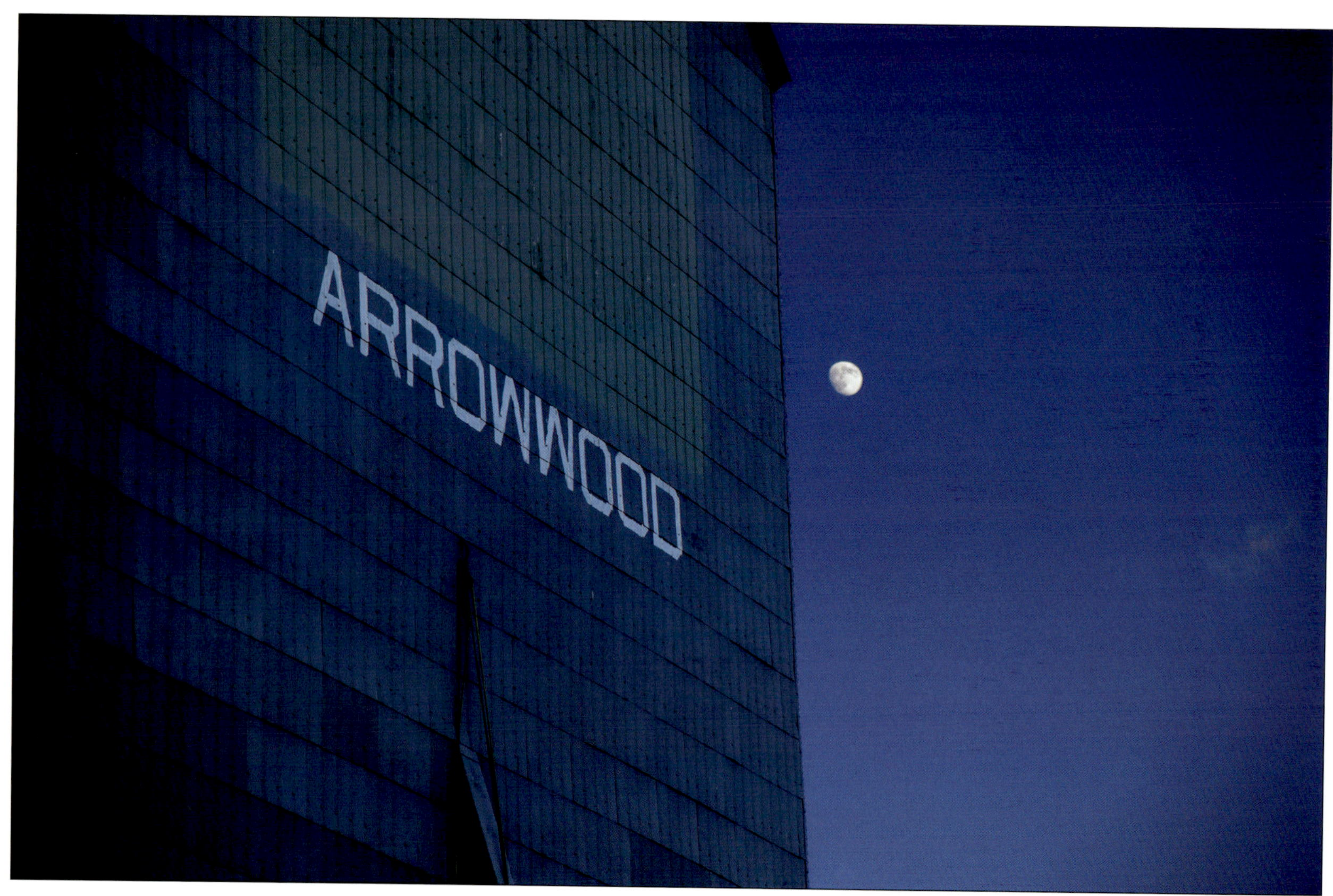

Moonrise at Arrowwood.

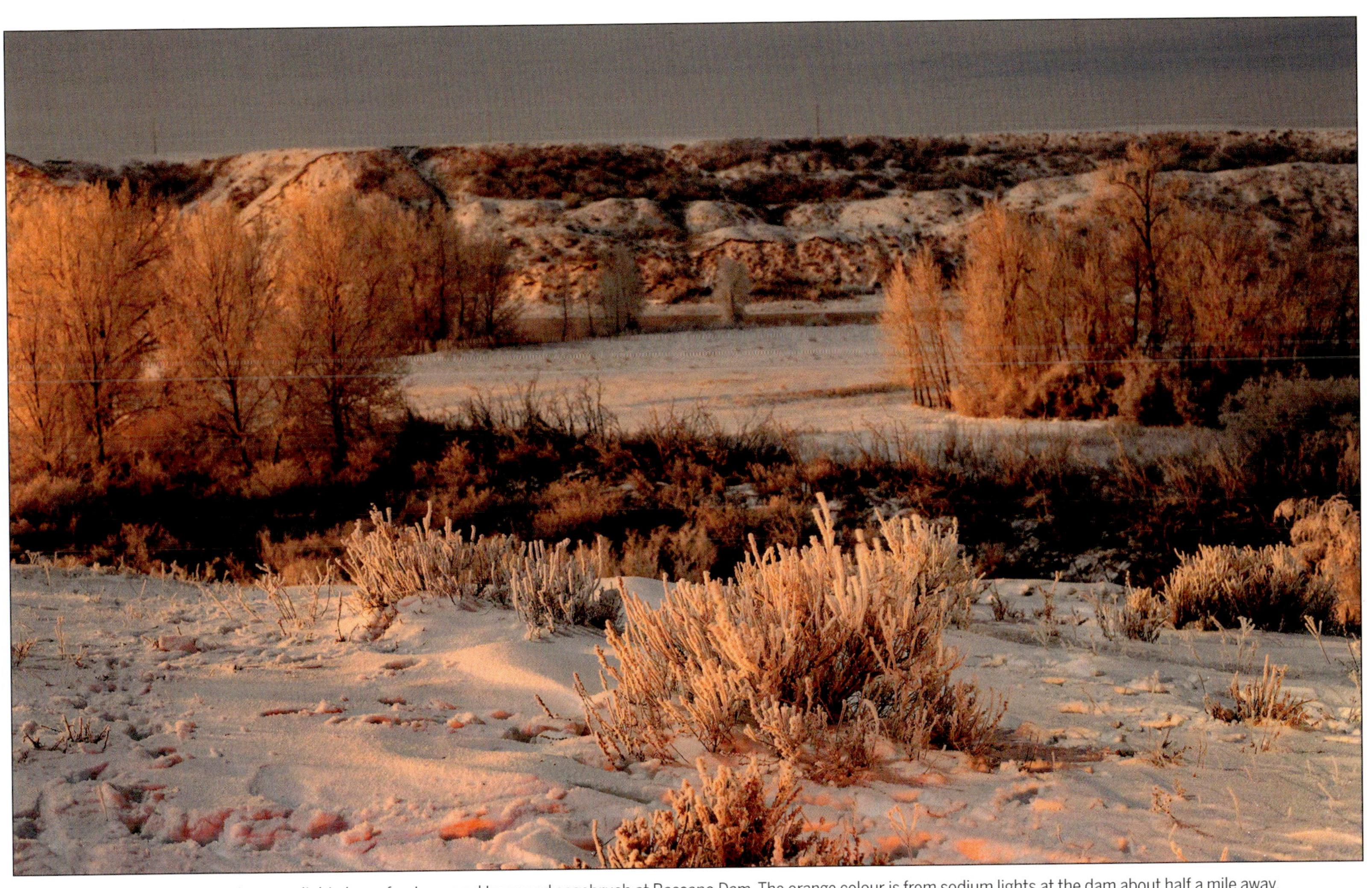

A long exposure under moonlight shows frost-covered trees and sagebrush at Bassano Dam. The orange colour is from sodium lights at the dam about half a mile away.

SNOWY PLAINS

I JUST BARELY PICKED OUT THE big ears poking through the snow as I drove by.

Turning around up the road I eased back to where I'd seen the ears for another look. There were the ears again, right on top of a pair of curious eyes. But the snow was so deep that was about all I could see.

No, I wasn't up on Smith-Dorrien Trail headed to Spray Lakes and, no, I wasn't in those lovely Porcupine Hills. I was out on the prairie along the Red Deer River just north of Buffalo.

This is normally dry country, not much rain in summer and not much snow in winter. But this year, the snow clearly didn't get the email.

The little mule deer I had lined up in my lens was lying down among some cottonwoods along the river, and when it stood up for a better look at me, the snow there in the riverine forest came nearly up to its belly. Just up the road momma and a sibling were relaxing in a more open part among the trees. The snow there was almost as deep.

I noticed the snow as the sun was coming up near Brooks. I'd pulled off onto a side road to shoot a picture of a tree against the sunrise, and I could immediately see that there is a whack more snow out there than there is near the city.

Now that might not be much of a surprise given all the news coverage of blizzards out that way, highway closures and all that stuff, but as a boy who grew up on the prairie I can tell you that there is more snow out that way right now than I can remember seeing in a very long time.

Heading north from Tilley toward Dinosaur Park as the day brightened, I passed pastures with cattle standing hock-deep and stands of buffaloberry and willows nearly buried under mounds of snow. I had to abandon my original plan of wandering the snowy badlands at Dinosaur because the snow in the public-access area of the park was nearly knee-deep. Not a lot of fun pushing through that.

But the day was shaping up to be pretty nice so I rolled on east anyway.

The sagebrush country past Patricia and Princess was covered in snow, and when I made the turn to follow the old railroad tracks to Iddesleigh I had to pick my way along a path between fresh snow drifts. The wind had picked up a bit at Jenner and little finger drifts were starting to form along the highway.

The clouds were changing constantly overhead, alternating eyeball-searing snow glare with blue shadows on the vast white expanse laid out in front of me. The grasslands of the Suffield army range were completely covered and big drifts filled every farmyard along the roadway. Turning north at Buffalo, I crossed the Red Deer River.

After stopping for a few minutes to photograph the family of mulies, I rolled on across the snowy valley and headed farther north. In a more normal year there would be grass showing through the snow on the south-facing slopes of the valley and cattle would have stomped their way through to the pasture grass in at least a few places on the valley bottom.

But there was no grass showing anywhere. The wind was blowing just hard enough to move a little bit of loose snow, and I could see where drifts had piled up in places. But the snow was consistently deep everywhere, drifts or not.

There were antelope on the benchlands above the valley, a herd of maybe a hundred or so that were in a big open field. It's amazing how well they blend in with the landscape in their pale winter coats. In a normal year you could roll right past one, thinking that the mass lying there was a patch of grass with a couple of splashes of snow, until it got up to run away.

Snow buntings wheeled away in front of me as I continued along the north side of the Red Deer River valley. In summertime this is a good place to look for rattlesnakes, but now they're deep underground waiting out the winter and, let me tell ya, they've got a lot of winter to wait out.

Ranchers hauling feed to their cattle had packed down the snow in places but the rabbit brush and sage barely stuck through anywhere and the huge patches of cactus I know line the hillsides were nowhere to be seen.

Herefords and longhorns share these pastures with horses, antelope and deer. The Herefords are thick-bodied and look like they can pretty much ignore most weather, but those longhorns don't have the bulk and those runway-model hips don't look like they could push much snow. Makes me wonder how they survive on the northern plains.

I stayed on the north side of the river past Jenner and rolled on to Wardlow before turning back south again. The snow stayed heavy all the way and the bright sun glaring off it was starting to give me a squint headache. Mule deer seemed to be everywhere – I must have seen more than 200 of them – and I saw at least a dozen prairie falcons. Okay, maybe a couple of them were gyrfalcons. I have trouble telling them apart at a distance. Never did get a picture of any of them.

Heading back west through Rosemary and on to Bassano, I could feel the temperature rise as I drove. It had been pleasantly warm out east but by the time I hit the hills northwest of Gleichen I was driving in slush. There were patches of dry gravel here, too, and for a few kilometres I was kicking up dust.

Which is what usually happens out east any time of year. But not right now. There's more snow on the prairies along the Red Deer River than I can ever remember seeing.

And it is an awesome sight, all that glittering whiteness stretching off to the horizon in every direction. And maybe it's not that unusual. I don't live out there so I don't know for sure.

All I do know is that when it melts those coulees are going to run like rivers and there won't be a dry dugout anywhere.

I hope the mulies don't mind wet feet.

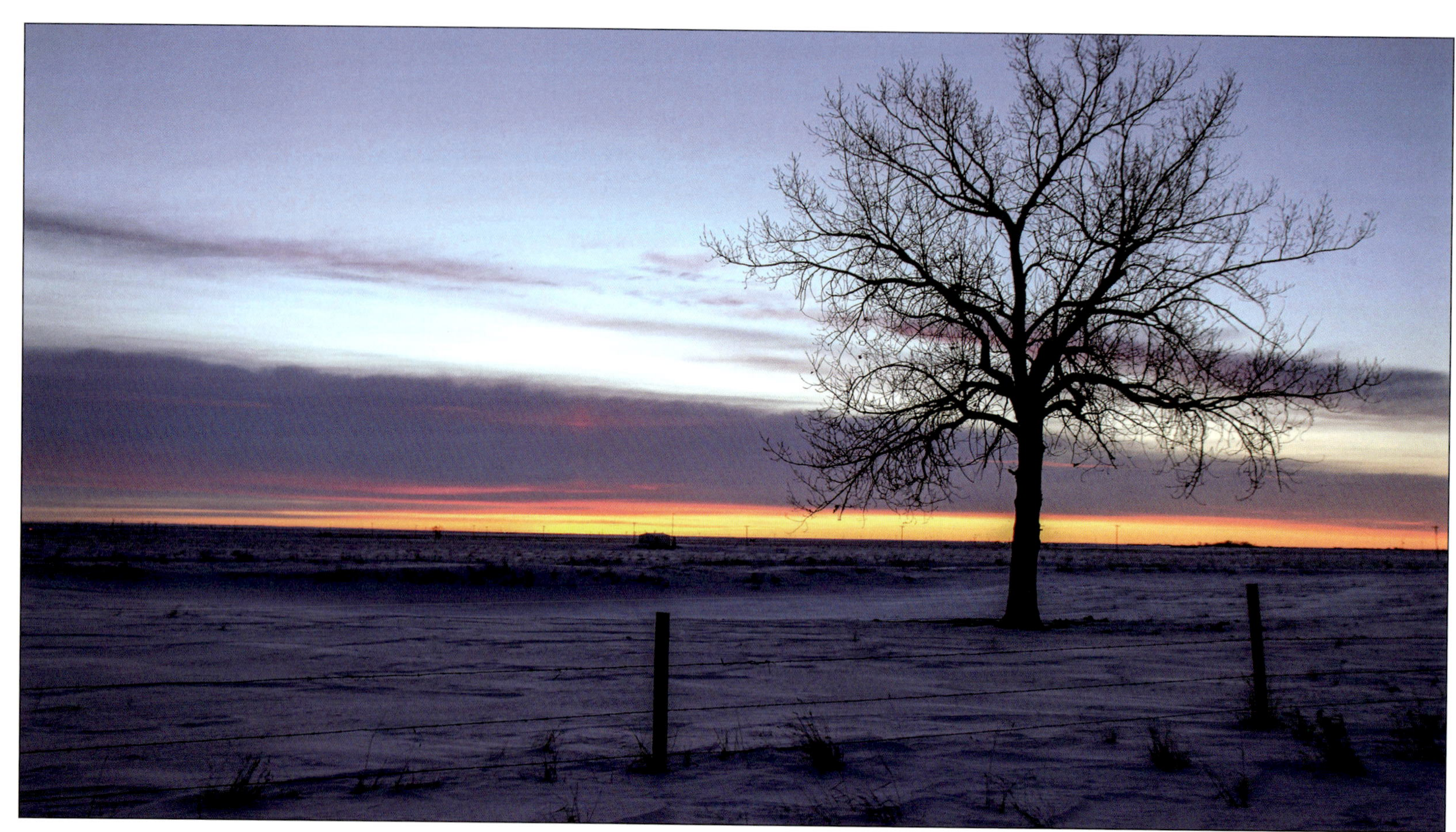

Chinook sunrise on the prairie near Tilley.

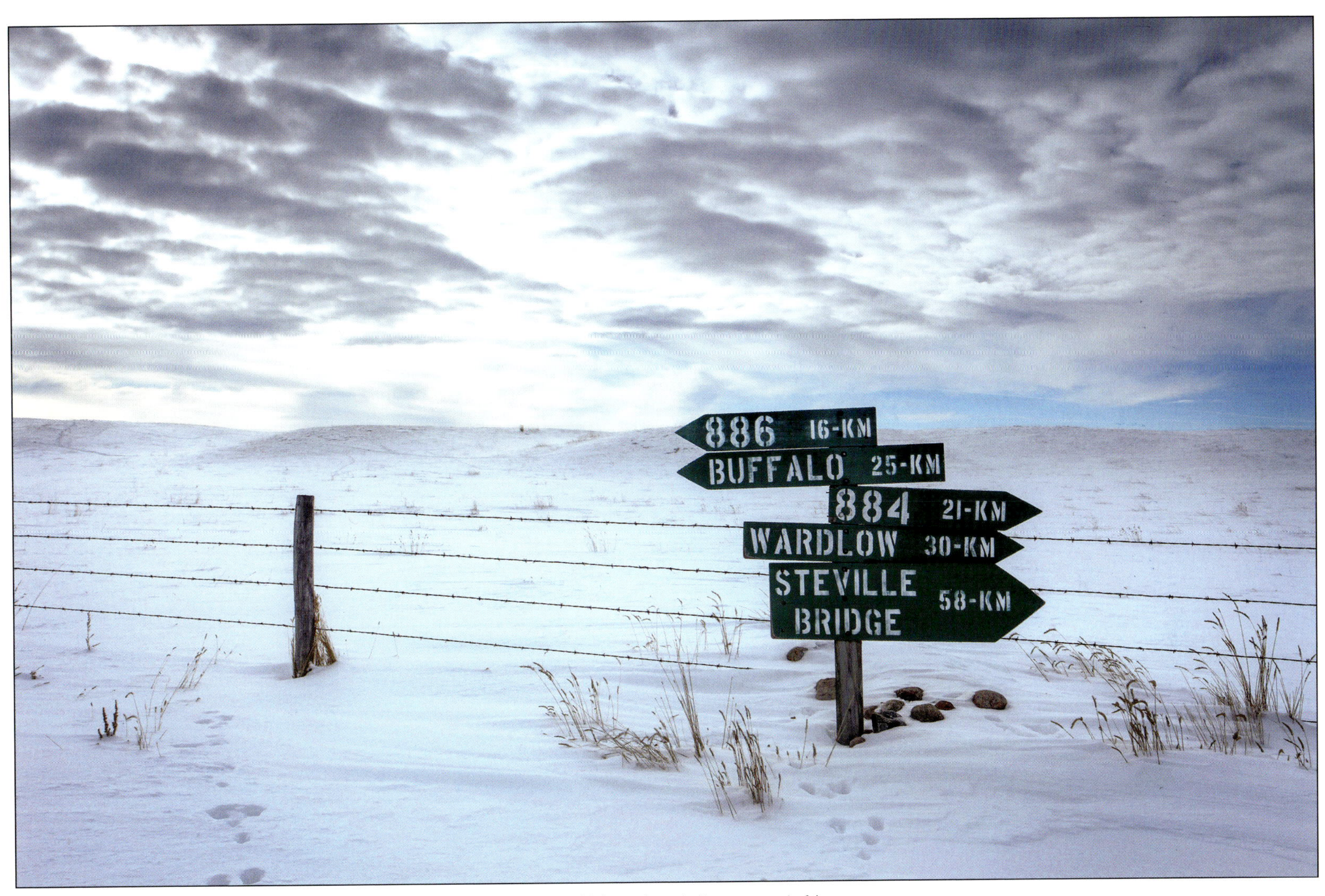

So you know which way to go in the snow east of Jenner.

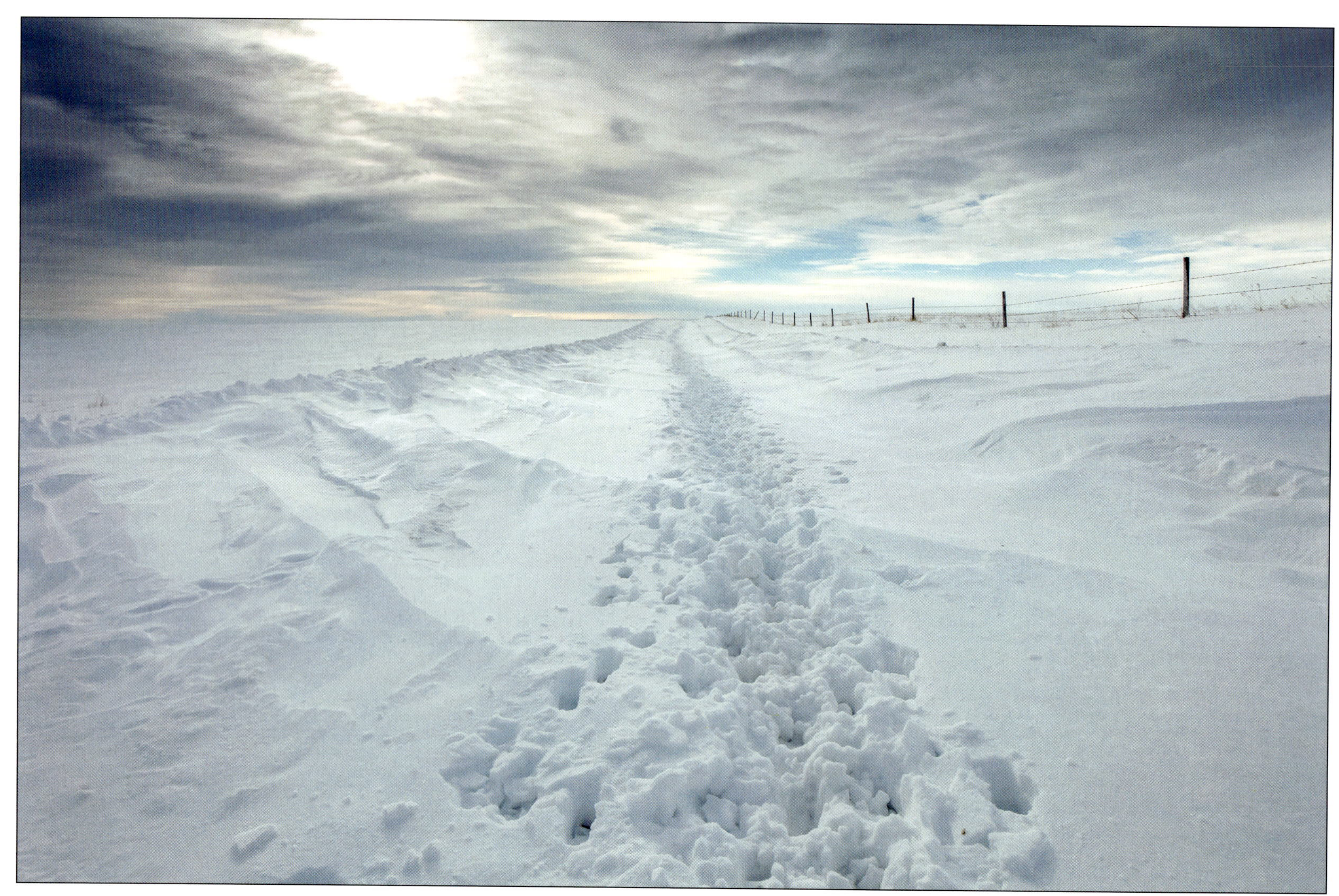

Antelope tracks in the snow along the Red Deer River benchlands north of Buffalo.

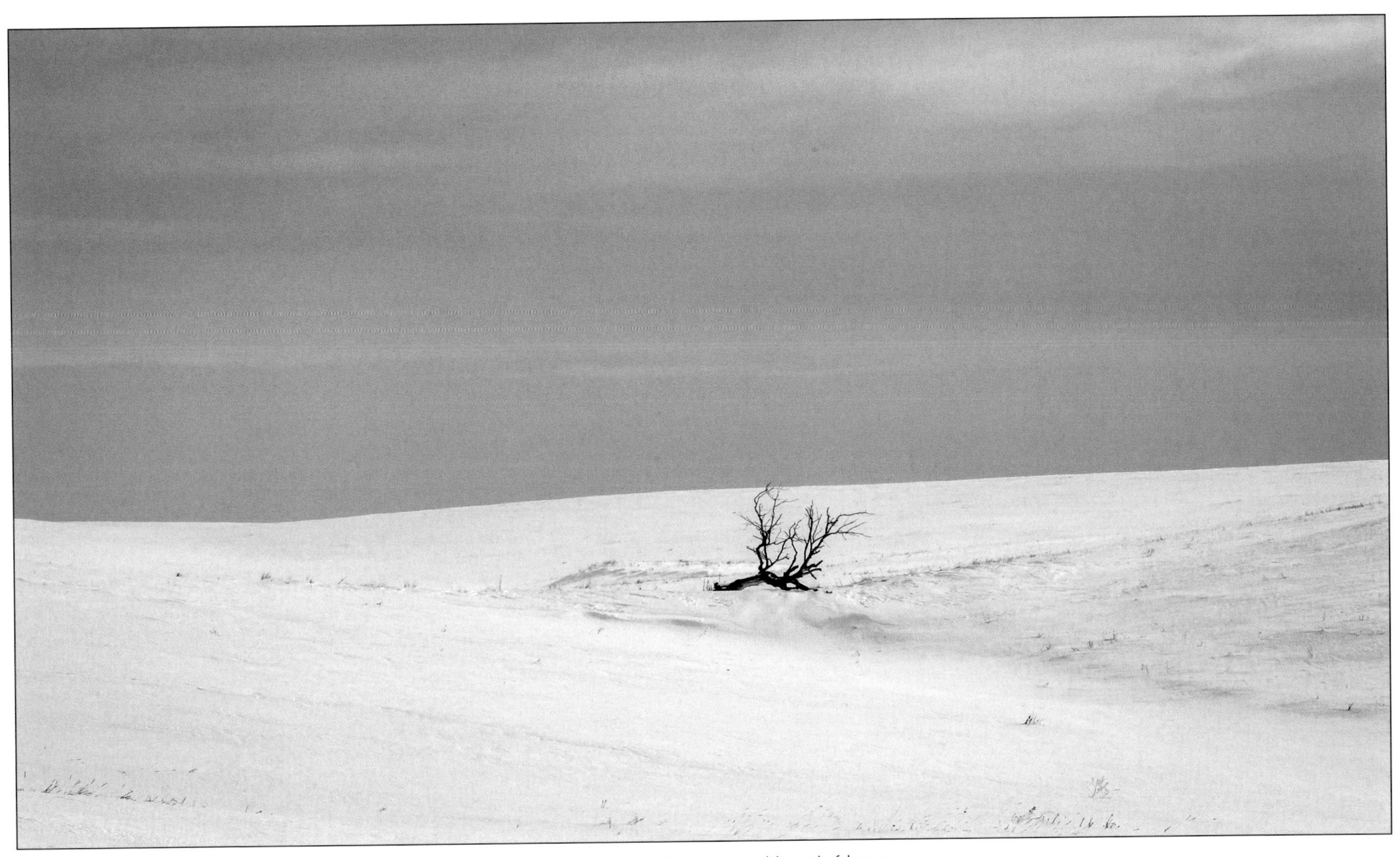

Snow meets sky on the snowy prairie east of Jenner.

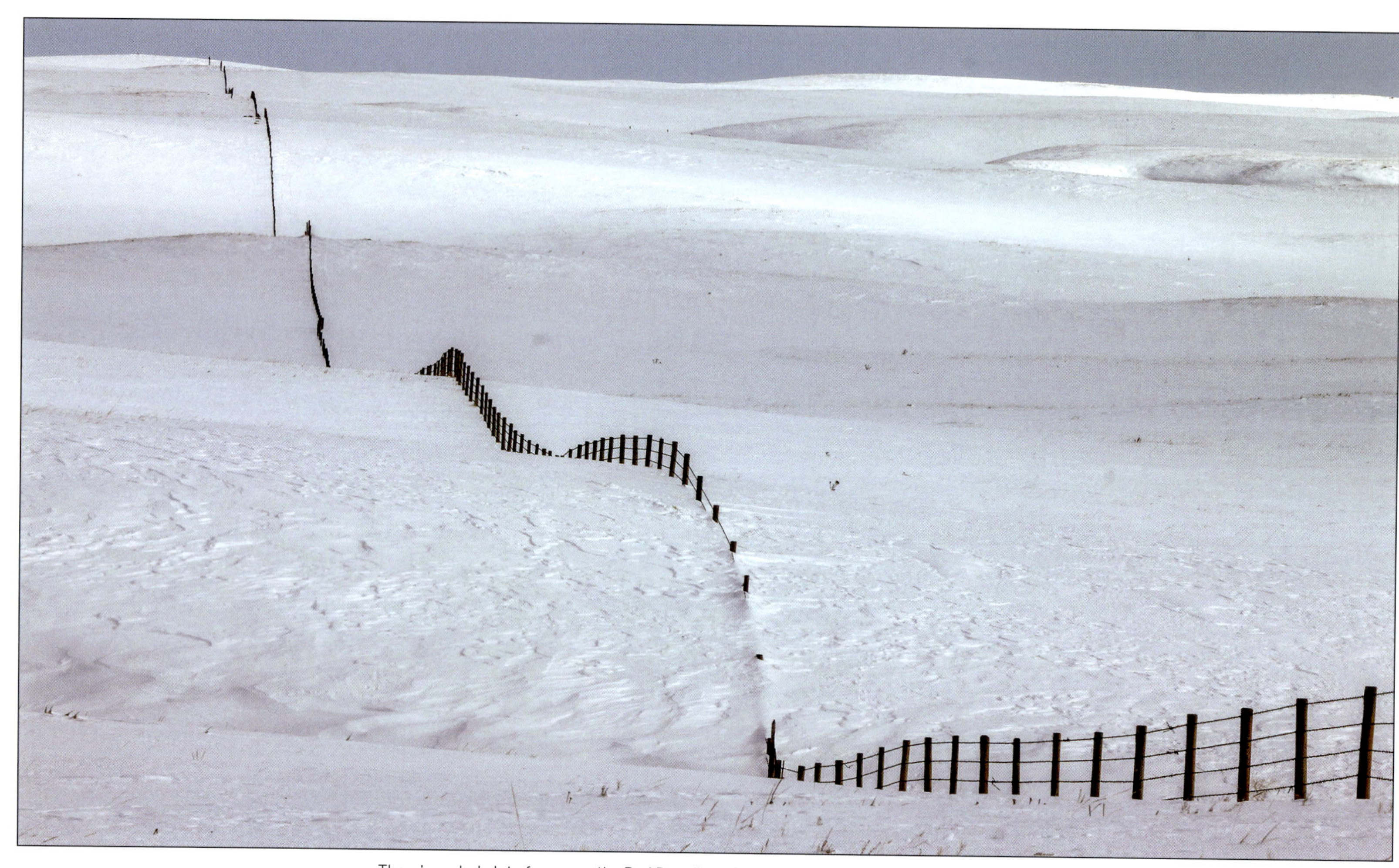

There's a whole lot of snow on the Red Deer River benchlands between Buffalo and Jenner.

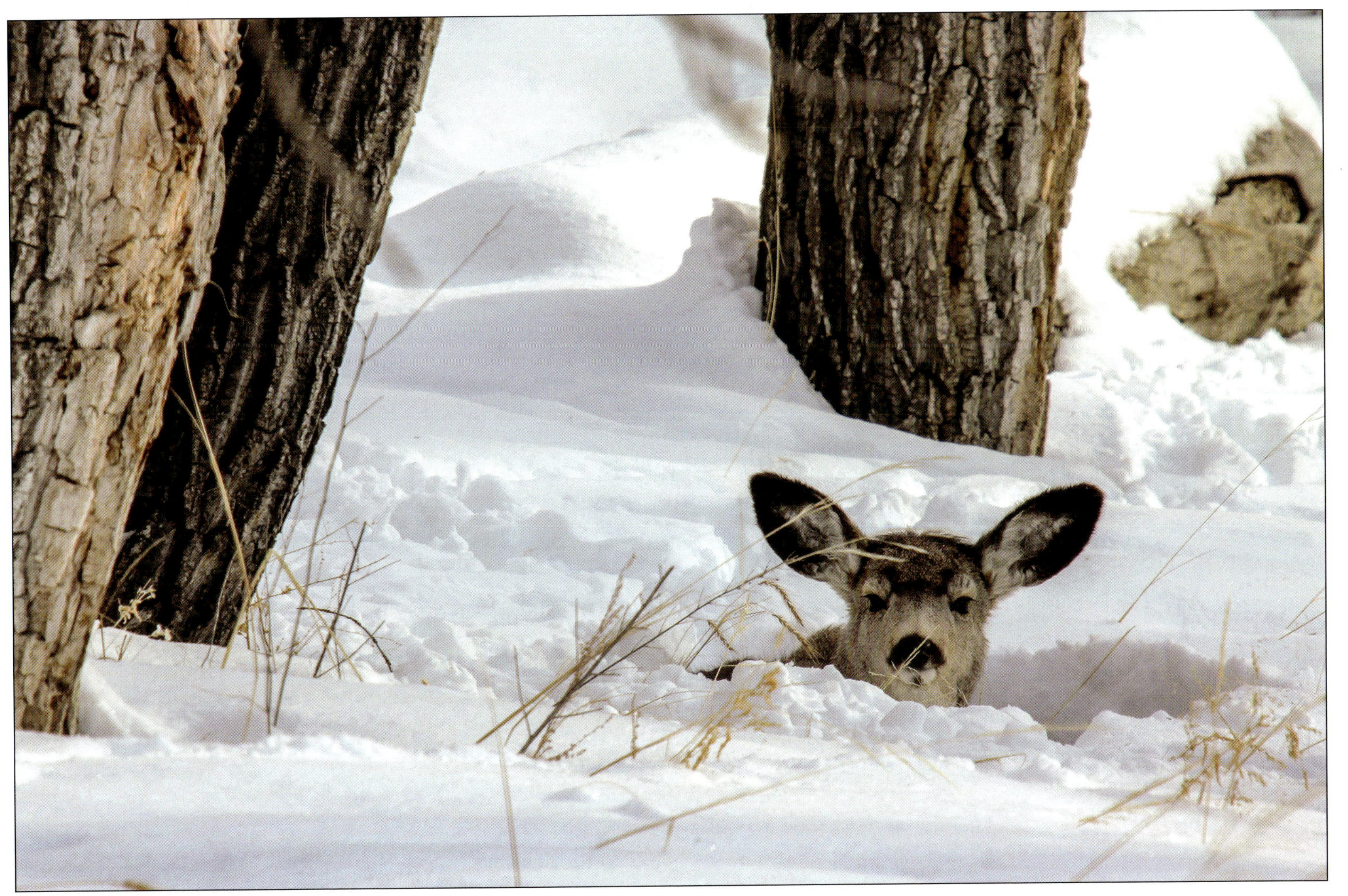

A young mule deer relaxes in the deep snow in the Red Deer River valley between Buffalo and Jenner.

PRAIRIE FROST

I TOOK A RIGHT TURN AND headed south on a gravel road just east of Tilley.

Like the rest of the countryside it was covered with snow, and in my mirrors I could see snow crystals hanging in the still air behind the truck as I sped along. Ahead of me was open prairie dotted with the dark shapes of oil pumps. Not a tree in sight.

I came to a T-intersection and turned right for no particular reason and was surprised to see a sign that told me I was on the old Trans-Canada Highway, a simple gravel road that paralleled the railroad tracks. I'd always assumed that the present highway was just built over the original.

But it soon petered out and turned into a drifted-over track, so I cut left at the next crossroads and headed farther out onto the plains.

I was looking for antelope. In the summer they're pretty common out here so I figured they'd be pretty easy to find. But no, I'd been poking around on the plains for the past two hours and not an antelope in sight.

Not that it wasn't pleasant. It was cold, true, colder than back in Calgary but not bitter. There were frost crystals on everything, backlit and glittering in the sun with just the tiniest breeze to give them a bit of animation.

The still air carried sounds from the new Trans-Canada road, by now about ten kilometres to the north of me, and they mixed with the rumble and pop of the oil pumps.

I turned back and followed the railroad tracks east, scanning the passing prairie for antelope. Nothing. But I found a plaque that told of Alberta's first natural gas well, an accidental discovery made in 1883 by a CPR crew drilling for water. A while later the gas ignited and destroyed the drilling rig. Must have been quite a sight.

I backroaded all the way to Suffield, cut north and then headed east again. I spotted a couple of empty ferruginous hawk nests that I'll check out come summertime and found a few cattle but no antelope. Not even a deer.

South toward Medicine Hat, back west just a tick to Redcliff and then south to the river valley park along the South Saskatchewan. Finally, some animals.

There was a handful of mule deer there poking around a hay field and it made a lovely scene. The cliffs along the river shone golden where the snow had fallen away and the soft blue of the winter sky soared above. But the road dead-ends here so I had to head back up to Redcliff and motor on.

I cut north from Redcliff and back west. By now it was getting to be late afternoon and I was running out of time. Some cattle posed nicely for me in a snowy field and I found some frosted horse hair hanging on a fence. I just can't resist shooting that picture even though I've done it a thousand times.

I think I might have seen a couple of antelope lying down way out in a field, but even through my long lens I couldn't be sure. And that was it.

I drove on north, cut west then went back south again. I followed oilfield roads out onto the prairie northwest of Tilley, sure I'd see antelope out there. I photographed them last spring right near here having their babies.

But pretty as the countryside was, it suffered from a paucity of antelope. They were there, I'm absolutely sure of it. But I never saw them.

The sun was heading west and throwing long shadows from the snowdrifts and making the frost on the grama grass and sagebrush shimmer with amber light. The shadows turned a deep blue and the rust on old farm equipment I found in a field glowed like copper.

On west again. The sun sank into a wall of mist and fog started to form in low spots on the plains. I photographed an oil pump as the sun dropped and then it was gone.

No antelope. Not this time, anyway. But a day on the prairie is never a disappointment. I drove on west into the winter dusk.

I'll find the antelope next time.

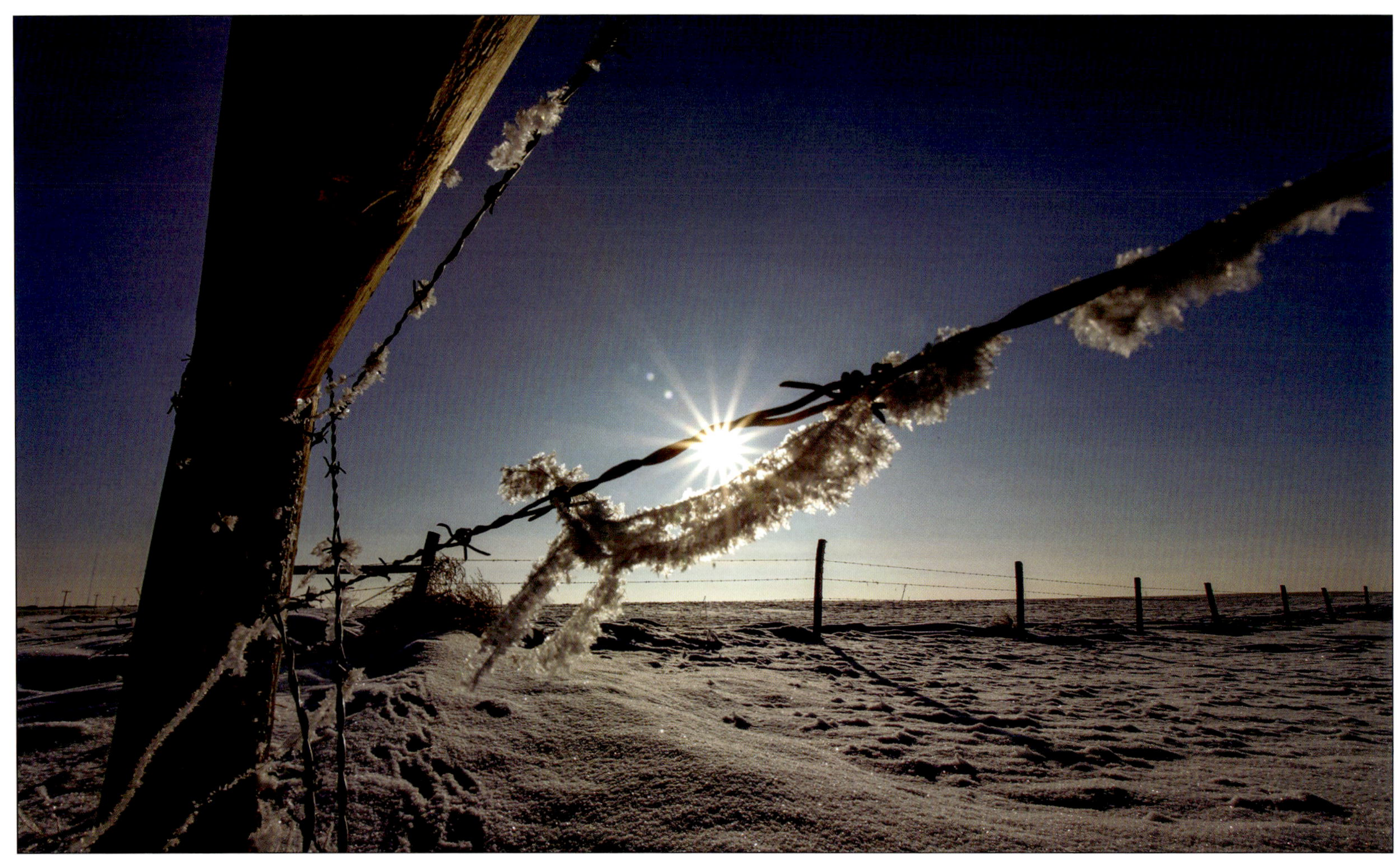

Frost, fence and the winter sun near Tilley.

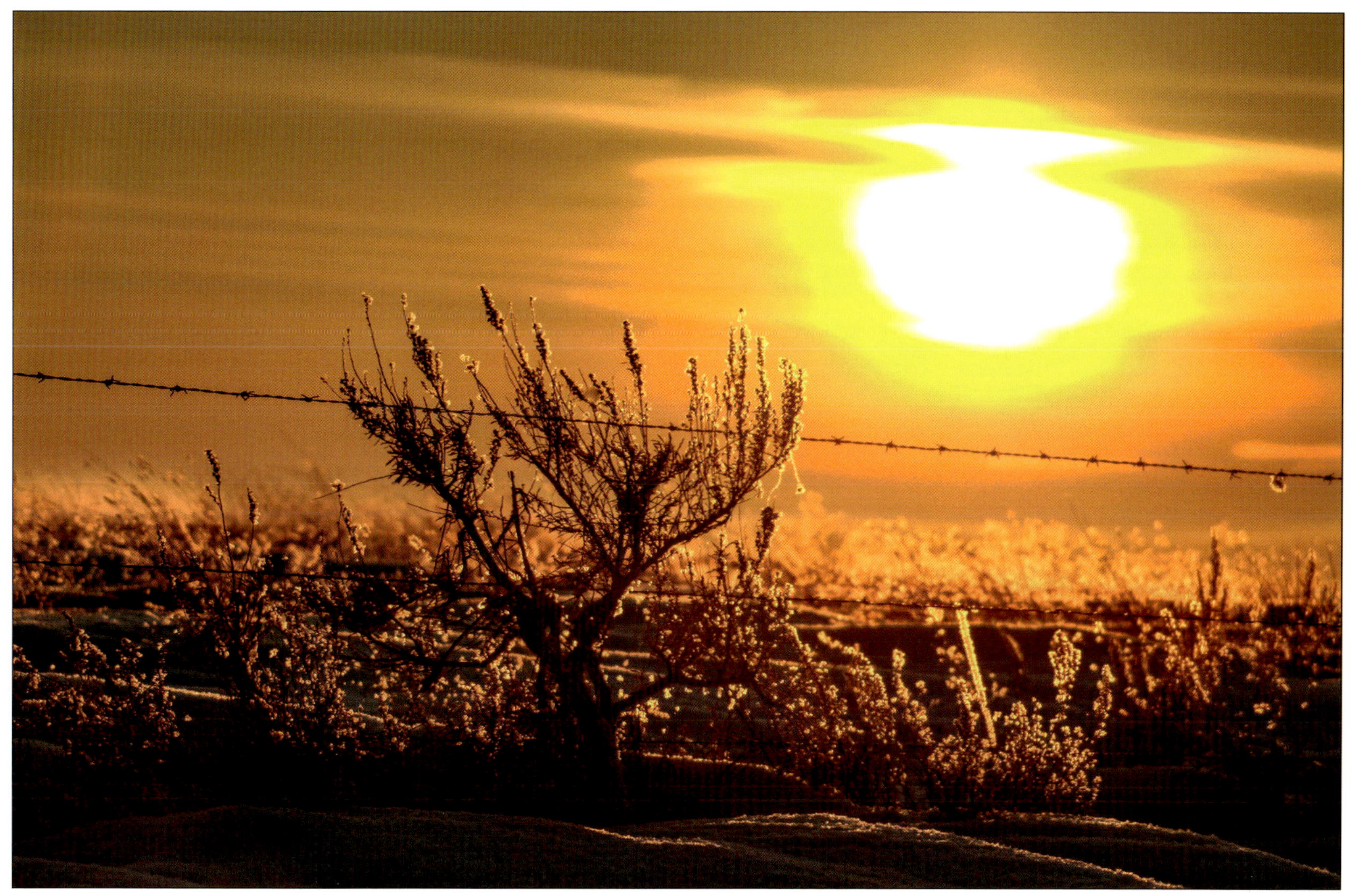

Frosty sagebrush and the setting sun on the prairie near Tilley.

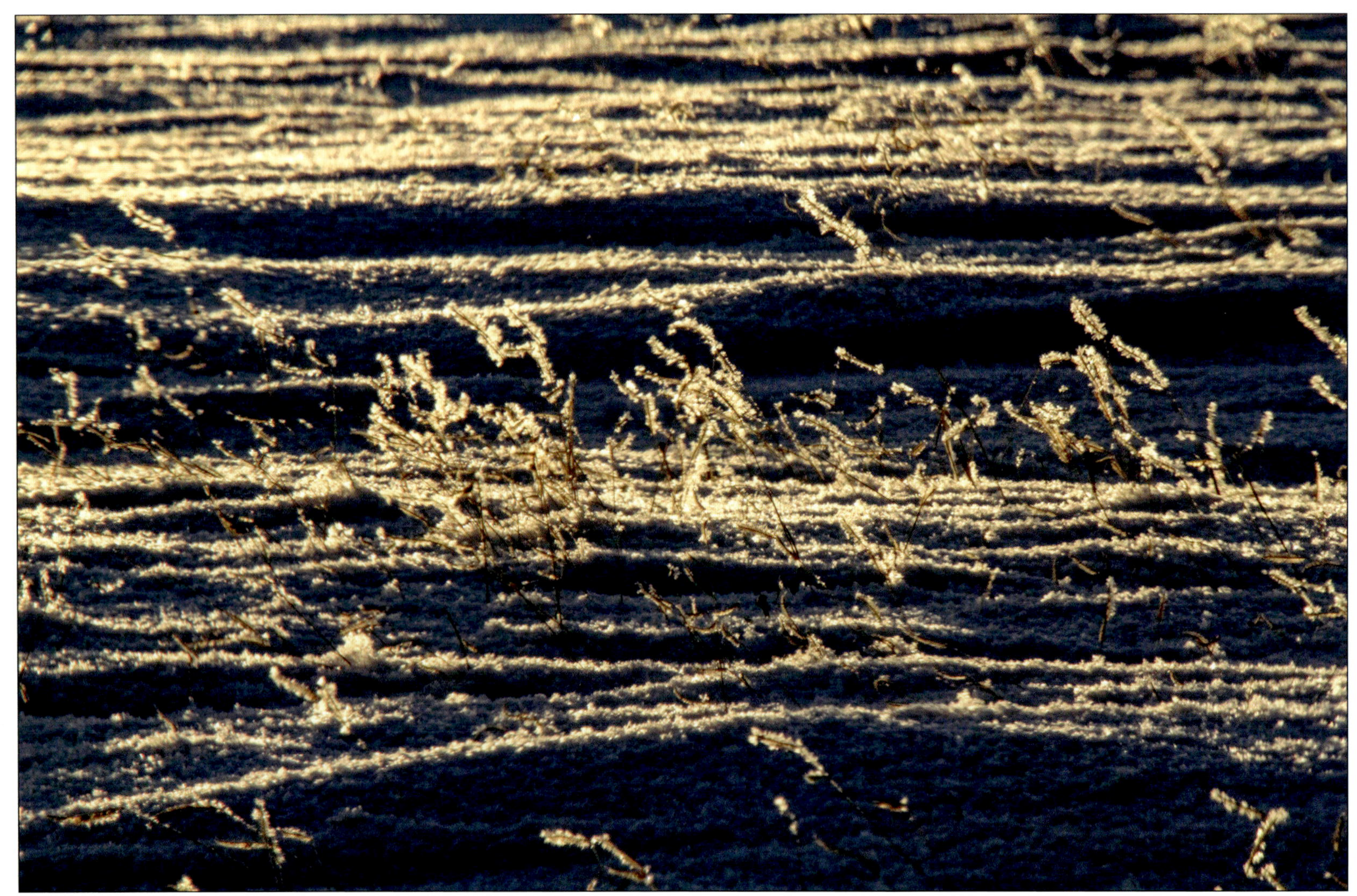

All kinds of frost and snow near Tilley.

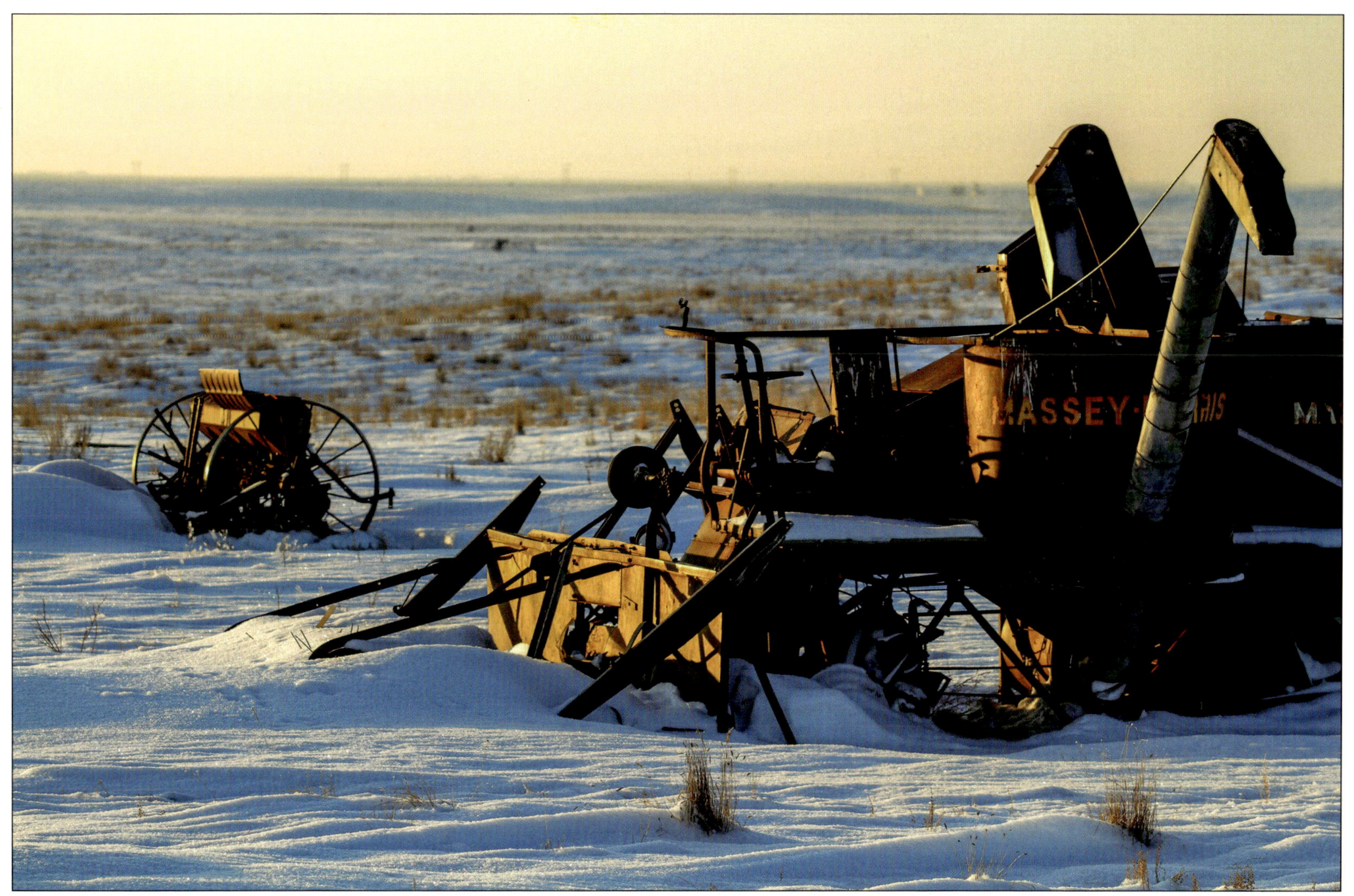

Old combine and a seed drill near Tilley.

CHRISTMAS EVE DAY

I WAS SORT OF HOPING THAT my second last adventure before the end of the year might turn out to be something special, but alas, it was not meant to be.

Once again the wind was blowing hard from the west and a grey spread of chinook cloud hung over the mountains. I could see the peaks through the cloud, snow sifting down from the clouds above and tearing off the summits in long streamers as I headed west across Morley Flats, but by the time I reached the turn to Bow Valley Provincial Park they were completely obscured.

I often see elk here this time of year but on Monday the wind was so strong they were likely all hunkered down in the trees. Even the ducks on the open water of the reservoir at Seebe kept tight to the lee side of the long split in the ice. I saw a muskrat pop up on the ice for a second or two but it dropped back into the water before I could get a picture.

There were no bighorn sheep near the road at Exshaw, and the green waters of the Bow were so choppy that even if there had been any birds to see I couldn't have shot a decent picture anyway. I finally found some sheep by Gap Lake but as I was about to take some pictures a truck pulled up and couple of guys got out and started walking up to the herd. The sheep bolted.

So I headed to Banff. Always animals around there. My friend Mike shot a cool picture of a couple of bull elk with a black wolf walking behind them just a couple of weeks ago. Maybe if I hit the Banff Parkway I'd get lucky too.

It looked good when I found the bighorn ram licking salt off the road. He was an almost full-curl, healthy, big sheep and he let me pull up right beside him to take pictures. I got close enough to count his eyelashes.

The wind here on the east side of the Bow River valley wasn't too bad. The tops of the trees were swaying and when I stopped the truck I could hear the creak of rubbing branches as they thrashed around. But along the ground it was nearly calm. I drove on hopefully.

But there was nothing else. Not a deer, not an elk. Wolves? Of course not. I drove all the way to Lake Louise and never took a picture. I never even saw a squirrel.

And then I did something I almost never do. I turned around and drove back on the same road.

Don't much like doing that. I'd much rather make a circle than a ricochet. But my only other choice was to go back on Highway 1. There, even if I'd seen anything, I likely wouldn't have been able to stop for a picture anyway. So I decided to take a chance on a rebound trip.

It wasn't much better than the outbound leg. I saw a couple of elk at the far edge of a clearing but they were in too much brush to make a picture. That was about it.

Maybe the animals all went somewhere for Christmas. Nah, more likely it was just the wind. But I wanted some pictures. I even drove down to Vermilion Lakes to see if there was anything. There's often elk down there, but of course, not today. There were a couple of coyotes far out on the ice but I couldn't get a picture.

I moped back through Canmore, thinking I'd just have to write off the day. But then as I looked up at the Three Sisters I saw a rainbow in the sky.

Okay, not a rainbow. But there was prismatic colour in the sky, the sunlight breaking into its component colours through the tiny crystals of ice blowing off the peaks. And then a little farther east, beyond Exshaw – I did another rebound on that road, too – a long, ropy cloud hung above Yamnuska, with just a slight glow seeping through the clouds to the west lighting the face of the cliff.

But best of all were the horses. Ponies in the big pasture by the Goodstoney rodeo grounds. It was all there, the warm glow in the sky, the golden grass, the shaggy horses with their faces in the wind. It wasn't the wildlife I'd set out to find but it would do just fine. Yeah, that's what I needed.

I sat in the ditch listening to the wind howl by the truck window as the colour faded from the sky before I pulled back onto the highway. I glanced over my shoulder to see if the horses were still there. And had I been clever I would have rolled down the window and shouted back at them, "Merry Christmas to all and to all a good night!"

That might have made the adventure something special. But alas, it was not meant to be.

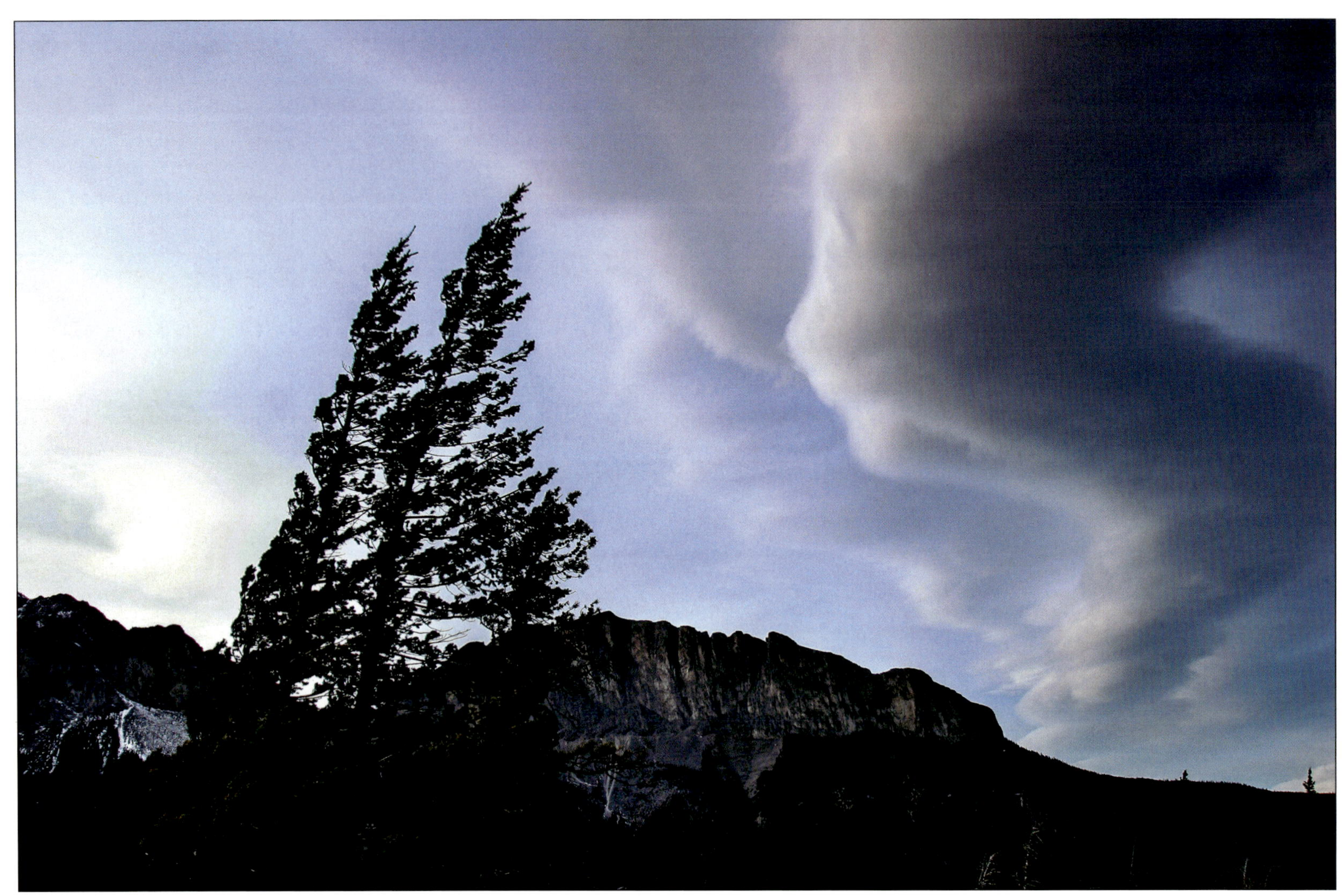

Chinook cloud and Yamnuska.

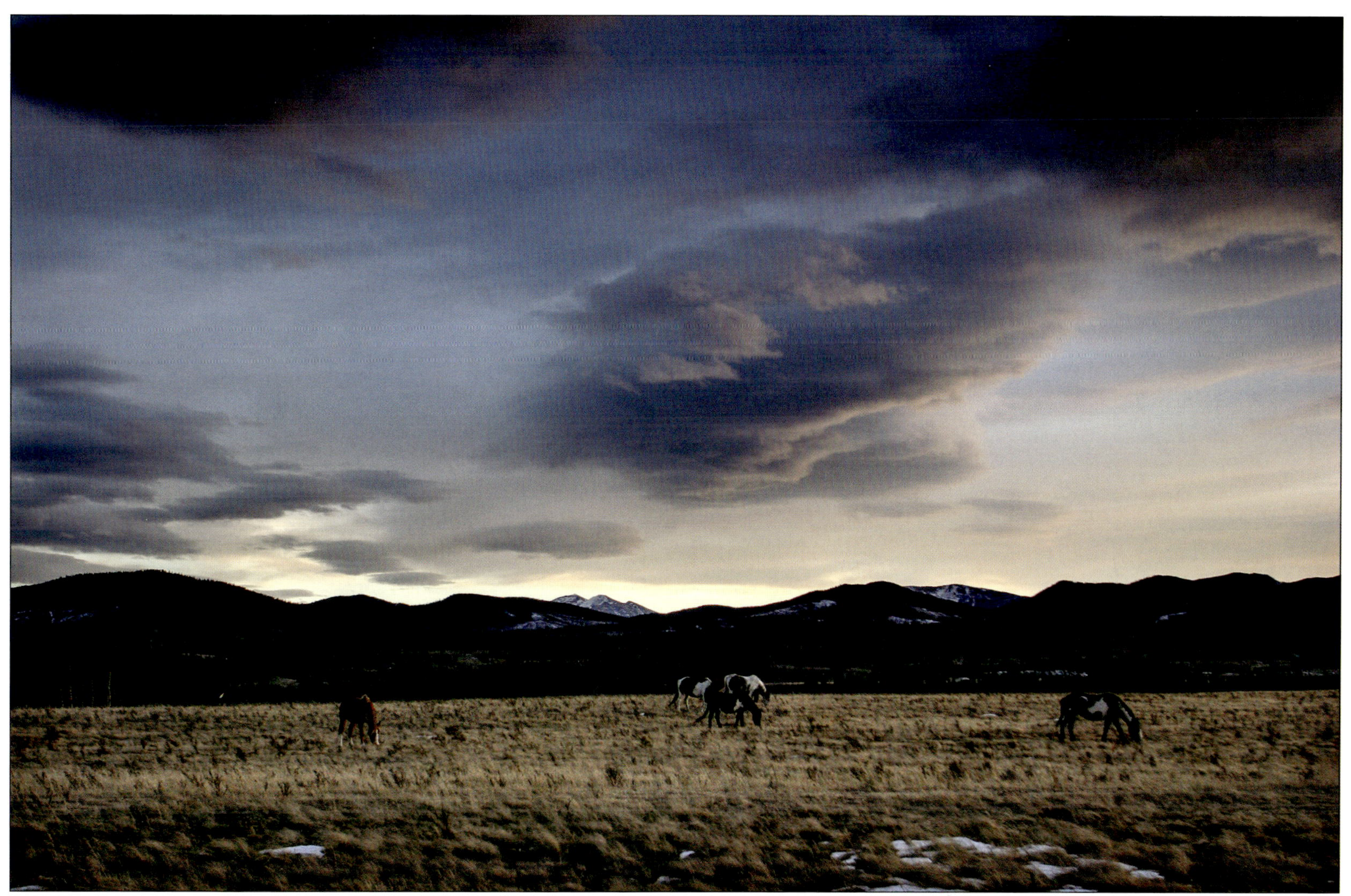

Chinook cloud and horses near Morley.

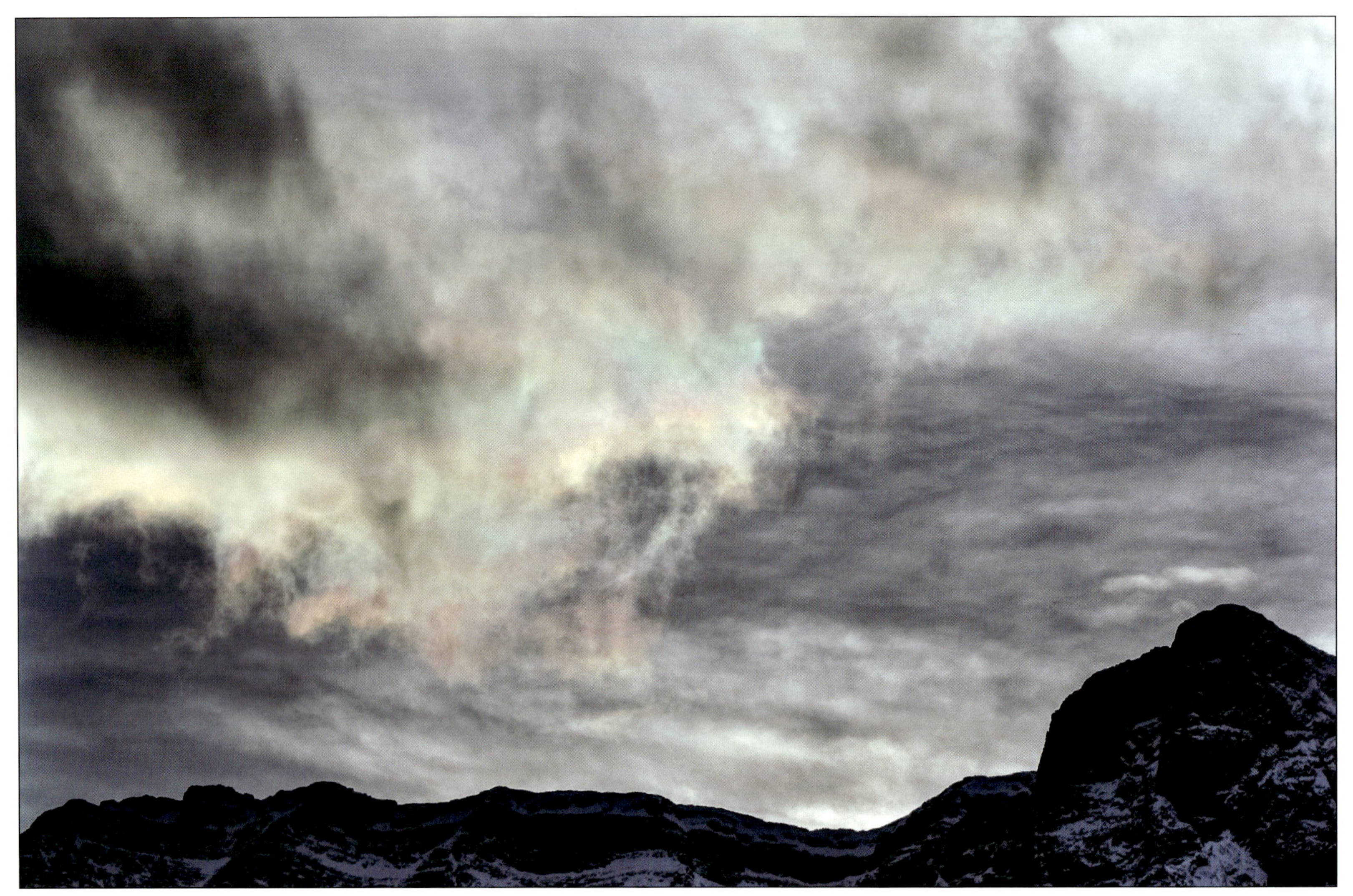

Prismatic spread of sunlight in blowing snow coming off the peaks near Canmore.

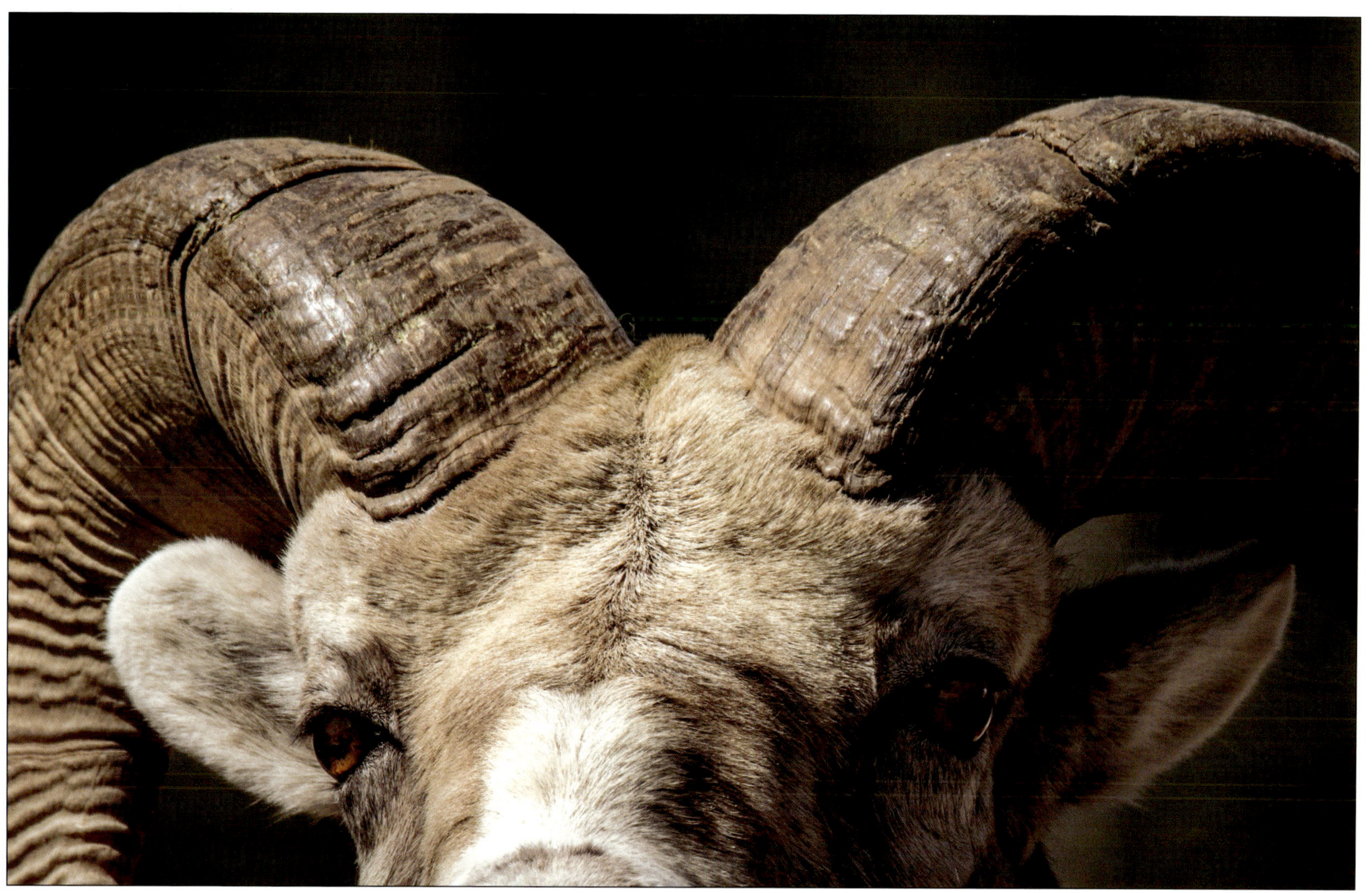

A bighorn ram in the sunshine of the much-warmer Kananaskis valley in the still-wintry high country in Peter Lougheed and Spray Lakes Provincial Parks.

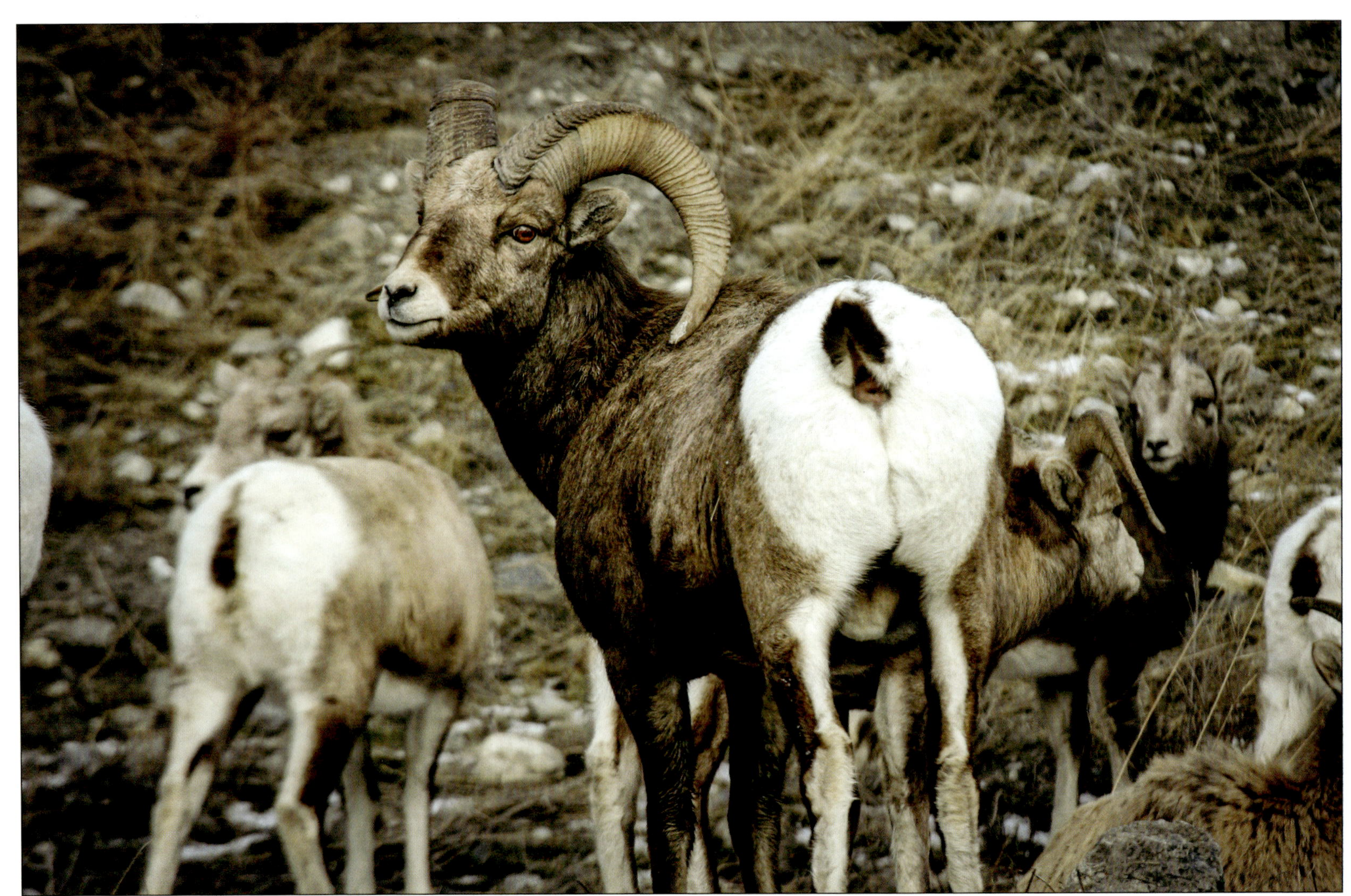

A bighorn ram hangs out with ewes and younger rams at Gap Lake.

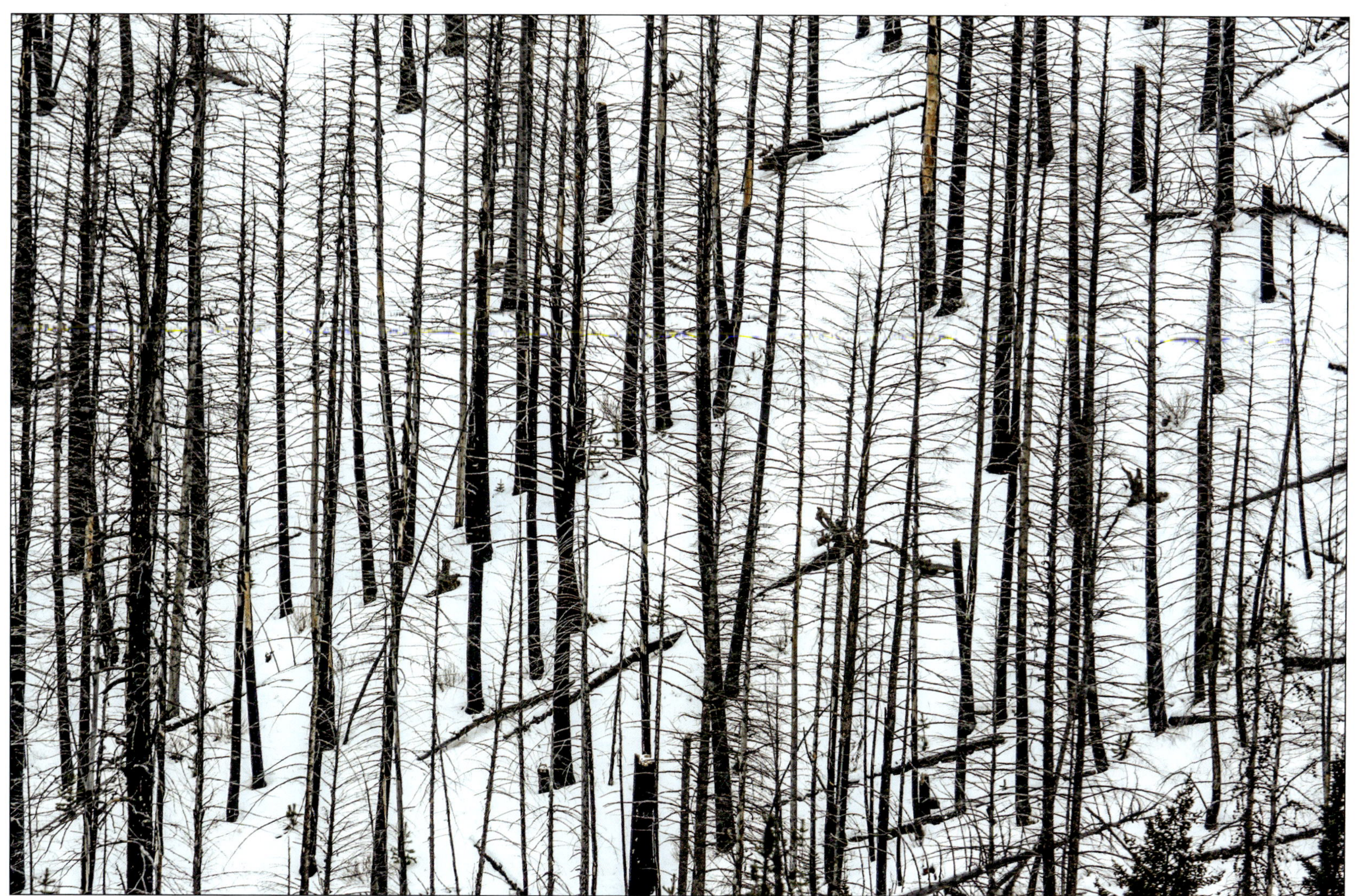

Stark, bare trees in a burn area along the Banff Parkway.

ACKNOWLEDGEMENTS

Thanks to all my friends at the *Calgary Sun* who put up with my eccentricities for more than 30 years and pals, both old and new, that have offered encouragement and advice, some of which I've actually taken.

I'd especially like to thank Al Charest, Jim Wells, Darren Makowichuk, Stuart Dryden, Lyle Aspinall, John Gibson, Neil Zeller and, of course, my great pal Todd Korol.

But more than anyone, thanks to my best pal Leah Hennel. For more than 20 years we've had each other's backs and I know we will forever. She's the second best friend a boy could ever have!